W9-APR-090

SOTHEBY'S
CONCISE ENCYCLOPEDIA OF
SILVER

JUL 2007

SAN RAFAEL PUBLIC LIBRARY
SAN RAFAEL, CALIFORNIA

DATE DUE	
8-21-07	

GAYLORD   PRINTED IN U.S.A.

SOTHEBY'S
CONCISE ENCYCLOPEDIA OF
SILVER

GENERAL EDITOR · CHARLES TRUMAN

San Rafael Public Library
1100 E Street
San Rafael, CA 94901

CONRAN OCTOPUS

First published in 1993
by Conran Octopus Limited
37 Shelton Street, London WC2H 9HN

This paperback edition published in 1996 by
Conran Octopus Limited

Copyright © Conran Octopus Limited 1993

Sotheby's illustrations (see p.208) © Sotheby's
Sotheby's is a registered trade mark.

All rights reserved. No part of this book may be reproduced, stored
in a retrieval system, or transmitted in any form or by any means,
electronic, electrostatic, magnetic tape, mechanical, photocopying,
recording or otherwise, without the prior permission of the publisher.

British Library Cataloguing-in-Publication Data
A catalogue record for this book is available from the British Library

ISBN 1-85029-759-2

SERIES EDITOR Denny Hemming
ART EDITOR Helen Lewis
DESIGNER Sally Powell
PICTURE RESEARCHERS Kathy Lockley, Liz Heasman, Celia Dearing
PICTURE RESEARCH ASSISTANT Clare Barraclough
COPY EDITORS Patricia Bayer, Christine O'Brien
PRODUCTION Sonya Sibbons
EDITORIAL ASSISTANT Emma Wheeler
ILLUSTRATOR Coral Mula

Typeset by Servis Filmsetting Limited
Printed in China

The Publisher would like to thank Asprey plc, Roy Davids, the
Gallery of Antique Costume and Textiles, P.J. Hilton, Peter Hurford,
Katie Klitgaard, E. & C.T. Koopman, David Lee, Mallett and Son
Antiques Limited, S.J. Phillips, Peter Waldron, Lucilla Watson,
Elizabeth White and the Silver Departments of Sotheby's, London
and Sotheby's Inc.

ILLUSTRATIONS ON PAGES 1–12

*Page 1: Silver soup tureen with cover, liner and stand (detail), Henry Auguste,
Paris, 1804.*
Page 2: Pieter de Ring, Still Life with Fruit, *17th century.*
Page 4: Tea infuser, silver and ebony, Marianne Brandt, Weimar, 1924.
Page 4–5: Giulio Romano, The Salon of Psyche, A Peasant Banquet, *16th century.*
Page 6: Silver and gold plaques, Thracian, 4th century BC, from Latzina.
Page 9: The Parabiago Shield, detail of Mithras's Chariot, 5th century AD, from Italy.
Page 10: Pieter Gerritsz. Roestraten, Still Life with Silver-Gilt Cup and Cover
and Silver Porringer, *17th century.*
Page 12: A selection of Islamic silver jewellery from Arabia.

CONTENTS

PATRICIA BAYER
Art Deco

Patricia Bayer is a freelance writer and editor specializing in nineteenth- and twentieth-century decorative arts and design, with an emphasis on the Art Deco period. She is the author of *Art Deco Source Book* (1988), *Art Deco Interiors* (1990) and *Art Deco Architecture* (1992), and the co-author of *The Art of René Lalique* (1988) and *Lalique Perfume Bottles* (1990). She has also contributed to *Sotheby's Concise Encyclopedia of Furniture* (1989) and *Sotheby's Concise Encyclopedia of Glass* (1991).

LESLIE GREENE BOWMAN
American Silver

Leslie Bowman is head curator of the decorative arts department of the Los Angeles County Museum of Art. She has written extensively on various aspects of American decorative arts. Her most recent publications include *American Rococo, 1750–1775: Elegance in Ornament* (1992), with co-author Morrison H. Heckscher, and *American Arts and Crafts: Virtue in Design* (1990).

VANESSA BRETT
Forgeries, Fakes and Concoctions

Vanessa Brett worked at Sotheby's from 1970 until 1979 and now lectures on silver and pewter. Her books include *The Sotheby's Directory of Silver* (1986) and, as co-author, *Lighting in the Domestic Interior* (1991). From 1986 to 1989 she edited *Sotheby's Guide – Antiques and their Prices Worldwide*.

SHIRLEY BURY
Empire and Regency
(The Nineteenth Century)

Shirley Bury joined the Victoria & Albert Museum, London, in 1948 and retired in 1985 as Keeper of Metalwork. A Fellow of the Society of Antiquaries and a Liveryman of the Worshipful Company of Goldsmiths, she has organized exhibitions and written extensively on silverwork and jewellery. Her publications include *Victorian Electroplate* (1971) and *Jewellery 1789–1910*, 2 vols. (1991).

MARIAN CAMPBELL
Gothic Silver
(The Medieval Period)

Marian Campbell, F.S.A., is a Deputy Curator in the Metalwork Collection, Victoria & Albert Museum, London, responsible for medieval metalwork and enamels, and whose interests include fakes and fakers of medieval art. She has lectured widely and her publications include *An Introduction to Medieval Enamels* (1983), and contributions to the exhibition catalogue *The Age of Chivalry; Art in Plantagenet England, 1200–1400*, J. Alexander and P. Binski (eds), Royal Academy of Art, London (1987). She is currently researching a book on English medieval goldsmiths' work.

JOHN CULME
True and False Principles
(The Nineteenth Century)

John Culme joined Sotheby's London in 1964. He has written extensively on various aspects of the eighteenth- and nineteenth-century London goldsmiths' trade. The present editor of *The Silver Society Journal*, John Culme is also a Liveryman of the Worshipful Company of Goldsmiths.

GODFREY EVANS
Baroque Silver
(Baroque, Rococo and Neoclassicism)

Godfrey Evans has been Curator of European Metalwork and Sculpture at the National Museums of Scotland, Edinburgh, since 1982. He has organized a number of exhibitions, including the 1985 Edinburgh International Festival Exhibition entitled *French Connections: Scotland and the Arts of France*, and has also published and lectured on a wide range of subjects. He is currently working on the Sir Thomas North Dick-Lauder collection of continental silver.

PETER FUHRING
Rococo Silver
(Baroque, Rococo and Neoclassicism)

Peter Fuhring is a Dutch freelance art historian living in Paris, specializing in drawings and prints of ornament, architecture and the decorative arts. He is the author of *Design into Art. Drawings for Architecture and Ornament. The Lodewijk Houthakker Collection* (1989), and of the forthcoming book on the life and work of Juste-Aurèle Meissonnier, goldsmith, designer and architect.

MALCOLM HASLAM
Arts and Crafts & Art Nouveau

Malcolm Haslam was an antiques dealer for several years before becoming a writer and lecturer specializing in the decorative arts. He is a regular contributor to magazines and the author of several books, including *English Art Pottery 1865–1915* (1975), *Marks and Monograms of the Modern Movement* (1977), *In the Nouveau Style* (1989) and *Arts and Crafts Carpets* (1991).

JAMES LOMAX
Neoclassicism
(Baroque, Rococo and Neoclassicism)

James Lomax joined the staff at Leeds City Art Galleries in 1977 and later worked at Manchester City Art Gallery. He has been Keeper of Temple Newsam House since 1985 and has recently published a catalogue of its silver collection. He lectures and writes extensively on various aspects of the fine and decorative arts and was editor of the Furniture History Society journal for four years.

ANTHONY NORTH
Romanesque Silver
(The Medieval Period)

Anthony North has been a curator at the Victoria & Albert Museum, London, since 1964. He is a specialist in arms, armour and base metalwork, and is the author of several books on these subjects, including *European Swords* (1982) and *Swords and Hilt Weapons* (1989). He has also lectured extensively both to associated societies and at international conferences.

IAN PICKFORD
Mid-Nineteenth-Century Eclecticism
(The Nineteenth Century)

Ian Pickford worked in the antique silver trade for some years, and now lectures extensively to the National Association of Decorative and Fine Arts' Societies, the National Arts Collection Fund and the National Trust, as well as the Universities of London and Surrey. He is a Freeman of the Worshipful Company of Goldsmiths and a Freeman of the City of London. He has written numerous books and articles on silver and is editor of *Jackson's Silver and Gold Marks* (1989).

TIMOTHY SCHRODER
Renaissance and Mannerism

Timothy Schroder joined the silver department at Christie's in 1976 and from 1984 to 1988 was curator of decorative arts at the Los Angeles County Museum of Art. He became a director of Partridge Fine Arts in 1991. His publications include *The National Trust Book of English Domestic Silver* (1988) and *The Gilbert Collection of Gold and Silver* (1988). He is currently Chairman of the Silver Society.

ERIC TURNER
Post-War Silver

Eric Turner has been a curator in the Metalwork Department of the Victoria & Albert Museum, London, since 1976. His particular areas of expertise are associated with the collections of post-1880 metalwork and Sheffield plate. He has contributed to many publications and several conferences on these subjects both in Britain and abroad.

MICHAEL VICKERS
Early Silver

Michael Vickers is a Senior Assistant Keeper in the Department of Antiquities at the Ashmolean Museum, Oxford, responsible for the Greek, Etruscan, Roman and Byzantine collections. He is the co-author with Oliver Impey and James Allen of *From Silver to Ceramic* (1986) and with David Gill of *Artful Crafts: Ancient Greek Silver and Pottery*, to be published by Oxford University Press in 1993.

FOREWORD

Although the history of silver has a large literature stretching back at least to the mid-nineteenth century in English and French, the last decade has seen an explosion of scholarly publications on both sides of the Atlantic and across Europe from Lisbon to Moscow. A burgeoning spirit of enquiry and cooperation across frontiers has stimulated exhibitions and catalogues of English, German and Danish silver collections in Russia, French silver in Denmark and Portugal, Portuguese silver in London, and major private and public collections in, for example, Lugano, London, Leeds and Los Angeles. Shipwrecks in Ireland and Florida have yielded up previously unknown forms of Spanish domestic silver. War has played its part, too; for example, Greek silver has been unearthed from ancient graves in Afghanistan. Economic pressures have teased out on to the market and into the public eye such important silver as the astonishing dinner service made for the Prince-Bishop of Hildesheim or the tableware copying Greek vases designed for Kedleston. Simultaneously, new themes are being explored that draw on the riches of local archives and family papers, especially in France, Germany and England. Many simplistic assumptions, for example, that in England the master's mark necessarily identifies the maker, have been swept away to be replaced by a new understanding of the complex nature of production and design. The free flow of design ideas across national boundaries and their transmogrification is better understood, thanks to exhibitions such as Rococo *(London, 1984),* Wenzel Jamnitzer *(Nuremberg, 1985),* The Age of Chivalry *(London, 1987),* Un Age d'Or des Arts Decoratifs 1814–1848 *(Paris, 1991),* Le Trésor de St Denis *(Paris, 1991) or* Silver of a New Era *(Rotterdam, 1992). Curators and scholars have played a leading role in this flowering of knowledge as the diverse contributions to this volume demonstrate.*

PHILIPPA GLANVILLE

INTRODUCTION

Silver is a unique medium in the arts. For most of history it has had a value exactly that of coin, and it is infinitely recyclable. As fashion changed, silver was melted to emerge in new forms, or if funds ran short silver was converted into coin. Because of its intrinsic value most European centres of production devised a system, probably beginning in Byzantium, of assaying silver to determine its purity, subsequently indicating this with a hallmark. These marks frequently provide an accurate method of dating the piece, and even identifying the maker. Thus it is the most reliable barometer of wealth and taste available to the historian. With its highly reflective surface, silver was the ideal medium for display; whether as jewellery, or in a Roman triumph, a cathedral treasury or in the great houses of Europe and America. The secular display of silver was largely restricted to two principal areas: the eating room and the bedroom of a grand house. In the eating room silver was piled high on a buffet, although the table was also dressed with silver, especially at the dessert, to sparkle and delight. In the great bedrooms, or in ante-rooms to them, elaborate toilet services were laid out, as much to impress as for use. Indeed, much silver was made solely for display, without any thought being given to its function. The decline of lavish displays of silver during the nineteenth century coincided with the taste for collecting antique silver. Whereas before outdated silver was melted and refashioned, now it was collected for its aesthetic appeal. From the middle of the last century, when hallmarks were first deciphered for the general public, silver studies have progressed at a remarkable speed, and never faster than in the last two decades when new discoveries have changed the conventional view of the industry of silversmithing.

A comprehensive history of silver in Europe and America, from rare pre-classical survivals to contemporary work by leading international designers, this book traces the development of silver as a craft and as a trade, the technical innovations, the craftsmen and the major artistic movements reflected in its designs through the centuries.

EARLY SILVER

From the dawn of civilization, in the fertile lands between the Tigris and the Euphrates, silver and gold have been known to man. Whilst gold occurs naturally, silver had to be extracted from ores, notably galena or lead sulphide. The process of refining silver by cupellation was known at least in the third millennium BC. The legendary wealth of the Ancient World in Mesopotamia, Babylon and Egypt is belied by lack of surviving pieces, but contemporary records confirm huge quantities of precious metals. In classical Greece, descriptions of lavish plate survive and King Croesus has today become a byword for wealth while the riches of ancient Rome are well documented. The uncertainty of life in the late Roman Empire led to the burial of a large number of hoards of silver whereas the destruction of the great treasuries during the Dark Ages has left little extant evidence of the wealth of the time, which so far as England was concerned was the principal attraction for marauding Danes.

ROMAN FRESCO, POMPEII, 1ST CENTURY AD

———

The fresco depicts an informal drinking party, with silver – cups, a ladle and a long spoon – placed on a table in the foreground. The man drinks from a silver rhyton which he holds above the level of his head to enable the wine to flow out.

The hierarchy of materials which prevailed in the Ancient World is demonstrated by two examples. First, a fresco, illustrating the contents of an Egyptian royal treasury in the fifteenth century BC, shows shelves of gold objects ranged above silver, and silver above objects made from precious stone, bronze, copper and alabaster. Second, a text of the Roman period, discussing how application might be made for public assistance, states: 'If a man formerly used golden vessels, he must sell them and use silver vessels; if he used silver vessels, he must sell them and use bronze vessels; if he formerly used bronze vessels, he must sell them and use glass vessels.' Ownership of precious metals was a mark of rank and status, whether of an individual, a city or a shrine. Although gold and silver is often mentioned in ancient texts, very little has survived in the archaeological record.

There seems to have been little respect for antiques in antiquity, and it was usual for objects of precious metal to be melted down and remade when they became old-fashioned or worn, were stolen or looted. Only rarely was the family silver placed in the grave: it was usually kept above ground for the living. Even when precious materials have been buried, grave robbers have usually gone in and taken rich pickings. Ceramic surrogates were sometimes used instead, and these can often serve as a guide to lost silver. Occasionally, gold and silver survive in hoards, but for this to occur there had to be doubly disturbing circumstances: conditions had to be critical enough for precious objects to be buried in the first place, and so dire that no one was able to return to dig them up. Thus, few objects are extant from periods that were characterized by centuries of peace. Very little Greek silver has survived, and gold vessels remaining from Roman times are rarer still.

It was the desire for rich and exotic objects on the part of élites that generated long-distance trade, the desire to cut a fine figure in the world that caused rich men to commission beautiful objects from skilled craftsmen in gold and silver. Aesthetic judgements in antiquity were usually only made with regard to objects of precious metal; it is in this sphere that patronage flourished, and in connection with which the names of famous artists are occasionally mentioned. Another constant element throughout history has been the close relationship between vessels of gold and silver and the consumption of alcohol, whether at banquets or religious festivals. Wine containers, mixing bowls and drinking cups are by far the most frequently mentioned items in the ancient sources relating to precious metal, and they also figure large among extant plate.

EARLY MESOPOTAMIA

c.3000 TO 2167 BC

The land between the Tigris and Euphrates rivers was the site of the first cities (and the first writings) in about 3000 BC. The techniques of extracting and working precious metals were already known. Gold presented relatively few problems because it was often found in alluvial deposits and was readily malleable. Silver had to be recovered by means of more complex metallurgical processes from ores and natural alloys. Silver was probably imported into Mesopotamia from Cilicia (in southern Anatolia), and gold from Elam (in Iran) or northern Syria. Notable examples of Sumerian gold and silver work have survived in the royal cemeteries at Ur. There was much work in hammered sheet gold and silver, a technique which involved annealing. The coffin of a young man called Meskalamdug was found to contain a gold helmet in the form of a stylized wig, a silver belt with a gold dagger and several gold bowls. The latter were raised from discs by means of hammering. The burial of Queen Puabi was even more resplendent. She had been interred with a profusion of precious objects: 'a mass of beads of gold, silver, lapis lazuli, cornelian, agate and chalcedony'. She

EARLY MESOPOTAMIAN LYRE WITH SILVER REVETMENTS, UR, LATE 3RD MILLENIUM BC (H60cm/23⅔in)

One of the many lavish articles found in the royal cemeteries at Ur.

wore spiral earrings and a triple headdress of plain ring pendants, beech leaves and willow leaves, all in sheet gold. In the same tomb were four lyres, two wholly plated with silver: one with a cow's head in front of the soundbox, and another shaped like a boat supporting a stag. A model boat in silver, 60cm (2ft) long, was another striking find, attesting to the variety of shapes in the Sumerian silversmith's repertoire.

The limitations of Sumerian silver refining are indicated by the high lead content of a vase from Lagash, said to be made, according to the Sumerian inscription on its neck, from 'purified silver'. This vase is also curious on account of its copper ring-foot

OLD BABYLON

c.2081 TO 1576 BC

In a letter preserved in the royal archives at Mari, on the Upper Euphrates, Mukannishum, the director of the palace workshops, ordered to be made 'two drinking vessels of silver in the form of a bull's head, weighing [650 grams/23oz]; eight drinking vessels in the form of an ibex head and one drinking vessel of red gold,

capacities: '73 drinking vessels [for] Hammu-shagish, two [of which are] bull's head [vessels]. 6 drinking vessels, [for] Asqudum. 10 drinking vessels, 2 [of which are] bull's head [vessels for] Yasim-Sumu'. Royal banquets were often the occasion for the presentation of gifts; plate was always an acceptable present even after the invention of coinage in the sixth century BC.

Animal-head imagery was also used on such articles as votive axe-heads, sometimes incorporating a model of the object of the hunt, such as a wild boar.

ELAMITE VOTIVE AXE-HEAD OF SILVER AND ELECTRUM, TCHOGA-ZANBIL, NEAR SUSA (IRAN), MID-13TH CENTURY BC (L12.5cm/4$\frac{9}{10}$in)

BABYLONIAN SILVER VASE MOUNTED ON COPPER FEET, TELLO, LOWER MESOPOTAMIA (IRAQ), 2404–2375 BC (H35cm/13$\frac{3}{4}$in)

A Sumerian inscription is engraved on the neck.

resting on four lion's paws, also of copper. (Copper was a strengthening material which was to have a long tradition in silversmithing: Bronze Age and classical Greek silverware had copper bands at points of potential damage, and today's sterling silver has an admixture of copper, again to prevent wear.) The surface of the main field is engraved with pairs of lion-headed eagles and groups of lions and goats. On the shoulder are seven heifers, perhaps sacrificial animals for the cult of the god Ningirsu, for whose temple the vase was made, as indicated by the inscription around the neck. The dark incised lines contrast with the lighter surface of the metal.

weighing [nearly 3 kilos/6lb], one silver drinking vessel in the form of a gazelle's head weighing [200 grams/7oz], weighed with the king's personal set of weights'. Although no Old Babylonian animal-head silver survives, there are glimpses here of early examples of a genre of plate which was to be widespread throughout the ancient Near East. The drinking vessels would have been used at royal banquets, displayed on elaborate silver stands themselves adorned with animal heads: lions, roebucks and stags are mentioned in another letter. These would have been made in the palace workshops, although vessels imported from 'Tukrish' (locality unknown) were also prized.

Plate was not merely used for show, but was also stored in treasuries and served as currency in what was still a pre-monetary society. A list from Mari includes silverware given to court officials either as personal payments, or for them to use in their official

ANATOLIAN DRINKING VESSEL IN THE FORM OF A BULL, c.1400–1200 BC (H18cm/7in)

EGYPTIAN SILVER VASE IN THE FORM
OF A POMEGRANATE, TOMB OF
TUTANKHAMUN, VALLEY OF THE
KINGS, *c.*1325 BC (H13.4cm/5¼in) (RIGHT)

EGYPTIAN SILVER VASE IN THE FORM
OF A POMEGRANATE, TOMB OF
TUTANKHAMUN, VALLEY OF THE
KINGS, *c.*1325 BC (H13.4cm/5¼in) (RIGHT)

PART OF A HOARD OF SILVER VESSELS,
INGOTS AND CURRENCY-RINGS, AND
LAPIS-LAZULI, TÔD, UPPER EGYPT,
1938–1904 BC (BELOW)

*The shapes, and fluted and spiral decoration of these
silver vessels suggest that they were made in Crete.*

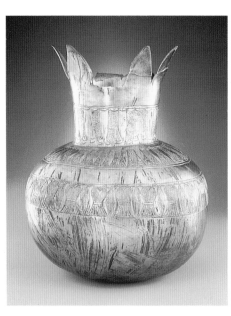

EGYPT

*c.*3000 TO 1325 BC

The Egyptians enjoyed rich local sources of gold, and their gold-smiths were mounting amethyst, turquoise and lapis lazuli on jewellery as early as the First Dynasty (*c.*3000 BC). Silver by contrast was rare, and was indeed more valuable than gold until the end of the Middle Kingdom (*c.*2060–1786 BC). Copper chests containing silver ingots, rings and silver cups of this period were found in a temple at Tôd in Upper Egypt. Only ten cups were in their original form; 143 were crushed and folded. They were apparently used as currency, and perhaps came as tribute from abroad. Their forms and fluted decoration resemble pottery influenced by silverware traditions from Crete. A strap-handled cup resembles a vase with a scalloped rim from Gournia on Crete, and the rivets on another vessel recall the handle attachments on silver and gold work from Mycenae. The tomb of Tutankhamun (d. 1325 BC) is justly famous for its profusion of gold: the funerary mask, rings, collars, gilded wooden shrines and attendant figures. Only one silver vessel was found, a vase in the form of a stylized pomegranate, engraved with bands of petals and leaves. A carved wooden throne, covered with sheet gold, was inlaid with polychrome glass paste, glazed terracotta (for the flesh of human figures) and silver leaf (for their drapery).

BRONZE AGE

AEGEAN

*c.*3000 TO 1100 BC

Frescoes from Egyptian Thebes can be used as evidence for close relations between Minoan Crete and Egypt. The gold and silver objects, identifiable by their yellow and dark blue colouring, carried by tribute bearers are clearly Minoan in form. There had been a long tradition of work in precious metal in the Aegean, aided by the existence of gold and silver mines in the Cyclades, in Attica and in Thrace. A few Cycladic shallow silver bowls survive, some decorated with incised chevron patterns. Stone vases and lamps would have been covered with sheet gold. Knowledge of Aegean metalwork is aided by the fact that potters imitated both the form and colour of vessels of gold, silver and bronze. Fine-walled pottery ('eggshell ware') echoes Cretan silver wares, but it is the rich contents of the shaft graves at Mycenae that give a real sense of Bronze Age splendour. There are inlaid swords and daggers, gold and silver cups – some conical, some with spool handles, some decorated with repoussé relief. A unique cup was made from electrum and inlaid with both gold and niello. These objects help archaeologists to envis-

CYCLADIC
SILVER BOWLS,
POSSIBLY FROM
EUBOEA, *c.*3000–
2300 BC (Left:
D19.6cm/7⅞in; right:
D24.6cm/9⅔in)

*The islands of the
Aegean were early
centres of metallurgy,
with extensive deposits
of lead ores from which
silver was extracted.
Most Cycladic silver
objects are of beaten
metal.*

ELECTRUM CUP, MYCENAE, c.1650–
1500 BC (H15.5cm/6in) (BELOW)

GOLD LIDS INLAID WITH SILVER,
VULCHITRUN (BULGARIA), 13TH–12TH
CENTURIES BC (D37cm/14½in) (RIGHT)

PHOENICIA AND

ETRURIA

c.750 TO 400 BC

age the opulence of the heroic age described by Homer. There are echoes of Aegean and Near Eastern work in precious metals in Europe. Vulchitrun in Bulgarian Thrace has produced a hoard of gold vessels weighing 12.5 kilos (27½lb), including two lids the surfaces of which are adorned with delicate spiral patterns of dark, overlaid silver. In Britain, the gold Rillaton Cup in the British Museum serves as a reminder of the formal sources of the ubiquitous Beaker Ware pottery, so typical of Bronze Age burials throughout northwest Europe.

ISRAEL

c.1300 TO 950 BC

One of the earliest craftsmen in precious metal whose name is known is Bezalel, who was entrusted with the construction of the Tabernacle during the exodus of the Jews from Egypt. The Lord is said to have blessed him with 'ability, with intelligence, with knowledge, and with all craftsmanship, to devise artistic designs, to work in gold and silver and bronze, in cutting stones for setting, and in carving wood, for work in

every skilled craft'. Much of the surface of the Tabernacle was overlaid with gold plates, and the liturgical vessels, 'the plates and dishes for incense, and its bowls and flagons with which to pour libations', were made from 'pure gold', as was the seven-branched candlestick 'made of hammered work'. Silver was used to inlay the columns and capitals which supported the surrounding screens. The total weight of precious metal is given in biblical sources as equivalent to a tonne of gold and three-and-a-half tonnes of silver. Weight and purity were always of paramount importance throughout antiquity.

Some centuries later, Solomon was to construct the Temple in Jerusalem. The whole of the inner sanctuary and the altar was overlaid with gold. The lavishness of the biblical descriptions has often been doubted, but probably unnecessarily: 30 grams (1oz) of gold can be beaten into a sheet 30 metres (c.300ft) square (not that Solomon's gold need have been that thin). Olivewood statues of cherubim, each ten cubits high, were also covered with gold; this was a regular practice so far as the most costly and venerable statues of antiquity were concerned, and can be matched by cult images at Babylon, Sparta, Athens, Olympia and elsewhere.

The material culture of the world Homer describes is that of his own day, the eighth or seventh century BC. The first prize in the foot race at the Funeral Games of Patroclus was 'a mixing bowl [crater] of silver, well wrought, which only held six measures, but far surpassed all others on earth in beauty, for skilled Sidonian craftsmen had made it well, and Phoenicians had brought it across the misty sea'. The most beautiful and most costly of the treasures in the house of Menelaus was a 'crater, well wrought in solid silver, with a rim of hammered gold, given to me by the king of Sidon'. Phoenician silver bowls have been found at Nimrud in Syria, in Cyprus and in central Italy. Many of them are decorated with scenes inspired by Egyptian art: rows of sphinxes, hunting scenes, pharaohs slaying their enemies, hieroglyphs.

Phoenician imports of silverware to Italy underlie Etruscan black *bucchero* pottery, which survives in vast quantities. The Etruscans exported gold libation bowls, seen in banquet scenes on frescoes in Etruscan tombs. An exquisite specimen in the Victoria & Albert Museum, London, is decorated with chevrons, meanders and an interlace pattern in fine granulation.

LYDIA AND

PERSIA

c.650 TO 325 BC

The wealth of Croesus, King of Lydia, was legendary. One source of it was the gold-bearing River Pactolus which flowed by his capital, Sardis. In the mid-sixth century Croesus made some impressive dedications at Greek sanctuaries:

those at Delphi included a gold *crater* weighing 225 kilos (495 lb), and a silver one that could hold sixty amphorae of wine for use at religious festivals. The latter was said to be made by Theodore of Samos and to be 'of no common work'. Theodore also made a gold *crater* for the bedroom of a Persian king, a chamber which doubled as the state

PERSIAN SILVER AMPHORA, DUVANLI (BULGARIA), 5TH CENTURY BC (H27cm/10⅝in)

This vessel is of a kind carried by tribute bearers on the reliefs of the Apadana at Persepolis. (FAR LEFT)

PERSIAN SILVER RHYTON, BOROVO (BULGARIA), 4TH CENTURY BC (H16.5cm/6½in)

The horizontal grooves on the body of the vessel are characteristic of Achaemenid Persian work in precious metal. A rhyton was used to aerate wine: here it would have poured from an aperture between the bull's forelegs. (LEFT)

treasury and contained a jewel-studded golden vine which extended over the bed. Many wine vessels and pieces of jewellery were carried in procession by tribute bearers from all over the Achaemenid Empire, as seen on reliefs at Persepolis. A distinctive form is an amphora with a spouted handle; a silver-gilt specimen with the spout ingeniously concealed within the body of a horned goat-lion has been preserved in a burial mound at Duvanli in Bulgarian Thrace. The Persian king could be lavish with his gifts. In the fifth century BC a Cretan gentleman was presented with, in addition to slaves, concubines and pieces of gold, a silver-footed bed with its coverings, a tent with a gaily coloured canopy, a silver throne, a gilded sunshade, twenty gold *phiales* (shallow libation bowls) set with jewels and a hundred large silver ones, and an unspecified number of silver *craters*.

GREECE

c.1000 TO 325 BC

'I owe a debt of 200 drachmas. How can I pay it?' asks a character in *The Babylonians* of 426 BC by Aristophanes. His companion replies: 'Here, take this silver cup and pay for it with that.' Gold and silver objects were usually made to round figures according to one weight standard or another, and in effect served as large-denomination bank notes. Phidias's gold and ivory statue of Athena Parthenos, which stood more than 11 metres (36ft) high, was made in such a way that the gold plates could be taken off and weighed, should accusations of embezzlement be made (as they were). Athens had a rich local supply of silver in the Laurium silver mines: 'A

fountain of silver lies beneath her soil', says one of Aeschylus's characters. The richer inhabitants of the city ate and drank from gold and silver, and Athenian plate was exported throughout the Mediterranean and beyond. Pindar mentions 'Athenian cups' in a poem written for a Sicilian patron. When the Athenian fleet left for Sicily in 415 BC, the whole of Piraeus was 'ringed with silver *craters*', from which libations were poured using gold and silver bowls, and brief descriptions of publicly owned plate still exist in the inventories of shrines and temples. Silver was a mark of gentility in Athens. A public pension paid to a descendant of a national hero included, in addition to a daily allowance, 100 Greek pounds of silver, presumably intended for his household plate. The Athenian Xenophon was stating the obvious in saying that, in times of prosperity, 'people have a very great use for

HEAD OF SILENUS: DETAIL OF GREEK
SILVER WINE-JUG HANDLE, VERGINA,
4TH CENTURY BC (Head: H6.5cm/2½in)

*The high degree of characterization is typical of the
skill of the foremost craftsmen in the 4th-century
Greek world.*

A few examples of Athenian silverware
have survived, notably a libation bowl
(*phiale*) and a drinking cup (*cantharos*) from
Duvanli (now in Plovdiv, Bulgaria), with
figure decoration in gold foil laid over the
surface. This effect was aped by the manufacturers of the infinitely cheaper red-figure
pottery which has survived in rather greater
numbers, and which serves as a useful guide
to the range of shapes and the nature of the
decoration on silver vessels given as prizes at
games or used at Athenian symposia. The

used by craftsmen in the Roman period.
They must also have been used by potters,
who very occasionally and erratically copied
the names of designers and silversmiths –
such as Exekias, Euphronius, Polygnotus or
Brygos ('the Phrygian') – on their wares.
The presence of names on silverware would
have served as a guarantee of the purity of
the metal in the days before official assay
offices were set up to determine the precise
quantities of impurities present in either
silver or gold articles.

DETAIL OF A
GREEK SILVER
LIBATION BOWL
(*PHIALE*)
DECORATED
WITH A GOLD-
FIGURE SCENE
OF A CHARIOT
RACE, DUVANLI
(BULGARIA),
5TH CENTURY BC
(D20.5cm/8in)

money: for the men are willing to spend on
fine armour, good horses, and impressive
houses and plate, while women are eager for
expensive dresses and gold jewellery'.

The poets Aeschylus and Pindar refer to
wealth in terms of 'gold-wrought and silver
cups' or a 'solid gold bowl, the peak of
possessions'; and Euripides describes a festival at Delphi at which the guests are
entertained with wine served from gold
craters in gold and 'silver inlaid' cups, whose
size increased as time went by – a discreet
security device. When the sanctuary was
sacked in the fourth century BC, the Del-
phians subsequently claimed to have lost
10,000 talents – equivalent to 260 tonnes – of
silver. Even allowing for exaggeration, this
would leave ample room even for 'big cups'
of gold and silver. A remarkable find at
Delphi was a life-size silver statue of a bull,
dedicated in the sixth or fifth century BC.

tendency for silver to become oxidized near
the sea probably accounts for the blue-black
aspect of the imitative fine Greek pottery.
The extreme purity (98–99 per cent) – and
hence softness – of the silver in question
would in any case have inhibited frequent
cleaning (although sulphur, the cleaning
agent for precious metal that is mentioned in
Homer's writings, would have rendered it
black in any case).

The gold-figure *phiale* from Duvanli
shows a chariot race and is full of finely
observed characterization. One youthful
charioteer is shown with his hair swept back,
and the first down just visible on his
receding chin; another bares his teeth in
grim determination to win. The horses are
exquisitely rendered, with tossing heads and
flaring nostrils, impressive musculature and
flowing tails. Artists' designs for Athenian
metalwork (called *graphides*) were still being

GREEK SILVER DEER-HEAD RHYTON,
POSSIBLY FROM THE BLACK SEA AREA,
4TH CENTURY BC (L29cm/11½in)

SCYTHIA AND

THRACE

c.600 TO 300 BC

It was said of the Scythians in antiquity that 'they despise gold and silver, much as other men covet them'. This used to be taken to mean that the Scythians lived a simple life, free from greed and acquisitiveness (and as a consequence, precious metal). However, the rich finds of precious metal objects from Scythian tombs in the Crimea and the Ukraine indicate that, unlike most other peoples, the Scythians were so careless of gold and silver that they even placed them in the grave, rather than keeping them for the use of the next generation. From the small gold and electrum plaques, stamped in great numbers to be sewn on garments, to the sheet metal overlays for wooden vessels and the elaborate jewellery and bow cases, finds from Scythian graves display a wide variety of motifs and styles. Activities from the everyday life of nomads, including milking time, lion hunts and warriors feasting, were rendered in low relief in a manner closely akin to Greek and Persian workmanship, and highly stylized stags and elks, and attacks by lions and griffins on helpless deer, horses and cattle, are evocative of the Scythians' Central Asiatic origins. Silver from Thrace displays a similar mixture of Greek, Persian and local styles. Numerous hoards of gold and silver objects have been found in Thrace, buried in the second half of the fourth century BC. Notable among these

THRACIAN
SILVER RHYTON,
PARTIALLY GILT,
DUVANLI
(BULGARIA),
c.400 BC
(H20.6cm/8in)

The form of this elegant vessel was based on a drinking horn.

THRACIAN SILVER PLAQUE OF A LION ATTACKING A STAG, PARTIALLY GILT, LUKOVIT (BULGARIA), 4TH CENTURY BC (L8.7cm/3$\frac{7}{10}$in)

This motif was extremely common in the art of the Near East and was taken over by Greek and Thracian craftsmen.

is the collection of 167 silver vessels from Rogozen, in northwest Bulgaria. Their total weight was 3,600 sigloi (nearly 640 oz), and in view of the fact that some of them were damaged in antiquity, they were probably on their way to the melting pot when they were hurriedly buried.

HELLENISTIC AGE

LATE 4TH

CENTURY TO 31 BC

Rapid changes in fashion took place as a direct result of Alexander the Great's conquest of the Achaemenid Empire between 334 and 323 BC. Depending on the amount of gold involved, Alexander's Persian booty could have been worth as much as £20 billion (nearly $40 billion). The sudden cessation of red-figure vase painting in Greece is a signal that gold-figure work (which was in essence a means of greatly enhancing the appearance, and doubtless the price, of a vessel with the minimum expenditure of material) ceased to be made. So much gold was suddenly available to Greeks in the eastern Mediterranean that it was no longer necessary to eke out limited supplies by using gold foil on silver. Instead, rather more vessels might be made from solid gold than hitherto.

The many new cities founded by Alexander and his successors, at Alexandria, Antioch and elsewhere, had aristocracies whose requirements were met by court craftsmen. At Antioch, in Syria, there was a temple the walls and roof of which were plated in gold, and it was not unique. King Antiochus Epiphanes (*c*.215–163 BC) would occasionally slip out of his palace and visit the shops of 'silver beaters' and 'gold casters' (a distinction which perhaps reflects the different ways in which the materials were worked). He would air his views on art before the 'relief makers and other craftsmen'. But this was regarded as eccentric behaviour and contributed to his nickname

Epimanes ('the Mad'). He also put on lavish games accompanied by a procession of thousands of finely accoutred soldiers and courtiers, hundreds of sacrificial animals, elephant tusks and statues. One of the king's friends alone contributed 1,000 slaves, each of whom carried silver vessels, none weighing less than 1,000 drachmas (4.3 kg/9½lbs). Following them were 80 women in gold-footed litters, and 500 in silver-footed litters, all richly caparisoned.

But these celebrations were as nothing compared to a procession held in Alexandria in the eighties of the first century BC, the cost of which amounted to more than 3,000 tonnes of silver. Golden tripods, thunderbolts, eagles, armour and crowns of colossal size were carried through the streets. One float carried a gigantic silver spear and another a gold phallus 54 metres (180ft) long with, at the tip, a gold star 2.7 metres (9ft) across. Huge gold *craters*, libation bowls and drinking cups were outdone in size by a silver *crater* with a capacity of more than 2,300 litres (600 gals). The cart it stood on was drawn by 600 men. This vessel is said to have had figures in relief beneath the rim and handles, as well as under the base, while around the middle it was wreathed with a gold band studded with jewels. (Hellenistic literary sources frequently mention gem-studded plate, but none survives; the nearest equivalent is turquoise-studded Bactrian jewellery.) There was in addition a solid silver table 6 metres (20ft) long, and a further thirty tables which were 3 metres (10ft) in length. The procession culminated in '400 cartloads of silver vessels, 20 of gold vessels and 800 of spices'.

None of these objects has survived in its original form, and only relatively small items can be discussed with any confidence. For example, the bowl of the East, as opposed to the handled cup of Greece, became the drinking vessel of preference in the Hellenistic world. While only ceramic analogues of the gold vessels are extant (in the form of red-glazed mould-made pottery), some silver examples of the period have survived. Their decoration is frequently characterized by rich floral and vegetal motifs. Sometimes they were raised in one piece, sometimes they were cast and then chased, and sometimes the craftsman employed an ingenious device to make the metal go further. From the second century BC, and into the first century AD, vessels might be made in two pieces: an outer casing that carried the embossed decoration, and an inner, smooth liner. The space between would be hollow. They would thus look as though they were of great intrinsic value, while in reality they were not.

A related technique was to adorn the centre of a dish with a pictorial emblem: a circular tondo ornament would be worked in high relief with the head of a deity, a full-length figure or even a group. Such an emblem would be soldered on to the centre of a larger dish, rather as, on a smaller scale, a silver coin might serve as the tondo ornament of a drinking cup. Only South Italian black-glazed ceramic versions of the latter are known, whereas some silver emblems still survive, though usually parted from their original settings.

Information concerning ancient silversmiths at work is rare. An inscription from Delos of 279 BC tells of the silversmith Aristarchus, who had been employed to do odd jobs during the previous year: he was paid 2 drachmas for 'attaching the handle of the silver *crater* which had fallen off'; the 3 obols' worth of coals, which is the next entry, was presumably part of the expenditure for the same job. Later Aristarchus was paid 1 drachma 1½ obols (6 obols equalled 1 drachma) 'for making a cup', and then 1 drachma for 'repairing the handle of a bronze *cothon*, a vessel of unknown shape', in connection with which a drachma's worth of coals and another of wax (for modelling?) were used. Aristarchus's income cannot have been very high. The fact that mercury gilding was regularly practised from the third century onward cannot have made the ancient silversmith's job a pleasant or healthy one.

The immense wealth of the eastern Mediterranean attracted the attention of Celtic tribes of central Europe. A determined attempt was made by Gaulish invaders of Greece in 279 BC to take and sack Delphi, on account of the great riches the sanctuary contained, but it was repulsed. More than a century later, invaders from the north carried away from Thrace a splendid silver vessel which was found in a bog in northern Denmark in 1891. The 'Gundestrup Cauldron' consists of a large plain bowl edged with a double row of embossed plates

HELLENISTIC SILVER BOWL, 2ND CENTURY BC (D12.7cm/5in)

An elaborate piece, this bowl is made in two parts: a smooth interior and an outer casing, joined at the rim. Erotes, birds and a butterfly are to be found among the floral decoration.

THRACIAN SILVER CAULDRON,
GUNDESTRUP, DENMARK,
1ST CENTURY BC (H42cm/16½in)

*One of the most enigmatic objects to have survived in
northern Europe, the imagery of the scenes embossed
on the panels of the Gundestrup cauldron is thought to
have originated from India.*

surmounted by a tubular rim, but it is now in
a fragmentary condition. On what survives
there are scenes of war and sacrifice, of
strange deities wrestling with ferocious
beasts and of a goddess flanked by elephants.
The closest parallels to this iconography are
to be found in contemporary India, albeit at
several removes. Not only do these serve as
reminders that Alexander's conquests
extended as far as the Indus, but also that
artistic motifs might travel long distances
across the Eurasian landmass. It is interesting to note the apparent survival of the
Persian weight standard in Thrace, for the
total original weight of the Gundestrup
Cauldron has been estimated as being equivalent to 1,666 sigloi.

ROMAN REPUBLIC

c.200 TO 31 BC

It was through conquest and despolia-
tion that the Romans enriched themselves, gradually becoming the effective successors to the Hellenistic kingdoms.
It was through the acquisition of booty that
the use of precious metal became at all
widespread in Roman society – much to the
disgust of the traditionally minded, who
were still condemning luxury in the first
century AD. The Greek cities of southern
Italy and Sicily were looted first (Syracuse
in 211 BC, Capua in 210, Tarentum in 209),
then Greece itself (beginning with Eretria in
198 and ending with Athens, Olympia and
Epidaurus in 87–85 BC).

The principal means by which the Roman
public became aware of the range and
splendour of Hellenistic plate was through
seeing quantities of it carried in the triumphal processions celebrated by victorious
generals on their return to Rome. In 167 BC

Aemilius Paulus had 3,000 men carry
'coined silver in 750 vessels, each holding
three talents [*c*.75kg/165lb]. . . . Others
brought silver *craters* and drinking horns
and drinking bowls and cups, each well
arranged for display, and all extraordinary
for their size as well as for the thickness of
their embossed work.' Also exhibited was all
the gold plate used at the Macedonian king's
dinner table, as well as a 'sacred bowl which
Aemilius had made, weighing ten talents
[about a quarter of a tonne] of solid gold and
set with jewels'. Court goldsmiths had
evidently been captured as well.

By 161 BC there was a sumptuary law
controlling the amount of plate that could be
used at banquets at Rome. The limit of 100
Roman pounds' weight of silver (*c*.33kg/
73lb), suggests how resplendent some banquets may have been.

The last century of the Roman Republic
was one of those rare periods in antiquity
when there was an interest in the silver wares
of the past. The bequest of Pergamum to
Rome in 133 BC by its last king is said to have
brought much silver onto the Roman
market and to have encouraged an interest in
early pieces. It was probably on this occasion
that Gaius Gracchus (d. 121 BC) acquired
some silver dolphins for more than ten times
their bullion value. Even higher prices are
recorded for the first century BC: Lucius
Crassus had a pair of cups decorated by the
Greek silversmith Mentor, active more than
three centuries earlier, for which he had paid
100,000 sesterces (*c*.70kg/154lb of silver),
but 'he confessed that for shame he never
dared to use them'. More shameless were
Roman provincial governors of the period:
Cotta 'appropriated untold gold and silver'
from Heraclea in Bithynia, while Verres in
Sicily would hold whole communities to
ransom until they had handed over their
plate. Verres was especially interested in the
emblems on drinking vessels, which he
would cut out and have remounted by his
palace goldsmiths. It was a relatively easy
matter for Verres to locate his victims, for it
had been the practice in Sicily for rich men
to exhibit their plate on stands (*abaci*).
Verres's rapacity led to greater controls

ROMAN SILVER CUP, ALISE-SAINTE-REINE, COTE-D'OR,
1ST CENTURY BC–1ST CENTURY AD (H11.5cm/4½in) (BELOW)

ROMAN SILVER DRINKING VESSEL, BOSCOREALE, NEAR
NAPLES, 1ST CENTURY AD (H10.4cm/4in) (RIGHT)

being placed on officials posted abroad.

Comparatively little silver of the first century BC survives. One silver service (*ministerium*) probably comes from Tivoli, and was perhaps buried during the disturbances of the civil wars (49–31 BC), but never recovered by its owners. The thirty items include: a pair of drinking cups (cast and lathe-spun, with delicate bands of once-gilded ornament on the rim, at the shoulder and on the foot); a ladle with a duck's-head handle; a small spouted pitcher (raised, with a long hammered spout, and a cast foot and handle soldered on); a mug (raised, with chased and punched ornament at the rim and base, lathe-finished, with added feet and handle); a platter (edged with very fine beading); a dish in the form of a shell; three dishes and three cups (all with added ring feet); ten spoons with elliptical bowls; and seven others with round bowls and pointed handles intended, it is thought, for eating snails. Many pieces are inscribed with the name of 'Sattia, daughter of Lucius', as well as their weights. The total comes to just over ten Roman pounds.

EARLY ROMAN
EMPIRE
31 BC TO *c.* AD 300

Pliny the Elder's friend Pompeius Paulinus, who was governor of Germania Inferior in the mid-first century AD, never travelled without taking with him 12,000 pounds (nearly four tonnes) of silverware (an English ambassador in the eighteenth century only needed 4,000 oz [124kg] to make the necessary impression on those he did business with). Even the most apparently lavish hoards of Roman silver known are modest by comparison with such flamboyance. A few such hoards from the Naples area, containing silver of the first century AD, exist because of the eruption of Vesuvius in AD 79, which covered nearby cities and settlements with ash and lava. Most people escaped, presumably with their valuables, but some of these were left behind. Thus, at Pompeii, a chest full of

silver (118 items weighing 23.5 kg/52lb) was found in the House of the Menander, and at nearby Boscoreale a cache of 109 pieces of silverware (weighing nearly 30kg/66lb) and a thousand gold coins – clearly an individual's total wealth – was found hidden in a farmhouse cistern.

The cups in the Boscoreale hoard are especially ornate. One two-handled, low-walled cup (*skyphos*) carries a representation of a triumphal procession and an official sacrifice, another the Emperor Augustus receiving a statue of Victory from his legendary ancestor Venus, and the submission of barbarian captives. Some have exquisitely rendered still-life scenes, others show exuberant putti riding on animals. Long-legged marsh birds feed their young amid delicate plants on a series of two-handled goblets on high feet (*canthari*), and a pair with horizontal ring handles are covered with plant scrolls inhabited by birds and game animals. The surfaces of other cups bear plane leaves or olive leaves and fruits, in low and high relief respectively. A pair of handled beakers are decorated with

ROMAN SILVER CUP, HILDESHEIM (GERMANY), LATE 1ST CENTURY BC (H12.5cm/4⅞in)

One of a pair of magnificent cups from the Hildesheim hoard. Allusions to the cult of Bacchus and to the theatre adorn the main frieze. The rim and inner lining were made separately. The foot was cast and lathe-spun.

ROMAN SILVER BOWL DECORATED IN HIGH RELIEF WITH AN EMBLEM OF AFRICA, BOSCOREALE (NEAR NAPLES), 1ST CENTURY AD (Bowl: D22.5cm/8⅝in; emblem: D14.5cm/5⅔in)

A masterpiece of the Roman silversmith's art, this bowl was deposited with 117 other items by someone about to flee from the eruption of Vesuvius in AD 79.

the skeletons of famous Greeks: Euripides, Sophocles, Zeno and Menander, and graffiti of macabre humour. All are made with the double-walled technique described earlier, and most were partially gilded. The emblems of some of the bowls are hollow as well: two bowls have emblems in the form of the heads and shoulders of two Roman gentlemen, while a larger one contains a magnificent bust of the personification of Africa, who carries a horn of plenty, wears an elephant-skin hat and is laden with other attributes. A pair of splendid jugs (*oenochoae*) are *tours de force* of repoussé work, for the winged Victories and their sacrificial animals were hammered from the inside. The last-mentioned motifs are certainly Greek, and could still have been seen outside the Nike Temple on the Athenian Acropolis. They illustrate well the classicism which

marks early Roman Imperial decorative art.

Perhaps the finest of all early Imperial silverware is the wine *crater* from Hildesheim, one of seventy silver objects found in a hoard 250 kilometres (156 miles) beyond the Rhine frontier. Its surface is covered with spiral tendrils of great delicacy inhabited by playful putti. The Hildesheim hoard is puzzling in that it is incomplete: sets of cups have been broken up, suggesting that the hoard was a share of booty taken from the Romans before burial in the sixties or seventies of the first century.

Several dozen hoards of Roman silverware are known from around the empire (and beyond), which reflect the disturbed conditions of the third, fourth and fifth centuries. Even though most of them are modest by the standards of what is known to have existed, they serve as reminders of how

ROMAN DECORATIVE PLAQUE
SHOWING HERCULES AND THE
LERNAEAN HYDRA, 4TH CENTURY AD
(H18.8cm/7⅓in)

Bronze is here inlaid with copper and silver.
(FAR RIGHT)

ROMAN SILVER SAUCEPAN AND CUP,
RUFFIEU (ISÈRE), 2ND–3RD
CENTURY AD (Saucepan: L19cm/7½in; cup:
H4.7cm/1⅚in) (RIGHT)

ROMAN SILVER
BOWLS, PLATES
AND SPOONS,
VIENNE (ISÈRE),
3RD CENTURY AD
(Largest plate:
D33.4cm/13in)

*These articles form
part of a hoard found
during a rescue
excavation in the
French town of Vienne
in 1985.*

tempting the wealth of the Roman Empire must have been for those living beyond its borders. But buried in haste, and usually found by chance, such hoards do not tell the full story. And even when they are found in a controlled excavation (which happens rarely), there are still outstanding questions. The group of silver objects found in 1984 in a rescue excavation in Vienne (Isère) – plates, bowls, a mirror, a pepper pot and a spoon neatly packed inside a hanging bowl embossed with shells, more spoons, a 'fork', a tooth/ear-pick, and a small jar embossed with a marine chariot race located nearby – illustrate all the various techniques employed by the third-century silversmith: hammering, embossing, casting, lathe-turning, gilding, chasing and inlaying with niello. The decorative repertoire is characteristic: sea monsters, banqueting, farming,

the hunt. There was, however, a total absence of drinking cups from the Vienne hoard (which is far from unique in this respect). There are two possible explanations: the owner may have used glass vessels which, being intrinsically valueless, were not hidden, or he or she may have used gold vessels which were not buried, but (as Krugerrands might be today) carried away for expenses incurred in flight. Although the latter may not be applicable to the Vienne hoard (which was found in a house in an artisans' quarter), there is circumstantial evidence, in the form of inventories referring to both silver and gold objects, that this may have been the case elsewhere. Although large quantities of gold on the tables of rich Romans have been described, only three vessels of the early Imperial period have actually survived; the ubiquitous – and

imitative – red-glazed pottery of the period illustrates the kind of object made in gold.

With regard to imitation in other media, the status of glass in Roman antiquity has been somewhat overrated. It is widely believed that a variety of silver drinking cup, found, for example, in the Chaourse, Notre Dame d'Alençon, Wettingen and Water Newton hoards of the third and fourth century, and decorated with a series of hollow facets, was made in imitation of glassware. Rather, both the silver and glass examples will have been imitations of vessels of rock crystal or sardonyx, truly luxurious materials of great intrinsic value. The Greek silversmith Mentor is said also to have been a worker in rock crystal, and it is likely there was a close relationship between practitioners of luxury crafts in the Roman period as well.

Very little wrought gold has survived from this period: a large plate, an elaborate bowl and a tall ewer found in a hoard at Pietroasa in Romania. Very many pieces of silver, by contrast, are known. This will not, however, have reflected ancient reality, but is a by-product of the fact that silver was a relatively cumbersome commodity, whereas gold was more readily convertible into goods and services in an emergency. It is not too difficult to imagine the owners of the richest deposits of silverware that are extant, the hoards from Mildenhall and Kaiseraugst, the Esquiline hoard (named after one of Rome's seven hills) and the so-called Seuso hoard having possessed wine cups (and quite possibly other vessels) of gold. The same considerations would have applied to ecclesiastical plate. Pagan temples were stripped of their possessions by Constantine the Great in 311, and thenceforth Christianity became the official religion of the empire. In practical terms, much gold and silver plate would have been melted down and remade. Even before this event, an inventory of the plate belonging to a church at Constantine in Numidia (present-day Algeria), dated 303, records '2 gold chalices, 6 silver chalices, 6 silver ewers, 1 silver paten, 2 silver lights'. No known hoard of church plate contains gold vessels; perhaps they were deposited by communities too poor to possess them, or perhaps they were carried away by those who hid the rest. Gold vessels, jewellery and coins figure large in representations of imperial largesse, as does silverware.

One of the most characteristic forms of late Roman silver was the picture plate. An outstanding example is the Mildenhall Great Dish, 60.5 cm (24in) in diameter and decorated in low relief with the bearded head of Oceanus in the centre, surrounded by successive rows of nereids riding sea monsters,

ROMAN
RECTANGULAR
SILVER PLATE,
KAISERAUGST,
SWITZERLAND,
4TH CENTURY AD
(L41.5cm/16¼in)

*The central panel
depicts Ariadne,
Bacchus and a satyr.*
(ABOVE)

ROMAN SILVER
PICTURE PLATE,
PARABIAGO,
LOMBARDY, 4TH
CENTURY AD
(D39cm/15⅛in)

*Cybele and Attis are
shown seated in a
chariot drawn by lions.*
(RIGHT)

and of Dionysus and Heracles accompanied by energetic – and naturalistic – satyrs, maenads and Pan figures. The rim is heavily beaded. Such a plate would have been made for display rather than for practical use. The largest known picture plate was made for the celebrations in 388 of the tenth anniversary of the accession of Emperor Theodosius I. Found bent in half, it measures 74cm (29in) across, and shows the emperor enthroned before his palace and accompanied by princes and courtiers. Almost as big is a plate found in the River Rhône showing a similarly enthroned Achilles quarrelling with Ulysses over the slave girl Briseis, one of the themes of *The Iliad*. The earlier story of Achilles, from his birth to his discovery disguised as a woman on the island of Skyros, appears on two more picture plates: one from Kaiseraugst near Basle (one of more than sixty vessels found inside the Roman fortress there in 1962), unusually signed by the silversmith, Pausylypos of Thessalonica, and another which is from the newly publicized Seuso hoard. Episodes are spread out around the rims, with the culminating scene in the tondo.

The Seuso hoard consists of 14 magnificent silver vessels and the large bronze cauldron in which they were deposited. The place of discovery is open to question, but since it is impossible to establish the place of manufacture even of objects whose findspots are known (it is safest to think in terms of an international style), this need not concern us. What is important is that the hoard in question includes some of the finest late Roman plate known. Even the simplest items in the assemblage – a pair of tall, slim ewers decorated with geometric designs, a bowl with fluted ornament and a plate with a tondo of interlocking hexagons – are splendid objects.

Three more ewers are considerably more elaborate. One is covered with a series of 120 hexagonal panels on which intricate niello-inlaid motifs alternate with engraved and gilded busts, amphorae, and wild animals (lions, boars, bears and hares) and their keepers. Even the small domed lid has a series of small portrait heads. Another is of

ROMAN SILVER PICTURE PLATE, THE RHÔNE, NEAR AVIGNON, 4TH CENTURY AD (D70cm/27⅖in)

Scenes from the life of Achilles were common on late Roman picture plates. He sits enthroned, addressing Ulysses, while the slave-girl Briseis is led towards him. (ABOVE)

ROMAN SILVER PICTURE PLATE, ALMANDRALEJO, SPAIN, AD 388 (D74cm/29in)

This plate celebrates the 10th anniversary of the accession of Emperor Theodosius I. (LEFT)

ROMAN SILVER
CANDELABRUM,
PARTIALLY
GILDED AND
INLAID WITH
NIELLO,
KAISERAUGST,
SWITZERLAND,
4TH CENTURY AD
(Extended: H1.17m/
45⅝in; retracted:
78cm/30½in)

*The stem is hexagonal,
and the upper part can
be retracted into the
lower part. The elegance
of the alternating
openwork and nielloed
zones has been won at
the expense of a certain
fragility.*

ROMAN SILVER AMPHORA, PORTO
BARATTI, TUSCANY, 4TH CENTURY AD
(H61cm/23¹¹⁄₁₂in)

the same basic form, with an angled handle, an openwork thumb plate, the junction of neck and body disguised with a wreath of oak leaves, a faceted body and a scalloped foot. Each face of the body contains the embossed figure of an ecstatic Dionysus, Pan, a satyr or a maenad, akin to those on the Mildenhall Great Dish. Details are gilded. The third of these ewers is embossed with three narrative bands: hunting scenes above and below, and in the main field the story of Hippolytus and Phaedra. It in turn is part of a set, for the same principal motif of the chaste youth and his stepmother is repeated on a pair of buckets (*situlae*) which have separately cast, heavily beaded rims and loop handles. All three vessels have details picked out in gold. Together they weigh nearly 40 Roman pounds.

An amphora combines several of the themes found on other pieces. In the main field there is a Dionysiac rout, with a marine scene, including shrimps, below, and the hunt and fighting animals above. The handles are in the form of a pair of lively leopards, repeating motifs that occur within the decorative schemes. The body of the amphora was made in two pieces, the join at the shoulder being concealed with a classical ovolo pattern. The base-ring was made separately and soldered on. The panther handles were cast. Until recently, this kind of amphora was extremely rare, the best known example being a piece from Romania depicting a battle between Greeks and Amazons in the main field and with centaur handles. Then, in 1968, another – without its handles – was found in the sea off Porto

Baratti in Tuscany. This probably ranks as the finest of all extant late Roman silver objects. Its surface is covered with 112 oval medallions, each embossed with a tiny figure.

A circular toilet box, embossed with a lady surrounded by attendants carrying items for the bath and the toilette, is matched by a similar box from the Esquiline hoard, and only surpassed in splendour by the Projecta Casket, also from the Esquiline. The latter was a wedding present, and shows Projecta and her husband Secundus in a roundel on the lid, and marriage rites on other panels. These decorative features are all in repoussé and surrounded by bands of formal ornament.

But the plates are perhaps the most eye-catching pieces in the Seuso hoard. One is relatively plain, with a central medallion of interlocking hexagons surrounded by a wave pattern, all inlaid in niello. A picture plate has the Achilles legend, described above, as well as a version of a scene shown on the west pediment of the Parthenon, namely the struggle between Athena and Poseidon over the land of Attica. The Parthenon group commemorates Athenian victories over barbarians in the fifth century BC; it has been suggested that the similar scene on the Achilles plate may have been intended to recall the reported appearance of Athena and Achilles which put heart into the defenders of Athens against the Goths in AD 396. The scenes on the flange are divided by theatrical masks. The same device is used on the largest picture plate in the hoard, the central tondo of which shows Meleager resting after the hunt of the Calydonian boar. Somewhat unusually, the interior of this plate is decorated with finely chased acanthus leaves.

The most informative of the picture plates, however, is the one that bears Seuso's name in the metrical inscription around the central medallion: 'May these little vessels, O Seuso, last for you for many ages, so that they might profit, and be a source of honour for your descendants.' This well expresses the principal purpose of ornamental plate throughout antiquity: to add to the dignity of a family or an institution, and to be at the same time a realizable asset in time of need. The Seuso plate was clearly a gift, a fact which recalls the role played by gold and silver in the gift exchange system which prevailed in late antiquity. The presence of a discreet Chi-rho symbol (the first two letters of 'Christ' in Greek) must mean that both Seuso and his benefactor were Christians. The main scene is akin to that on a plate from Kaiseraugst, which shows a seaside city, and one from Cesena, Italy, on which an outdoor banquet, a duck pond and a horse, its groom and a stable are depicted. There are stag and boar hunts, and another banquet on the Seuso plate, as well as horses (one of which is named), dogs, a rabbit, and men fishing in a stream, cutting up meat and cooking: the 'good life' in the eyes of a late Roman aristocrat. The miniature scenes on the flange include more hunts and a villa.

SASSANIAN
EMPIRE
AD 226 TO 651

The Persian Sassanians, who ruled Mesopotamia and Iran, regarded themselves in many ways as the successors of the Achaemenids. The imagery of their work in precious metal centres around idealized kingship. Several Sassanian bowls are known which show kings hunting (the regal activity *par excellence*), and a silver-gilt head of a king survives as a reminder of the role played by gold and silver in ancient sculpture. Sassanian silversmiths shared many forms, motifs and techniques with their Roman contemporaries (ewers, for example, resemble those in the Seuso hoard, and bear comparable decoration) and influenced Chinese silverwork, but the high relief on some of their bowls was achieved by means of separately cast or hammered figures fixed into place in ridges on the surface. There is much use of niello and mercury gilding.

ROMAN SILVER PLATE, PARTIALLY GILDED WITH NIELLO INLAY, KAISERAUGST, SWITZERLAND, 4TH CENTURY AD (D59cm/23in)

EARLY
BYZANTIUM
c. AD 500 TO 670

Much silver of this period bears official hallmarks – as many as five – but neither their purpose nor the mechanism of the procedure is as yet fully understood. There is no observable difference between the purity of stamped and unstamped silver (94–98 per cent), and it is uncertain whether the stamps were added in Constantinople or in local mints. It is clear, however, that there was far more government control than hitherto. Liturgical plate figures large in both the historical sources and the surviving silver (although the latter mostly comes from village churches, rather than metropolitan centres). Lavish donations of silver revetments – to cover screens, altars, *ciboria* (free-standing shrines), doors and thrones – are thus recorded: 40,000 Roman pounds were given to St Sophia in Constantinople by Justinian in 537. The practice survives in the way icons in Orthodox churches today are usually covered with metal. Votive plaques, with representations of the organs to be healed, or with prayers of thanks for cures, are also found in the archaeological record. This tradition goes back to pagan times, and a variation occurs in what is the earliest known collection of Christian plate, the Water Newton (Cambridgeshire) hoard of the fourth century, comprising 20 silver

BYZANTINE
SILVER PATEN
WITH THE
COMMUNION OF
THE APOSTLES,
KAPER KORAON
(SYRIA), 6TH
CENTURY AD
(D35cm/13¾in)

*One of several silver
objects dedicated at a
village church by
parishioners. The
inscription reads: 'For
the repose of the soul of
Sergia, daughter of John
and of Theodosius, and
for the salvation of
Megas and of Nonnous
and of their children.'*

DARK AGES

c. AD 500 TO 1000

The discovery of the seventh-century ship burial at Sutton Hoo in Suffolk provides a rare insight into courtly life in early Anglo-Saxon England. Intricate jewellery – a gold buckle with interlace decoration in a style with close parallels in Sweden, and gold cloisonné work set with garnets recalling the adornments of Merovingian France – as well as silver plates and spoons from Constantinople attest to the wide contacts of the original owner. Surviving Anglo-Saxon work in precious metal is negligible which, in one respect, is extraordinary as contem-

plaques bearing Chi-rho symbols, bowls, jugs, a two-handled cup and a strainer.

The church silver from the village of Kaper Koraon in northern Syria has been preserved in a hoard (recently reconstructed thanks to painstaking detective work). More than 50 objects – chalices, patens, crosses, spoons, strainers, plaques, a ladle and a mirror – were presented to the church of St Sergius between 540 and 640 by members of four or five important families. One donor is described as an *arguroprates* (silver seller), and may have held a position in a state silver factory. Among these donations are two patens made in the tradition of late Roman picture plates, showing the Communion of the Apostles: Christ is shown twice on each paten, distributing wine from a chalice to six Apostles on one side, and bread to six others on the right. Both were hammered, burnished on the front, embossed with relief decoration from the back, then gilded with foil. Inscriptions (in niello) appear on the flanges. The shape of chalice in these scenes – a bulbous cup on a high conical foot with a knob between them – is the same as that of those in the hoard. All are inscribed beneath the rim, and one is embossed with figures of Apostles standing within arcades. It became the customary shape for eucharistic chalices.

ANGLO-SAXON
CHALICE OF
PARTIALLY
GILDED, SILVER-
PLATED COPPER
WITH NIELLO
INLAY,
KREMSMUNSTER,
AUSTRIA, c.AD
777 (H27cm/10⅔in)

*Made for Duke
Tassilo, whose name it
bears, the bowl of the
chalice is decorated with
images of Christ and
the Four Evangelists.*

porary accounts give the impression that England was awash with gold and silver in both churches and private houses. According to a twelfth-century report, a chalice found in the coffin of St Cuthbert had a bowl of onyx mounted on a lion 'of the purest gold'; at York altars were covered with gold, silver and precious stones; and at Ely an effigy of the Virgin 'of gold, silver and gems' was 'priceless because of its size' and sat on a throne 'as long as a man'. It was in the expectation of rich booty that England was constantly attacked by the Danes; in 1066 Norman adventurers came into possession of 'vessels of silver and gold, the description of whose number and beauty would strain credulity'.

Ireland enjoyed an equally rich Dark Age material culture, and one that was likewise the object of envy by Norsemen. Thanks to fear of marauding Vikings, the magnificent jewellery and ecclesiastical plate from the Ardagh and Derrynaflan hoards has survived. The latter was discovered near the site of an important monastery in County Tipperary, and included a large silver communion chalice, a silver paten with its stand and a bronze strainer inlaid with silver panels. The chalice is the most splendid of its kind, with intricately wrought gold filigree panels and amber set beneath the rim, over the handles and around the base. The paten is made up from numerous parts, and was assembled with the aid of a code of engraved letters and symbols. It is ultimately based on late Roman plates with richly decorated flanges, its upper edge enriched with 24 gold filigree panels of men, beasts, an eagle, snakes, and interlaced and spiral decoration.

EARLY ISLAM

c. AD 622 TO 1000

The presence of lavish silver revetments and furnishings in the Kaaba at Mecca and at the Dome of the Rock in Jerusalem shows that there cannot have been a very strong resistance to silver

in religious circles, despite the slogan recorded as early as 735–8: 'He who drinks from a silver vessel will have Hellfire gurgling in his belly.' It was the close association between precious metal and the drinking of alcohol which led to the proscription of gold and silver in many Islamic societies. By the same token, it was a love of wine among royalty and military aristocracies, especially in Iran, that led to the manufacture of gold and silver vessels. These are frequently mentioned in chronicles and literary sources, but, as so often, very few actually survive.

VIKING SILVER HOARD, CUERDALE, LANCASHIRE, 9TH CENTURY AD

IRISH SILVER CHALICE, ARDAGH, CO. LIMERICK, MID-8TH CENTURY AD (H17.8cm/7in)

A liturgical vessel, this piece was made in the tradition of late Roman chalices, intended for the distribution of Communion wine to a congregation.

THE MEDIEVAL PERIOD

The destruction of much medieval goldsmith's work makes it difficult to envisage the riches, both religious and secular, produced in the period from approximately the end of the first millennium until the beginning of the Renaissance. However, a number of pieces have survived the ravages of war and the vagaries of fashion, preserved in the ecclesiastical treasuries of Europe. These include many gilt-metal wares which have remained intact, if often restored at later dates, since they lacked the intrinsic value which caused pieces to be melted down for specie in times of hardship.

The two styles associated with the Middle Ages in Europe are the Romanesque and the Gothic. The first, almost by definition, was a classicizing influence, born of a time of revival and expansion following the disintegration of empires and invasions; the second, which evolved during an era of crusades, castles and chivalry, drew on the preceding style, but in many ways was a reaction to it. From a technical standpoint, craftsmen had a valuable treatise in Theophilus's De Diversis Artibus, *probably written in the early 1100s, and significant decorative techniques, such as the use of translucent enamels and enamelling in the round, were developed at this date. Later, printed designs enabled patterns to be circulated throughout Europe cheaply and speedily, thus laying the foundation for new ideas from which sprang the Renaissance.*

PLAQUE FROM THE KLOSTERNEUBURG PULPIT, *CHAMPLEVÉ* ENAMEL AND COPPER-GILT, MOSAN, 1181 (DETAIL)

———

An inscription records that the pulpit was made for Provost Wernher, head of the Augustinian Canons, by Nicholas of Verdun, in 1181. Damaged in a fire, the pulpit was converted into an altar retable in 1331, using the original plaques. The scene from the second book of Kings shows the prophet Elijah being drawn up to heaven by the chariot and horses of fire.

ROMANESQUE SILVER

The full story of the stylistic development of goldsmiths' work during the Romanesque period is virtually impossible to tell. Losses and destruction over the centuries have left few vessels extant, and these pieces give a very one-sided view of form and style. Many surviving wares have been damaged or substantially altered to suit the tastes of a later period, thus bearing little resemblance to their original Romanesque forms. Manuscript illustrations and period inventories can be helpful in terms of showing, respectively, the general form and range of silver and gold vessels in use, but not their precise details. Knowledge of Romanesque goldsmiths is also sparse: few names are known, and few signed wares survive.

The work that has survived has done so under very specific circumstances. Controlled excavation of sites such as abbeys and churches in the latter part of the twentieth century has led to the discovery of numerous important Romanesque metal objects, but these finds are mostly fragmentary and damaged. Although intact vessels have been found in datable graves, by far the most significant extant wares are those carefully preserved objects associated with an important personage, such as the reliquary of a saint. These have been kept in cathedral treasuries or museums, carefully inventoried over the centuries and rarely, if ever, used. Many of these pieces have been subjected to drastic restoration and alteration, but in a good number of cases such treatment has contributed to their survival. Deliberate concealment has also played its part in the survival of Romanesque rarities. At times of iconoclasm important relics and shrines were carefully hidden, such as the twelfth-century Eltenberg Reliquary, which was stored up a chimney. It is from finds and fragments such as these that the history of goldsmiths' work in the Romanesque period has to be constructed.

ENGLISH METALWORK

The origins of Romanesque metalwork in England must be sought in earlier Viking and Anglo-Saxon stylistic traditions. The late Anglo-Saxon period was celebrated for its metalwork, attested by the wealth of descriptions of shrines, altar plate and reliquaries in contemporary documents. Most have disappeared, but a few examples of early eleventh-century goldsmiths' work have survived and give some indication of the maker's skill, such as a circular hammered-silver brooch of *c*.1000 from Sutton on the Isle of Ely, Cambridgeshire. The brooch is engraved on the front with intersecting circles, stylized animals

and plant motifs, and on the back with the name of a former owner, Aedvwen, coupled with a curse on any who might take the brooch from her. An example of the 'Ringerike' style of Viking ornament, characterized by the use of lobed tendrils, the brooch was found in the seventeenth century in a lead casket with coins, a dish and some rings. Although its engraving and crosshatching are not particularly well done, the intensity and vigour of the design more than compensate for weak execution.

Ecclesiastical metalwork of this period from England includes a group of base metal censer covers dating from the tenth century, the forms of which resemble church towers; the finest examples are inlaid with engraved silver plates and animals are incorporated into the openwork designs.

One of the most outstanding masterpieces of English Romanesque art is the candlestick commissioned between 1107 and 1113 by Abbot Peter for the Benedictine monastery of Gloucester. It was cast by the *cire-perdue* method in three separate parts from a copper alloy with a very high silver content, which has led to the suggestion that silver vessels had been melted down to make it. The openwork design comprises animals and human figures among foliage. Its triangular base has three feet in the form of dragons, the central knop contains the symbols of the four Evangelists within silver roundels with niello work and the mid-section features scenes of men fighting beasts and centaurs. In addition, three winged dragons with prominent tails bite the upper rim's edge, while on the base the clawed feet of monsters reach down to grip the heads of human figures held fast in foliage. The entire surface presents an impression of intense activity, yet the design is executed so skilfully that the usual proportions of contemporary candlesticks, made up of spreading feet and cone-shaped upper sections, have been kept.

The candlestick bears several Latin inscriptions. Two narrow bands twisting around the stem extol 'the kind devotion of Abbot Peter and his flock [who] gave me to the Church of St Peter at Gloucester', while the outer edge of the pan reads 'This burden of light, this work of virtue shining with holy doctrine, teaches us so that man will not be shadowed in vice'. A later inscription notes that the candlestick was given to the Church of Le Mans by Thomas of Poché. Comparisons between the Gloucester candlestick and contemporary manuscripts, as well as its symbolism and inscriptions, suggest it was to be used on an altar.

Closely related to the Gloucester candlestick in terms of its high quality and subject matter is a cast base formerly in the Von Hirsch Collection. The only surviving segment is the foot, which could have supported either a cross or candlestick stem. Like the Gloucester candlestick, dragons form the feet of the triangular base and finely cast seated figures, dragons and animals are incorporated in the design. It is almost certainly the work of an English goldsmith and, like the candlestick, dates from the early twelfth century. The design of the figures is of interest: one pulls a thorn from his foot, a motif deriving from classical sculpture (the *Spinario* theme is derived from an ancient bronze statue, recorded as being in Rome as early as the twelfth century); another holds a dragon and a third is accompanied by a seated bird of prey. Analysis of the base has

THE ELTENBERG RELIQUARY, COPPER AND GILT BRONZE, WITH *CHAMPLEVÉ* ENAMEL AND CARVED WALRUS IVORY, RHENISH (COLOGNE), *c.*1180 (H54.5cm/21½in)

The reliquary came from the Benedictine nunnery at Eltenberg on the German border. Other reliquaries in the form of basilica are known and it is likely that this example once formed the container for an important relic. (FAR LEFT)

THE GLOUCESTER CANDLESTICK, GILT METAL, ENGLISH, *c.*1100 (H51cm/20in) (LEFT)

THE SUTTON BROOCH, ENGRAVED SILVER, ANGLO-SAXON, *c.*1000 (D14.9cm/5 9/10 in) (ABOVE)

shown a very high copper content in its alloy, as is the case with many other Romanesque gilt-metal wares. This was probably a deliberate choice by goldsmiths, as a high percentage of copper in an alloy makes it easier to gild.

In terms of object type, the Gloucester candlestick cannot have been unique. Indeed, earlier works of related form are known, such as a pair of cast silver candlesticks said to have been buried with St Bernward of Hildesheim (their association with the saint is confirmed by inscriptions on the base). Made in about 1000, the candlesticks feature stems decorated with climbing figures amongst foliage and triangular-shaped bases cast with lively human figures with turned heads.

FIGURATIVE WORK

A distinctive feature of the Romanesque style, as illustrated by the above examples, is the extensive use of figurative, especially human, subjects as part of the ornament. Another significant example is the small gilt-bronze figure of a

CROSS OF HENRY THE LION, SILVER-GILT, FILIGREE, SET WITH PRECIOUS STONES, GERMAN (HILDESHEIM), c.1172 (H40.7cm/16in)

According to tradition this was presented by Henry the Lion to the Convent of the Holy Cross, Hildesheim, and incorporates relics brought back from a pilgrimage to the Holy Land in 1172.

FIGURE OF A KNIGHT, CAST COPPER ALLOY, ENGLISH, c.1140 (H7.6cm/3in)

This knight may have formed one of the sleeping figures from a Holy Sepulchre group. Other similar figures have survived; all of them once belonged to the same object, probably an elaborate pyx.

knight in the Wallace Collection, London, which was once part of a pyx (the small box in which the Eucharist was reserved for veneration within that Christian Church, and carried during processions). Dating from about 1140 and almost certainly English in origin, the knight wears a conical helmet and supports a long, kite-shaped shield with rounded top, as seen in the Bayeux Tapestry and contemporary manuscripts. The figure has been cast and details such as the design in the centre of the shield have been engraved. The skilful modelling of the knight's hand and details of his costume reveal the work of a master goldsmith. Other fragments of what must once have been a very splendid pyx have been recorded, including a group of three knights

from the same piece in the Burrell Collection, Glasgow; additional figures were recorded in the eighteenth century but have since been lost.

TECHNIQUES

The manufacture and decoration of precious metals in the early Medieval period required the knowledge of various specialized techniques. Modern scientific analysis has been able to identify groups of enamels, for example, and metallurgists have identified various alloys in use during the period. In addition, *De Diversis Artibus*, a treatise written by 'Theophilus' in northwest Germany in the first half of the twelfth century, gives in considerable detail recipes and methods used by Medieval artists and craftsmen. The author has been identified plausibly as Roger of Helmarshausen, who is known to have made a gold cross and reliquary in *c*.1100. Helmarshausen was an important centre during the period, especially for metalwork and manuscripts, and enjoyed the patronage of prominent figures such as King Henry the Lion (1129–95), Duke of Saxony and Bavaria. The treatise explores gilding, soldering, gem-setting, niello work, repoussé and other techniques, as well as how to make a chalice and paten from both silver and gold, and was clearly written from personal experience.

Many of the objects described by Theophilus were for church use, such as chalices, censers and bells, but purely secular pieces, including spurs, are also mentioned. At the time the treatise was written, some of the methods and decorative techniques described were no longer fashionable, for example *cloisonné* enamelling, which by this period in Germany had been superseded by the *champlevé* technique. Nonetheless, *De Diversis Artibus* is an invaluable resource in terms of both the history of metalworking and other Medieval arts and the Middle Ages in general.

ENGRAVED SECULAR WARES

In spite of losses and depredations over the centuries, the treasuries of a few cathedrals and abbeys remained relatively intact, and it is in such collections that some of the most important secular plate of the Romanesque period has been preserved. One of the best-known treasuries is that of the Abbey of St Maurice d'Agaune in Sion, Switzerland. Among its treasures is a masterwork of casting and engraving: a cast silver flask embellished with key patterns, foliage and a quartet of winged dragons arranged vertically, their tails formed as scrolling flowers. The decoration combines punched and niello work with engraving, of which the latter has been compared to ornamental borders found on English illuminated manuscripts of the 1130s (leading to speculation that the vessel was made by an English goldsmith). The flask's form – a tapering bottle with stopper and a suspension ring on the neck – indicates that it was meant to be hung from a belt, a popular fashion accessory of the time. The bottle may have contained perfume or medicine originally, although its survival is probably due to the fact that it was later used as a relic container: a label attached to the stopper (a later, inferior replacement) refers to a tooth of St Maurice and bears the abbey seal. Several other flasks of this form feature bodies of rock crystal imported from Fatimid Egypt; these are usually fitted with silver mounts made by Western goldsmiths.

Some important silver vessels, now in the Historical Museum, Stockholm, were excavated in Dune, on the Swedish island of Gotland, and have also been attributed to an English goldsmith. This treasure includes a series of drinking cups that provide an insight into the appearance of what must have been a common secular vessel in wealthy twelfth-century households. One example, a footed drinking cup, bears a series of Latin inscriptions that identify not only the goldsmith who made the vessel, Simon, but also the patron who commissioned the piece, a Slav named Zhalognev; on the plain foot is a further inscription naming a subsequent owner. The parcel-gilt cup is engraved with scenes showing figures hunting lions, set within scrolling foliage. Despite the Slav patron, there is strong evidence to suggest that this cup is the work of an English goldsmith: its ornament has been compared with architecture of the 1180s, with enamels and with contemporary manuscripts, all of English origin. Indeed, the vessel also provides an interesting glimpse into European trade during the last quarter of the twelfth century. Unfortunately, nothing is recorded about Simon, who is known only from this cup.

The footed bowl from Dune represents one of many different forms of Romanesque drinking cup. Another is the tapering cylindrical beaker, a silver-mounted, wooden example of which is in the treasury of the Soeurs de Notre Dame in Namur. Its surface is decorated with alternating bands of scrolls and dragons that are gilded and filled with niello. The goblet of *c*.1200, of which the original domed cover decorated with quatrefoils and griffins is still intact, owes its preservation to an association with Ste Marie d'Oignies.

Although few secular silver wares survive

DRINKING CUP, ENGRAVED AND GILT SILVER, ENGLISH, *c*.1180 (D4.7cm/5⅛in)

On the bowl are the names of the maker Simon and that of a Slav patron Zhalognev, possibly a Russian merchant. The foliage and figures are typically English and there seems little doubt that the maker Simon was an English goldsmith. The cup comes from a hoard of gold and silver found at Dune on the Isle of Gotland.

from the twelfth century, some idea of the shape and decoration of bowls can be determined from parallels in base metal. Fortunately, a large series of engraved bronze bowls has survived. Known as Hansa (or Hanseatic) bowls because of their association with the Hanseatic League, they are made of heavy-gauge metal, which was cast and then turned on a lathe. Their interiors are roughly engraved with scenes from the classics, accompanied by Latin inscriptions, and the similarity of their shape and decoration suggests they were mass-produced in one centre, probably in Germany. In fact, many of the bowls were clearly made in one workshop, as evidenced by the curious triangular pattern of punched work on their rims.

Hansa bowls have been discovered in France, England, the Low Countries and Germany and were clearly traded extensively all over Europe. An example found in England in the River Severn has a typical form; its central print is engraved with a picture of King Cadmus of Thebes demonstrating his alphabet, while the remainder of the bowl contains scenes from the life of Hercules. If indeed these bowls are German, they are fascinating precursors of the well-known Nuremberg brass dishes of the fifteenth and sixteenth centuries.

ENAMELWORK

One of the greatest artistic achievements of the Romanesque period was its enamelled ware. Fortunately, a considerable number of objects decorated with various enamelling techniques have survived, some in outstanding condition. Although several types of enamelwork were fashionable in the twelfth and thirteenth centuries, the *cloisonné* and *champlevé* techniques dominated. The first necessitated the use of narrow ribbons of metal which were soldered on to the surface of a vessel edge to form 'fenced-off' areas, which were then filled with the enamel as required. The *champlevé* technique required the actual surface of the metal to be cut away, the resultant shallow depression then being filled with enamel. *Cloisonné* was a particularly delicate and complex technique that was used for small objects like jewels, which, since they were made of precious metal, could be easily soldered. *Champlevé* was used for larger vessels such as reliquaries, bowls and crucifixes. Since by about 1100 *champlevé*

HANSA BOWL, ENGRAVED BRONZE, GERMAN, 12TH CENTURY (D10.2cm/4in)

The engravings show King Cadmus of Thebes and scenes from the life of Hercules. It is likely that similar vessels were made in silver. This was found in England in the River Severn. (ABOVE)

THE HENRY OF BLOIS PLAQUES, *CHAMPLEVÉ* ENAMEL AND COPPER-GILT, MOSAN, *c*.1150 (D17.8cm/7in)

These plaques may have come originally from a shrine of St Swithun associated with Henry of Blois, Bishop of Winchester (1129–71). (RIGHT)

work had become far more common than *cloisonné*, the majority of enamelled wares in the Romanesque style are decorated by this method.

The numerous ecclesiastical foundations established in the twelfth and thirteenth centuries commissioned a great quantity of enamelled pieces from goldsmiths, leading to an increase not only in the number of craftsmen producing the wares but also of their workshops. Art historians have succeeded in identifying different workshops and schools, including the Mosan and Rhenish schools. They took their names from the areas around the Meuse and Rhine valleys, which in the early twelfth century became notable enamelling centres; later in the century southern France and Spain also produced outstanding enamelwork. As with silver, however, few objects are signed by the artist who made them but several bear inscriptions.

MOSAN ENAMELS

Two semicircular copper plaques in the British Museum, both decorated with *champlevé* enamel, offer a rare instance in which a Romanesque decorative-art object can be directly associated with a known historical figure. One plaque shows a pair of censing angels, the other a kneeling figure with a crozier; both are engraved with Latin inscriptions referring to a donor described as 'Henricus Episcopus'. He has been identified as the Bishop of Winchester, Henry of Blois (d. 1171), the brother of King Stephen and a prominent figure in the turbulent politics of the period. The shape of the two plaques suggests that they were originally attached to a cross or altar that was probably commissioned by Henry. The first lines of verse on the plaque depicting the bishop translate as: 'Art comes before gold and gems, the author before all things'. The inscription on the other plaque contains a direct reference to England and states that the choice of peace or war depends on the bishop. The plaques have been compared with a larger group of enamels scattered in several museums. The general consensus is

FRONT OF A RELIQUARY CROSS, COPPER-GILT WITH *CHAMPLEVÉ* AND *CLOISONNÉ* ENAMEL, MOSAN, *c.*1160–70 (H15cm/6in)

The scenes on the front show incidents taken to prophesy the Crucifixion. The reverse side of the Cross, now in Berlin, depicts the discovery by Empress Helena of the True Cross. It is likely therefore that a relic of the True Cross was once contained within it.

that these were produced, probably *c.*1150, by a Mosan goldsmith, who was perhaps working in England.

The portable altar from Stavelot dating from about 1160 is another outstanding manifestation of the Mosan style. Decorated with enamels and supported at the corners with three-dimensional figures of the Evan-

PORTABLE ALTAR FROM STAVELOT ABBEY, *CHAMPLEVÉ* ENAMEL AND COPPER-GILT, MOSAN, *c.*1160 (L25cm/9¾in)

The top is set with a crystal covering a relic. The enamelled scenes include Samson carrying off the gates of Gaza, Jonah and the Whale and scenes from the Old Testament.

ARMILLA (ARM ORNAMENT),
CHAMPLEVÉ ENAMEL AND GILT-
COPPER, MOSAN OR RHENISH, *c*.1165
(H11.5cm/4½in)

This is one of a pair of armillae *from the coronation
vestment of the Emperor Frederick I Barbarossa. It
is thought to have been presented to the Russian
Prince Boguloubski (1111–74) when on an embassy to
Aachen in 1165.*

gelists, the altar includes a crystal plaque
covering the relic within. Also from the
Mosan School is an important pair of
armillae (arm ornaments), one in the Louvre,
the other formerly part of the Von Hirsch
Collection. The latter depicts the Crucifixion in *champlevé* enamel on a gilt-copper
ground; its figures are finely engraved and
its colours bright and striking. It has been
claimed that the two ornaments once formed
part of the imperial regalia of Emperor
Frederick Barbarossa and were presented to
Prince Andrew Boguloubski of Russia when
the prince visited Aachen in 1165.

IMPORTANT WORKSHOPS

The quality of the workmanship of the
armillae has led experts to attribute them to
the craftsman Godefroid de Claire, although
it has also been suggested that they exhibit
characteristics of the workshop of Nicholas
of Verdun. Godefroid's only certain work is
the shrine of Saints Domitian and Mangold
at Huy (hence he is also known as Godefroid
de Huy). Indeed, his work was highly
acclaimed: an account of *c*.1240 stated 'he
had no equal as a goldsmith and he made
many shrines in many places and objects for
kings'.

Nicholas of Verdun (*fl*.1181–1205), a key
figure in the study of Romanesque metalwork, is known by two signed works, the
Klosterneuberg pulpit, later converted into
an altar retable, and the shrine of the Virgin
at Tournai Cathedral, completed in 1205.
Other masterpieces, such as the reliquary of
the Magi at Cologne Cathedral, have been
attributed to him. The enamels on the
Klosterneuberg pulpit are of outstanding

quality: the colours are glowing shades of
red, blue, turquoise, green and white, and
the drawing of the figures resembles a
manuscript in its attention to detail and
liveliness. The Magi reliquary, on the other
hand, shows the master's skill as a sculptor,
especially on the figures surrounding the
body of the piece. Nicholas had a considerable influence on other workshops working
in both the Mosan and Rhenish traditions.

LIMOGES ENAMELS

It is not clear when enamels were first
produced in Limoges, but there seemed to
be well-established links between the French
city and Spanish enamelling centres in the
early part of the 1100s. By the latter years
of the century, however, a recognizable
Limoges style had emerged, characterized
by features such as engraved arabesques in
the ground of the design. In addition to such
stylistic traits, Byzantine influence has also
been detected in some of these enamels.

One of the most familiar types of Limoges
enamelled object is the *chasse*, a form of
reliquary. An example of *c*.1180 in the
Metropolitan Museum of Art has the usual
architectural form, its pitched roof and
cresting set with crystals. Figures enamelled
in characteristic Limoges blue occupy a
ground of scrolling foliage, with the central
design of Christ in Majesty surrounded by
the Evangelists' symbols. The mounts are of
gilt-copper.

THE CHURCH AS
PATRON

Most of the vessels and enamelled
reliquaries that adorned Romanesque treasuries were the result
of special commissions or donations by
wealthy patrons, such as Abbot Suger of St
Denis. He was abbot from 1122 until 1151,
during which time he restored and beauti-
fied the abbey. Some of the vessels mentioned by Suger in the account of his

leadership, *De Administratione* (*c.*1144), are still extant. In the Louvre is a plain porphyry vase dating from the late classical period which was supplied with silver-gilt mounts in the form of an eagle with wings, claws, feathers and strikingly powerful head and beak. On the mounted rim is a Latin inscription, which translates as 'This deserves to be mounted with stones and gold, it was marble but in this form it is more precious than marble'. Suger's account relates how a vessel was made for the service of the altar from 'a porphyry vase after it had lain idly in a chest for many years, converting it from a flagon into the shape of an eagle', which clearly relates to this vessel.

RELIQUARIES

Attributed to a workshop in Cologne and dating from *c.*1160 is a gilt-copper plaque from a reliquary at Darmstadt. On it is a finely drawn image of the prophet Jonah amid scrolling bands that enclose vari-

THE EAGLE VASE, ANTIQUE PORPHYRY MOUNTED IN SILVER-GILT, FRENCH, *c.*1150 (H43cm/17in)

In his text on administration, Abbot Suger of St Denis describes the conversion of an antique vase to an altar vessel by the addition of mounts in the form of an eagle. (LEFT)

RELIQUARY *CHASSE, CHAMPLEVÉ* ENAMEL AND ENGRAVED GILT-COPPER, FRENCH (LIMOGES), *c.*1180 (L23.5cm/9¼in, H22cm/8⅔in)

The style of the figures suggests that a strong Byzantine influence prevailed at the workshop where it was produced. (BELOW LEFT)

THE JONAH PLAQUE, *CHAMPLEVÉ* ENAMEL AND GILT-COPPER, RHENISH (COLOGNE), *c.*1150–75 (H12.4cm/4⁹⁄₁₀in)

The Latin inscription comes from Jonah 1:12: 'Take me up and cast me forth into the sea.' This is the missing plaque from a twelve-sided tower reliquary, now in Darmstadt. (BELOW)

THE WILTEN CHALICE AND PATEN, SILVER-GILT AND NIELLO, GERMAN, *c.*1160 (Chalice: H16.7cm/6½in)

An inscription records that the chalice was made for Abbot Berthold of Zähringen (1148–84). (ABOVE)

THE BALFOUR CIBORIUM, *CHAMPLEVÉ ENAMEL AND GILT-COPPER*, ENGLISH, *c.*1150 (H18.3cm/7½in, D16.5cm/6½in)

The ciborium is decorated with scenes from the Old and New Testaments on the theme of Redemption executed in champlevé *enamel. The vessel held the consecrated wafers for the Communion Service and was said to have been given by Mary, Queen of Scots to Sir James Balfour of Pittendreich.* (ABOVE RIGHT)

CHALICE AND PATEN, ENGRAVED AND GILT-SILVER, ENGLISH, *c.*1160 (Chalice: H14.2cm/5½in; paten: D14cm/5½in)

These come from the grave of Archbishop Hubert Walter (1193–1205). The tomb in Canterbury Cathedral was opened in 1890 and the furnishings removed. (RIGHT)

coloured flowers. Also from Cologne come several splendid reliquaries in the form of a basilica, among them the Eltenberg Reliquary of *c.*1180 (now in the Victoria & Albert Museum). The gilt-bronze and copper reliquary is set with carved ivory panels and features a roof and pillars decor-

ated with *champlevé* enamel. The ivory figures around the dome represent Christ and the Apostles, and the prophets are set below. It seems likely that an important relic was once enclosed under the dome, which can be lifted off by turning a series of heads set above the niches.

CHALICES, CIBORIA AND CENSERS

The chalice was an important vessel in the Medieval liturgy and some fine examples in the Romanesque style are extant. A parcel-gilt silver chalice from the grave of Archbishop Walter (d. 1205) is preserved at Canterbury Cathedral; it has been dated to about 1160. The Wilten chalice in the Kunsthistorisches Museum, Vienna, is of silver engraved and decorated with niello. Made for Berthold of Zähringen (1148–84), it also dates from the 1160s.

Like the pyx, the ciborium was a receptacle to hold the Host. Its usual form was a footed vessel resembling a large cup. The Balfour ciborium in the Victoria & Albert Museum, made in England in *c.*1150–75, is decorated with biblical scenes in *champlevé* enamel on a gilt-copper base. Its subject matter can be compared with English wall-paintings and sculpture of the time.

Censers, or thuribles, formed an important part of church ritual and a number of them have survived. In fact, Theophilus gives a detailed account of the manufacture of a cast bronze censer in his treatise, *De Diversis Artibus.* Unusual shapes and designs, the upper sections often inspired by architecture (later accentuated in Gothic art), were the product of considerable ingenuity on the part of the maker.

OTHER ECCLESIASTICAL OBJECTS

In the Cathedral Treasury at Essen is an important eleventh-century sword, the hilt and scabbard of which are decorated with gold. Associated with Kosmas and Damian, the patron saints of Essen, the sword is traditionally believed to be the weapon with which the two holy men were executed. The hilt has the standard cross and pommel of swords from this period but is of gold set with stones and overlaid with filigree. The scabbard is a fine example of goldsmiths' work and is covered with plates embossed with animals set amid scrolls.

A vessel which must have frequently been made in silver and rarely in gold is the aquamanile, which seems to have been used for washing the hands both in sacred ceremonies and for secular use. A number of bronze versions survive that demonstrate the rich imaginations of their makers. Lions are the most common models, but examples with mounted knights, griffins and, far less commonly, human figures are found. A bronze aquamanile excavated in the Baltic area was once part of the Von Hirsch Collection. In the form of a youth in classical costume, it dates from about 1200 and has been attributed to a workshop at Magdeburg or Hildesheim.

Theophilus devoted a section in his treatise to the setting of gems and pearls into precious-metal objects. An idea of these ornate decorative techniques can be formed by looking at extant Romanesque crucifixes, among them the Cross of King Henry the Lion of 1172, preserved in Hildesheim Cathedral. Of silver-gilt and some 40cm (16in) in height, it is decorated with filigree and set with pearls and precious stones.

TRANSITIONAL WORKS

Objects of religious importance were regularly restored and usually incorporate the work of many different craftsmen. For example, a book cover from the treasury of St Maurice d'Agaune has suffered many alterations. The *cloisonné* enamels and borders date from the eleventh century, the text is an eleventh-century gospel-book, and the central figure dates from the twelfth century. In addition, some of the surface was also restored in the nineteenth century.

Elements of the Gothic style can be detected in some late Romanesque chalices and reliquaries but in reality the move towards a new style – especially in metalwork – was a gradual transition rather than a rapid transformation.

SION BOOK-COVER, GOLD, *CLOISONNÉ* ENAMELS AND PRECIOUS STONES, GERMAN (TRIER) (L25.4cm/ 10in, W22cm/8⅔in)

The manuscript is an 11th-century Evangelistary and the cloisonné *plaques are 11th-century with later restoration. The figure of Christ is 12th-century. The cover was stolen from the Treasury of St Maurice d'Agaune in the 14th century. According to a 15th-century inscription inside, the book then belonged to the Cathedral Church of Sion.*

GOTHIC SILVER

Although it has been argued that in some parts of Europe – notably the north – the Gothic style persisted in metalwork well into the eighteenth century, the more conventional dating ranges from *c*.1200 to *c*.1530. In silver the Gothic style is characterized by the dominance of elaborate, often fantastic, architectural forms and by naturalistically modelled figures, animals and foliage, all frequently framed within pointed arches. Two styles of lettering generally occur on silver of the period: the rounded capitals of the Lombardic hand, in use until *c*.1400, and the spiky, lower-case hand known as 'black letter', dating from about 1350 until 1500 (but much later in northern Europe).

In the history of European silver the Gothic period is notable for several dramatic technical innovations. Advances in enamelling brought about the invention of several new forms – *basse-taille*, *ronde bosse* and painted enamel – which significantly expanded the goldsmith's repertoire. Also, in fifteenth-century Germany, specialist goldsmith-engravers developed the technique of making multiple impressions on paper from an engraved metal plate. Until then, there had been no quick method for reproducing a design, so the advent of this revolutionary process meant that a design could be printed in quantity and disseminated anywhere. Work betraying Italian or German stylistic influence might now simply be the product of a goldsmith with a foreign pattern-book, as is clearly the case

EWER, SILVER-GILT WITH *BASSE TAILLE* ENAMEL, FRENCH (PARIS MARK OF FLEUR-DE-LIS), *c*.1320–30 (H22.5cm/9in) (ABOVE)

CASTLE CUP, COPPER-GILT, PAINTED, GERMAN (NUREMBERG), *c*.1475–1500 (H37.1cm/14⅝in) (RIGHT)

RELIQUARY OF CHARLES THE BOLD, GOLD AND SILVER-GILT, WITH *RONDE BOSSE* ENAMEL AND COLD PAINT, BURGUNDIAN, 1467–71

Charles, Duke of Burgundy (d. 1477) is shown kneeling. He holds a crystal reliquary containing a fragment of the finger of St Lambert, patron of Liège, a city sacked by Charles in 1467 and 1468.

with the English silver pax of *c.*1510 at New College, Oxford, its border decoration inspired by an engraving in a Parisian Book of Hours of some ten years earlier.

Beginning in the thirteenth century, guilds of goldsmiths throughout Europe increasingly standardized and regulated the quality of the metals worked. And from around 1300, for the first time, significant records survive – where the objects often do not – describing the wide range of goldsmiths' work owned by ecclesiastical foundations as well as royal, noble and mercantile households. Goldsmiths – the craftsmen responsible for working both gold and silver – produced a remarkable variety of pieces, objects which today are either made in other materials or are obsolete. The Church needed plate for liturgical and sacred purposes, primarily for the service of the Mass and to enclose relics, and the laity needed, or aspired to own, precious metal jewellery (worn by both sexes) and domestic plate, principally for display or use at table.

Until well into the Gothic period, the term goldsmith was often applied to an artist who was competent in many crafts, including various types of metalworking. Many artists may still have possessed the versatility of Hugh of Bury (St Edmunds), the illuminator of the Bury Bible of *c.*1135 who was also known as a sculptor and metalworker.

SURVIVALS AND STYLE

The present-day picture of what was made in the Gothic period, as in the earlier Middle Ages, is seriously distorted by historical accident. The impression gained from what survives is that an immense amount – indeed, the majority of silver and gold plate – was made for the Church, but this is false. It is probable that by the fourteenth century far more silver and gold plate was made for secular purposes, whether for use or display. In an age without banks, gold and silver domestic plate was an

asset which could be, and often was, melted down in a crisis to pay debts or soldiers' wages. Although vulnerable to similar pressures, church plate has more often survived, through being hidden, buried or associated with an important personage. The scale of losses is such as to make highly difficult any assessment of the relative popularity of gold or silver, and of the evolution of style and ornament. Judging from the evidence of surviving objects, goldsmiths seem to have been rather slow to adopt the Gothic idiom, although given the destructive vagaries of war and fluctuations of taste and fashion it is likely that the complete picture of stylistic development in metalwork is too episodic to be coherent.

The records suggest that from the thirteenth century onward, plate and jewellery were increasingly made of gold (which was roughly ten times more costly than silver). In the fourteenth century, when there seems to have been a shortage of silver, several European countries established a gold coinage. Bullion supply is bound to have affected the plate and jewellery that goldsmiths produced. Pieces of jewellery – largely rings and brooches – are the most common survivals by the fifteenth century, and these are predominantly of gold, suggesting the growing availability of this precious metal.

Notably indebted to Mosan precedent, French High Gothic art was the dominant artistic influence in Europe during the thirteenth and fourteenth centuries, and the patterns and figures that were engraved, enamelled or depicted in niello work by goldsmiths are often close to those rendered in contemporary manuscripts. The elegant 'International Style' of *c.*1400 was a court style, its characteristics transcending regional boundaries. More distinctively national features developed in much of Europe from around 1420 and flourished throughout the century, only to give way in general to Renaissance motifs by *c.*1530. The exception is Italy, where the Gothic style was ousted by the mid-fifteenth century.

THE SHRINE OF ST ALBAN, FROM 'THE LIFE OF ST ALBAN', INK ON VELLUM, COLOURED, ENGLISH, *c.*1240–50 (Folio: H *c.*24.5cm/9¾in)

This drawing is by the great English historian, artist and goldsmith, Matthew Paris, himself a monk of St Alban's Abbey.

TECHNIQUES

The techniques of working gold and silver changed little during the Gothic period, although fashions in superficial decoration varied. There were two principal methods of working metal: by casting it in moulds and by shaping it with a hammer. The surface might then be embellished in a number of ways: by embossing, engraving, enamelling, gilding, setting with gems and the use of niello, a decorative technique that was popular in the thirteenth and fifteenth centuries.

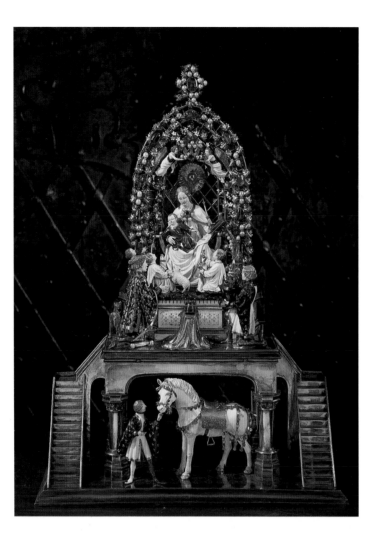

GOLDENES RÖSSEL, GOLD, WITH ÉMAIL EN RONDE BOSSE, FRENCH (PARIS), c.1403 (H62cm/24½in)

This is the most famous surviving example of this difficult technique, and shows the Virgin and Child with Saints John the Baptist, John the Evangelist and Catherine. In the foreground on the left is the figure of King Charles VI of France, with his squire on the right and his horse and pageboy below. It was given to Charles on New Year's Day, 1404, by his wife, Queen Isabel.

MONKEY CUP, SILVER WITH PAINTED ENAMEL, FRANCO-FLEMISH, *c.1430–40* (H20cm/7⅞in)

This masterpiece of painted enamelling was probably made for one of the Dukes of Burgundy or their entourage. It is decorated with scenes from a story of monkeys who rob a sleeping pedlar of his goods.

It should not be forgotten that during this period the craft of the goldsmith encompassed that of the jeweller as well. Very few gems were cut; rather, they were simply polished, their colour and 'virtue' being their chief attractions to medieval eyes. Precious stones were used not only on jewellery and shrines, but also on clothing and, above all, ecclesiastical and secular plate of any distinction. A cathedral chalice and a ducal drinking cup might be equally studded with gems.

ENAMELLING

The most common type of added decoration in the Gothic period was enamelwork, in which coloured glass powder was fired and hence fused on to metal. This method allowed the gold, silver or other surface to be coloured permanently, either with pure pattern (as it might be with gems), or with heraldic badges, or figurative scenes from the Bible or romances, as on the pages of an illuminated manuscript. As in the earlier Middle Ages, *cloisonné* and *champlevé* enamel were used, but important advances were made in these techniques.

The first Gothic innovation in enamelwork was *basse-taille*. This enamel type was possibly invented in Siena, where the earliest surviving piece on which it appears, the chalice for Pope Nicholas IV (1288–92) by Guccio di Mannaia, was made. *Basse-taille*, a development of the *champlevé* technique, consists of translucent enamel used on a gold or silver base on to which a design in low relief has been chased or engraved. Great tonal richness and subtlety in the modelling of forms can be achieved by variations in the depth of the engraving and hence the thickness of the enamel, through which light is reflected back from the metal base.

The second advance in enamelling – *émail en ronde basse*, or encrusted enamel – was developed in Paris in the second half of the fourteenth century. This technique allowed the enamelling of irregular surfaces of figures and objects in the round or in very high relief. These small-scale sculptural compositions are invariably of gold or silver, the surface of which has been roughened to hold the enamel coating in place.

Painted enamel, the third innovation, originated in around 1420, probably in the Netherlands. This technique was fundamentally different from the others, in that the various colours are not separated from each other by metal ridges of any sort, and the metal ground requires no special preparation. The skills required, in fact, are less those of a goldsmith than of a painter. At first, the metals used were gold and silver, but later copper was more common.

GUILDS AND MARKS

In the thirteenth century the growing economic pull of towns and the wealth of the nobility and merchants led to the establishment of urban associations, or guilds, of goldsmiths, all regulated by rules which determined the quality of both the metals used and the workmanship, as well as the working hours. Craftsmen tended to hand down their tools from father to son, and these often included moulds, which were valuable because they were laborious and expensive to make. The use of the same moulds over several generations is sometimes demonstrable even from the comparatively few extant objects, and there can be no doubt that this must have curbed innovation. Some English goldsmiths used the same moulds for spoon finials for two or more generations, that is, for up to fifty years. This conservatism highlights the dangers of relying entirely on style as the indicator of the date of a piece of metalwork, especially of such everyday items as spoons. Special commissions were a different case.

Although the records are far from clear or complete, France probably led the way in legislation over the quality of the metals worked. In England the Goldsmiths' Company of London was the authority principally responsible for the implementation of hallmarking gold and silver wares throughout the country. This complex system, with different marks to represent, respectively, the standard of metal, the maker, the town and the year, was almost certainly inspired by developments in France, where the standard mark had apparently been introduced in Paris in *c.*1260 and the date-letter system in Montpellier in 1427. In 1275 a royal ordinance decreed that every town with goldsmiths should have a mark. In fourteenth-century England two marks were introduced: a standard mark in 1300 in the form of a leopard's head, which was to represent the sterling standard for silver vessels and jewellery, and the 'touch of Paris' (19.2 carats) for those of gold. Secondly, in 1363, legislation was introduced to the effect that each goldsmith should have his own mark.

In the fifteenth century the English system was more or less finalized. A statute of 1423 nominated seven towns other than London to be set up as assay towns, each with its own mark (Bristol, Coventry, Lincoln, Newcastle, Norwich, Salisbury and York). In 1478 the standard mark was altered to a crowned leopard's head, and a system of alphabetical date letters was introduced in London, beginning with the letter 'a', the letter to be changed each year on 19 May (the feast day of St Dunstan, patron saint of English goldsmiths). Even though French and English goldsmiths were perhaps the most firmly regulated, marks on surviving pieces of the period are a rarity and not always identifiable. Elsewhere in Europe, whatever the theoretical controlling powers of guilds, the use of marks is sporadic. For instance, marks are fairly common on fifteenth-century Hispanic pieces, but rare on German ones.

CHURCH SILVER

Ecclesiastical patronage was extremely important in the later Middle Ages, so it is not surprising that the greater number of surviving Gothic works in precious metal are those intended for liturgical use. Chalices, cruets, monstrances, paxes and pyxes were needed for the Mass, and other religious objects in silver and gold included altarpieces, crosses, croziers, reliquaries and embellishments for vestments. The most significant items intro-

SPOONS, SILVER PARCEL-GILT, WITH MARKS OF A LAMB AND FLAG (FOR ROUEN) AND A LEOPARD'S HEAD (LONDON, STERLING STANDARD), ENGLISH (RIGHT, CENTRE) AND FRENCH (LEFT), *c.*1400–50 AND 1300–50 (L max. 20.2cm/8in)

duced during the period were the pax, the plaque on which the priest passed the kiss of peace to the faithful before Communion, and the monstrance, a crystal container mounted in precious metal on a stand (and devised after the establishment of the feast of Corpus Christi in 1264), in which the host was displayed.

SHRINES AND RELIQUARIES

The most expensive and prestigious ecclesiastical commissions were for the great shrines which enclosed the relics of saints and martyrs revered by a particular church or cathedral. One of the most famous European shrines was that of St Thomas Becket in Canterbury Cathedral, a magnificent work of pure gold plates studded with sapphires, diamonds, rubies and emeralds. Becket had been martyred by Henry II's supporters in 1170, and the shrine holding his body was first placed in the crypt of the cathedral but moved to the choir in 1220, when the new shrine was made (it was destroyed during the Reformation). Such a significant commission would have been in the latest style, Gothic, and an idea of its appearance can be gleaned from the slightly later St Taurin shrine in Evreux, France.

Designed c.1240–55 as a miniature Gothic church with pinnacled niches, gabled transepts and pointed arches, the silver shrine is a thoroughly Gothic work and represents a considerable stylistic advance on the Notre Dame shrine in Tournai, Belgium, created by the great Flemish goldsmith, Nicholas of Verdun, in 1205. This piece stands at the crossroads between Romanesque and Gothic in concept, its design inspired by a sarcophagus rather than a church. Even the

quickly through France and Flanders. It appears fully developed on Flemish pieces like the silver-gilt reliquary-triptych of c.1254 from the Abbey of St Floreffe (now in the Louvre) and the silver shrine of St Gertrude of Nivelles of 1272–98, as well as in German and Italian works by the late thirteenth century. Fourteenth-century German examples include the Charlemagne head reliquary and the 'Three Towers' reliquary in Aachen Cathedral. In Italy the

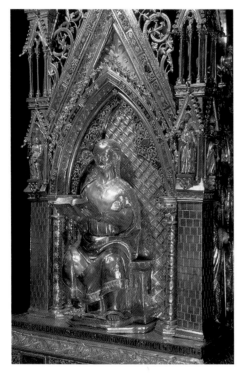

SHRINE OF SAINT TAURIN (DETAIL), COPPER AND SILVER-GILT, WITH *CHAMPLEVÉ* ENAMELS, FRENCH, c.1240–55 (H70cm/27½in; L1.05m/41½in)

Made in the shape of a Gothic cathedral, the shrine was commissioned by Abbot Gilbert to house the relics of the abbey's patron saint, the 4th-century Bishop of Evreux. A scene of Christ in Majesty decorates the end of the shrine. (ABOVE)

RELIQUARY OF THE HOLY CROSS OF FLOREFFE, SILVER AND COPPER-GILT, PRECIOUS STONES AND NIELLO, BELGIAN, c.1255 (H79cm/31⅛in) (RIGHT)

shrine of St Elisabeth of Marburg of c.1236–40 is essentially a Romanesque piece, despite Gothic details in the arches.

The new style of shrine was perhaps inspired by the model of Sainte Chapelle, the exquisite Rayonnant church built in Paris for Louis IX in the 1240s to house the Crown of Thorns and other relics. The Gothic style in shrines and reliquaries spread

most splendid, and probably the largest, is the silver and *basse-taille* enamel reliquary of the Corporal of Bolsena in Orvieto Cathedral. Made for the Bishop and Chapter of Orvieto by Ugolino di Vieri of Siena in 1338, it takes the form of a giant altarpiece, rather than following the shape of the relic. The panels relate to scenes of the life of Christ and the Miracle of the Corporal.

LITURGICAL OBJECTS

As it was the focal point of the Mass and the symbol of Christ and the Last Supper, the altar became the subject of lavish goldsmiths' work. No surviving Gothic altar surpasses that of St James the Apostle in Pistoia Cathedral, Italy. Made of silver, embossed and engraved with scenes from the life of Christ and images of saints, it is the work of several goldsmiths from the thir-

teenth to the fifteenth century and represents the evolution of the Gothic style in Italy.

The most important objects for the Mass were the chalice, paten and pyx. The form of the chalice and paten remained largely unchanged, but the size of the chalice had markedly diminished by the late thirteenth century, when the laity no longer received wine with their bread at Communion. The large silver-gilt Dolgelly chalice of c.1250, made by Nicholas of Hereford, is engraved

with the 'stiff leaf' characteristic of early English Gothic ornament. By contrast, from the late thirteenth century there is the much smaller chalice by Guccio di Mannaia in Assisi. It is notable, too, for its *basse-taille* enamel and its use of both copper and silver-gilt, a combination of precious and base metals found only in German and Italian goldsmiths' work from this date onward. The foot shape is distinctively Italian, an elaborately cusped octofoil.

RELIQUARY OF THE CORPORAL OF BOLSENA, SILVER-GILT WITH *BASSE TAILLE* ENAMEL, ITALIAN, 1338 (H1.39m/55in)

The reliquary was made for the Bishop and Chapter of Orvieto by the Sienese goldsmith Ugolino di Vieri and his assistants, at a cost of 1,374 ½ gold florins. It depicts scenes from the Life of Christ and the Miracle of the Corporal, framed in an architectural structure which echoes that of the cathedral itself, built between 1305–50. (LEFT)

CHALICE, SILVER WITH *BASSE TAILLE* ENAMEL, ITALIAN, c.1288–92 (H22.5cm/8¾in)

The chalice is inscribed with the name of its maker, the Sienese goldsmith Guccio di Mannaia, and its donor, Pope Nicholas IV. (ABOVE)

OTHER RELIGIOUS OBJECTS

The cross, often containing a relic of the True Cross, symbolized Christ's triumph over death. Altar crosses at first remained on the altar only during Mass. Processional crosses were carried through towns on feast days and sometimes had removable bases, thus enabling them to stand on the altar. The Flemish Oignies altar cross in the Victoria & Albert Museum, London, c.1230, is notable among thirteenth-century pieces: it is set with gems and miniature paintings on vellum with lists of the relics within. It combines an engraved copper-gilt back with a silver-gilt front enriched by realistically cast openwork leaves. Its style is closely associated with that of Hugo d'Oignies, who made several pieces for the priory of St Nicholas, Oignies, characterized by the use of filigree, niello and finely cast openwork with animals and foliage.

Censers, used during the Mass and in processions from the Romanesque period onward, took on the prevailing architectural form, as in the English silver-gilt Ramsey Abbey censer of c.1325, which is a miniature polygonal chapter house in contemporary 'Decorated' style. The crozier, or pastoral staff, was the symbol of authority carried by an abbot or bishop. Its shape was a stylized shepherd's crook, which by the fourteenth century and throughout the fifteenth had developed an almost standard design common to Britain, France, Germany and Italy. In this the silver crook is supported by an angel, the knop consists of tiers of architectural niches and the whole is enamelled.

SECULAR SILVER

The great men of the Middle Ages lived lives of conspicuous ostentation, in which the display of wealth – in the form of jewellery and of gold and silver plate (often embellished with gems and enamel) – was an essential indicator and attribute of status and power.

Inventories of the time show that considerable quantities of domestic silver and gold plate, including dishes, ewers, cups, spoons and salt-cellars, were in use in the fourteenth and fifteenth centuries in the noble and princely households of Europe.

There can be little doubt that an average goldsmith would have spent the greater part

of his working day providing for these customers rather than for the Church. Yet the vagaries of time and fashion have consigned almost all such secular pieces to the melting pot, for plate and jewellery were the liquid assets of an age without banks. In addition, there was no desire to preserve plate for the sake of its antiquity – a fashion prevalent only since the nineteenth century – but, rather, a constant wish to be up-to-the-minute. To that end, plate was frequently sent to goldsmiths to be remodelled.

BUFFET DISPLAYS

Magnificence was an important social requirement in the later Middle Ages, and the holding of feasts of splendour was an increasingly indispensable expression of power on the part of the medieval nobleman. Manuscripts and tapestries clearly

A GREAT FEAST, WOVEN WOOL, BELGIAN (TOURNAI), c.1511 (L5.60m/17ft 9in)

In this tapestry, one of a set of ten made for the Duke of Lorraine, a great tiered dresser displaying plate is shown on the left. On the table a nef with Venus as its masthead has been placed in the centre, and diners drink wine from shallow bowls or beakers.

EWER, SILVER-GILT, WITH COLD PAINT, GERMAN (NUREMBERG), c.1450–1500 (H63.5cm/25in)

This ewer is one of a pair, elaborate versions of those visible on top of the sideboard in the Great Feast tapestry (ABOVE). The wildmen originally held shields with the arms of the owner, Hartmann von Stockheim, Master of the Order of Teutonic Knights of the Hospital of St Mary in Jerusalem, based from 1457 in East Prussia.

TABLE FOUNTAIN, SILVER-GILT WITH *BASSE TAILLE* ENAMEL, FRENCH (PARIS?), *c*.1350 (H31cm/12¼in)

Fountains for dispensing wine or water became fashionable during the 13th century. This example is said to have been found in Istanbul. (LEFT)

MÉRODE CUP, SILVER-GILT AND GOLD, WITH *PLIQUE-À-JOUR* ENAMEL, FRENCH (PARIS), *c*.1400 (H17.5cm/6⅞in) (BELOW)

reflect the sort of life enjoyed by the wealthy men and women of the day. The early sixteenth-century Flemish series of tapestries in Nancy shows various aristocratic feasts, one, *Le Bancquet*, featuring a fine four-tiered buffet, or open-shelved cupboard. The lowest shelf clearly holds plate in use, but the upper levels may have displayed items which, on account of their value and fragility, were solely for show.

It was a common practice in the fifteenth-century Burgundian court to have several buffets in the banqueting hall, at least one being entirely 'to make men marvel', according to the court chronicler Chastellain. His account of the feast held by Philip the Good, Duke of Burgundy, in 1456 at The Hague, for the Order of the Golden Fleece, describes a hall hung with tapestries representing the tale of Jason. In it were placed three buffets, one bearing silver vessels for

the ordinary guests to use, one with gilt vessels for the knights and one with gold and gem-encrusted vessels for show.

In 1468, on the occasion of the marriage feast of Charles the Bold of Burgundy and Margaret of York, a lozenge-shaped buffet was placed in the middle of the hall, hung with cloth bearing the ducal arms. The largest silver vessels were placed at the bottom and above them were those of gem-covered gold, with the most precious cup at the very top. The Nancy tapestry shows large silver ewers in use, probably holding water and wine; these are simpler versions of the fifteenth-century silver-gilt Nuremberg ewers, 91cm (3ft) high and decorated with wild men, in New York's Metropolitan Museum of Art. The company drink mostly from wide, shallow bowls, one from a beaker, a plainer version of the Parisian beaker at Oriel College, Oxford. Another

vessel, still used on ceremonial occasions in northern Europe, was the mounted drinking horn. The coy centrepiece in the tapestry has no surviving parallel, nor does the magnificent and unique fourteenth-century French silver and *basse-taille* enamel table-fountain in the Cleveland Musem of Art, Ohio. Wine would have cascaded down the tiers into a large basin, causing the bells to chime as the wheels rotated.

OTHER SHOWPIECES

Two other items which must have been intended for display rather than use are the Monkey Cup and the Mérode Cup, both from the early fifteenth century. The silver body of the beaker is painted in enamel inside and out with mysterious scenes, probably inspired by a romance of monkeys scrambling amid foliage and robbing a sleeping pedlar, and a fantastic forest. It is thought to have been made in Flanders for the Burgundian court, which is known to have employed goldsmiths from cities such as Bruges and Ghent. The sides of the silver-gilt Mérode Cup are pricked out in *pointillé*, also known as pounce work, with birds and vine leaves. Into the sides, cover and base have been let panels of *plique-à-jour* enamel. When the cup is placed in a shaft of light, it appears to be set with miniature stained glass windows. Pieces decorated with this type of translucent enamel are known from inventories, such as that of Jean, Duc de Berry, brother of Charles V of France and the great fourteenth-century patron of the arts, but this is the only example in the world known to have survived.

An English royal feast illustrated in a late fifteenth-century Bruges manuscript depicts a simple table setting and a very plain buffet holding ewers and bowls, evidently for use. However, in the foreground a figure holds a silver nef, a ship-shaped ceremonial salt-cellar. This special salt was one of the few medieval table objects with a dual function. It was placed to the right of the host in front of his guest of honour, and, unlike other vessels, remained symbolically on the table throughout the meal. These grand salt-cellars tended to hold comparatively little salt for their size and were of lavish workmanship, as befitted such an emblem of opulence and hospitality.

Typically English are the hourglass salts of the late fifteenth century, of which nine examples survive. The exotic forms, often gem- or enamel-encrusted, are more familiar from descriptions. Such pieces include the silver-gilt salt set with crystal, pearls and enamel that was made for Richard Fox, Bishop of Durham, in *c*.1494 and given by him to Corpus Christi College, Oxford, and the late fifteenth-century silver-gilt and enamel 'Huntsman' salt, perhaps of German origin, at All Souls College, Oxford. One of the finest examples of the boat-shaped salt is the Burghley Nef in the Victoria & Albert Museum which, although Renaissance in date, is stylistically transitional. It bears Paris hallmarks for 1527–8, but its type is of

medieval origin, as described and illustrated in French and English sources from at least the fourteenth century. The ship, in full sail, carries under its main mast the diminutive figures of Tristan and Iseult playing chess, a subject derived from the popular medieval romance of *Tristan*. The actual container for the salt is semi-oval, placed in the poop of the vessel.

UTILITARIAN OBJECTS

To modern eyes there are noticeable omissions in the Bruges manuscript, for spoons, forks, plates and glasses are absent. Yet plates were then unknown, their place being taken by trenchers (from the Old French *trancher*, 'to cut'), usually made up of very thick square slices of stale bread, pieces of wood or sometimes silver or pewter. Forks were used only occasionally for delicacies like green ginger or fruit. Glasses were a rarity; instead, drinking vessels consisted either of beakers (plainer versions of the Mérode Cup), chalice-shaped cups, sometimes with lids, like the English Lacock Abbey Cup of *c*.1450, and bowls, at times used communally. Other types included the drinking horn, mounted in silver or gold, and the *hanap*, a cup with a broad, flat bowl. An example of the latter is the British Museum's Royal Gold Cup, made in Paris *c*.1380 and presented by Jean de Berry to Charles VI, his nephew. Enamelled in *basse-taille* on gold with the life of St Agnes, it is one of the finest surviving masterpieces of the Gothic goldsmith.

As well as being fashioned of silver or gold, bowls might be made of wood, frequently of a type known as mazer, the name given to the burr grown by the maple tree. Since it had no grain and was therefore not liable to shrink or split, this wood was particularly suitable for vessels subject to the continual tensions of being wetted and dried. The distinctive wide, shallow shape of mazer bowls was determined by the natural form of the maple burrs; the disadvantage of shallowness was overcome by mounting the bowls with broad lips of silver. Further decoration included a silver or enamel

CUP AND COVER FROM LACOCK ABBEY, SILVER-GILT, ENGLISH, *c*.1450 (H35cm/13¾in)

Although long owned by a parish church, and used as a chalice, this is a very beautiful secular cup.

roundel, set into the bottom of the bowl. It seems likely that the shape of mazers influenced those of the wide, shallow drinking bowls produced by goldsmiths and seen in the Bruges manuscript and other contemporary tapestries.

The Rouen Treasure, consisting largely of bowls and spoons, is a classic instance of a long-hidden hoard that came to light only in the last century. Although the circumstances of its discovery are mysterious, it was probably found in Rouen in about 1865, having been bricked up behind the wall of an old house being demolished. This story is echoed in the discovery in about 1953 of the Coëffort Treasure, a spectacular collection of fourteenth-century French domestic silver, 21 pieces in all, many of them bowls and spoons. The spoons from the Rouen Treasure include a pair with diamond knops (bearing Paris hallmarks and the fleur-de-lis) and a pair with acorn knops (bearing Rouen marks, the lamb and flag), each with biting beasts joining bowls to stems. Their styles are also found in England in the fourteenth and fifteenth centuries, and are doubtless typical of the serviceable spoons used by merchants or noblemen.

The beautiful silver-gilt Studley Bowl is engraved with the letters of the alphabet. An English object dating from *c*.1400, the vessel owes its preservation in part to having been for many years the property of Studley Royal Church, near Ripon, Yorkshire, where it was used as an alms bowl. Its original function is uncertain; it may have been a child's porridge bowl or it may represent yet another form of drinking vessel. Another piece, some decades earlier, is a crystal ewer, mounted in silver-gilt (not hallmarked), engraved with fleurs-de-lis and decorated with enamel. Its style indicates

EWER, SILVER-GILT, CRYSTAL AND ENAMEL, FRENCH, *c*.1350 (H27cm/10½in)

The ewer, its crystal, like the mounts, probably worked in Paris, might have held wine or water. Pieces such as this would have been used at the tables of the wealthy.

that it must be French, made about 1350, as similar crystal vessels are described in contemporary royal French inventories. A very rare survival, the ewer is perhaps another instance of an object that was too fragile for use and was intended for display.

An important part of the ceremony of eating was the washing of hands, particularly since the absence of forks meant that fingers had to play an active role as implements. From as early as the eleventh century, sets of gold and silver basins and ewers, often called *aquamanilia* (literally, 'water carriers'), were made for this purpose in the shapes of various animals; no medieval silver or gold examples have survived, although two silver lion *aquamanilia* from Lüneberg, Germany, dated 1540 and 1541, are in the medieval tradition. Similar vessel types were known as *gemellions* (from the medieval Latin *gemellio*, or 'twin') and were used in pairs, water being poured from one bowl into the other. Shallow vessels decorated with *champlevé* enamel on copper, they were made in the thirteenth and fourteenth centuries in Limoges, an area long renowned for its enamelled products.

Apart from jewellery and items associated with eating, few of the precious metal vessels or implements of daily life from the Gothic period survive today. The Gothic style in silver was inspired by the example of France; indeed, there were more goldsmiths working in Paris at this time than in any other European city. Only gradually was Gothic overtaken by the new Renaissance fashions; first in Italy, then in France, Spain and England, later in Germany and Austria, and later still in Scandinavia.

DRINKING HORN, SILVER AND ENAMEL MOUNTS ON HORN, AUSTRIAN, *c*.1500 (H28cm/11in)

Drinking from animal horns is a custom of ancient origin, which remained popular in remoter parts of northern Europe until well after the Renaissance. This horn is thought to have been made for an Archbishop of Salzburg.

RENAISSANCE AND MANNERISM

The artistic styles known as Renaissance and Mannerism both originated in Italy. The sheer wealth of classical remains, and new discoveries from excavations in and around Rome led to a reappraisal of the classical traditions of form and ornament. Since Greece was suppressed by a Muslim colonial power, Italy was the obvious source of inspiration for such a classical revival, and as Italian wealth dominated Europe during the fifteenth century all the factors necessary for a cultural rejuvenation were present.

The Renaissance had been established for about one hundred years in Italy before its impact began to be felt in northern Europe, where, throughout the fifteenth century, the predominant style continued to be the Gothic. In consequence, by the time the style had moved north of the Alps, a new interpretation of classicism was already taking place in Italy. This new style, which we now call Mannerism, reworked the grammar of classical ornament, incorporating motifs of Islamic origin. This highly intellectual movement spread rapidly throughout Europe, and was used with greatest effect by the goldsmiths of northern Europe whose patrons delighted in the free expression and intellectual stimulus that the style afforded.

Portrait of Wenzel Jamnitzer,
Nicholas Neufchatel, c.1562

In the niche behind the goldsmith is a piece in a technique particularly associated with Jamnitzer: a silver-gilt vase profusely chased with Mannerist ornament and strapwork and filled with silver flowers and ferns that have been cast from nature.

PLATE AND ITS ROLES IN SOCIETY

During the Renaissance, as in other periods, plate had a number of different though complementary roles. Most sprang from the two main characteristics of precious metal: first, that in the form of coinage it was the principal instrument of commercial transactions and second, that unlike most other materials it could be melted down and refashioned. Equally, in times of financial need, it could be readily converted back into specie. One of the most important functions of plate was pure display. An impressive show of silver and gilded vessels was a telling measure of the wealth – and consequently the standing – of its owner. Almost as conspicuous was its role as an index of taste, which encouraged patrons to commission plate in the latest styles and to turn in old vessels for refashioning as frequently as circumstances allowed. These purposes were well illustrated by Cardinal Wolsey's plate at the banquet he gave for the French ambassador in 1527. The occasion is described by Wolsey's contemporary biographer, George Cavendish: 'there was a cupboard made [the full length] of the same chamber, six desks high, full of gilt plate, very sumptuous and of the newest fashions. ... This cupboard was barred about that no man might come nigh it; for there was none of the same plate occupied or stirred during this feast, for there was sufficient besides'.

Wolsey's banquet was a state occasion, and state or institutional patronage was probably as important to the goldsmith as that of individuals. For example, the presentation of plate played a major role in diplomacy, New Year gifts of plate were customarily exchanged at the English court, and colleges and civic bodies throughout Europe accumulated sizeable holdings of plate. In addition, while Protestant churches were not notable sources of work for goldsmiths, the Roman Catholic Church remained one of the most important

'JANUARY' FROM THE GRIMANI BREVIARY, c.1515

Formal dining in the early 16th century was still essentially medieval. Knives were used but food was eaten with the fingers rather than a fork. The array of plate on the buffet to the left is as much a display of wealth and status as for practical use during the meal.

patrons, and princes in Protestant and Catholic Europe alike commissioned intimate and intricate works of art in precious metal for their personal pleasure.

Plate was also the preferred material among the wealthiest aristocratic and merchant classes for ordinary domestic wares. At the beginning of this period tin-glazed earthenware was still a novelty in Italy (although a well-known luxury ware in Spain), and glass had yet to develop into the sophisticated material for which Venice was to become so famous in the sixteenth century. At most social levels domestic wares in coarse lead-glazed pottery or even wood predominated. Pewter and brass were widely available and found across a broad spectrum of society, but where they could be afforded similar wares would generally be chosen in silver.

The enormous breadth that these different functions gave to the goldsmith's craft is illustrated in contemporary manuscripts, such as a miniature from the Grimani Breviary of about 1515, which shows with great realism the luxury in which a lord in France or Flanders dined. The 'duke' sits alone, as was the custom, attended by supplicants and servants. He eats off a silver plate and drinks from a sumptuous rock crystal vessel. On the table is set a nef – a traditional status symbol in France, fashioned in the form of a ship, which was often used to contain the personal eating utensils of a person of such rank – and various other vessels; on the credenza, or buffet, to the left stands a variety of vessels, including flagons, a decorated gilt cup and cover, and plain utilitarian beakers and bowls, stacked upside down in the usual manner.

THE GOLDSMITH AND HIS CRAFT

The high intrinsic value of the material in which he worked and the special roles played by plate in society accorded the goldsmith the highest status among craftsmen; the modern distinction between artists and craftsmen had little meaning before the sixteenth century. Many of the most famous artists of the time trained initially as goldsmiths and either continued to practise the craft themselves or supplied designs for others to work from. In Italy, for example, Lorenzo Ghiberti, Filippo Brunelleschi and Andrea del Verrochio in the fifteenth century and Benvenuto Cellini in the sixteenth were all goldsmiths by training; in Germany Albrecht Dürer's father was a leading goldsmith in Nuremberg and in England the father of the miniaturist Nicholas Hilliard was a notable goldsmith in Exeter. Such associations reflected, and helped reinforce, the prominence of goldsmiths' work among the arts of the Renaissance.

Yet the goldsmith seldom enjoyed the privileged independence that one might equate with such status. His freedom of action was strictly limited by his patrons and by his guild. The powers of the guild, especially in northern Europe, were considerable and were used to regulate both the trade and the lives of its members. Apprenticeship usually lasted at least seven years, followed by a period as a journeyman. In Nuremberg the aspiring master would have to show competence in all the fields and techniques of goldsmiths' work and would be required to produce, as his 'masterpiece', a highly decorated cup, a ring and seal-die. Before this, as a journeyman, he would undergo a *Wanderjahr*, a period abroad or in another city employed in a goldsmith's workshop. But the guild also looked after its own, protecting the interests of its members like a modern trade union, acting as arbitrator in case of disputes and ensuring that only its own members could sell plate within the area of its jurisdiction. The only way in which a goldsmith could escape its authority was by entering the personal service of a ruling prince, and while this allowed him greater freedoms in certain respects, it also exposed him to the risk of expulsion from the guild.

Despite comprehensive training, the craft was highly specialized. A large workshop, although producing a wide range of work from utilitarian plate to jewellery, would have many workers concentrating on a single technique such as casting, chasing, gem-setting or enamelling. Control of costs was important to proper business management, and it was common for workshops to buy in ready-made components, casting patterns and steel dies for striking repeated decoration. Such considerations also account for the discrepancies that are often found between an important object and the original drawing for it, if such survives; not only would patrons sometimes require changes to be made, but also it made economic sense for the goldsmith to use a component he happened to have to hand rather than making up a special one.

THE SURVIVAL OF PLATE

While comparatively little plate from the early Renaissance survives, this is the first period from which significant quantities from most categories still exist. Yet this still falls short of a representative cross-section of all goldsmiths' work and rates of survival within different geographical areas or classes of object have been quite uneven. The early plate of Oxford and Cambridge colleges, for example, and of the London City livery companies, although but a fraction of their original holdings, at least gives some idea of the range of plate these institutions possessed. Likewise, the sixteenth-century princely collections that remain intact or partially intact in Munich, Dresden, Florence and elsewhere serve as an impressive indicator of the far greater number of treasures that have been lost. With domestic plate, on the other hand, where the luxury of choice existed, decorated silver tended to be preserved in preference to plain utilitarian wares. Of the latter next to nothing remains despite being far more plentiful at that time. Similarly, pre-Reformation church plate, which in the Middle Ages accounted for some of the greatest examples of the goldsmith's art, suffered in some countries, notably England and France, from systematic and almost complete destruction, while in Spain far more has survived.

Variations in the purity of silver used in different countries have also affected the survival of secular plate. German silver, generally made at a standard of about 80–85%, would yield less value per ounce than English silver (92.5%) and has thus survived in relatively large quantities, while Flemish sixteenth-century plate, made to an even higher standard (about 94%) and Spanish (about 93%) have fared even worse.

Consequently, to arrive at a balanced picture of the range and relative importance of the different categories of plate that were made, it is necessary to consider various kinds of evidence in addition to that of surviving objects. Contemporary inventories and other written records are of enormous value in assessing the sheer quantities of plate found in wealthy households of the time. Depending upon the literary skills of the inventory clerk, these can also shed light on the appearance of types of plate that are entirely unknown today. Paintings, too, add greatly to knowledge of current styles. Biblical subjects, such as the Adoration of the Magi and the Last Supper, show the types of plate in contemporary use, as do group portraits and paintings illustrating banquets or more informal domestic scenes. In addition, sixteenth-century designs and printed pattern-books produced for goldsmiths' work survive in extraordinarily large numbers. All these sources taken together create a fuller picture of the nature of plate in the Renaissance period than for any previous time.

THE RENAISSANCE

ITALY

The Renaissance style in early fifteenth-century Italy was in part an artistic response to the archaeological remains of ancient Roman civilization that were starting to be excavated and studied. No ancient plate had yet come to light, however, and the adaptation of the new style to silverware depended upon the reinterpretation of motifs that were essentially architectural. Among the first secular works which allude to the Renaissance style are the series of magnificent mounted hardstone vases made for Lorenzo de' Medici (1449–92). Lorenzo was one of the greatest patrons of his day and an avid collector of small works of art. He was also deeply fascinated by the art and culture of the Ancient World. Some of the hardstone vases in his collection, made from valuable materials such as sardonyx, jasper and amethyst, were themselves ancient, and the mounts he commissioned were intended purely to enhance their beauty as works of art.

Without doubt the most important surviving example of the early Renaissance style in Italian silver is the altar cross of 1457–9, made for the Baptistry in Florence by Antonio del Pollaiuolo and Betto Betti. The tabernacle motif in the stem bears a striking resemblance to the recently completed cupola of Florence Cathedral and clearly refers to Brunelleschi's design.

Severe economic conditions in Florence during the late fifteenth and early sixteenth centuries led to the destruction of much of the finest plate, such as the massive altar candlesticks executed by Pollaiuolo to accompany the cross in 1465. It is consequently difficult to reconstruct the development of Italian plate over this period, and such insights as can be gained depend upon the chance survival of a handful of key objects. Among these, perhaps consistently

the most outstanding are the works of Valerio Belli (1460–1546), whose chief patron was the Medici pope, Clement VII. Belli was famous as a rock crystal cutter and surviving works attributed to him include a casket in the Museo degli Argenti in Florence and a dish with the arms of Clement in the Residenz Museum in Munich. These objects are composed in a clear and rational architectural manner; the dish is characterized by simple lines, balanced proportions and scrolling enamelled foliage of an excep-

tionally pure Renaissance design. The casket, with its brilliantly carved rock crystal panels, is typical of one of the major preoccupations of the Renaissance, namely a fascination with the history and mythology of the Ancient World.

The mass destruction of Italian secular plate from this period has made it particularly hard to trace the character of the more standard vessel types, but contemporary paintings provide some evidence. One of Andrea Mantegna's great canvases of the

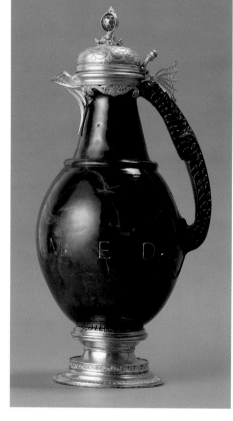

SASSANIAN SARDONYX EWER, WITH SILVER-GILT MOUNTS, FLORENCE, c.1460 (H41cm/16⅛in)

The ewer is inscribed LAVR MED *for Lorenzo de Medici and the mounts were added to his order.*

Triumphs of Caesar at Hampton Court, 'The Corselet Bearers' (*c.* 1500–06), shows an impressive array of vases and bowls, many of which are inspired by classical architecture.

The adoption of a fully developed Renaissance style, however, was probably not as rapid or as universal as such paintings might lead one to suppose. Outside the most accomplished humanist circles much of the plate being made or still in use at the end of the fifteenth century was evidently still Gothic in style. A recently discovered fresco of about 1480 in the Palazzo Altemps in Rome, for example, shows a well-stocked credenza of dishes, flagons, vases, bowls and candlesticks, all of which have a decidedly

Gothic character. The relatively conservative taste of some patrons, indeed, is a recurring theme in the history of art and one of the greatest surviving monuments of the mature Renaissance style in Italian silver is the extraordinary service of 12 silver-gilt tazzas owned in the late sixteenth century by Cardinal Ippolito Aldobrandini, later Pope Clement VIII (1536–1605). The dishes, each of which is chased with scenes from Suetonius's *Lives of the Caesars* and surmounted by the figure of one of the emperors, were made in *c.*1550–60. Their comparatively late date is betrayed by small contemporary decorative details, but the proportions and overall plan of the tazzas are a definitive essay in the mature Renaissance style.

NORTHERN EUROPE

Throughout the fifteenth century northern Europe remained largely ignorant of the Renaissance style and it was not until the first quarter of the sixteenth century that new elements began to appear in fashionable plate. Surviving objects of English or French origin within this category are extremely rare, but two that illustrate this transitional phase are the Burghley Nef, made in Paris in 1527 (Victoria & Albert Museum, London), and the London-made Howard Grace Cup of 1525.

CROSS, SILVER AND ENAMEL, ANTONIO DEL POLLAIUOLO AND BETTO BETTI, FLORENCE, 1457–9 (H250cm/98⅜in) (LEFT)

'THE CORSELET BEARERS' FROM *THE TRIUMPHS OF CAESAR*, ANDREA MANTEGNA, *c.*1500–06 (detail) (ABOVE)

TAZZA, SILVER-GILT, ITALY, *c.*1550–60 (H43.2cm/17in)

One from a set of twelve tazzas which belonged in the late 16th century to Cardinal Ippolito Aldobrandini. Each is surmounted by one of the Caesars and chased with scenes from his life. They are in the fully developed Renaissance style with pure architectural decoration and balanced, stable form.

THE HOWARD GRACE CUP, SILVER-GILT, IVORY AND PRECIOUS STONES, LONDON, 1525–6 (H30.5cm/12in)

One of the first surviving English objects to incorporate the new repertoire of Renaissance ornament, such as vases, bearded masks, cherubs and flutes. The ivory bowl is earlier and is traditionally said to have belonged to St Thomas Becket.

DESIGN FOR THE SEYMOUR CUP, HANS HOLBEIN, 1536

The solid gold cup, melted down in 1629, was made to commemorate the marriage of Henry VIII to Jane Seymour. The design is filled with allusions to the King and his bride: the repeated initials IH, Jane's personal motto 'Bound to Obey and Serve', and the finial, presumably bearing their coats of arms.

The latter incorporates an ivory bowl of much earlier date. Its overall form, the style of the inscription around the lip and the choice of a chivalric finial all betray its essential Medieval character, and yet much of the ornament is distinctly Renaissance.

Both England and France were propelled toward a fully Renaissance court style by the personal ambition and taste of their two young kings, Henry VIII (ruled 1509–48) and François I (ruled 1515–47). Both invited leading Italian artists to work for them, such

as Pietro Torrigiano in London and Francesco Primaticcio in Paris. Henry's most productive court artist was the German painter Hans Holbein the Younger (*c.*1497–1543). Primarily a portraitist, Holbein also produced designs for goldsmiths' work, the most impressive of which is for a gold cup ordered in 1536 to commemorate the marriage of Henry VIII to Jane Seymour. An epitome of Renaissance court style, the cup is designed to appear as sumptuous as possible and is enhanced with jewels and

enamels. Yet this richness of effect does not detract from the disciplined organization of the cup into a series of carefully controlled horizontal zones which balance its sense of verticality.

As striking as the overall artistic qualities of the design is the choice of ornament, all of which is of a fully developed Renaissance character. Much of this would have been appropriate only to such an extravagant commission, but one of its decorative features, the engraved arabesque, or moresque, became quite popular on English mid-century decorated plate. So-called because of its origins on Saracenic metal-work which entered Europe through Venice and Spain, this abstract, interlaced foliage ornament did not include animals or figures and was particularly suited to frieze decoration. The rapid dissemination of the arabesque was largely due to its appearance in printed pattern-books of the 1540s by Francesco Pellegrino, Jean Gourmont and others.

Apart from Paris and excluding Germany, the other great centres of goldsmiths' work in northwest Europe in the second quarter of the century were in Flanders, notably Antwerp and Bruges. At this time the court style in Paris, illustrated by a silver-gilt and rock crystal ciborium made for François I in the Paris court workshops (Louvre, Paris), was remarkably similar to that being promulgated by Holbein in London. Flanders was probably the most prosperous part of northern Europe and had a greater concentration of large and medium-sized towns than anywhere outside Italy. It had a strong tradition of goldsmiths' work, with a number of guilds hallmarking plate by the end of the fifteenth century and important centres of court patronage in Malines and Liège. Too little is left of the greatest Flemish plate from this period to form a clear view. A few chance survivals, however, such as the jewelled Michael Cup (Kunsthistorisches Museum, Vienna), hint at the importance of goldsmiths' work in this region and support the rich evidence of fine craftsmanship as portrayed in Flemish paintings of the period.

GERMANY

Probably the most productive region in Europe for silver was Germany. Partly because it was not a single country but a loose aggregation of many different states, plate was made and marked in many towns. But the most important were Augsburg and Nuremberg in the south and Strasbourg, Frankfurt and Cologne farther north. In the far north, Lübeck and Lüneburg should also be mentioned. One reason for this high productivity was that, before the discovery of the vast silver deposits in

the New World, some of the richest known silver mines were in Germany. Another may be the relatively high German demand for plate that was related to the political structure of the country. The assimilation of the Renaissance style in Germany was less systematic than at the courts of Paris and London, a fact that may be due to the lack of either direct Italian influence or a strong central court, as well as the relatively conservative taste of many patrons. Even Albrecht Dürer, who had travelled to

Venice in 1494 and 1506 and would have been familiar with the works of Bellini and Mantegna, remained loyal to the Gothic style in his designs for plate. A drawing of 1526 for a double cup in the Albertina, Vienna, for example, has absorbed something of the Renaissance sense of proportion, but in its overall form and decoration (namely, the scrolling foliage and pronounced lobes) it is still Gothic.

The most outstanding Nuremberg goldsmiths of the early part of the century were

DESIGN FOR A DOUBLE CUP, ALBRECHT DÜRER, 1526

The double cup was a traditional German form, often given at weddings. This is typical of Dürer's designs for plate, combining a Renaissance sense of proportion with Gothic characteristics, such as scrolling foliage and pronounced lobes. (FAR LEFT)

CUP AND COVER, PARCEL-GILT, LUDWIG KRUG, NUREMBERG, c.1525 (H44cm/17$\frac{5}{16}$in)

Covered cups were one of the most important forms of late Medieval and Renaissance plate and were subject to highly innovative design. This cup combines Gothic and Renaissance detail. (LEFT)

THE HOW CUP, SILVER-GILT, LONDON, 1514–15 (H21.5cm/8$\frac{1}{2}$in)

Recently acquired by the British Museum, this piece represents one of the standard forms of standing cup and cover in England and Flanders in the early 16th century. The engraved decoration is still of a Gothic character and the flat finial would originally have been engraved or enamelled with the arms of the owner. (ABOVE)

CUP AND COVER, SILVER-GILT, PROBABLY STRASBOURG, *c*.1540 (H37.2cm/14⅝in)

This unmarked cup is a magnificent example of the German Renaissance style. The coins betray the patron's interest in the ancient world, although in fact several of them are 16th-century fakes.

Ludwig Krug (*c*.1480–1532) and Melchior Baier (fl. 1525–77). Krug, who probably collaborated with Dürer on some commissions, was also essentially a Gothic goldsmith addressing the challenge of Renaissance ideas. The result in much of his surviving work is an appealing combination of old and new motifs that have a strange and idiosyncratic vitality. A covered cup in the Museum of Decorative Arts in Budapest, for example, combines the organic, vegetable forms of the late Gothic with classicizing cameos, while another of about 1525 in the Kunsthistorisches Museum,

Vienna, combines Gothic foliage and figures with tiers of Renaissance flutes. That the taste of the patron was crucial to the character of important plate, however, is illustrated by a cup of about 1530 attributed to Krug's elder brother, Erasmus, who moved to Strasbourg in 1506. The cup was made for Wilhelm Honstein, Bishop of Strasbourg and Count of Alsace, who had his personal medallion set into the foot and cover. He was a confidant of the emperors Maximilian I and Charles V; he had attended the university of Pavia and had clearly received a cosmopolitan education. The design of the cup is as rigorous an expression of Renaissance principles as anything made outside Italy at this time. Not only are the proportions quite unlike those of Gothic plate, but virtually all the ornament, including the collection of inset classical coins, betrays a strong interest in the ancient world and its culture.

DECORATED DOMESTIC PLATE

Outside court circles the impact of the Renaissance style on decorated plate throughout northern Europe was more diluted. Forms and ornament gradually evolved over the first half of the sixteenth century. While the main repertoire of plate types seems to have remained fairly constant, basic shapes gradually began to reflect Renaissance norms of proportion. At the same time a restricted range of new ornament began to filter down from the luxury objects made in the court style during the 1530s. In particular, symmetrical chased flutes begin to replace the swirling ones of Gothic plate; engraved arabesques and busts are found in place of the highly naturalistic foliage of previous decades; and simple stamped dentil ornament derived from classical architecture is introduced in place of the often highly complex stamped patterns of earlier decades. A typical form of ornament in the middle years of the century,

probably popularized by the circulation of pattern-books such as those of Francesco Pellegrino and Hans Brosamer, consisted of panels of naturalistic leaves and tendrils. A rare survival of this type of ornament is an English casting bottle of 1553 in the Gilbert Collection, Los Angeles. As one might expect, there is more evidence of the transition between Gothic and Renaissance in decorative plate made for what might be termed the middle market than in court objects. A silver-gilt beaker of 1541 by the Basle goldsmith Johann Rudolf Fäsch-Glaser, for example, is decorated with typical engraved foliage and simple geometric stamped ornament but has retained a beautiful and sinuous Gothic sense of form, especially in the curvature of the body and elegant ogee outline of the cover.

Examples of plain and decorative plate in common use by a prosperous family around the middle of the century are well illustrated by the 1559 portrait of the Basle goldsmith Hans Rudolf Fäsch, who was presumably related to the maker of the covered beaker. The family drink from typical German beakers of a type known as *Satzbecher*, which would have been stacked together when not in use. The exception is the goldsmith himself who is drinking from one half of a fine gilt double cup. On the table are two plain vase-shaped casters, or casting bottles, and a faceted jug which must date from late in the previous century. Knives are to be seen on the table, but until the end of the sixteenth century forks were almost unknown north of the Alps and food was usually eaten with the fingers or a spoon. The picture also shows what other materials were in use at the table of a relatively prosperous family; whilst the drinking cups and other small vessels are of silver, the larger ones are of pewter; the dishes and the great flagons contained in the brass or copper cistern on the floor also seem to be of pewter. Most revealing of all is the fact that the family is eating off plain wooden plates, or 'trenchers'. Silver plates and flagons, which required the use of a great deal of precious metal, were only for the very rich in the mid-sixteenth century.

CASTING
BOTTLE, SILVER-
GILT, LONDON,
1553–4
(H14.5cm/5 11/16 in)

*These small vessels for
sprinkling scented water
are commonly found on
16th-century inventories,
although very few
survive today. The
decoration is typical of
a kind fashionable for a
few years around the
middle of the century
and popularized
through printed
pattern books.*

COVERED
BEAKER, SILVER-
GILT AND
ENAMEL,
JOHANN RUDOLF
FÄSCH-GLASER,
BASLE, 1541
(H33cm/13in)

*Made for a member of
the Bärenfels family,
who lived near Basle,
the finial of the beaker
includes their enamelled
coat of arms. The
'wildman' finial was a
common symbolic device
in the 16th century,
supposedly representing
freedom from moral
turpitude.*

PORTRAIT OF
THE FÄSCH
FAMILY, HANS
HUG KLUBER,
1559

*Hans Rudolf Fäsch,
seen drinking from one
half of a fine gilt double
cup, was a prominent
Basle goldsmith. The
portrait shows a
mixture of silver and
pewter vessels, and
reminds us that not all
plate in use was new:
the double cup was
probably about 50 years
old and the faceted jug a
15th-century example.*

BEAKER, PARCEL-GILT,
CHRISOSTHEMUS FEDERER,
STRASBOURG, *c.*1595 (H8.8cm/3½in)

A typical example of simple but elegant domestic plate with engraved strapwork.

WINE CUP,
SILVER-GILT,
LONDON, 1557–8
(H15.7cm/6³⁄₁₆in;
D17.8cm/7in)

Some of the finest surviving Tudor plate was presented or sold to the Tsar of Russia in the late 16th and early 17th centuries and has been preserved in the Kremlin. This shallow-bowled cup is a rare example of the form of wine cup fashionable at this time.

Not all the standard repertoire of plate is represented in the Fäsch portrait, however, and while a thorough survey is not possible here, some at least should be mentioned. The resources of the family perhaps did not extend to a silver ewer and dish, but before the introduction of the fork this was essential to civilized dining. Often made in brass or pewter, when in silver the set formed one of the most expensive items of practical plate and few from the first half of the century have escaped destruction. They were made throughout Europe, although they were not generally supplied as matched sets until the early sixteenth century.

Other kinds of decorated plate had stronger regional traditions, such as the double cup in Germany and the nef in France. In England one of the most important status symbols in silver was the ceremonial standing salt. It performed a comparable social function to the nef and its design was consequently subject to more variation than elsewhere. During the late Middle Ages inventive sculptural forms had been favoured; by the early sixteenth century it

had begun to take on more standardized patterns, the most popular in the first quarter being the 'hour glass salt', a form on a broad foot with waisted stem and spreading upper part mirroring the foot. In common with other ceremonial plate, the salt generally had a cover.

Of all the most prestigious decorated plate of the late Middle Ages and Renaissance, the standing cup and cover was probably the most universal. Its use was primarily ceremonial and its design and manufacture formed an area of special importance for goldsmiths throughout northern Europe. Nevertheless, distinct regional differences existed. In Germany, for example, cups of Gothic form or modelled as naturalistic fruits continued well into the sixteenth century. In England and Flanders, the most typical form in the early part of the century has a bulbous, flat-topped finial which would generally be engraved or enamelled with the owner's coat of arms. By the second quarter of the sixteenth century the type represented by the Seymour Cup became the standard form.

A more practical form of drinking vessel favoured in both countries was the shallow-bowled and high-stemmed wine cup, as exemplified by an Antwerp cup of 1542 in the Provinciaal Museum Sterckshof, Antwerp, or a magnificent London cup of 1557 in the Kremlin. With their strong emphasis on horizontal divisions, these vessels are fine illustrations of a typical Renaissance form.

Other vessels that were widely used in northern Europe were conical beakers and tankards. The latter appear not to have entered general circulation until around the middle of the sixteenth century and were anyway more popular in predominantly beer-drinking regions, such as Germany and England. Although reflecting current decorative fashion, these vessel types did not undergo radical changes in form over the rest of the century.

Mounted vessels had always been popular in England. A common late Medieval type was the mazer, a shallow turned wood bowl with silver lip, and another category of vessel, often associated with drinking but more likely to have been for pouring, was the covered pot, usually made in ceramic and mounted in silver or silver-gilt. The most commonly found silver-mounted vessels in England were Rhenish stoneware jugs, which were imported in large quantities. Around the middle of the century, when these jugs first appeared in England, the mounts were often of the finest quality, but the standard tended to decline later in the century, presumably reflecting the declining social status of such vessels. Mounted vessels were also popular in the German-speaking lands, and were often fashioned in the form of animals or birds with detachable heads. Frequently made of diverse materials such as coconut, turned wood or ceramic with silver mounts, these objects were probably intended to be more decorative than practical.

ORDINARY DOMESTIC PLATE

Just as the division between court and decorated domestic silver is only approximate, so that between decorative and purely practical wares is less than clear-cut. The mazer bowl in England, for example, and its Germanic covered equivalent, were among the most utilitarian forms of early sixteenth-century plate, although occasionally they could be finely wrought and embellished with enamelled coats of arms. Spoons were often plain, but many were decorated with sculptural finials in the form of apostles or other figures. Likewise, the silver-mounted stoneware jugs of the second half of the century were not very different in form from their luxurious equivalents in *façon de Venise* glass and Isnik pottery. Yet very plain utilitarian plate was made in prodigious quantities for the grandest households. For the most part this has almost entirely disappeared and survives only in isolated cases and by chance. A dinner service of 26 dishes made in London between 1581 and 1601, for example,

recently acquired by the British Museum, survives only because it was buried in the seventeenth century and rediscovered in the nineteenth. Similarly, a single plate of the 1560s from a service made for King Eric XIV of Sweden escaped the melting pot only by being lost in a moat. Although the greatest families had possessed extensive holdings of plate for generations, many more people aspired to its possession by the latter part of the sixteenth century. This is chiefly because a great deal more silver was in circulation: between 1503 and 1660 (and mainly after about 1560) some 16 million kilograms of silver were imported into Spain from the New World, sufficient to increase Europe's existing resources three-fold. The majority of this holding went straight into the service of foreign debt and was also used for the payment of troops rather than the enrichment of Spain. As a result, a commodity that had been in desperately short supply in the fifteenth century now came into greatly increased circulation, a fact that was directly reflected in a significant increase in plate production.

GERMAN STONEWARE JUG WITH SILVER-GILT MOUNTS, LONDON, 1567–8 (H21cm/8in)

Rhenish stoneware jugs were frequently embellished with silver mounts in England during the second half of the 16th century. The mounts on this one are unusually elaborate. The neck is engraved with a typical design of arabesque foliage and linear strapwork and the cover is chased with strapwork cartouches. (ABOVE LEFT)

OWL CUP, SILVER-GILT AND COCONUT, CHRISTOPH ERHART, AUGSBURG, *c.*1600 (H26.6cm/10½in)

Drinking vessels formed as animals or birds, sometimes incorporating other materials such as coconut or turned wood, were very popular in Germany. Owl cups were often presented as archery prizes. (ABOVE)

MANNERISM

By the time the northern interpretation of the Renaissance style had fully matured in the late 1530s, the Italian principles of design on which it was based, first evident nearly a hundred years earlier, were starting to be overturned in Italy in favour of what was, at its most extreme, a radically different style. While the relatively conservative taste of some patrons ensured that plate in the mature Renaissance style, such as the Aldobrandini Tazzas, continued to be made after the middle of the century, others were already looking for new inspiration considerably earlier.

The term Mannerism has its origins in *maniera*, a word used by Vasari in his *Lives of the Artists* (1550; expanded 1568) to describe a certain type of pictorial representation in which emotion is expressed through the manipulation of construction and colour and by exaggeration of the human form.

The first major architectural project with strong Mannerist features was the Palazzo del Te (1526–34), built in Mantua by Giulio Romano (?1499–1546) for Federico Gonzaga. A similar collaboration between Romano and the Gonzaga family was responsible for the earliest Mannerist plate of which there is any record. Although the objects themselves no longer exist, a number of drawings survive for ewers, tureens, candlesticks and other items of table silver. The common feature to these designs is an abandonment of the formal sense of order that typified Renaissance plate in favour of a search for novelty and wit. A drawing for a candlestick of about 1539 at Christ Church, Oxford, for example, shows lions crawling from under acanthus leaves on the base and putti emerging from a calyx of leaves to support the fluted candle socket. The ingredients here are classical; their combination is not.

Contemporaries of Romano who also produced Mannerist designs for plate included Perino del Vaga (1501–47), Enea Vico (1523–67) and Francesco Salviati (1510–63). Certainly the most talented of these was Salviati, and his drawings illustrate many of the features of the fully developed Mannerist style: an exaggeration of form to the detriment of function, a constant search for originality and a rejection of architectural construction (though not the vocabulary of architecture). In place of the balanced stable vessels of the Renaissance, elongated forms of complex profile on precariously diminutive feet became fashionable. A significant development, also evident in Salviati's drawings, was a predilection for subtle and often obscure allusion to philosophical or classical subjects and an ever-increasing complexity of ornament. The latter, dubbed *difficultà*, was another key element of Mannerism. This notion embraced both technical and intellectual

DESIGN FOR A CANDLESTICK, GIULIO ROMANO, *c.*1530

The drawing is inscribed Illmo sʳ. feran[te] [Gonz]aga. *This is a highly spirited design with all the main elements of early Mannerism, mixing architectural and figural components in a novel way.*

THE FARNESE CASKET, SILVER-GILT AND ROCK CRYSTAL, MANNO DI SEBASTIANO SBARRI AND GIOVANNI DEI BERNARDI, ROME, 1547–61 (H49cm/19¼in)

Commissioned by Cardinal Alessandro Farnese, this is now in the Museo di Capodimonte in Naples. In its density of ornament and virtuosity of craftsmanship, and in its philosophical references, it is an epitome of Mannerism.

virtuosity and was intended to express the taste and sophistication of the patron as well as the skills of the goldsmith.

Virtually all the great Mannerist plate of Italy has been lost, but two works that have survived must be as splendid as any that were made. The altar candlesticks from the Vatican Sacristy, completed in 1581 by Antonio Gentile da Faenza, and the gilt and rock crystal casket of 1547–61 by Manno di Sebastiano Sbarri were commissioned by Cardinal Alessandro Farnese. Both are highly architectural in conception and derive very obviously from Michelangelo – especially his work in the Medici Chapel – in the style of the figures incorporated into the designs. The design of the Farnese casket has been attributed to Francesco Salviati. Like the candlesticks, it incorporates rock crystal plaques by Giovanni dei Bernardi and is highly architectural and sculptural. In its density of ornament, its virtuosity of craftsmanship and the complexity of its philosophical references it represents the epitome of Mannerism.

NORTHERN EUROPE

The migration of Mannerism to northern Europe was, in comparison with that of the Renaissance style, almost immediate and owed a great deal to François I of France, who invited some of its leading exponents – Rosso Fiorentino, Francesco Primaticcio and Benvenuto Cellini – to work for him in Paris. Cellini (1500–71) is probably the most celebrated of all goldsmiths and although only one piece that is indubitably his work in precious metal has survived, his lasting fame was ensured by two important books: his *Treatise on Goldsmithing* and his delightful if not always reliable *Autobiography* (1558–62).

By remarkably good fortune his single known surviving piece of goldsmith's work – the gold salt-cellar now in the Kunsthistorisches Museum, Vienna – was also one of his most important. Started in Rome for Ippolito d'Este in 1539, it was completed in Paris in 1543 for François I. The king's praise was, according to Cellini, nothing if not extravagant: 'This is a hundred times more divine than I could ever have imagined. The man is a wonder! He should never lay down his tools'. Wrought entirely in gold and enriched with enamels, the salt is essentially a work of sculpture. Its design is based on an elaborate symbolic programme which Cellini describes at length in both his *Autobiography* and *Treatise*.

Of much wider significance for the spread of Mannerism in northern Europe was the work of Rosso Fiorentino (1495–1540) who, together with Primaticcio, was responsible between 1533 and 1535 for the plaster ceiling decoration of the Galerie François I at Fontainebleau. This was distinguished by a novel form of ornament that resembled three-dimensional cut and curling straps of leather. Known as strapwork, it was soon recognized to have a potential as abstract ornament for all kinds of objects. Rosso is thought to have made designs for plate and although none survives, they were probably

SALT CELLAR, GOLD, WOOD AND ENAMEL, BENVENUTO CELLINI, ROME AND PARIS, 1539–43 (L33.5cm/14in)

The only goldsmith's work of Cellini known to survive, the salt cellar was made for François I of France and given in 1570 to Archduke Ferdinand II of Tirol. The figures are symbolic of the Earth and the Sea, their interaction being the origin of salt.

close in manner to the printed designs for plate by René Boyvin which illustrate nefs, tureens, table fountains and so on, characterized by prominent embossed or engraved scenes contained within strapwork surrounds and with applied putti.

The spread of strapwork in a short time from an isolated novelty to the most ubiquitous decorative motif in northern Europe is due almost entirely to printed pattern-books. By the third quarter of the century its potential in many contexts had been realized, not only by the leading French designers such as Etienne Delaune and Androuet du Cerceau, but also by the great ornamentalists elsewhere. Erasmus Hornick of Nuremberg, Virgil Solis, Cornelis Floris and others were all incorporating strapwork into their designs by the 1560s and earlier, and these, in the form of woodcuts and engravings, found their way into goldsmiths' workshops all over the Continent.

WENZEL JAMNITZER AND SOUTH GERMANY

Without question the most famous northern European goldsmith was Wenzel Jamnitzer of Nuremberg (1508–85). Jamnitzer was a true 'Renaissance man', whose accomplishments embraced goldsmithing, sculpture, draughtsmanship and mathematics. He was born in Vienna – itself a notable centre of goldsmiths' work in the early sixteenth century – and moved to Nuremberg, where he became a master of the goldsmiths' guild in 1534. In most techniques he showed a virtuosity that, with rare exceptions, exceeded that of his contemporaries and won him great fame. These are skills that are suggested in Nicholas Neufchâtel's portrait of Jamnitzer, painted in about 1562 when he was at the height of his career. The portrait shows the master surrounded by tokens of his prosperity and accomplishments: sober

DESIGN FOR THE MERCKEL
CENTREPIECE, WENZEL JAMNITZER,
1548–9 (ABOVE LEFT)

EWER, SILVER-GILT, TROCHUS SHELL
AND ENAMEL, WENZEL JAMNITZER,
NUREMBERG, c.1570 (H33cm/13in) (LEFT)

GLOBE CUP, SILVER-GILT, ABRAHAM
GESSNER, ZURICH, c.1600 (H49cm/19¼in)
(ABOVE)

but costly clothes, instruments for measuring and weighing silver, a part-finished silver figure of Neptune and the drawing he has prepared for it.

The most sensational work of Jamnitzer to have survived, described by John Hayward as 'the *non plus ultra* of artistic virtuosity', is the Merckel centrepiece of 1549 in the Rijksmuseum, Amsterdam, for which the goldsmith's finished design is also extant.

A radically different late work is a trochus shell ewer of about 1570. This is a brilliant composition which achieves an extraordinary unity out of a rich diversity of elements and in which any relationship of scale between the different parts has been dismissed as secondary to the sense of movement and energy which it inspires.

Wenzel Jamnitzer was the founder of a family of goldsmiths whose younger members, Hans and Christoph, worked into the seventeenth century. His work was much imitated by his contemporaries, including other leading Nuremberg goldsmiths such as Jakob Fröhlich and Christoph Ritter. An important factor in the dissemination of the Jamnitzer style was the availability of much of his intricate ornament in the form of lead casting patterns, which found their way into other workshops in Nuremberg and elsewhere. Sophisticated Mannerist plate bearing a close affinity to Jamnitzer's work is thus known from towns as far apart as Augsburg, Strasbourg and Cologne.

Until the middle of the sixteenth century Nuremberg's dominance of south German silver production remained unchallenged; but although it continued to spawn great goldsmiths, from then on it was gradually superseded by Augsburg. This was a natural result of the increasing financial and political importance of the latter: it was the headquarters of the Fugger banking empire and in 1530 hosted Charles V's Diet. By the last quarter of the century it was probably the most significant producer in Germany of both useful plate and fine decorated pieces such as ewers and dishes, tankards and tazzas. The last of these survive in small numbers, although a remarkable set of 24 preserved in the Pitti Palace in Florence serves as a reminder of how splendid these could be. The decorative possibilities of the wide, flat surfaces inside tazza bowls were frequently used to maximum advantage with finely chased embossed scenes.

During this time, Augsburg goldsmiths developed a number of distinctive techniques that made a special contribution to German silver. Among these are the use of panels of etched moresque ornament and the application of strips of filigree decoration, a technique that was also practised in nearby Ulm. The most interesting development, however, was the perfection of a highly sophisticated form of translucent enamel decoration that is particularly associated with David Altenstetter (*c.*1547–1617).

One other town among many in the southern German cultural region that calls for special mention is Zürich. Not only was the city a prolific centre with a thriving community of goldsmiths, it also happened to produce two of the most outstanding craftsmen of the sixteenth century. Hans Jacob Stampfer, working in the middle of the century, was a master of Renaissance ornament. At the end of the century Abraham Gessner is distinguished for the supreme quality of his embossed work and is particularly famous for a series of engraved globe cups, borne either on a baluster stem or by a figure of Atlas.

ANTWERP AND LONDON

By the middle of the century Antwerp was the most important commercial centre in Flanders and was said to have over a thousand resident foreign merchants. It suffered a violent reversal, however, as a result of the brutal uprising in 1576 of Spanish troops garrisoned in the city, followed in 1583 by further rioting on the part of French troops and by the subsequent imposition of the Spanish Inquisition, which had the effect of driving away any remaining Protestant merchants and craftsmen.

In the middle years of the century Antwerp's commercial strength was reflected in a thriving school of goldsmiths and the evolution of a highly distinctive interpretation of the Mannerist style. As early as the 1540s this is evident in a small group of plate including the Founder's Cup of 1541(?) at Emmanuel College, Cambridge, and the Aspremont Lynden ewer and dish of around 1550 at the British Museum. Both retain a strong sense of Renaissance design and proportion, with distinct horizontal divisions and broad, stable bases, but the decoration is quite new. The cup is characterized by bold freestanding strapwork and bizarre acrobatic figures, while the ewer is decorated at the base of the handle with an applied faun which is held down, as it were, by manacles of strapwork. This avant-garde ornament was strongly influenced by Cornelis Bos, a prolific and talented Antwerp designer who had trained in Rome in the 1530s and who is thought also to have visited Fontainebleau. His work thus shows an acute awareness of most of the key elements in the developing Mannerist style and his bizarrely imaginative grotesques became widely known through engravings. Other influential designers of plate from Antwerp included Cornelis Floris, Hans Vredeman de Vries and Balthazar Sylvius.

Little of the finest sixteenth-century plate from Antwerp has survived, but its influence was extensive, both through the movement of artists and craftsmen and also from actual plate that found its way abroad. Erasmus Hornick, for example, one of the most influential figures in south German Mannerism, was born and trained in Antwerp. The Founder's Cup has been in England since at least 1584, when it was presented to the college by Sir Walter Mildmay, and a number of the finest pieces listed in the various royal inventories compiled for Henry VIII and Elizabeth I are described as 'of Flaundours making'. Even before the collapse of Antwerp's economy

THE ASPREMONT LYNDEN EWER AND DISH, SILVER-GILT, ANTWERP, *c.*1550 (H33.9cm/13¼in; D47.4cm/18¾in)

The form and decoration of this ewer is typical of the distinctive character of early Antwerp Mannerism in the use of grotesque beasts entangled in strapwork.

LEOPARD, SILVER-GILT, LONDON, 1600–1 (H98cm/38⁹⁄₁₆in)

One of a pair, these massive sculptural heraldic leopards are the greatest of all the Tudor plate surviving in the Kremlin. They were sold to the Tsar by Charles I in 1626. (RIGHT)

THE BOWES CUP, SILVER-GILT AND GLASS, LONDON, 1554–5 (H48.9cm/19¼in)

One of the few treasures of the Goldsmiths' Company to escape destruction in the Civil War, the cup was presented to the Company by Sir Martin Bowes in 1561. Although made in London, it is reminiscent of the designs of Balthazar Sylvius of Antwerp. (ABOVE)

STANDING SALT, SILVER-GILT, LONDON, 1594–5 (H41.5cm/16⁵⁄₁₆in)

In the second half of the 16th century this example and the cylindrical drum salt emerged as the most usual types of standing salt. Intended for display, they could reach enormous sizes and this salt, from the Kremlin, is one of the largest surviving, although its mediocre chasing reflects declining standards. (CENTRE)

many of its natives were working in London as goldsmiths and some of the most stylistically advanced surviving plate from the 1550s and 1560s with London hallmarks may well have been made by or with the assistance of immigrant Flemish craftsmen. The London-made Wyndham ewer of 1554 in the British Museum, for example, is close in form to the Aspremont Lynden ewer and was almost certainly inspired by a Flemish ewer or design. Similarly, the Bowes Cup, also of 1554 and presented to the Goldsmiths' Company by Sir Martin Bowes in 1561, is very close in a number of respects to the designs of Balthazar Sylvius.

The Continental influences on English silver were not limited to Flanders and there

was probably an even greater presence in London of German plate and German craftsmen than of Flemish. Certainly the royal Jewel House was rich in 'Allmaine' cups and there are frequent references in the minutes of the Goldsmiths' Company to the illegal sale of German silver in London. The market in England for German silver might in part be explained by the fact that it was of a lower standard of purity and appreciably cheaper. But equally there is no doubt that the standard of workmanship among English silversmiths was not as high as that of the best German and Flemish masters.

The apparent decline in the quality of English silver during the second half of the century is probably partly illusory, however, to the extent that almost all the great plate made for royal and wealthy aristocratic patrons has been lost. Most surviving objects were made for a less exacting clientele, although exceptions exist. From the latter part of the century, for example, a small corpus of outstanding engraved silver associated with the monogrammist 'P over M' and the Flemish engraver Nicaise Roussel survives, while a remarkable group of plate from around 1610 by the anonymous 'TYL' maker testifies to the existence of the finest skills, even if on a limited scale.

Equally characteristic of late Tudor and early Stuart silver is a certain insularity of taste. This is evident not only in a somewhat repetitive use of ornament, but also in a more limited range of forms than is encountered on the Continent. Yet such insularity itself created the conditions for the evolution in the late sixteenth century of certain specifically English types of plate. These included the standing salt-cellar, which developed along lines unparalleled elsewhere. From the middle of the century the usual form was a pedestal of either square or circular section with a domed cover. Most surviving examples are not more than about 15 cm (6 in) high, although the Kremlin's example of 1594 (41.9 cm/16½ in) and the Mostyn Salt of 1586 in the Victoria & Albert Museum (40.9 cm/16⅛ in, lacking finial) give an idea of the prodigious size these preposterous objects of display could reach. An innovation, also without Continental parallel, was the steeple cup. This was a tall cup with baluster stem and ovoid bowl and cover surmounted by a steeple-shaped finial. The form became standardized at an early stage and its decoration seldom deviated from a set repertoire of flat-chased and embossed strapwork and foliage. In most cases their quality was indifferent. Surviving examples tend not to exceed about 40 or 45 cm (16 or 18 in) in height, although the remarkable survival of a group in the Kremlin, one of which reaches as much as 89 cm (35 in), reminds us that the principal purpose of such plate was to create a display of wealth that impressed more through mass than taste or craftmanship.

THE SCHATZKAMMER

A parallel development to the evolution of the court style in Renaissance and Mannerist plate was the phenomenon of the *Schatzkammer*, or treasury. Intimately connected with the humanist

THE PASTON TREASURE, DUTCH SCHOOL, *c*.1660

This extraordinary collection of exotic objects belonged to the Paston family of Norfolk and several pieces still survive. Most appear to be of contemporary manufacture, although some, such as the nautilus cup behind the globe, evidently date from earlier periods.

interest in categorizing and collecting artefacts, the *Schatzkammer* was developed to demonstrate both the learning and taste of its owner and the dynastic antiquity of his family. In 1565 Duke Albrecht V of Bavaria decreed that some 45 objects in his treasury be designated 'inalienable heirlooms', never to be disposed of by his successors, the intention being to demonstrate by virtue of such a perpetual inheritance the continuity of the family.

With Duke Albrecht's heirlooms lay the origins of the great *Schatzkammer* at Munich. This was not an isolated phenomenon and around this time a number of such collections were initiated: in 1560 the Elector Augustus I of Saxony founded his *Kunst-*kammer in Dresden and Emperor Rudolf II's collections were started in Prague in the 1580s. The fact that these collections were deliberately held apart from useful plate and were esteemed principally as works of art accounts for their survival in relatively large numbers. The basis on which they were established varied widely. The treasures of the Paston family of East Anglia, painted in about 1660, represent what might be termed an informal 'Cabinet of Curiosities'. The collection of tropical shells with silver-gilt mounts emphasizes exotica rather than wealth or learning. A further instance of exoticism is the Chinese Wanli blue-and-white dish in the centre of the painting. Although by this date Chinese porcelain was

TANKARD, SILVER-GILT AND ROCK
CRYSTAL, DIEBOLT KRUG,
STRASBOURG, c.1595 (H26cm/10¼in)

*Rock crystal was one of the most treasured materials
in Schatzkammer collections and was given silver-gilt
or gold mounts of the highest quality. Diebolt Krug
was a member of the famous family of Nuremberg
goldsmiths.* (RIGHT)

BIRD, GOLD AND ROCK CRYSTAL,
PROBABLY MILAN, c.1500 (H31.5cm/12¾in)

*The leading rock crystal carvers were the Saracchi and
Miseroni families of Milan, who produced brilliant
and virtuoso carved and engraved vessels in bizarre
forms for the princely collections of Europe. This one
is from the Medici collection in Florence.*
(BELOW RIGHT)

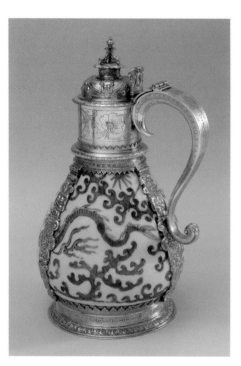

CHINESE PORCELAIN EWER WITH
SILVER-GILT MOUNTS, LONDON, c.1600
(H28.5cm/11¼in)

*Chinese porcelain, relatively well-known in England
by the late 16th century, was often embellished with
fine silver-gilt mounts. The foliage around the neck is
close in manner to that of the immigrant Flemish
engraver, Nicaise Roussel.* (ABOVE)

many, but in the late sixteenth century a school of talented rock crystal carvers and engravers was established in Milan, associated especially with the Saracchi and Miseroni families. The most virtuoso products of these workshops were pure fantasies in the form of beasts and birds embellished with gold mounts. They were prodigiously expensive and were supplied only to the wealthiest princely patrons, such as the Medici and the Electors of Bavaria and Saxony, but vessels of a more practical appearance, such as cups, tankards and candlesticks, were also produced for the *Schatzkammer*.

SPAIN, PORTUGAL AND THE NORTH

The physical isolation of the Iberian Peninsula, coupled with its tendency to look as much to its empires overseas as to Europe, had always resulted in a rather separate line of artistic development. The Spanish and Portuguese transition seems in the early sixteenth century to have been less from a specific Gothic tradition than from a sort of ill-defined Medievalism. The decorative programme of early sixteenth-century Portuguese embossed dishes, of which there are many, is typically concerned with subjects such as chivalry, courtly love and the Last Judgement, all of which had been preoccupations of the northern European mind a hundred years earlier.

Practically no Spanish secular plate from the early sixteenth century is known, however, and it is impossible to reconstruct more than an outline of its history. Before the development of its empire in the New World, Spain was not a wealthy region. Divided into a number of separate kingdoms, principally Castille and Aragon, it was moreover highly regionalized and the development of artistic styles was far from synchronous. The main centres of goldsmiths' work in Castille included Burgos,

becoming more common in Europe, at the beginning of the century it was highly prized and often given silver-gilt mounts.

One of the favourite materials in the *Schatzkammer* collection of the sixteenth century was rock crystal. Before the perfection of glass this naturally occurring mineral was the only known perfectly clear material; as such it had a special beauty that, coupled with its rarity, made it an ideal material for precious drinking vessels. The main centre for rock crystal carving in northern Europe was Freiburg im Breisgau in southern Ger-

Cuenca, Toledo and Valladolid, and the leading Aragonese towns were Barcelona and Saragossa. From the evidence of religious plate, which is relatively plentiful, both kingdoms were very conservative while Aragon, the poorer of the two, was perhaps the slower to adopt Renaissance form and ornament. Even as late as 1550 echoes of Gothic ornament are not unusual on Spanish plate.

The paucity of secular silver partly reflects the overwhelming economic strength of the Church in Spain. While the most splendid examples of northern European plate were made for ruling princes or city councils, the greatest monuments of Spanish silver were the *custodiàs*, great portable tabernacles carried in procession on major feast days, some of which could reach

enormous proportions. Indeed, to assess the artistic and technical skill of Spanish goldsmiths' work in the sixteenth century, both at home and in its colonies, it is exclusively to religious plate that one must turn.

As with earlier styles, Spain and Portugal were less influenced by Mannerism than other countries and continued to develop in relative isolation. Under Phillip II there was a short-lived period of Italian influence, although it did not take root. By the end of the century the more austere and monumental Herrara style, named after the architect, Juan de Herrara, had established itself. This style has been aptly described by the late Charles Oman as 'the affectation of a rich austerity emanating from the Escorial'. Yet Oman's assertion that such plainness might reflect cost-saving motives must be reas-

sessed in the light of the extraordinary treasure recently recovered from the wreck of the *Atocha*, sunk off the Florida coast in 1622. In addition to the cargo of bullion, the ship also carried a quantity of plate in the personal baggage of its passengers. These included ewers, candlesticks, drinking vessels and salvers, some of solid gold and some of silver or silver-gilt. Much of it was austerely decorated, but it was mostly of a heavy gauge that would have more than compensated for any savings of cost through minimal decoration. In short, the style was clearly an expression of taste rather than economics.

At the other end of Europe – in northern Germany and Scandinavia – developments also followed a distinct course. Knowledge of north German silver of the first half of the

CHALICE, SILVER-GILT, ROCK CRYSTAL AND BOXWOOD, MEXICO CITY, *c.*1600 (H33cm/13in)

The most impressive Spanish 16th-century plate was liturgical and Spanish colonial masters followed home styles very closely. The colonial origins of this chalice are reflected in the use of humming-bird feathers as a background for the carved boxwood panels.

STILL LIFE OF SPANISH PLATE, JUAN BAUTISTA DE ESPINOSA, *c.*1624

This illustrates a well-dressed credenza of fashionable plate in the Herrara style. The forms are simple but strong and the decoration is mostly flat-chased and confined to clearly organized patterns. Relief ornament is restricted to small geometric enamelled panels on the salt cellars.

sixteenth century is limited, since destruction of plate from that area was relatively greater than the loss of plate from the south. However, the survival of 29 pieces from the town council plate of Lüneburg, many of which date from the early or mid-sixteenth century, shows a preference for massive objects characterized by a fine sense of proportion, but with a certain looseness of execution that lacks the jewel-like refinement of the finest Nuremberg and Augsburg goldsmiths' work. The most important of the Hanse towns in the early sixteenth century was Lübeck, although toward the end of the century Hamburg gradually eclipsed it as a trading power. These towns were known for the production of massive cups and a distinctive type of tall and slender tankard known as a 'Hanse tankard'. The importance of Hamburg as a centre of plate

STANDING DISH, PARCEL-GILT AND ENAMEL, LÜNEBERG, 1541 (H25cm/9⅞in, D40.5cm/15⁷⁄₁₆in)

One of a pair of dishes from the Lüneberg City Council plate, preserved in the Kunstgewerbe Museum in Berlin, this piece gives some insight into the scale and character of north German Renaissance plate.

production was enhanced in the late sixteenth century by the presence of two outstanding goldsmiths, Lüneburg-born Dirich Utermarke and Jacob Mores, the latter of whom is known not only as a maker but also as an important designer of plate.

THE AURICULAR STYLE

A form of loosely organized Mannerist ornament continued in fashion in Germany during the early seventeenth century, but the very artificiality of the style in a sense ensured its eventual demise. A new direction was required, and to an extent was supplied by the gifted and prolific Nuremberg goldsmith, Hans Petzolt (1551–1633). Petzolt began working in the Mannerist style, but by the end of the

EWER, SILVER-GILT, ADAM VAN VIANEN, UTRECHT, 1614 (H25.4cm/10in)

The entire body, modelled as a crouching monkey on a rippling base, is raised from a single sheet of silver. The cover is equally amorphous, rising to a finial that suggests a sea monster and with a naked figure whose head dissolves into the loop of the handle. (RIGHT)

THE IMHOFF CUP, SILVER-GILT, HANS PETZOLT, NUREMBERG, 1626 (H46.3cm/18¼in)

Made for one of the great patrician families of Nuremberg, the Imhoff cup incorporates the crest of the family – a lion with a fish's tail – into the stem and finial. It is decorated with an elaborate programme of ornament illustrating silver mining and refining. (ABOVE CENTRE)

EWER, GOLD AND JASPER, THE JASPER BY OTTAVIO MISERONI AND THE MOUNTS BY PAULUS VAN VIANEN, PRAGUE, 1608 (H35.9cm/14⅛in) (ABOVE)

extreme, it even exaggerates this quality by suggesting an impression of objects modelled in a semi-molten state.

The earliest intimations of the Auricular style appear on a gold-mounted jasper ewer of 1608 made by Paulus van Vianen at Prague under the patronage of Emperor Rudolf II. A more confident expression of the style, however, can be seen in his ewer and dish of 1613 in the Rijksmuseum, Amsterdam, which are decorated with brilliantly accomplished relief scenes of the story of Diana and Actaeon, contained within cartouches formed of fleshy scrolls and residual masks.

The Auricular style continued to enjoy some popularity during the second quarter of the century. It was promoted in England by Adam's son Christiaen van Vianen, who worked at the court of Charles I. In Amsterdam it was taken up most notably by Johannes Lutma. The style also became popular for engraved ornament and carved picture frames until the middle years of the century. Although almost too dramatic a departure to be considered part of the mainstream of European stylistic development, it nevertheless did form a crucial element in the early development of the Baroque style. A sort of proto-Baroque, it

DESIGN FOR A
SILVER DISH,
PETER PAUL
RUBENS, *c.*1630

Commissioned by Charles I and subsequently made up in silver with a ewer, this design is a powerful statement of the early Baroque style in silver. An important feature is that it is intended to be read like a picture, with all the figures orientated to the same vertical axis.

century led a brilliant if short-lived Gothic revival which recreated many of the most ambitious forms of Dürer's style.

While such stylistic experiments were taking place in Germany, a highly original and plastic style evolved in Holland. Known as the Auricular style, this is mainly associated with the Utrecht goldsmiths, Adam van Vianen (1569–1626) and his brother Paulus (*c.*1570–1613), and was Holland's most original contribution to European goldsmiths' work. The style is characterized by the use of amorphous, lobate scrolls and relief ornament which emphasize the malleable nature of the metal. At its most

The most dramatic and fully plastic of all the early works in the style is undoubtedly the silver-gilt ewer of 1614 made by Adam van Vianen in Utrecht for the Amsterdam guild of goldsmiths in memory of his brother. The ewer was celebrated in its own time as a work of brilliant originality and a technical *tour de force*. Nothing like this had ever been seen before and Adam never rose to the same level of inspiration again. Most of his later works, such as figural salt-cellars, tazzas and ewers, are less abstract and take the form of naturalistically modelled groups, the abstract elements being restricted to bases and borders.

embodied a number of features that were central to the new style. In particular the seminal works of Paulus and Adam van Vianen have a unity of conception and an integration of form and ornament that are at variance with Mannerism. There is more than a passing resemblance between the design of Paulus van Vianen's Diana dish and the bold, sculptural treatment indicated in a design by Rubens for a dish for Charles I. With its dramatic representation of the Triumph of Neptune within a flowing border of river gods and marine subjects, this is an object that stands on the threshold between Mannerism and the Baroque.

BAROQUE, ROCOCO AND NEOCLASSICISM

The full effect of the goldsmith's art becomes a reality in the seventeenth century. Whilst great melts abound during the century and after, there is sufficient evidence, both extant and in pictorial sources, to justify a thorough study of silver works of art. The immense confidence of the Baroque style swept across Europe largely due to the power of the Papacy and the influence of Louis XIV in France. The style was that of grandeur; the ultimate embodiment of the princely state. In almost direct contrast, the Rococo style was the product of peace. In silver, the style was characterized by asymmetry, frequently mixed with elements of naturalism. A style that was born in Italy, but which developed into maturity in France, it was interpreted by each nation in Europe in a different manner.

Almost as soon as the Rococo had taken its wayward hold on Europe, a new renaissance was underway. This Neoclassical style, born of an accurate study of the ruins of ancient Greece and Rome, sought to reintroduce the 'true principles' of design: those constants in design which had endured since the ancient world. Beginning in France and swiftly moving to England, an Anglo-French style emerged in the mid-eighteenth century built on the foundation of the Palladian tradition. Elsewhere in Europe, where the style was adopted later, 'light and insignificant forms prevailed', which nevertheless maintained an etiolated elegance.

THOMAS GERMAIN AND HIS WIFE, NICOLAS DE
LARGILLIÈRE, 1736

———

The goldsmith Thomas Germain is shown with a ewer, the sculptural details of which he is modelling in wax. He points to a candelabrum of the same design as those he supplied to the King of Portugal, c.1732–3. Beside it is another model for a candlestick, after a design by Meissonnier.

BAROQUE SILVER

The Baroque was a reaction to Mannerism, which was characterized by highly contrived, non-naturalistic compositions, an emphasis upon minute, hard-to-read details and a subject matter that was sometimes only fully intelligible to the patron and his or her own immediate circle. In contrast, the Baroque was a big, bold, dramatic and dynamic style, intended to be sensuous and emotive and capable of making a profound impact upon a wide range of people. Whereas Mannerism was an ideal style for meeting the needs of the very rich, sophisticated and introverted collector, the Baroque was the propagandist style *par excellence*. It could convincingly suggest the majesty of the Trinity and the heroism of the saints, and promote the Roman Catholic Church after the Counter-Reformation. Equally, it could be used to create magnificent, triumphalist and intimidating settings for secular rulers and others with wealth.

ITALY

The Baroque style was developed in Rome, which became the most important artistic centre in Europe in the 1590s and early seventeenth century, with Annibale Carracci, Caravaggio, Guido Reni and Guercino undertaking major innovative projects and paintings for the leading Roman families and churches. The principal practitioner of the Baroque style was unquestionably the sculptor Gian Lorenzo Bernini (1598–1680), who worked for various popes and created such seminal Baroque works as the bronze baldacchino (1624–33) and Cathedra Petri (1657–66) in St Peter's. These great theatrical sets and other works by Bernini exerted a tremendous influence on contemporaries and subsequent generations. Another great sculptor, Alessandro Algardi (1598–1654), was also active in Rome during these decades, albeit in a calmer, less dramatic style.

Both Bernini and Algardi were called upon to design silver. Bernini designed the gold and silver reliquary of St Helena, set with rubies, which Cardinal Francesco Barberini commissioned for Queen Henrietta Maria of England to be made by Francesco Spagna in 1636. Subsequent designs included those for the great silver bowl executed by Francesco Perone for Cardinal Antonio Barberini in 1643 and the jewel-encrusted silver-gilt cradle which Olimpia Maidalchini presented to her daughter-in-law, the Princess of Rossano, in 1653. Among Algardi's models and designs were those for the silver fountain and brazier which Fantino Taglietti made for Prince Marcantonio Borghese in 1636. Not surprisingly, all these salient pieces have disap-

DRAWING OF A RELIQUARY CASKET, ALESSANDRO ALGARDI, ROME, 1644–55 (H43cm/17in)

Drawings such as this give some idea of the silver designed by Bernini and Algardi. The base of the reliquary is decorated with the arms of Algardi's important patron, Pope Innocent X, who reigned between 1644 and 1655. Reliquaries with pairs of Algardi-related kneeling angels survive in Florence and Siena.

peared. A number of minor Algardi-related works have survived, however, including a silver frame which Francesco Perone is believed to have made in 1648. Fortunately, a great deal can also be learned from drawings by the major sculptors and artists, from the works of such lesser lights as the Austrian artist Johann Paul Schor (1615–74) and his brother Egid, and by studying contemporary sculpture and metalwork.

One of the few significant, surviving items of mid-seventeenth-century Roman secular silver is the cast and chased dish decorated with the Rape of Europa and the arms of Tavora of Portugal, now in the Al-Tajir Collection. The workmanship is not of the highest order and it is clear that the dish was not meant to be viewed in splendid isolation. It is therefore useful to refer to an engraving which shows a great buffet in the grounds of the villa of Cardinal Flavio Chigi (the nephew of Alexander VII) in 1668, with silver arranged on seven tiers to impress the viewer with quantity and size, if not necessarily quality.

Unfortunately, the greatest surviving religious pieces of this period – the four candlesticks made by Carlo Spagna for Cardinal Francesco Barberini between 1670 and 1672 – are not fully representative of the Baroque. They were the result of a commission to lengthen and embellish the stems of the two candlesticks and cross which Antonio Gentile da Faenza had made for Cardinal Alessandro Farnese about 1581 and to supply four further candlesticks *en suite* (all seven items are now in the Treasury of St Peter's, Rome).

Some appreciation of late seventeenth- and early eighteenth-century Roman silver can be gained from the activities of Giovanni Giardini (1646–1721), who was in charge of the papal foundry from 1698. A surprisingly large corpus of his work survives, including a processional mace, made between 1696 and 1710, and the reliquary for the head of San Mercuriale, of 1719–20. Giardini is of particular interest because he combines silversmithing with casting bronze artillery and sculptural decoration and in 1714 published two volumes, *Disegni*

Diversi, each with fifty plates. Giardini's oeuvre does not reveal an innovator, but it does provide a remarkable insight into both ecclesiastical and secular silver in Rome in the late Baroque period.

The Baroque style continued in Rome and elsewhere in Italy long into the eighteenth century, and indeed beyond that in terms of ecclesiastical silver. Among noteworthy late examples are reliquaries and other items by Angelo Spinazzi (*fl.*1721–67), bearing the arms of Clement XII, 1730–40 (now in the Treasury of S. Giovanni in Laterano, Rome), and the major pieces commissioned for King João V's new royal chapel of St John the Baptist in the Church of São Roque in Lisbon (now in the Museu de São Roque). The latter include the candlesticks by Giuseppe Gagliardi (1697–1749), after a design by the sculptor Giovanni Battista Maini (1690–1752), and the *carteglorie* (altar cards) by Antonio Vendetti (1699–1796), all made between 1744 and 1749. Many of the late works tend to have a swollen, lumpen appearance, rather than the vigorous quality of the earlier pieces.

Work produced in Rome exerted a strong influence on the other Italian centres. This is clearly evident in Florence, in the silver and other items produced to the designs of the

CANDLESTICK, SILVER-GILT, GIUSEPPE GAGLIARDI, ROME, 1744–9 (H285cm/112¼in)

Many magnificent pieces of late Baroque Roman silver were supplied for King João V's Chapel of St John the Baptist in the Church of São Roque, Lisbon. (LEFT)

DISH DECORATED WITH *THE RAPE OF EUROPA*, MEMBER OF THE TRAVANI FAMILY, ROME, *c.*1670 (H100cm/39⅜in)

Assayed after 6 December 1668 and bearing the arms of Tavora of Portugal used prior to 1671, this dish was probably presented to the Marquez Don Luis Manuel de Tavora in connection with a Portuguese embassy to Rome, by Pope Clement IX or his successor, Clement X. (ABOVE)

CHALICE, SILVER-GILT, MARKED GOC 91, POSSIBLY FOR GIACINTO OMODEI AS CONSUL AND MAKER, PALERMO, 1691 (H30.5cm/12in)

The decoration on this little-known chalice includes the Last Supper (on the bowl) and the Last Judgement. (ABOVE)

RELIQUARY OF ST SIGISMUND, DESIGNED BY GIOVANNI BATTISTA FOGGINI, FLORENCE, 1719 (H57.7cm/22¾in)

This is one of many reliquaries designed by Foggini and Massimiliano Soldani Benzi. The silver figures are closely related to Foggini's small bronzes, while the ebony-veneered structure and polished stones draw on the skills of the cabinet-makers and stone cutters and polishers in the Grand-Ducal workshops. (ABOVE RIGHT)

court sculptor Giovanni Battista Foggini (1652–1725), one of the first students at the Florentine Academy in Rome, and the Master of the Mint Massimiliano Soldani Benzi (1656–1740), who had also studied in Rome. Interestingly, Florentines drew on the services of northern goldsmiths for some actual fabrication. 'Arrigo Brunich' (d.1683), who is described in documents as a Flemish silversmith but may have been German, was selected to execute the silver antependium designed by Foggini for the Church of the Santissima Annunziata, Florence (1680–2). By 1688 the German goldsmith Bernardo Holzmann was working in the grand-ducal workshops and he assisted the head silversmith Cosimo Merlini with another major Foggini-designed altar frontal for the Basilica of Santa Maria at Impruneta, outside Florence (1711–14). Some Florentine works incorporate *pietre dure* (hard stones), a speciality of the grand-ducal workshops.

Naples was a major centre of production in this period and the designs published in 1642–3 by the goldsmith Orazio Scoppa (*fl.*1608–50) can be contrasted with later work. Most of the major surviving pieces are ecclesiastical and in the form of altar frontals and bust reliquaries. The most outstanding is the altar frontal executed by Giandomenico Vinaccia between 1692 and 1695, after the design of Dionisio Lazzari, in the treasury of San Gennaro, Naples. This relates to the life of St Januarius and the central area comprises a three-dimensional scene of Archbishop Alessandro Carafa carrying the relic of the saint's blood on horseback, with Heresy being trampled underfoot and the saint flying overhead, protecting the city. Neapolitan works were also influenced by Roman models but are definitely the products of a strong independent city-state culture. To the south, Palermo and Messina in Sicily were significant centres, influenced by Naples but with sufficient wealth to support first-rate silversmiths and major work.

It is hard to assess the output of the northern centres because of the huge losses, partly due to Napoleon's Italian campaign and the subsequent meltdowns. From the surviving evidence it seems that Genoa produced little to rival the quality of its early Baroque ewers and basins (see p.77). That said, one should not overlook the throne of the Virgin of Sagrario in Toledo Cathedral, executed in 1670–2 by the Genoese Virgilio Fanelli and the Madrid goldsmith Juan Ortiz de Rivilla. Venice suffered particularly badly at the hands of Napoleon but enough survives to reveal that the city could be very conservative, especially in the field of ecclesiastical silver. Milan was capable of fine work, as is shown by the over-life-size statue of St Ambrose with jewelled mitre by the goldsmith Policarpo Sparoletti and others, of 1681–95, in Milan Cathedral. Indeed, some of the very best surviving northern pieces are by the Milanese Carlo Giuseppe Grossi (1663–after 1716), including the exceptional 'Seminary Chalice' in Bergamo Cathedral (attributed to the Grossi workshop).

FRANCE

The magnificent silver of Louis XIV's reign was a development of earlier French (and French-owned) silver, rather than something radically new. Both Louis XIV's mother, Anne of Austria, and Cardinal Mazarin owned superb silver and silver furniture and the quality of earlier work is revealed by the gold chest of *c.*1645 in the Louvre. It seems that the civil strife of the Frondes had little serious effect on Parisian goldsmiths. Moreover, the Louis XIV style was basically a development of the Italian Baroque and its foundations were laid in the decades leading up to 1660. The long-established taste for things classical was increased by contact with Italy. Between 1630 and 1660 key painters like Charles Le Brun and Pierre Mignard visited Rome and gained a thorough knowledge of the Italian Baroque, which they subsequently used in their own work and disseminated. At the same time, craftsmen began to draw upon prints of classical or classicizing vases, scrolling foliage and a wide range of other 'Italian' decoration by both Italian and French artists. There would, therefore, have been considerable continuity in silver types, shapes and decoration between, approximately, 1640 and 1675.

Louis XIV began his personal rule after Cardinal Mazarin's death in 1661 and almost immediately gave an enormous boost to the decorative arts by the sheer scale and example of his patronage. Louis saw himself as the most important monarch in Europe, and he desired wonderful settings to reflect his glory and to impress and intimidate foreign powers, as well as his own aristocracy and people. To achieve some of these ends, his chief minister Colbert began to reorganize and develop the royal workshops and placed them under the control of Charles Le Brun (1619–90), the *premier peintre* to the king from 1664. Thus, a great artist was designing or overseeing the design of the items for Versailles and the other royal palaces, coordinating decorative schemes and ensuring uniform quality. The

CHATSWORTH TOILET SERVICE, PIERRE PRÉVOST, PARIS, 1670–71

Embellished with the arms and monogram of William III and Queen Mary, this is the largest surviving Louis XIV toilet service. One of the octagonal boxes is a replacement by the Nuremberg goldsmith Hans Conrat Brechtel, who worked in The Hague.

result was superb silver in immense quantities: solid silver and silver-veneered furniture, mirrors and candelabra, even figures and balustrades.

Sadly, little of this silver survives because the Sun King over-extended himself in his disastrous wars of the League of Augsburg and Spanish Succession and had to issue edicts in 1689 and 1709, requiring the surrender of silver to the Mint so that it could be melted down and turned into coins to pay for troops and munitions. Nevertheless, some idea of the court's splendour can be gleaned from the French royal archives and from various visual sources. Charles Le Brun and the goldsmiths Claude Ballin I (master 1637–78) and Nicolas Delaunay (master 1672–1727) were the cardinal figures and some of their designs for individual pieces survive. In addition, many large pieces are represented in the tapestries designed by Le Brun, notably the design entitled *Louis XIV's Visit to the Gobelins.*

Although almost no French royal silver survives from the first half of Louis XIV's reign, a number of major Parisian pieces escaped the melting pot (generally because they had been exported). The most important early examples of secular silver include a mirror of 1659 or 1660–1 (now in the Louvre), which is believed to have come from a toilet service owned by Anne Hyde, the first wife of James II, and the fountain from Kedleston of 1661–3 (now in the Getty Museum). Slightly later survivals include four silver-gilt toilet services, the most important being the 23-piece service by Pierre Prévost, at Chatsworth, which was owned by Queen Mary, the wife of William III. Then there are the 17-piece service of Frances Teresa Stuart, Duchess of Richmond and Lennox, of 1661–77 (Royal Museum of Scotland, Edinburgh); the closely related but unmarked 15-piece service formerly in the Chatsworth and Stonor collections but now in the Toledo Museum

BAPTISMAL FONT FOR THE SWEDISH ROYAL CHAPEL, JEAN-FRANÇOIS COUSINET AND BERNARD FOUQUET, STOCKHOLM, 1696–1707 (H106cm/41¾in)

The Swedish court followed artistic developments in France very closely and commissioned French and French-inspired works. Cousinet, originally a Parisian goldsmith, moved to Stockholm in 1693.

EWER, NICOLAS DELAUNAY, PARIS, 1697 (H33.2cm/13in)

This remarkable ewer demonstrates the Baroque interest in classical antiquities and the Neoclassical style of the 17th century. The great table service made for Louis XIV by Delaunay, and very probably in this style, was regrettably melted down by the King in 1709.

over, it is clear that the pieces were intended to complement elaborately decorated rooms. This is most obvious in the case of candlesticks and royal furniture with figurative supports, which would have echoed the figures in paintings, sculpture and tapestries, but the shapes, scrolling foliage and mouldings of leaves on the toilet services also mirror the shapes and decoration found on ceilings, carved woodwork and carpets.

The same restraint, symmetry and classical vocabulary are also to be seen in French ecclesiastical silver. The most important surviving group is the altar set by Nicolas Dolin in the treasury of Troyes Cathedral, but a relatively large number of chalices, shrines, candlesticks, holy-water stoups and

other items are also extant, two of them meriting particular attention. The first is the four-foot high baptismal font (Swedish Royal Collections) made in Stockholm between 1696 and 1707 by the French goldsmith Jean-François Cousinet and the sculptor Bernard Foucquet for the royal chapel. This is of considerable interest in its own right, but it also provides a vivid insight into the appearance, quality and

construction of the French royal furniture and other large items which perished in 1689–90 and 1709. The second item is the little-known reliquary bust of Father Jean de Brébeuf, who was martyred in Huronia, Canada, in 1649. Commissioned by the priest's family and made in Paris in 1664–5, this rare type of Parisian product was presented to the Jesuits in Quebec and is now in the Musée des Augustines de l'Hôtel-Dieu, Quebec City.

The development of Parisian silver in the second half of Louis XIV's reign (1690–1715) is hard to chart because of the huge losses. Nicolas Delaunay remained a major figure, becoming director of the Mint and of the coining press in 1696. An extremely fine secular ewer bearing his mark and the date letter for 1697 survives in the treasury of Poitiers Cathedral and exhibits an almost proto-Neoclassicism, which was not confined to Delaunay. There was, in fact, considerable variety in these later years. On the one hand, some designers and goldsmiths explored the possibilities of an austere style with plain shapes and limited decoration, both of which could be given classical form such as urn shapes and Vitruvian scroll ornamentation. On the other, there was a developing interest in bands of repeating small-scale decoration using strapwork, tassels, shells, masks, guilloche with rosette or beading and other elements associated with the designer Jean Bérain (1640–1711). Both features are reflected, and indeed combined, in Delaunay's drawings, as well as in the rectangular casket and oval basket of 1712–13 by Claude Ballin II (master 1688–1754), in the Residenz, Munich. Some of the more expensive later works seem to suffer from a *horror vacui* and are covered with panels of repeating small-scale decoration. However, goldsmiths like Nicolas Besnier, working in the 1710s and 1720s, continued the more austere style with plain areas and bands of decoration. The silver made from 1700 to 1730 is generally called Régence, although it obviously includes the product of the last twenty years of Louis XIV's reign as well as the regency of Louis XV.

of Art, Ohio; and the 18-piece service of the Princess Hedvig Sofia of Sweden, made between 1658 and 1676 (Rosenborg Castle, Copenhagen). The first three are decorated with scrolling foliage and other foliate motifs but the last also includes putti and other figurative decoration.

Both the royal and non-royal pieces share the same restraint, rigid symmetry and a classical or classicizing vocabulary. More-

ENGLAND AND HOLLAND

Much of the best English and Dutch silver produced in the Baroque period is linked with developments in France. During the reign of Charles II, both the English and Dutch courts were inspired to attempt modest imitations of the grandiose silver and silver furniture owned by Louis XIV and the French aristocracy. The major survivals are the pier suites, consisting of a console table, pier glass and two flanking candlesticks. Garnitures of display vases, perfume burners, andirons and sconces were also made and survive in reasonable numbers. Most of the major pieces, along with many lesser items, are decorated with curling foliage, acanthus leaves, putti and swags, which relate to features on French silver.

The influence of France is particularly noticeable in the case of Dutch and English toilet services. Goldsmiths at The Hague were quick to respond to Parisian models, as can be seen by comparing the plain toilet service of Veronica van Aerssen van Sommelsdijk of 1653–8 with the richly decorated service of Elisabeth van Nassau-Beverweerd by Adriaen van Hoecke of 1665. The situation in England is less clear, partly because of major losses and the absence of Paris, but the majority of items represent putti and scrolling foliage, with the figures and foliage on the sides of the small circular boxes related to prints by Stefano della Bella and others.

The most sophisticated London-made toilet services made around 1679–84 incorporate cast reliefs. An interesting example is the service decorated with lovers in contemporary dress, now in the Virginia Museum of Fine Arts, Richmond, which bears the maker's or sponsor's mark of a goose or a duck in a dotted circle, attributed to John Duck, and the date letter for 1679–80. However, the finest services with cast relief decoration reached a peak in the group associated with the goldsmith 'WF', which

SILVER TABLE, MIRROR AND TWO GUERIDONS OR CANDLESTANDS, LONDON, *c.*1680

Decorated with the cypher of Charles II, this set – sometimes called a triad or pier suite – is made of embossed silver attached to wooden forms.

THE CALVERLEY TOILET SERVICE, MAKER'S MARK WF WITH KNOT ABOVE AND STAR BELOW, LONDON, 1683–4

'WF's' services reflect the profound influence of France upon the English court and leading craftsmen during the reign of Charles II.

date letters on many surviving pieces. In the 1660s some members of the royal family are known to have owned French toilet services and their ready availability may well have delayed the production of first-rate London examples. In the 1670s Jacob Bodendick and others were producing high-quality services with embossed and cast decoration. Some of Bodendick's large boxes are decorated with mythological scenes relating to the shepherd have cast plaques of Venus and Adonis, Phaëthon and other mythological scenes. The Calverley service in the Victoria & Albert Museum and the service now in the Al-Tajir Collection are struck with this maker's mark and the date letter for 1683–4, and other partly marked and unmarked, closely related services are known. It seems likely that the plaques on the Virginia and 'WF' services were either imported or made using imported models or moulds, with France the obvious source.

Rich relief decoration soon fell out of favour, mainly due to developments in France and the emigration of many skilled Huguenot, or French Protestant, craftsmen. Huguenot craftsmen were already leaving France in the 1670s and early 1680s to seek livelihoods in London, Amsterdam, Berlin and other Protestant centres and the stream became a mass exodus after 1685, when Louis XIV revoked the Edict of Nantes, which had given the Huguenots limited protection.

In Holland, the two main arrivals were the goldsmith Adam Loofs (d. 1710), who had worked in Paris for many years, and the Parisian architect-designer Daniel Marot (1663–1752). Loofs became 'Ordinary gold- and silversmith and Keeper of the Silver' to William of Orange in 1680, subsequently producing many large items, such as chandeliers and candelabra, and becoming alderman of the goldsmiths' guild (1687–99). Marot fled from France in 1684 and soon found employment with the Stadholder, designing houses, gardens, interiors and items in the Parisian style. He was extremely important and influential and even today his significance tends to be underestimated.

Among the many Huguenots who settled in London in this early period were Peter Harache and David Willaume of Metz. However, the process of change was greatly speeded up when James II lost his throne and was replaced by his daughter Mary and William of Orange in 1688–9. Marot and the goldsmith Pierre Platel of Lille came to London in the wake of the joint sovereigns and other goldsmiths arrived or settled down permanently. Many London goldsmiths were annoyed at the influx of Huguenots, who challenged their products and sales and were prepared to work for less, but the Huguenots were soon established, either in their own workshops or working for Huguenot or English masters. By the turn of the century the dominant style was that of the Huguenots and it was reinforced by the next generation of Huguenot goldsmiths, notably Peter Harache II, Philip Rollos II,

Paul de Lamerie, Paul Crespin and David Willaume II. The consequence was that medium-sized items such as ewers, two-handled cups and punchbowls were still being made in the Huguenot style in the 1740s and smaller items even later.

In essence, the Huguenot style was founded on the idea of simple, massive, handsomely proportioned shapes, economically decorated – in both the visual and financial senses – with cast or cut shapes of silver soldered to the sides, and with large gadrooned borders. The large plain surfaces could be engraved with a bold coat of arms and thus formed impressive, aggrandizing display pieces, which were relatively inexpensive because they did not require large-scale embossing, chasing or decorative engraving. The style was doubtless shaped by Calvinism and the provincial background of many of the makers, but also reflected a general movement away from the elaborate relief style of the previous generation.

The Huguenots achieved a major stylistic breakthrough in Holland, England and elsewhere in Europe. In the course of time, they were also responsible for introducing or promoting new French forms such as the

HUGUENOT-STYLE PILGRIM BOTTLES AND TWO-HANDLED CUPS, THE BODIES UNMARKED, PROBABLY LONDON, *c*.1700 (Bottles: H45cm/17¾in) (TOP)

WINE COOLER, DAVID WILLAUME I, LONDON, 1700–1 (H23.2cm/9¼in)

Wine coolers for single bottles of wine were introduced at the fashion-setting court of Louis XIV. This refined piece (one of a pair) is an early English example in the French Régence style, later engraved with a coat of arms. (ABOVE)

helmet-shaped ewer, the wine cooler for a single bottle of wine, the double-lipped sauce boat and the centrepiece. They also introduced and promoted the Régence and Rococo styles. It is surprising to see just how early the Régence style is mirrored in Huguenot work. The watershed seems to have been the ending of the 1689–97 war and the resumption of contact with France, leading to the appearance of French types around 1700 and the basic Régence vocabulary of enriched Vitruvian scrolls, guilloche with rosettes, strapwork, masks and shells. Cast strapwork for vertical and radial decoration appears in the first decade of the eighteenth century, with trelliswork appearing in the 1710s and 1720s. Between 1700 and 1745 thousands of well-proportioned, massive shapes with combinations of Huguenot and Régence decoration were produced by dozens of makers, with the most sophisticated English versions of the Régence by Paul de Lamerie.

GERMANY

Augsburg was the most important German centre in the Baroque period. As the century progressed, its goldsmiths swamped the German cultural area with their wares, smothering and stifling production in other towns, not only in south Germany but further afield, and profoundly influencing work undertaken in central, north and eastern Europe.

Two main lines of secular silver in the seventeenth century were the ubiquitous cylindrical beaker with rounded base, generally set on three ball feet and supplied with a cover, and the tankard. However, Augsburg goldsmiths also produced very fine embossed display plate (notably the works associated with the Jäger family and Hans Jakob Mair in the mid-seventeenth century), elaborate mounts which transformed carved ivory cylinders into splendid tankards and large table decorations in the shape of animals, equestrian figures and Atlas carrying the world.

In the middle of the century there was a definite move toward classical subject matter and vocabulary with mythological scenes, putti, the heads of classical rulers and various types of classical-Baroque foliage. The Mannerist tradition continued, especially in table decorations, but was not in conflict with new developments.

After 1680 Augsburg began to excel in two areas: cased services of both luxury toilet items and tea wares, and figurative reliefs. The former are frequently called travelling services, because they are packed in chests, but in fact they were intended for private display. In the early period, the principal maker-supplier of such services was Tobias Baur (c.1660–1735), who made extensive use of agate but was also responsible for examples with applied painted enamels. The leading producer of silver reliefs was Johann Andreas Thelot (1655–1734), who concentrated initially on classicizing and religious subjects but subsequently turned to reliefs of landscapes and hunting scenes and even to tea wares.

Augsburg was also the main centre in central Europe for the production of silver furniture and display plate. Major surviving examples of seventeenth-century furniture include the Swedish throne of state, commissioned from Abraham Drentwett for the coronation of Queen Christina in 1650, and the small X-shaped throne decorated with the heads of putti and dolphins, of c.1675, at Schloss Köpenick, Berlin. Eighteenth-century pieces survive in greater quantity. Two early eighteenth-century pier suites – each consisting of a table, mirror and pair of candlesticks – are in the Maximilianmuseum, Augsburg, and the palace of Het Loo, Apeldoorn, while a number of important items are at Rosenborg Castle, Copenhagen,

RELIEF OF *THE BAPTISM OF CHRIST*, JOHANN ANDREAS THELOT, AUGSBURG, 1685 (H39cm/15⅜in)

Thelot embossed and chased his reliefs, adding small projecting parts where necessary.

Dssein du grand Buffet de vermeil d'ore. Dressé dans la Sale des chevalliers au chateau Royal de Berlin.

THE 'LEPANTO MONSTRANCE', JOHANNES ZECKEL, AUGSBURG, c.1708 (H124cm/48¾in)

This outstanding monstrance celebrates the great naval victory of the Christian forces under Don Juan of Austria over the Turks led by Ali Pasha at the Battle of Lepanto, 1571, which ended Turkish control of the Mediterranean. (FAR LEFT)

THE SILVER BUFFET OF KING FREDERICK I OF PRUSSIA, ENGRAVING, EOSANDER VON GOETHE, 1707

The original arrangement in the royal palace in Berlin was destroyed during the Second World War and the pieces are now displayed in a reconstruction at Schloss Köpenick, Berlin. (LEFT)

including a firescreen, table, mirrors and candlestands bearing the mark of Philipp Jakob Drentwett VI and Augsburg marks for 1732–40. Between about 1690 and 1710 Johann Andreas Thelot and other craftsmen were involved in the production of a number of other, different types of display furniture, the most impressive consisting of a clock in an altar-like structure supported by semi-nude figures. Smaller works include tabletop display cabinets fitted with clocks and decorated with openwork mounts, and clock cases with decorated silver faces.

Many of the best pieces of display silver were supplied by the Biller family. The largest surviving group is the famous silver buffet which Johann Ludwig Biller I and Albrecht Biller created for the Elector Frederick III of Brandenburg shortly before he became Frederick I, King of Prussia, in 1701. The decoration on the ewers and pilgrim bottles includes variations on the Prussian eagle and the royal lion. Among other major Biller pieces are vases with putti in motion by Albrecht Biller, of c.1700, and shaped vases with three-dimensional figures

around the sides by Lorenz Biller II, of about the same date. The latter are in the Museo degli Argenti, Florence, and are of particular interest because they seem to be related to ewers designed by Massimiliano Soldani Benzi and other Italian works. Among the other suppliers of display vases and other plate were Johann Bartermann I and Abraham Drentwett II. Drentwett's pieces include an urn-shaped vase of c.1708–10 in the Green Vault, Dresden which features a classical scene on the side and is supported by three mermen.

Around this time, Augsburg goldsmiths were also executing extremely fine ecclesiastical silver, notably spectacular monstrances. In one type, the central circular area for the display of the Host is surrounded by a half-length representation of the grieving Virgin Mary; in another, the centre is heart-shaped. In around 1705, Johannes Zeckel developed this idea by surrounding the heart with a crown of thorns and creating a background which gave the illusion that the heart was on fire. The German love of colour is fully demonstrated in these and other pieces of ecclesiastical silver. Whereas French and English silver is generally gilt or white, German silver is frequently parcel- or partly gilt, creating a rich, painterly effect. Ecclesiastical silver was made even more colourful by the addition of cut, precious or semiprecious stones, coloured glass and even painted enamels.

Hamburg was the chief silver-making centre in the north, meeting some of the needs of north Germany and Scandinavia, while Viennese goldsmiths produced excellent silver for the imperial court and the churches; not surprisingly, artisans in both cities were heavily influenced by Augsburg. Dresden was a centre of excellence, although primarily in terms of mounted, virtuoso pieces rather than wrought silver. These amazing cabinet works of art were created from the late 1690s to *c.*1730 by the Bavarian sculptor Balthasar Permoser (1651–1732), the Swabian jeweller Johann Melchior Dinglinger (1664–1731) and others for the court of Augustus the Strong of Saxony. Rather than essays in the Baroque, however, these objects were a continuation of the Mannerist tradition.

Many of the finest non-Augsburg pieces are, in fact, the tankards that were made in the north, notably in Berlin, Danzig and Scandinavia. A keen taste for these and other items decorated with coins developed in Berlin, where Daniel Mänlich (1625–1701) produced some superb '*Münzhumpen*', as such tankards are known. Between about 1660 and 1710, the goldsmiths of Danzig (now Gdansk) fashioned a large number of

CHALICE, SILVER-GILT, JOHANNES DUMEISEN, RAPPERSWIL, EARLY 18TH CENTURY (H28.5cm/11¼in)

Decorated in repoussé *with angels carrying the Instruments of the Passion, this chalice is set with six painted enamels of the Passion of Christ in silver mounts adorned with garnets and blue glass.* (BELOW)

TANKARD, PARTLY-GILT, MAKER'S MARK BG ABOVE PELLET, DANZIG, 18TH CENTURY (H26cm/10¼in)

The sides of Danzig tankards are generally embossed with narrative scenes. This example appears to be decorated with three scenes based on the classical story of Narcissus and Echo. (BELOW RIGHT)

impressive tankards for the merchant patriciate. These vessels are a development of the thin-gauge, embossed and partly gilt tankards made in Augsburg and north Germany, and are sometimes surmounted by swan-shaped finials. Moving further north, most top-quality Scandinavian tankards belong to a different 'family' grouping. They are generally made of thick-gauge metal and have broad, cylindrical bodies, three sculptural feet (which normally take the form of balls, bursting pomegranates, lions or clusters of fruit and flowers) and a matching thumb-piece. In most cases, the flat covers are engraved with flowers and foliage. Some tankards also have inscriptions or coats of arms, and partly or completed engraved sides are not uncommon.

Looking back at all the material discussed in this chapter, one is struck by the enormous variety of Baroque silver – arguably a far greater variety than in any other stylistic period – and by the strong continuity of the various traditions. Looking forward, it is hardly surprising that Baroque works inspired a revival in the nineteenth century.

ROCOCO SILVER

The Rococo style in France originated during a period of prosperity, and the dominant position of the French court that had been established under the Sun King, Louis XIV, resulted in the hegemony of Gallic culture in Europe.

After the Treaty of Utrecht in 1713, the royal manufactories once again began production, and under the Régence (1715–23), Paris became the centre of artistic creation. When Louis XV ascended the throne in 1723, he found himself the ruler of a country blessed not only with a prosperous economy but also with an important group of artists and craftsmen, whose most innovative creations in the early decades of the century materialized in the decorative arts.

For an understanding of French silver production in the eighteenth century, it is important to recall the multiple melting programmes. The first dates from 1689, when France was at war with the Palatinate (although Louis XIV's extravagances as well as hostilities with the German territories were the cause), and the second from 1709, during the War of the Spanish Succession (1701–14). The third, in 1759, took place in the midst of the Seven Years' War (1756–63), and the fourth in the years following the Revolution. According to the writer of memoirs, Saint Simon, after 1709 many people replaced their silver with ceramics, but large numbers of candelabra, candlesticks and centrepieces were executed in silvered or gilt copper or bronze. For these, the goldsmiths used the models they had created for silver or gold wares, and such pieces should therefore be considered a major secondary source for later knowledge of original works in precious metals. During the Régence, the fear that silver was going to be used as a refuge for capital was instrumental in the renewal of the earlier sumptuary laws forbidding the production of silver above a certain weight; as a result, commissions for silver declined, although only

temporarily. Also, the fascination for gold became paramount during the period, possibly contributing to the success of gilt-bronze objects.

After Louis XV's coronation a new phase of silver production was inaugurated. From 1724 to 1725 the Duc de Bourbon, as *grand maître* of the royal household, presided over the reconstitution of the king's silver and gold services. They were executed by the three *orfèvres du roi*: Claude Ballin II (1661–1754), Thomas Germain (1673–1748) and Nicolas Besnier (1685/6–1754). Some of these royal pieces are depicted in the paintings of Alexandre-François Desportes, but the majority are only known today from written descriptions. It is difficult to visualize many objects, such as Germain's *écuelle* (a two-handled bowl with cover) of 1736. The cover of this major piece, which was melted down after the Revolution, included two branches of fleur-de-lis reaching out to a centrally placed royal crown supported by cartouches, and its oval basin was decorated with gadrooning and enlivened by four crayfish and several vegetables, executed in different colours of gold. Not a single piece of metalwork is known today that illustrates such a use of gold. The nearest equivalents extant are several pieces in bronze gilded in various colours.

The increase in the demand for silver, stimulated by the renewal of the court tradition created by Louis XIV, was advantageous for the emergence of novel forms, which obviously resulted from an unparalleled competition among the goldsmiths. The centrepiece, or *surtout de table*, was a new product that became very popular. Probably dating from the late 1680s and illustrated for the first time in 1693, the centrepiece was composed of a base standing on feet, with an urn-shaped central section and branches for candles. At the base or tray there was enough space for casters, oil and vinegar cruets, and salts.

NATURE AND THE ROCOCO

The new style, Rococo, took its name in the nineteenth century from the word 'rocaille', an irregular-shaped form found in nature and used to decorate fountains, gardens and grottoes. Shells, stones and petrified wood were employed, as well as pieces of cut, coloured glass. Félibien stressed the 'rich choice of these beautiful productions of Nature' in his description of the Grotto of Thetis at Versailles (1667). Similar appreciations are found in descriptions of Rococo silver, wherein the aesthetic quality of the pieces is said to surpass considerations of material and technique. What was new about the Rococo was the gradual introduction of outdoor garden decoration into interior decoration and all other fields of the decorative arts, including silver. The word 'rocaille' never lost its traditional meaning, and it was only in colloquial French that it was employed for a new ornament, inspired by the irregular or asymmetrical shape of the shell. The first time it was used in this sense was to describe the corners of a picture frame designed in 1730 for Louis XV by Juste-Aurèle Meissonnier (1695–1750).

Apart from the use of rocaille ornaments, several other characteristics contributed to the style. One was the gradual abandonment of the traditional distinction between the border and the subject in the search for organic unity, and another was miniaturization, or the loss of interdependence of form and size, which made it acceptable, for example, to combine a small putto with architectural volutes, vegetables and game. The introduction of movement into traditionally static works is another aspect of the style, and this was brought about by the play of convex and concave shapes, serpentine contours, spiral fluting and the preference for the oval over the circle as an object's basic shape. All these characteristics, together with the inclusion of forms derived from nature and the increase in many types of fantastic ornamentation, led away from the traditional repertoire of goldsmiths' forms, which was broadly based on architectural ornaments. An early, representative example is Thomas Germain's silver tureen of 1729, the lid of which is decorated with a magnificent loose grouping of separately cast open oysters, asparagus, lemons, onions, mushrooms, artichokes, herbs, two small fish and a partridge.

In Italy, the permanence of works in the Baroque style necessitated only some changes or updating of details, and it is exceptional to encounter in the second quarter of the eighteenth century a form that can be considered French-style Rococo. In France, the Italian influence of the Baroque was perhaps least subdued in the theatre with its mixing of the genres, wherein singing, acting and dancing are combined and performed in an illusionary world. The importance of the theatre found its expression in the presence of actors in Jean Bérain's modern 'grotesques', the ornamental aspect of which was further developed by the next generation and found its final expression in Meissonnier's panels of ornament. These compositions combine all the arts in a single, unified picture, full of movement and unexpected vistas. Published from 1734, these designs were significantly based on snuff-box decorations dating from 1728 to 1732. In fact, related boxes, like one from 1728 that bears Meissonnier's mark, have a cartouche shape and comprise highly complex forms, the execution of which was technically challenging for the maker. Such boxes, made by the best *orfèvres* and *joailliers*, were enormously popular.

Although many characteristics of the Rococo were not novel as such, their combination was conscious and pushed to extremes, surpassing all that was known before and replacing a hierarchic unity with an organic unity. The ideas underlying this change are many, but the increase in the

TUREEN WITH STAND, THOMAS GERMAIN, PARIS, 1729–30 (Stand: L43cm/17in; tureen: H with cover 21cm/8¼in)

The ornamentation of the lid, with fish or game and vegetables, became a feature of prestigious tableware of the Rococo period.

contemporary passion for shells and minerals, as part of a more general interest in natural history, was significant. Asymmetry was appreciated in details, while symmetry was preserved in most cases for the composition as a whole, and irregular shapes were preferred to regular shapes.

'*Le genre pittoresque*' is today sometimes used to describe the best of the new style in France; it is considered an equivalent to the German-based term Rococo, and points to the successful choice of nature's effects or to a free and fantastic artistic arrangement. The paintings of Antoine Watteau and his peers clearly conveyed the new mode, the new feeling for nature, wherein men play their roles like actors on a stage. The appreciation of a novel equilibrium, in which asymmetry, implying movement and tension, plays a leading role, can be linked with the contemporary interest in the sublime, which envisages nothing other than the marvellous, the extraordinary, the surprising. In the visual arts, the *pittoresque* stresses inspiration and individual genius at the expense of rules.

The first significant new pieces in silver were made by Juste-Aurèle Meissonnier and Thomas Germain. Meissonnier's silver candlestick of 1728, known today in numerous versions of gilt-bronze or Meissen porcelain, was published in 1734 in three engravings, showing three viewpoints to explain the complexity of the original. The stem is composed of a succession of scrolls, or volutes, and shells, which embrace two

WINE COOLER, THOMAS GERMAIN, PARIS, 1727–8 (H22cm/8⁷⁄₁₀in)

Thomas Germain combined the skills of the metalworker and sculptor, translating the traditional shape of the wine cooler according to the rules of the new fashion.

putti in a spiralling upward movement, all contributing to a feeling of naturalness and balance. A pair of silver wine coolers of 1727–8 by Germain gives an idea of what the imaginative silversmith could achieve in the new idiom. The shape is no longer based on the cylinder but, rather, inspired by the form of a shell, placed on a square base and decorated with clusters of grapes and vine branches, which also form the handles.

VISUAL UNITY

The search for visual unity is an important characteristic of the Rococo. The introduction of novel ornament and forms in silver was a gradual process. Virtually all goldsmiths complied with the new aesthetic, albeit to different degrees and according to fashion. First, they introduced new but isolated features, like rocailles or other elements from nature, while retaining an essentially unchanged basic form. There are, for instance, isolated rocailles in the components of the *nécessaire* (travelling case) made by Henri-Nicolas Cousinet in 1729–30 for the queen, Marie Leczinska; the underside of the small silver-gilt pot shows the wrinkled form of a shell and rests on four small feet composed of shellfish and algae. Decorating the underside of a vessel with shell-inspired forms became very popular, as can be seen in several boar's-head tureens by Thomas Germain.

Another phase of the Rococo artist's search for visual unity was marked by the introduction or conscious exploitation of new forms and shapes. The silver wine cooler designed by Meissonnier for the Duc de Bourbon in 1723 is one of the earlier pieces; fortunately, it is known by an engraving. The inclusion of a bas-relief, a triton and siren supporting the handles, and the deliberate combination of convex and concave shapes of the body are representative of this phase of development, although some classical ornament, like the egg and dart, has been preserved. In the wine coolers made by Jean-Baptiste de Lens in 1732, movement is introduced by the discreet serpentine outline of the fluted body and the ribbon-tied and rocaille-capped handles, as well as vertically by the outward thrust of the four ribs flanked by rocailles and topped by dolphin heads. De Lens did not dissolve the shape of the wine cooler into a form taken from nature; all the traditional elements are still recognizable, like the shaped circular base and the vase body. On the other hand, the silversmith introduced in the ornament rocailles, shell motifs, foliage and dolphins, and in its application he tried to link the traditionally separated compositional elements and create a new unity.

A ewer and basin by Antoine-Sébastien Durand of 1752–3, made for the Portuguese king, João V, is a splendid example of the mastery of the Rococo idiom. Durand was able to employ elements from nature without distorting the equilibrium of the masses, which are both subtle and strong.

The third, and most remarkable, of the three successive phases of Rococo, on the basis of a full understanding of the artistic possibilities offered by the style, was the creation of entirely new forms and shapes. When contemplating such pieces, one easily forgets they were designed for specific, utilitarian purposes, like a candlestick, tureen or sauce boat. Indeed, the artistic creation prompts one to consider them as pieces of sculpture. It is only after detailed analysis that one is able to grasp the complexity of these works and to realize – in comparison with both earlier and contemporary pieces – the achievements of the goldsmith. The majority of Rococo silver production never attained this high artistic level, in which design, craftsmanship and material sublimely merged.

DUKE OF KINGSTON'S SILVER

An outstanding example of this high-quality Rococo silver is a candelabrum of 1734, designed by Meissonnier, that formed part of the silver of the Duke of Kingston. The

WINE COOLER, JEAN-BAPTISTE DE LENS, PARIS, 1732 (H19.2cm/7½in)

The discovery of a pair of wine coolers, of which this is one, together with two tureens, completely changed current knowledge of de Lens's work. The aquatic plants and rocailles reflect the new style.

EWER AND BASIN, SILVER-GILT, ANTOINE-SEBASTIEN DURAND, PARIS, 1752–3 (Basin: W36.8cm/14½in)

The elements so typical of the Rococo – the reeds, the triton and the rocaille border of the basin – received masterful treatment in Durand's hands.

CANDELABRUM, FOR THE DUKE OF KINGSTON, CLAUDE
DUVIVIER AFTER JUSTE-AURÈLE MEISSONNIER, PARIS,
1734–5 (H38.5cm/15⅛in)

This candelabrum is one of the earliest examples in the full Rococo style.

TUREEN, FOR
THE DUKE OF
KINGSTON,
HENRY ADNET
AND PIERRE-
FRANÇOIS
BONNESTRENNE
AFTER JUSTE-
AURÈLE
MEISSONNIER,
PARIS, 1735–40
(H36.9cm/14½in)

*Masterpieces of the
Rococo, the two tureens
made for the Duke of
Kingston, of which this
is one, were executed
under Meissonnier's
supervision.*

artist had already created a splendid silver candlestick in 1728, and a second model in 1729 for the Queen, known today by an outstanding pair in cast and chased gilt-bronze. The stem is again twisted, but the three sides are each decorated in a different way; sitting on top are tritons holding up the socket. A refined inter-play of forces is introduced by the upwardly sweeping movement of the major elements, countered by suspended garlands and decorative cartouches, which hang from ribbons held by children.

The same idea was used in 1734 for the three-branched Kingston candelabrum executed in silver by Claude Duvivier (1688–1747). However, the identifiable elements of the former two candlesticks have now been melted into one single form, starting from the base, spiralling upward into the three-sided, reversed baluster stem and terminating in a socket. This movement continues in the detachable nozzle that is placed in the

socket, as well as in the three branches that bend down and then rise again to support the sockets. A separate finial, cast as a cluster of leaves, surmounts the whole and can be taken off to make room for a fourth candle. The downward movement is created by a floral garland that hangs around the stem and terminates at the base of the candelabrum. The three upper parts of the stem, as well as the three branches, nozzle and drip pans, are decorated differently, with flowers, a moth and a cartouche with the engraved crest of Evelyn Pierrepont, Duke of Kingston.

The best illustration of the Rococo in silver can be found in the two silver tureens designed by Meissonnier in 1735, again for the Duke of Kingston. Both tureens were executed under Meissonnier's direction by two Parisian silversmiths, Henry Adnet (1683–1745) and Pierre-François Bonnestrenne (c.1682–after 1740), and they were delivered to the client in 1740. Meissonnier's

signature testifies to his involvement in the conception and production, as does the exceptional quality of the casting, embossing and chasing.

In judging the artistic achievement of Meissonnier, a comparison with Germain's tureen of 1729 is illustrative. For the sake of unity Meissonnier left not a single element of the tureen untouched, nor the basic shapes of the platter, body and lid. The suggestion of movement is created by introducing a pattern of forms that, although distinct, respond to each other and are part of an upward, spiralling movement. The sides of the asymmetrically shaped body, designed on an oval rather than on the more static shape of the classically circular tureen, are decorated with rock work, herbs and vegetable leaves. The choice of these motifs, in addition to game, oysters and fish, relates to the ingredients used to make the fashionable ragoût for which the tureen, or *pot-à-oille*, was primarily intended.

SILVERSMITHS' WORKSHOPS AND STANDARDS

For inspiration, many artists and craftsmen turned to the Parisian silversmiths, buying prints of their works or making their own drawings. The French court, nobility, bankers and rich bourgeoisie were all lovers of silver and gold, and they crowded into the artists' workshops whenever an important piece of silver was exhibited, as it often was before export. The public interest in goldsmiths' work found a parallel in the organization of art exhibitions, starting in 1727, and in the annual display of tapestries by the Manufacture des Gobelins. This situation is important in another respect, in that anyone visiting the ateliers of the goldsmiths could thus be made aware of the latest forms and fashions. The accessibility of the workshop stresses yet another point: information about models could be direct, the only requirement being one's presence in the right place at the right time.

The success of the workshop depended on a combination of design and craftsmanship. The techniques used in goldsmiths' work did not change significantly in the Rococo period, although both the casting of separate elements and chasing attained levels of excellence. The special qualities of French silver, that is its softness and colour, were due not so much to its high standard but to the addition of gold, a practice that had no parallel abroad and disappeared in France only in the nineteenth century. With increased public demand and stylistic changes, it was no longer possible to rely exclusively on a stock of models, formed and jealously preserved in the workshop. For small ornaments, the goldsmith relied on engravings. However, these prints generally did not provide for a complete model, nor did they show the shape of the piece and the relationship of the detail to the whole.

When new models were published, the author was not always a goldsmith himself, for example, Jean-Bernard Toro (1661–1731), who collaborated with two goldsmiths from Aix-en-Provence in the Régence period. The case of Meissonnier is different in another way, in that the publication of some of his models for silver took place after they had been executed, at a crucial point in his career when he wanted them to be known as his inventions. With the publication in 1748 of his *Eléments d'Orfèvrerie*, Pierre Germain (?1716–83) was

GOLD SALT CELLAR, FRANÇOIS-THOMAS GERMAIN AFTER THOMAS GERMAIN, PARIS, 1764–5 (H5.6cm/2⅕in)

Executed in gold, the shape and detail of the salt cellar, one of a pair, points to a creation by Thomas Germain. (ABOVE)

CANDELABRUM, CLAUDE BALLIN II, PARIS, 1739–40 (H49cm/19⅓in)

This candelabrum contains classical details, though the spiral movement finds a truly Rococo expression in the detachable four-light branch. (RIGHT)

DESIGN FOR A GIRANDOLE FOR LOUIS XV, 1739, ANONYMOUS ENGRAVER AFTER THOMAS GERMAIN, 1761

looking for a market by advertising his own drawings for secular and church plate, and he included, probably for reasons of prestige, some designs by the *orfèvre du roi* Jacques Roettiers (1707–84). Another exception is offered by François-Thomas Germain (1726–91), who published designs showing a pair of famous gold girandoles, designed in 1739 by his father and presented to Louis XV in 1748.

The Parisian goldsmiths and jewellers were organized as a corporation that applied a strict set of rules to check the standard of quality, which included both jury visits and a system of marking. In the mid-1730s, the corporation tried to stem the growing role of the retailers, or *marchands-merciers*, who sold pieces of silver and gold. In several official documents the goldsmiths stated that only they were able to distinguish good from defective work, while the retailer lacked the necessary training. Among themselves they formulated their position thus: they felt the status of the title '*ouvrier*' was equal to that of merchant; furthermore, they claimed to have the 'genius' that inspired designers, painters, sculptors, engravers and other practitioners of art. It comes as no surprise that the conservative French Academies, which refused to accept any member linked with craft or commerce, blocked the proposed candidature of both Germain and Meissonnier.

HUGUENOTS IN HOLLAND AND ENGLAND

Among the notable Huguenot Rococo silversmiths who fled France for Holland were Jean Saint (*fl.*1735–9) and Philippe Metayer (1699–1763). In addition, the English involvement with the Rococo relied greatly on the contribution of Huguenot silversmiths, who generally kept in touch with the latest French developments. Their designs were somewhat am-

DESIGN FOR A TUREEN AND STAND, THOMAS GERMAIN, *c.*1730–35.

This sanguine design is an important example of Germain's draughtsmanship.

TUREEN, PAUL DE LAMERIE, LONDON, 1736–7 (H31.5cm/12⅜in)

One of the major Huguenot silversmiths, Paul de Lamerie executed this tureen presumably after the print from The Modern Cook *(1733) by Vincent de la Chapelle, cook to the Earl of Chesterfield. The work is inspired by French designs of the early Rococo period.*

bivalent, often mixing motifs and shapes from the sixteenth and seventeenth centuries with those from the Rococo.

When one considers the silver tureen by Paul de Lamerie (1688–1751), made in collaboration with Paul Crespin (1694–1770) the basic shape recalls the work of the French goldsmiths of the Régence and Rococo periods, like the *pot-à-oille* designed by Thomas Germain. The proportions, however, are changed, and no precedent for the flattened body, or the elongated, dolphin-shaped feet, can be found on the Continent. De Lamerie and Crespin are also known to have worked together on the execution of the ambassadorial plate of Philip Dormer Stanhope, fourth Earl of Chesterfield, and de Lamerie may also have executed some pieces to Crespin's design. Although the design of the tureen shows a strong French influence, several details seem to point to a foreign interpretation of a French model, for example the laid-down relief ornaments on the lid. The shell motif decorating the underside of the tureen is reminiscent of the ridged ornamentation of the French pieces cited earlier, but the design of the motif and its application to the

tureen contrast sharply with French naturalism, in which the rocaille design merges perfectly with the border.

The silver-gilt ewer and basin executed in 1741 by Paul de Lamerie for the Worshipful Company of Goldsmiths in London exemplifies more clearly the multiple sources for both the general form and the ornamentation. De Lamerie must have been a great admirer of the Dutch Auricular style of

POSEIDON CENTREPIECE,
SILVER-GILT, MADE FOR FREDERICK,
PRINCE OF WALES, PAUL CRESPIN,
LONDON, 1741–2 (H49.5cm/19½in) (ABOVE)

SAUCEBOATS, SILVER-GILT, NICHOLAS
SPRIMONT, LONDON, 1743–4
(H22.7cm/9in) (RIGHT)

the seventeenth century. Recently, other sources have been tentatively pointed out; for example, ornaments were taken from the repertoires of the stucco workers and wood carvers of the Régence period. The Poseidon centrepiece of 1741–2, designed by Paul Crespin and made for Frederick, Prince of Wales, is an outstanding example of the French Rococo style, albeit executed in England. For the same patron and for the same service, Nicholas Sprimont (1716–71) executed four sauce boats in 1743–4. These are distinguished for the naturalness of the figures that perch on the rims of the small half-boat/half-shell bowls.

Among the extant works of George Michael Moser (1706–83), the Swiss-born chaser, enameller and medallist who worked

in London, is a design for a pair of candlesticks, dating from *c*.1740 and executed by an unidentified silversmith. The idea of the inclusion of a full-length figure forming the stem of the candlestick, or *torchère*, was used earlier by the Italians and the French. Moser chose Apollo and Daphne for his figures, thus linking both candlesticks as a pair, something that had previously been achieved by executing one in the reverse of the other. The inspiration from the French Rococo, notably Meissonnier for the base, does not result in a slavish copy, but in an original design.

ITALY AND GERMANY

In Italy the continuity of the Baroque style meant that silversmiths did not need to alter their designs radically, nor was this demanded of them. When a change finally did come about, it was due to French influence. As in France, Italian silver has suffered considerably from numerous melting programmes and it is no surprise to find

the major pieces of silver and gold abroad. From 1745 to 1749, a group of Roman goldsmiths executed two important church services for the Portuguese court, one of which, for the chapel of São Roque in Lisbon, survived the earthquake of 1755. The majority of the forms, probably conceived by a sculptor under the supervision of an architect, can be described as Baroque. It is mainly in details that Rococo ornament can be found, like the ridged surface of the incense boat by Leandro Gagliardi, although some full-blown Rococo silver was made, such as the silver-gilt *écuelle* by the goldsmith Bartolomeo Pagliani (*fl.*1753–75) of Turin, or the cruet stands by the Valadier workshop in Rome.

The centre of German silver production during the Rococo period was Augsburg, where output was mostly intended for export. Contrary to the French situation, German retailers had gradually eroded the dominant position of the individual silversmiths. They developed modern commercial strategies and could offer their pieces on any market for prices below those of local production. The surviving drawings that can be associated with their enterprises testify unequivocally to their international

SILVER-GILT
INCENSE BOAT,
FROM THE ST
JOHN THE
BAPTIST CHAPEL,
LISBON,
LEANDRO
GAGLIARDI,
ROME, *c*.1748
(H18cm/7in)

Part of a large service – which still exists in its entirety – commissioned by the Portuguese court in Rome. Almost all the important Roman goldsmiths of the period participated in its execution, including Gagliardi.

the well-organized print publishers who supplied a vast market that reached far beyond Germany. Designs in the Rococo style by Pier, Baur, Habermann, Hildt, Roth, Eisler and Wachsmuth, for example, were individual and did not copy French models, although the local tradition was open to both French and Italian influences. To characterize these models it is best to compare them to French production. First, the Germans were probably less bound by tradition and, second, their approach to form and ornament was different, with exuberance generally prevailing over restraint, and the exotic dominating the classical. Distinctive iconographic programmes were introduced in large centrepieces, like that made in 1763 by Bernhard Heinrich Weyhe (*c*.1701–82), often inspired by trellis work garden pavilions.

ROCOCO ON THE WANE

Jacques-François Blondel remarked in 1772 that some years ago 'our age seemed to be one of Rocailles, but today, without knowing exactly why, it is different'. In criticism of the Rococo style, the genius of the major artists was fully acknowledged. Their followers were condemned for failing to understand the original principles and for disregarding the relationship between form and function. Claude Ballin II was perhaps the first goldsmith known for his complaints about the loss of good taste, deriding the craftsmen who 'spoiled the beautiful shapes by replacing the wise ornaments of the ancients with crayfish and rabbits that were not made to be placed on top of silver vases, nor to decorate the outside' (from the artist's obituary, *Mercure de France*, 1754). The rocaille slowly began to lose ground from 1760, after which it was replaced by more restrained and classical forms, favouring shapes and ornaments inspired by the '*beau moderne*' of the Louis XIV period.

APOLLO AND DAPHNE CANDLESTICKS, UNIDENTIFIED SILVERSMITH AFTER GEORGE MICHAEL MOSER, UNMARKED, *c*.1740 (H34cm/14½in) (ABOVE)

CENTREPIECE WITH A MUSIC PAVILION, FOR BISHOP FRIEDRICH WILHELM VON WESTPHALEN OF HILDESHEIM, BERNHARD HEINRICH WEYHE, AUGSBURG, 1763 (H72.5cm/ 28½in) (ABOVE RIGHT)

scope, reaching from Germany, France, England and Russia, to probably all the other European countries. The draughtsmen and designers working for these retailers combined local models with French elements, and their drawings were sent to clients and retailers, including such details as weights and prices.

The publication of numerous sets of secular and ecclesiastical designs for silver in the years 1740 to 1770 was made possible by

NEOCLASSICISM

The emergence of the tasteful, refined Neoclassical style was a logical, understandable reaction to what many critics viewed as the excesses of the Rococo. Indeed, ever since the earlier style's first appearance in France, it had provoked enemies who ridiculed or criticized its flourishes, curves and spontaneity. Not surprisingly in a country with such a strong tradition of classicism, the modern style was considered to be an aberration: Voltaire had first poured scorn on it in 1733, and in 1745 the Abbé Le Blanc had mockingly questioned the sanity of any artist who could, for instance, draw a coat of arms at an oblique angle.

THE DECLINE
OF ROCOCO

The point at which *le genre pittoresque*, the purest form of Rococo, is generally considered to have lost its esteem among the avant-garde was in 1749–50. This was the date of the tour of Italy, fountainhead of classicism and antiquity, by Abel-François Poisson (1727–81), Madame de Pompadour's brother, later the Marquis de Marigny and from 1751 to 1774 the Directeur Général des Bâtiments (and effectively Minister of the Arts). His travelling companions were all opponents of the Rococo: the architect Jacques-Germain Soufflot (1713–80), the critic Le Blanc and the engraver Charles-Nicolas Cochin (1715–90). On their return to Paris, Marigny became a pragmatic supporter of a reversion to the principles of classicism, but it was Cochin who became its most ardent champion. In an important *Supplication aux Orfèvres*, published in the *Mercure de France* in December 1754, he attacked the goldsmiths for the absurdities in their decoration –

KING GUSTAVUS III OF SWEDEN AND HIS FAMILY AT TABLE, PEHR HILLESTRÖM, 1779

The silver of the royal family is French and in the extremely fashionable' 'goût grec'. (ABOVE)

SNUFF-BOX, PAUL BARBOT, LONDON, 1774, WITH A MEDALLION BY GEORGE MICHAEL MOSER (H7cm/2¾in)

This gold box, although English, is in the Parisian style of the late 1760s and may well be a direct copy of an imported French original. (LEFT)

tureens with figures of children the size of vine leaves, or twisted candlesticks that allowed wax to dribble over the furniture. He pleaded with them to follow 'simple rules governed by good sense', and for architects to 'return to the old style'. These arguments were entirely consistent with the spirit of the Enlightenment and the intellectual circle of the *philosophes* which was then gathering momentum.

While the group was in Italy, they might have observed that the classical tradition in French art was being maintained at the Academy in Rome. Here, artists would produce drawings after the antique – not only of figures but also of other classical forms and ornaments – which had been adapted for modern usage in the past and were available once again as infinitely variable source material. In addition, a new impetus was being given to archaeology by the recent discoveries at Herculaneum and Pompeii, which had revealed domestic interiors with a wealth of previously unknown ornamental material.

At almost exactly this time, one of the best connected and most influential figures among the arbiters of taste in Paris, the Comte de Caylus (1692–1765), was forming and publishing his collection of antiquities. He may well have been involved, together with the designer Louis-Joseph Le Lorrain (1715–59), with a new set of furniture for the rich art collector and affable courtier, Lalive de Jully. His surviving desk and *cartonnier* (filing cabinet), in the Musée Condé, Chantilly, are entirely classical and severely architectural in style, with straight tapering and fluted legs, pronounced Vitruvian scroll and Greek key mouldings, and rich laurel festoons in ormolu. They were also thought to recall the work of André-Charles Boulle and the classical period of Louis XIV.

THE 'GOÛT GREC'

As Lalive resided in the Rue St-Honoré (almost next door to Madame de Pompadour) and kept open house, it is hardly surprising that the new style – now nicknamed the '*goût grec*' – rapidly became the last word in chic. By 1763 the Baron von Grimm reported that all the smart young men in Paris had a gold snuff-box '*à la grecque*' about their person. This turnabout in taste is admirably demonstrated by a Parisian gold snuff-box by Jean Ducrollay of 1760–61 after a design by Pierre Philippe Choffard, dated 1759. This box, in the Gilbert Collection in the Los Angeles County Museum of Art, is paralleled by another slightly later English example in the same collection. Dated 1774, it is decorated with classical motifs and a laurel wreath, enclosing a relief medallion showing Love overcoming Strength; the box is signed by George Michael Moser, the Swiss gold chaser and enameller who is known better for his work in the Rococo style.

Unfortunately, so much eighteenth-century French silver has disappeared that it

TUREEN, COVER AND STAND FROM THE ORLOFF SERVICE, JACQUES-NICOLAS ROETTIERS, PARIS, 1770 (H33.7cm/13¼in)

is difficult to make a full assessment of the initial impact of the new style. Not only was a vast amount of plate melted down to finance the Seven Years' War (1756–63), but the royal family itself ceased ordering new pieces until after the hostilities had ended. Nevertheless, it is possible to see that the French goldsmiths responded with varying degrees of wholeheartedness to the new classicism. On the one hand, from 1756 onward Robert-Joseph Auguste (1723–1805) produced a series of tureens for the Danish court with somewhat modified oval and circular profiles, dead birds and naturalistic flora. On the other hand, Jacques-Nicolas Roettiers (b. 1736) supplied Catherine the Great's lover, Prince Orloff, with a vast service in a heavy classical style *à la grecque*. Another service with a simplified design can be seen in a 1773 illustration of Gustavus III of Sweden at table: the royal family is dining in public according to the convention of *le service à la française*, that is with the tureens and dishes set out in predetermined places on the table.

The Orloff service has been said to mark the end of the *goût grec*. From this date onward, objects were to acquire more pleasing proportions and elegant small-scale ornament. The tureen which was made as part of a service for George III's use at Herrenhausen has scrolling acanthus leaves on the bowl and fluting on the base and elegant cover, as well as amorous putti similar to those on the Danish service.

As the century drew to a close, there was an increasing attenuation of forms and an ever more precious quality of execution in all the decorative arts across Europe. In French silver this can be seen in the work of Henry Auguste (1759–1816), Robert-Joseph's son, particularly when he appears to follow the designs of the sculptor Jean-Guillaume Moitte, and where he reveals a stark purity anticipating the style of the Directoire and Empire. The same characteristics can be seen in a mounted jasper cup of 1787 by Jacques Kirstein of Strasbourg, possibly made for William Beckford, the rich English eccentric. The designer, Jean-

THE ADAM STYLE

JASPER BOWL
WITH MOUNTS BY
JACQUES
KIRSTEIN,
STRASBOURG,
1787–8
(H14.6cm/5¾in)

DESIGN FOR THE
WEST END OF
THE DINING
ROOM WITH
NICHE AT
KEDLESTON
HALL,
DERBYSHIRE,
ROBERT ADAM,
1762

In Britain, where the understanding of the Rococo had never been as profound as in France, a new classicism emerged in fashionable circles at almost exactly the same time as the *goût grec*, although it took on a remarkably different appearance. Whereas in France it was a reaction to the old-fashioned style which led the way, in England it was the careful orchestration of a new taste by Robert Adam (1728–92), the ambitious Scottish architect, after his return from Italy in 1758. By cultivating the right influential patrons and by a very subtle use of public relations, Adam remained almost

publications, notably *Ruins of Palmyra* by Wood and Dawkins (1753), and by the experiments of James 'Athenian' Stuart (1713–88), author of *The Antiquities of Athens* (1762 onward), at Spencer House, London, and Kedleston Hall, Derbyshire. In 1761 Adam took over from Stuart the decoration of the latter house, then being rebuilt for Sir Nathaniel Curzon, and proceeded to make one of his most important early statements. A drawing for the dining-room niche, an idea which Adam revived, shows at once that the architect conceived his interiors as totally harmonious ensembles, with the permanent decoration of the room dictating the forms and disposition of its furnishings. Ideally, everything was to be coordinated and designed by a single hand: the plasterwork of the ceiling should echo the carpet on the floor, while matching decorative motifs should be followed through on the frieze, the overmantel and the furniture in a room. Naturally the design of silver, especially for the dining room, was included in this somewhat autocratic approach. Adam designed the main items for dinner services (especially tureens and epergnes, or centrepieces) for a number of his clients, as well as a new pattern for the humbler plates and dishes of at least one patron, Sir Watkin Williams Wynn.

Dining-room niches were to become a feature of Neoclassical houses until the end of the Regency. They generally possessed a single side table (or at Kedleston, three), sometimes with side pedestals and mirrors behind, and were intended to display the family plate in the age-old tradition. Here, the large dishes propped up on the knife boxes were probably old and venerated heirloom pieces, as were the fountains and cisterns, although the tripod perfume burner and ormolu-mounted vases had been designed by his predecessor and arch-rival, Stuart. It must have been somewhat galling for Adam to include these elements in his design, presumably at Sir Nathaniel's insistence.

Adam's attitude to classicism and antiquity was perfectly expressed by his contemporary, the painter Sir Joshua Reynolds,

Jacques Boileau, who was originally a decorative painter, also followed Moitte with purer vase forms, Egyptian-style water leaves and mask heads. He emigrated to England, where he joined the team of French craftsmen working for the Prince of Wales at Carlton House, and his influence was to extend into the early Regency period, when he worked as a freelance designer for Rundell's and Garrard's, among others.

unassailed for nearly 15 years. By the end of the century his style had been disseminated throughout the length and breadth of the country and into every sphere of artistic activity or craft. Indeed, in a panegyric in 1812, Sir John Soane was able to write that 'manufacturers of every kind felt, as it were, the electric power of this revolution in Art'.

At the very beginning of his career, Adam was greatly helped by recent archaeological

DESIGN FOR A
CANDLESTICK,
ROBERT ADAM,
c.1767

The rich classical details are taken from a variety of Antique sources but used in a completely modern way corresponding to the principles of 'invention'.

EPERGNE FOR LORD MANSFIELD,
ROBERT ADAM, *c*.1770

This shows how the refined Adam style could become 'all gingerbread and snippets of embroidery'.

in his *Sixth Discourse* (1774). Here he advocated the use of 'invention', or the uninhibited borrowing of features from the classical past for entirely modern purposes – the works of the ancients were to be considered 'as a magazine of common property . . . whence every man has a right to take what material he pleases'. This quite clearly allowed for the free interpretation of both the forms and ornamental vocabulary of antiquity (particularly, for Adam, from his favourite late Imperial period). The extraordinary epergne intended for Lord Mansfield's dining table precisely illustrates this principle. It takes the form of a colonnaded sequence of 'antique' garden temples standing on a plateau supported by sphinxes. The vessels themselves, which were meant to hold fruits and sweetmeats, are derived from classical sarcophagi, vases, urns and hanging lanterns and surround a central sacrificial altar, while the ornament consists of flimsy garlands and husks, palmettes or anthemion flowers, trailing *rinceaux* (decorative foliage), and spiral fluting and gadrooning. It is not known whether this object was ever made in silver, but it represents a virtual manifesto of the decorative possibilities of 'invention' from classical sources.

The centrepiece also exposes one of the weaknesses of the Adam style – the danger of it degenerating into 'gingerbread and snippets of embroidery', in the words of Horace Walpole, particularly in the hands of plagiarists. Another weakness is illustrated in candlesticks designed by Adam for an unidentified client. Although a preliminary drawing shows a beautifully proportioned classical baluster-shaped object, the finished product appears to be overwhelmed by fussy ornament. It has been pointed out that the architect must have overlooked the fact that silver is a reflecting material, with its own properties of highlights and shadows, and works best with a judicious balance between plain and ornamental surfaces. Later, when the Adam style had been absorbed by the craft as a whole, the most satisfying results derived precisely from this principle. In the case of these candlesticks, Adam also produced drawings for alternative square bases, probably because the original – with more correct 'antique' circular bases – would have been too unstable.

SIR WILLIAM CHAMBERS

Robert Adam was by no means the only architect designing silver in the progressive new style. Another of his great rivals, Sir William Chambers (1723–96), who once described himself as 'a very pretty connoisseur of furniture', also provided his clients with a distinctly francophile version of

CANDLESTICK, JOHN CARTER,
LONDON, 1767–8 (H35.4cm/13⅜in)

The over-abundance of classical ornament suggests that the architect had little first-hand experience of the silversmith's craft or material.

Neoclassicism, including, for example, the dining and chapel plate for the fourth Duke of Marlborough at Blenheim. Four massive tureens from this commission date from 1769 and are anglicized versions of the *goût grec*, with strong Vitruvian scroll bands (originally intended to be a Greek key pattern) and spiralling fluted and lobed

FRENCH IMPORTS

French silver was imported into Britain – as indeed everywhere in Europe – and provided models for native craftsmen. Examples of such inspirational pieces were candlesticks made by

TUREEN AND
COVER, MARKS
OF JOHN
PARKER AND
EDWARD
WAKELIN,
LONDON, 1769–
70, MADE BY
SEBASTIAN AND
JAMES CRESPEL
(H27.9cm/11in)

*This tureen represents
an anglicized Louis
XVI style of
Neoclassicism.*

TWO-HANDLED CUP, COVER AND
STAND, WILLIAM HOLMES AND
NICHOLAS DUMÉE, LONDON, 1774–5,
RETAILED BY WILLIAM MOORE
(H55.3cm/21¾in)

covers. Yet they retain bombé profiles and naturalistic artichoke finials, vestiges of the Rococo style. There was a distinct subgroup of English clients, mainly patrons of the London silversmiths Parker and Wakelin and Thomas Heming, who preferred this francophile style to Robert Adam's native version. Interestingly, the makers of the Blenheim tureens were Sebastian and James Crespel (working as subcontractors for Parker and Wakelin), who also produced at least four candlesticks to the above-mentioned Adam design. The Crespels' versatility makes it clear that silversmiths were perfectly capable of executing objects in either style – it was for the client and his architect-advisor to choose.

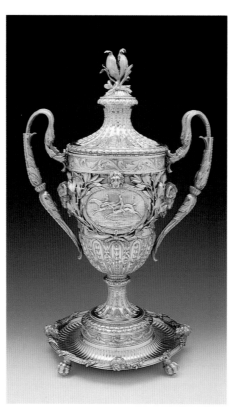

Robert-Joseph Auguste in 1766. Acquired by the Duke of Bedford, they were copied by Parker and Wakelin in 1770, and adapted and modified for that firm's repertoire thereafter. A magnificent race cup by William Holmes and Nicholas Dumée (fl.1758–76) reveals debts to French sources, not least in the fluting of the base and the split pomegranate finial. However, the form itself, a two-handled cup, is in the English tradition, although now assuming a shape more reminiscent of a classical vase. The exquisitely cast and chased medallions must have been executed by a specialist, as yet unidentified, possibly a German watch-case chaser, who interpreted the motif of classical cameos with entirely modern subjects (perhaps from prints after George Stubbs). A number of identical medallions survive on objects by different makers, indicating that buying in prefabricated parts from specialists was an established practice. There also exists a large group of objects, mainly by Andrew Fogelberg, with medallions of classical subjects derived from James Tassie's reproductions of classical gems.

BEGINNINGS OF
MASS PRODUCTION

Among the majority of silversmiths who were not working to bespoke designs from avant-garde architects, there was a slow transition toward the new style during the 1760s and early 1770s. The old Rococo style had allowed them to display their virtuoso skills in chasing, casting and engraving naturalistic ornament, whereas the new style was based on an established vocabulary with endlessly repeated motifs suitable for mass production on the new machinery. Seeming at first to allow fewer opportunities for imaginative interpretation, the simpler and more light-weight objects also prevented the silversmiths from charging high prices for 'fashion'. Thus there was only a half-hearted adoption of Neoclassicism in the 1760s: a

typical transitional coffee pot, for instance, may be given a classical garland around its neck, but still have a double bombé profile and a scrolling handle. By the late 1770s, however, the style had overcome all resistance. Silversmiths came to terms with the new ornament and also with the shapes, particularly the endless variations of the classical vase and the tripod, which by now had entered their everyday repertoire.

JAMES WYATT AND MATTHEW BOULTON

It was the third great Neoclassical architect, James Wyatt (1748–1813), who found himself, perhaps unwittingly, on the fringes of the beginnings of mass production. Wyatt had a large architectural practice and can be credited with the wide dissemination of a popular Adamesque style during the last years of the eighteenth century. His approach avoided the intransigence of Adam and provided clients with unfussy but

elegant classical interiors entirely suited to an increasingly informal mode of living. It was perhaps inevitable that he should meet and collaborate with the Birmingham entrepreneur Matthew Boulton (1728–1809), who was determined to raise his family business of traditional 'toymakers' into manufacturers of works of art. For this purpose, Boulton lobbied Parliament successfully for the establishment of assay offices at Birmingham and Sheffield (which were set up in 1773), and, in order to use nothing but the best in modern design, he became associated with Robert and James Adam, Sir William Chambers, James 'Athenian' Stuart and James Wyatt.

In a letter to Mrs Montague of 1772, Boulton wrote 'Fashion hath much to do in these things, and as that of the present age, distinguishes itself by adopting the most elegant ornaments of the most refined Grecian artists... I am humbly copying their styles and making new combinations of old ornaments'. The drawings supplied to him

A GENTLEMAN AT BREAKFAST, ATTRIBUTED TO HENRY WALTON, c.1780

The picture probably represents Sir Thomas Egerton of Heaton Hall, an early patron of James Wyatt. The vase-shaped tea urn (possibly made of Old Sheffield Plate) shows the impact of new technology.

JUG, MATTHEW BOULTON AND JOHN FOTHERGILL, BIRMINGHAM, 1776–7 (H34.2cm/13½in)

by Wyatt reflect his ideal of 'elegant simplicity'. They included designs for candlesticks, jugs and snuff-boxes incorporating decorative motifs such as guilloche patterns, or tripods with female masks and 'Grecian' hairstyles. Boulton felt free to interchange these motifs as and where appropriate, as on a jug deriving from a Wyatt drawing that combines plain shallow fluting on the bowl and cover with a plain horizontal band flanked by richer classical mouldings. Its

THREE CONDIMENT VASES, LOUISA
COURTAULD AND GEORGE COWLES,
LONDON, 1771–2 (Centre: H19.5cm/7¾in)

A SHEET OF DESIGNS FROM A
SHEFFIELD PLATE MANUFACTURER'S
PATTERN BOOK, *c.*1785

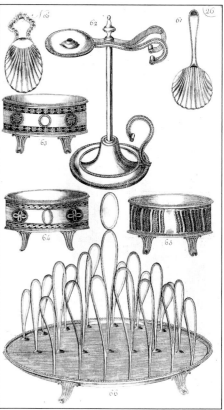

somewhat elongated form and more econo-
mical disposition of ornament is in contrast
to an Adam design, and a very long way
from French goldsmiths' work (once described by Boulton as 'troy Chargè').
Another version of this jug exists with an
incurved foot with a guilloche moulding,
originally intended by Wyatt for candlesticks but now transposed for a jug.

Both Wyatt and Boulton (and indeed the
more motivated London silversmiths) were
looking to the new design sources then
becoming available, particularly d'Hancarville's edition of Sir William Hamilton's
*Collection of Etruscan, Greek and Roman Antiq-
uities* (1766), with its wealth of decorative
borders, figures and ornamental details. In at
least one instance, Courtauld and Cowles
copied not only the shapes but also the
decoration from this source, for a set of
condiment vases for Sir Nathaniel Curzon.
Despite his determined provincialism, Boulton was also happy to borrow and then
imitate new objects from France, such as

cassolettes, perfume burners that were used to
waft away 'the Vapour of soup & all the
fulsome savour of dinner'. Following
Stuart's reconstruction of the Choragic
Monument of Lysicrates in the park at
Shugborough, and its adaptation for
domestic purposes at Kedleston, these
somewhat affected objects enjoyed a short
lease of life and took on a tripod form.

INDUSTRIAL DEVELOPMENTS

The determining factor in the appearance of
much late eighteenth-century silver was the
advance of industrial techniques for mass
production in the provincial centres of
Sheffield and Birmingham. As early as the
1740s, flatting mills had been developed to
create workable sheets of silver with a
consistent gauge, thus replacing the laborious method of beating from the ingot. Then
in 1743 a Sheffield cutler, Thomas Boulsover, discovered that copper and silver
would fuse under heat and that a plated

ingot of the new material would expand
equally under pressure. Thereafter a workable sheet of Old Sheffield Plate, as it came to
be known, could be used in the same way as
solid silver. In the 1770s, when a method
was devised for plating both sides of the
copper, its future use was assured. The
subsequent improvements in steel dies for
stamped ornament and the invention of fly
punches for piercing tin sheets could be used
equally well for solid silver and Old Sheffield Plate, and indeed many identical objects
were produced in both metals. The only
difference was the price: a pair of simple
candlesticks might cost £3 plated and £12 in
silver. Even so, both were out of reach of all
but the professional classes and above.

Timothy Schroder has pointed out that
the really significant price differentials at this
time were between objects made in solid
silver, for instance by Matthew Boulton in
Birmingham using the new dies, and those
made in London by traditional methods. A
'lion' candlestick made by the former

TEA URN, HESTER BATEMAN,
LONDON, 1790–1 (H24.4cm/9⅗in)

*The tea urn was a natural vehicle for Neoclassical
expression, seen here with 'bright cut' engraving.*

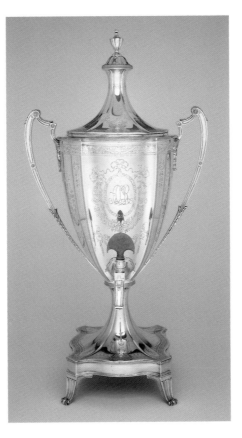

DESIGN FOR A TUREEN, COVER AND
STAND FOR THE ODESCALCHI
SERVICE, WORKSHOP OF GIUSEPPE
VALADIER, ROME, *c*.1795

*Giuseppe Valadier, well known for his architectural
talents, inherited his father's workshop in 1785.*

method might weigh only 33 ounces and cost a mere £17 2*s*, while if it were made by the latter technique, with cast ornament, it would weigh 108 ounces and cost £44. But for two significant factors, Boulton might have prospered with his method. On the one hand, his costings did not include the expense of sinking new dies, and on the other, the clientèle for any kind of solid silver still comprised only the very rich, who continued to regard silver as a recoverable investment and were not too concerned with the economics of 'fashion'. Thus Boulton's foray into the luxury arts was not the success it deserved to be and he was to find greater reward in the manufacture of Old Sheffield Plate (and, later, in the development of Argand lamps and, along with James Watt, the revolutionary steam engine).

The influence of the new machines and of plated goods on silver design grew increasingly obvious in the 1780s and 1790s. The flatting machines, which could now be driven by steam engines, were able to produce sheet silver with a very thin gauge of metal that was ideal for oval-shaped teapots, for example. Similarly, because dies for stamped ornament were expensive to create, they had a long life span and at Sheffield in particular were passed around within the trade quite freely. The fly punches originally developed for Old Sheffield Plate now produced highly decorative pierced silver useful for bottle stands, salt-cellars and sugar vases. An idea of the extensive range of simple domestic objects being mass-produced during this fecund period can be seen by looking at manufacturers' pattern-books of the time.

A particularly elegant new type of domestic object was the tea urn, which, like the two-handled cup, lent itself naturally to this classical shape. An example of the former type, dating from 1790 and made by Hester Bateman, has particularly fine 'bright

cut' engraving, a technique whereby the graving tool cuts an angled groove into the silver, making the surface sparkle in the light. The urn may well have been part of a set with a teapot, cream jug and sugar bowl. Bateman, who had one of the largest and most successful businesses in London, is particularly noted for just such exquisite pieces with an air of *fin-de-siècle* refinement about them. In fact, her extensive workshops were fully equipped for quick turnover with labour-saving devices, and by 1791 possessed their own steam engine.

The influence of English Neoclassical silver spread far into Europe, where Boulton's agents procured orders which were plagiarized and adapted by native craftsmen, most obviously in northern Europe, Scandinavia and Russia. Even the modest Sheffield goldsmith Daniel Holy was a creditor, and therefore supplier, of the Parisian *marchand-mercier* Granchez, whose shop Au Petit Dunkerque specialized in English wares. French influences were of course strongest,

but even the tureen from the Odescalchi service, made in Rome by the workshop of Giuseppe Valadier (1762–1839) *c*.1795, owes a debt to English sources.

It should be remembered that throughout this period goldsmiths were in severe competition with the producers of other luxury and useful wares, especially porcelain. The great days were over, at least temporarily, when it was normal to have a dinner service for 24 in white plate for the first two courses and gilt for the dessert, together with monumental displays at the sideboard and toilet table. Not only was Oriental porcelain highly acceptable as an alternative, but the new European varieties were positively *à la mode* for dessert and ornaments. Despite this, goldsmiths and silversmiths rose to the challenge and continued to expand their craft by evolving new designs and increasing their productivity by using new technology. They also produced some exceedingly beautiful and interesting objects worthy of their illustrious heritage.

THE NINETEENTH
CENTURY

*I*n *the nineteenth century more silver plate was produced than in any other period. This reflected new production processes, such as the steam-powered machines which replaced the earlier water and wind power. The emergence of Britain as a manufacturing nation during the Industrial Revolution transformed the established craft trades, including that of the goldsmith. Innovations such as rolled sheet metal components and decorative details stamped from steel dies emanated from the Sheffield plate manufacturers and spread throughout the country, enabling the commercial silver trade to flourish. Following the triumph of Napoleon's imperial pretentions, an exceptional confidence in what was perceived as imperial Roman design prevailed. Once again, France led the way stylistically, but each nationality interpreted the style in an idiosyncratic way. It was the mood of victory, and the associated peace, which led to a revival of the Rococo, and in turn of the Gothic. The conscious search for a 'correct' style led to an assimilation of many which were alien to Europe and North America. The result was on the one hand an elite striving for artistic perfection and on the other a clientele satisfied with the security of reproductions of earlier styles.*

Technical innovations set new standards in reproduction and, more universally, in finish, while electroplate provided a cheap, easily produced alternative to costly wrought silver. With the exception of an innovative few, contemporary design was completely submerged by a profusion of reproductions. A reaction against machinery, industrialization and mass-production in the latter part of the century, however, brought silver back to the domain of the craftsman and designer in both Europe and America.

CRAYFISH SALT, HUNT AND ROSKELL, 1844 (H16cm/6in)

This naturalistic salt is a copy of one made by Nicholas Sprimont and now in the Royal Collection. The design was also produced in porcelain at Sprimont's Chelsea factory.

EMPIRE AND REGENCY

EMPIRE STYLE IN FRANCE

The artistic hegemony of Rome was tested by the French Revolution of 1789. The subsequent military campaigns which transformed the face of Europe for over two decades enabled Napoleon to re-create Rome in Paris. After his successful invasion of the Papal States in 1796 he exacted tribute of a hundred works of art from Pius VI. The levies were arranged in the Louvre in 1800, along with other trophies. Bertie Greathead, one of the many English visitors who flocked to Paris during the Peace of Amiens in 1802–3, remarked that 'such an assemblage of art never existed before'. By 1815–16, it was largely dispersed.

The Borghese Vase, a renowned Greek *crater*, was sent to Paris between 1808 and 1811, having been purchased with other items by Napoleon from Prince Camillo Borghese. Paired with the Medici Vase (removed from Rome to Florence in 1780), it had been copied for garden ornaments from the mid-seventeenth century. In 1820, however, the German architect Karl Friedrich Schinkel (1781–1841) borrowed figures from the Borghese Vase for a cup of an entirely different shape. Indeed, early nineteenth-century goldsmiths throughout Europe produced miniatures which faithfully or loosely interpreted prints of vases and other objects by artists such as Piranesi.

To Napoleon, his treasures were manifestations of the might of ancient Rome with which he wanted his own empire associated. For his coronation in December 1804, the leading goldsmiths created suitably impressive plate. The trade, decimated during the Reign of Terror (1793–4), was newly revived. The old goldsmiths' guilds were

DETAIL FROM AN IMAGINARY GALLERY OF ANCIENT ROMAN ART, GIAN PAOLO PANINI, ROME, DATED *c*.1730

PENCIL DESIGN FOR A CUP IN SILVER OR GOLD, KARL FRIEDRICH SCHINKEL, BERLIN, SIGNED AND DATED 1820

WINE COOLER, SILVER-GILT, BENJAMIN AND JAMES SMITH OF RUNDELL, BRIDGE & RUNDELL, LONDON, 1810 (H33cm/13in)

legally abolished in November 1797 and a new system of marking introduced, modified versions of which were enforced in the Low Countries and in Rome during the period of French occupation. To encourage trade recovery, national exhibitions were instituted in Paris in 1798. They also gave rise to a powerful cultural establishment of jurors whose views helped to prolong the Empire style into the 1820s, when it dissolved under the international pressure of the Romantic movement.

Inevitably the French manner was emulated in many European countries, even those that were not vassal states of France. While Denmark and Norway inclined more toward England, particularly admiring the functional forms of Sheffield plate, Sweden turned to France. Despite the occupation of the Low Countries, goldsmiths such as François M. Simons of The Hague, although undoubtedly influenced by the French fashion, reinterpreted it. J.G. Dutalis of Brussels was among those more faithful to the original. Germany and Austria reflected Empire design at some distance. In Rome, two of Luigi Valadier's former assistants, G. Belli and R. Tombesi, married the Empire manner to local traditions. The Royal Factory of Spain turned out strongly ornamented Neoclassical work, as did Portuguese goldsmiths, whose work is illustrated by a large silver-gilt service presented by the Prince Regent to the Duke of Wellington in celebration of his defeat of the French. At Wellington's instigation, Portuguese craftsmen worked for a time at Garrard's of London.

LEADING FRENCH SILVERSMITHS

Jean-Baptiste-Claude Odiot (1763–1850), who had succeeded to his father's business in Paris in 1785, ceased trading during the Terror but resumed later. Like his great rival, Martin-Guillaume Biennais (1764–1843), Odiot on occasion executed plate from designs by Pierre-Paul Prud'hon (1758–1823) and the architect-designers Charles Percier (1764–1838) and Pierre-François-Léonard Fontaine (1762–1853),

acclaimed for their archaeological purism. Charles-Pierre-Joseph Normand, who engraved Percier and Fontaine's *Recueil de Décorations Intérieures* (1801), was responsible for the late eighteenth-century *Suite de Vases* and, with his son Louis, *Modèles d'Orfèvrerie*. The latter illustrated plate from the Expositions of 1819–23, which included designs by the painter Louis Lafitte for the goldsmith Jean-Charles Cahier.

The most characteristic forms of Empire silver exhibit strong profiles scarcely interrupted by disciplined ornament, sometimes polished on a matted ground, and frequently enhanced by cast sculptural elements. Its boldness derived from pre-Revolutionary plate by Robert-Joseph Auguste and his son, Henry (1759–1816). The younger Auguste used ornament that was often made independently and attached to the articles by nuts and screws, a technique adopted by many makers. Egyptian motifs – already seen on earlier Neoclassical plate – became more fashionable in the early 1800s in consequence of Dominique Vivant-Denon's *Voyage dans la Basse et la Haute Egypte* (1802). The vogue spread to other countries, including France and Germany, where in the early 1800s J.G.D. Fournie of Berlin produced a coffee pot with a lid in the form of an Egyptian bust.

Henry Auguste re-opened his workshops as the new century began and at the Exposition of 1802 was awarded a gold medal jointly with Odiot. Auguste received several major commissions for Napoleon's coronation, including a silver-gilt flagon and matching basin (now at Fontainebleau) and a large service for the City of Paris to present to the emperor. In order to complete the set Auguste adapted some items of pre-Revolutionary stock. The new work included two elaborately symbolic nefs for Napoleon and Josephine. Heavy debts forced Auguste to dispose of his models and tools at public auction at the end of the decade (many designs were acquired by Odiot). As a last triumph, he gained a gold medal at the 1806 Exposition for articles demonstrating a new application of die-stamping. This technological innovation,

probably prompted by the French adoption of Sheffield plating, was soon used by Biennais and Odiot. The latter's son, Charles-Nicolas, spent some time in London as a modeller with Garrard's, returning in about 1820 with equipment hitherto unknown in France (as well as an admiration for the relaxed shapes and naturalistic details current in England).

Biennais and J.-B.-C. Odiot were patronized not only by royals but by illustrious personages and institutions in France and elsewhere, many demanding sets of plate, preferably in silver-gilt. Both contributed to a huge service assembled between 1794 and 1814 by Prince Camillo Borghese. Biennais derived some of his designs from Percier and Fontaine, virtually replicating items executed for other commissions. Models and patterns were expensive and Odiot likewise

COFFEE POT WITH THE ARMS OF NAPOLEON I, SILVER-GILT, MARTIN-GUILLAUME BIENNAIS, PARIS, *c.*1810 (H35cm/13¾in)

reused designs: his hot-water urn in the Borghese service was duplicated with minor variations elsewhere. An amphora-shaped coffee pot by Biennais was plainly made to special commission, as Napoleon's arms, bee device and figures of Victory and Fame ornament the frieze. It probably dates to 1810, when Biennais executed a tea service at Napoleon's command for the Empress Marie-Louise. Biennais finally retired after showing a version of the Medici Vase at the Exposition of 1819.

Two oval soup tureens with figures of Victory, from a service commissioned from Odiot in 1817 by Count Nikolai Demidoff, evoke Prud'hon but were apparently designed by his occasional collaborator, Adrien-Louis-Marie Cavelier (1785–1867). Similar figures appear on two tureens from a set made in 1819 for the Polish general Count Branicki and his wife, Alexandra, illegitimate daughter of Potemkin and Catherine the Great of Russia. These splendid services attest to Odiot's continuing prosperity after the restoration of the Bourbon monarchy in 1814–15. Although Cahier, in succession to Biennais, was officially designated goldsmith to the king, Odiot was also patronized by Louis XVIII and his various relations.

The first sign that the Empire style was shedding its restraint during the 1820s was the increasing density of ornament, a trend in striking contrast to the simple shapes, almost bare of decoration, characterizing contemporary Biedermeier plate in Austria (*bieder* means plain or unpretentious; Meier is a common German surname). Josef Kern of Vienna demonstrated the French origin of the style in a tea-urn of 1820, a stripped version of a design in Percier and Fontaine's *Recueil de Décorations*. Stefan Mayerhofer's coffee machine of 1825 (Osterreichisches Museum für Angewandte Kunst, Vienna) is even more austere.

In some instances the saturation worked, as evidenced by a mirrored silver-gilt table plateau ordered from J.-B.-C. Odiot in 1825 for Dom Pedro I (1798–1834), Emperor of Brazil, and completed after the goldsmith's retirement in 1827 by his son, Charles-

OVAL SOUP TUREEN, SILVER-GILT, JEAN-BAPTISTE-CLAUDE ODIOT, PARIS, 1817 (H46.7cm/18½in)

Nicolas, working from designs by Cavelier. The figures of the Seasons were sand-cast; the gallery and other details die-stamped. Jacques-Frédéric Kirstein (1765–1838) of Strasbourg, however, preserved the old severity in a vase he designed in 1825; its frieze, representing the triumphal march of Alexander, is after the Danish sculptor Bertel Thorvaldsen.

J.-B.-C. Odiot was probably encouraged by his son to adopt a variety of Baroque-Rococo design in a service for the Duc de Penthièvre, which helped win him another gold medal in 1823. After succeeding his father, C.-N. Odiot treated the foliage ornamenting classical forms in a naturalistic manner, often introducing fruits and flowers. He showed several examples in the Exposition of 1834, together with wholly naturalistic pieces simulating plant forms. A year or so later he redeemed himself in critics' eyes by producing for Baron Salomon de Rothschild a service in the Renais-

sance style, designed by the modeller Pierre-Emile Jeannest and other artists.

Jacques-Henri Fauconnier (1776–1839), formerly head of the Odiot workshop, gained the patronage of the Duchesse de Berry. He essayed work in the manner of Percier and Fontaine in the 1820s, although he also used designs in a mixed Renaissance style by Aimé Chenevard. One of Fauconnier's chasers was Antoine Vechte. Another product of the Odiot firm, François Durand, won a silver medal for a ewer and basin in the Renaissance style in 1834; the immigrant German goldsmith Charles Wagner (1799–1841), a member of a distinguished Berlin firm, received a gold medal for his novel niello work.

REGENCY STYLE IN ENGLAND

The English were isolated from France and later the Continent by the French wars, which commenced with the declaration of war by France in 1793 and lasted with two brief intermissions until 1815. The great landowners profited from the high price of produce as the country had largely to depend on its own agriculture. Freed from the expense of dispatching their progeny on the Grand Tour, they were happy to invest some of their money in plate.

Royal patronage was of even greater importance to the leading London firms. To most it was represented by George, Prince of Wales (Prince Regent from 1811 to 1820, George IV from 1820 to 1830). An instinctive antiquary, he spent prodigally on plate. The great days of Matthew Boulton's Soho Manufactory in Birmingham were over, as neither Boulton nor his son and successor, Matthew Robinson Boulton, could compete with London for royal favour. The elder Boulton's former pupil, Edward Thomason, laboured in vain to obtain royal patronage for his Birmingham firm, while the Sheffield trade was mainly content to pro-

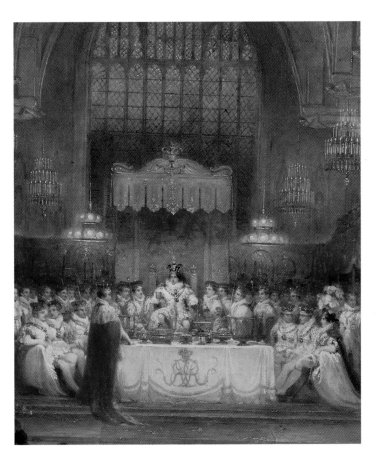

DETAIL FROM
THE BANQUET AT
THE CORONATION
OF GEORGE IV,
GEORGE JONES,
c.1821 (H109.2cm/
43in × 89.8cm/35¾in)

*George IV, seated
beneath a canopy in
Westminster Hall on
his coronation day (19
July 1821), is about to
drink the health of the
King's Champion.
Royal plate, including
two wine coolers, is set
out on the table. More
plate is piled on the
buffets behind him.*

duce standard domestic wares by machine.
London firms using similar equipment to
any extent tended to be manufacturers to the
trade, although Garrard's and Rundell's had
some machines.

Several firms in the West End of London
possessed royal connections. The retailer
Thomas Hamlet supplied the Prince of
Wales and, later, other members of the royal
family. Philip Gilbert of Jefferys, Jones &
Gilbert had been appointed 'Goldsmith in
Ordinary' to George III in March 1797.
Wakelin & Garrard, who ran a workshop
while continuing to use outworkers, from
time to time furnished the king and other
royals with plate on a modest scale. Robert
Garrard the elder took sole charge of the
firm in 1802 and was succeeded on his death
in 1818 by his sons, Robert, James and
Sebastian. Sebastian Garrard became royal
goldsmith in place of J.G. Bridge in 1843.
Garrard's was happy to open its doors to
Continental artists and craftsmen, from the

Portuguese workers who arrived during the
Peninsular War to C.-N. Odiot, c.1819–20.

In the City of London the retailers Green,
Ward & Green, although lacking the patronage of the Prince of Wales, remained an
irritant to their rival, Rundell & Bridge
(from 1804–5 to 1834 Rundell, Bridge &
Rundell) of Ludgate Hill. Appointed royal
goldsmiths in 1797, Rundell's nominally
shared the work on the royal plate with
Philip Gilbert for over 23 years, although
essentially they relegated him to the side-
lines. The two principals, Philip Rundell and
John Bridge, were jewellers by training who
used several outworkers, from the little-
known Philip Cornman to the esteemed Paul
Storr. In 1801–2 the partners persuaded
Digby Scott and his associate, Benjamin
Smith I, a chaser recruited from the Soho
Manufactory, to run a workshop for them in
Lime Kiln Lane, Greenwich. Scott with-
drew in 1807 and James Smith joined his
brother Benjamin until 1812, after which

Benjamin managed alone for two years
before removing to his own premises in
Camberwell, where he later took his son,
Benjamin II, into partnership. A second
workshop, in Dean Street, Soho, was
opened by Rundell's in 1807 and directed
until 1819 by Paul Storr in the name of Storr
& Co. Storr's departure forced Philip Rundell to register a maker's mark which was
used until 1823. John Bridge's mark was
employed from 1823 until his death in 1834.
In its final years before being dissolved in
1842–3, the firm produced plate that was
executed mainly by William Bateman II and
John Tapley & Co.

John Bridge, a brilliant courtier and
salesman, also looked after the firm's artists,
as did his nephew, John Gawler Bridge,
who joined him in about 1804. The sculptor
William Theed (1764–1817), Rundell's chief
artist until his death, was closely involved in
the practical realization of his models. He
was succeeded by the far more prestigious
John Flaxman (1755–1826), who in 1799
was proclaimed by the poet and dramatist,
Schiller, as 'the idol of all the dilettanti' for
his published line illustrations of classical
authors. Flaxman's drawings were represented in both English and French libraries,
as were Thomas Hope's *Household Furniture
and Interior Decoration* (1807) and d'Hancarville's catalogue, compiled in 1766–7, of the
vases and other antiquities collected by Sir
William Hamilton.

D'Hancarville's remarkable longevity is
evident in the Etruscan Revival of the 1840s
to 1870s. Stuart and Revett's *Antiquities of
Athens* (1762) was still consulted by Regency
goldsmiths, and Piranesi's *Vasi* (1778) was
cherished in many workshops. Besides etch-
ing the Borghese and Medici vases, Piranesi
also recorded (and restored) the Warwick
Vase (now in the Burrell Collection, Glasgow), excavated in 1771 and eventually sold
to the Earl of Warwick. As the earl long
refused to allow copies to be made,
designers were dependent on Piranesi or on
popular publications such as Henry Moses'
A Collection of Antique Vases (1814). Miniature versions of the Warwick piece in the
form of cups and wine coolers, and even an

unusual tea service, were produced in silver, most notably by Paul Storr from 1812, and in Sheffield plate.

The architect Charles Heathcote Tatham (1772–1842) acknowledged Piranesi's genius in the preface to *Ancient Ornamental Architecture* (1799). He followed this with *Designs for Ornamental Plate* (1806). As he

INFLUENCES FROM FRANCE AND ANTIQUITY

Fashionable English plate of the Regency, with its marked sculptured element, although heavier, reflects French preoccupations and perhaps in some instances Parisian models, but all derive from antique

prototypes. Like their French (and English) counterparts, Rundell's redeployed many of their models. There is, nevertheless, strong presumptive evidence that members of Rundell's visited Paris in 1802–3. Flaxman, however, went directly to antiquity modifying John Shaw's design for the Trafalgar Vase, a *crater* with patriotic motifs executed

TEA SERVICE, SILVER-GILT, COMPRISING TEAPOT, ROBERT HENNELL, LONDON, 1819 (L29.7cm/11¾in) MATCHING MILK JUG AND SUGAR BASIN, CHARLES GORDON, LONDON, 1831

worked for the architect Henry Holland, Tatham probably knew the mural painter Jean-Jacques Boileau, a French craftsman recruited by Holland in about 1787 to decorate Carlton House for the Prince of Wales. Boileau probably started designing plate in the late 1790s, developing bold, controlled forms reminiscent of those of Henry Auguste; a design in the Victoria & Albert Museum is based on Auguste tureens of 1787 in the Royal Collection. The artist also derived ideas from Piranesi, Tatham, Percier and Fontaine, and Vivant-Denon. Working mainly for Rundell's by the early years of the century, Boileau was probably responsible for a tea-urn in the Egyptian style executed by Scott & Smith in 1806, as well as a sizeable group of 'Egyptian' plate in the Prince of Wales's Grand Service. A Boileau drawing of a wine cooler combines the calyx and handles of the Medici *crater* with the bacchanalian frieze from the Borghese piece. Adapted to incorporate a base with griffins derived from Piranesi, his design was first used by Rundell's in 1808–9 for a set of eight royal wine coolers.

TEA-URN, SILVER-GILT, DIGBY SCOTT AND BENJAMIN SMITH OF RUNDELL, BRIDGE & RUNDELL, LONDON, 1806 (H36.9cm/14½in)

This vase-shaped tea-urn is ornamented with winged sphinx supports in the Egyptian style.

by Rundell's from about 1806 and presented by the Lloyd's Patriotic Fund to the admirals and captains who fought with Nelson. But his book illustrations also served to decorate plate. In 1826, the year of Flaxman's death, the Ages of Gold and Silver in his *Hesiod* (1817) were reused as reliefs on a wine bucket acquired by George IV.

Queen Charlotte gave her son, by now the Prince Regent, an example of the Theocritus Cup, a silver-gilt *crater* executed by Storr for Rundell's. Preliminary designs by Flaxman are in the Victoria & Albert Museum, as well as a record drawing (perhaps by Edward Hodges Baily). The cup is a gracefully luxurious re-creation of a description from the First Idyll of Theocritus of a vessel given by a goatherd to the shepherd Thyrsis.

George IV's restless desire for ever more glamorous and elaborate plate resulted in the gilding (and in some instances, refashioning) of much royal silver. A set of four dessert stands was apparently made by Paul Storr in stages between about 1811 and 1819 and gilded in 1816. But the king's liking for novelty actively stimulated a series of stylistic experiments, including in about 1807 the Rococo Revival, exemplified by a series of tureens made between 1813 and 1820. Characteristic ingredients of the style – scrolls, foliage, shells and masks – are present in a set of four silver-gilt candlesticks of 1828. The firm's knowledge of marine Rococo was gained from its additions to the service made by Nicholas Sprimont for Frederick, Prince of Wales, in the early 1740s. Rundell's likewise experimented with Renaissance and Baroque designs and made a few pieces of chinoiserie.

Shortly after its revival, the naturalistic elements of the Rococo affected the Neoclassical manner and gave rise to a separate style. The process was well advanced when a pair of double wine coaster waggons were executed in 1829 by Edward Barnard & Sons with vines trailing around the borders.

The melding of styles started in the second decade of the century, much earlier than in France, and was exploited with relish by the retailer Kensington Lewis. The output of his most prolific silversmith, Edward Farrell, ranged exuberantly from about 1816 to 1834 over a variety of manners from the sixteenth to the eighteenth century, and also borrowed from the Chinese. Storr, who had gone into partnership with John Mortimer in 1822, possessed a number of prints covering the same period. He clearly remained in touch with new developments while Rundell's declined. He poached the sculptor Edward Hodges Baily from his old employers in 1833, thus ensuring the continuance of the sculptural tradition, while Garrard's recruited their best-known modeller, Edmund Cotterill (c.1795–1860).

The self-appointed cultural establishment formed of witnesses to the Select Committee of Arts and Manufacturers in 1835–6 was united in deploring the passing of Regency design. Its answer, like that of the French, was to call for the archaeological treatment of historic prototypes.

THE THEOCRITUS CUP, A SILVER-GILT VASE ON A STAND, PAUL STORR OF RUNDELL, BRIDGE & RUNDELL, LONDON, 1811/12 (H35.7cm/14¼in) (TOP)

FOUR ROCOCO CANDLESTICKS, SILVER-GILT, JOHN BRIDGE OF RUNDELL, BRIDGE & RUNDELL, LONDON, 1828 (H31cm/12¼in) (ABOVE)

SIDEBOARD DISH, ONE OF A SET OF THREE, EDWARD FARRELL, PROBABLY FOR THE RETAILER KENSINGTON LEWIS, LONDON, 1822/3 (Diam 46.5cm/18½in)

MID-NINETEENTH-CENTURY ECLECTICISM

The middle years of the nineteenth century saw one of the most fascinating and, at the same time, complex periods in the history of design in general, and of silver in particular. The remarkable variety of design sources to be found in the silver of this period can be explained not by reference to any single cause, however, but rather as the product of a combination of factors, all of which influenced each other to a greater or lesser extent. The result was distinctive.

ECONOMIC FACTORS

During the eighteenth century the price of silver had averaged around six shillings per troy ounce, and until the early nineteenth century this relatively high cost had restricted the market to the wealthiest members of society. As the nineteenth century progressed this situation was to change, although the uncertainties of the post-Napoleonic era led to some extraordinary fluctuations in the price of silver, and indeed of gold, before levelling during the late 1820s. With the discovery of new deposits of ore in the United States, Mexico and Australia, silver flooded the market with the result that, by the end of the century, the price had fallen to just over one shilling per troy ounce. Such a reduction is all the more remarkable considering the insatiable demand for silver in India and the increasing use of silver in photographic processes from the mid-century onward.

Labour costs remained relatively low throughout this period, even for the most highly skilled craftsmen. The price of plate was therefore determined in most cases by the value of the basic material. As prices fell, silver became accessible to a wider market. The effects of the Industrial Revolution, and of the concomitant and less publicized commercial revolution, were becoming evident in the form of a marked change in the distribution of private wealth, an explosion in population numbers and a growth in the size of the middle classes. These factors acted as a trigger for an unprecedented increase in the production of plate. Large-scale emigration created a ready market in the United States, Canada and Australia for goods imported from the homelands; and manufacturers of silver in Europe were among the beneficiaries of this spread of European culture.

TECHNICAL DEVELOPMENTS

The technique of electroplating enabled all but the poorest to afford pieces with at least the appearance of silver. From about 1800, when Alessandro Volta developed the battery, great strides were made in researching uses for electricity. Its application, so far as goldsmiths' work was concerned, was the electro-deposition of silver or gold either onto another metal (electroplating) or as a coating inside a mould so as to produce an exact replica (electrotyping). As early as 1805 Brugnatelli had plated two silver medals with gold, and the technique was actively developed by Elkington & Co. of Birmingham, who took out their first patent in 1838. The most significant breakthrough came with J.S. Woolrich's invention of a plating dynamo in 1842, the patent for which was also acquired by Elkington's. Indeed, by 1847 Elkington's had obtained a virtual monopoly of the plating industry and began to license other firms, such as Barnard & Sons in London and Christofle in Paris, to use their techniques.

LACK OF RESTRAINT

The new market for silver inevitably had an influence on design. Mr Podsnap in Dickens's *Our Mutual Friend* (1864) was typical of his time, and the description of his silver is revealing: 'Hideous solidity was the characteristic of the Podsnap plate. Everything was made to look as heavy as it could and to take up as much room as possible.' The predominant interest of the Podsnaps was the creation of a show of wealth rather than any appreciation of the intrinsic design of the objects they acquired. The aristocracy and the landed gentry, who had been the traditional buyers of silver and might have exercised a restraining influence on design, appear to have been making few large-scale purchases at this time. Most families of this status had bought their banqueting services during the Regency and were quite content to continue using them. Those that did buy new silver for their own use frequently had pieces made to match their existing services.

Dickens was not the only critic of contemporary design. John Ruskin had been equally scathing in his lecture entitled 'The Political Economy of Art', which he delivered in 1857. Referring to what was being required of the contemporary goldsmith, he said, 'You ask of him nothing but a little quick handicraft – a clever twist of a handle here, and a foot there; a convolvulus from the newest school of design – a pheasant from Landseer's game cards – a couple of sentimental figures for supporters, in the style of insurance offices – then a clever touch with the burnisher, and there's your epergne.'

It could be argued that the manufacturers themselves might have taken a lead by producing well-designed silver on their own initiative. Some of course did, but the majority did not, a fact bemoaned by Chaffers in his *Gilda Aurifaborum* (1883): 'At the present day, when such quantities of plate are manufactured of tasteless design [it is] as much the fault of the employer as the employed.'

The origins of these problems go back to a much earlier period in history, for the mid-nineteenth century represents the culmination of a process which began during the Renaissance. Up to and including the early Renaissance, goldsmithing was, as Ruskin stated, 'generally the means of education of the greatest painters and sculptors of the day', but by the eighteenth century the designer was seen as having a more elevated status than the craftsman.

During the nineteenth century the basic division between so-called 'fine-arts' and 'applied arts' was compounded by a further division of the applied arts into 'works of high art' and 'industrial or useful articles'. With few exceptions (for example, the Frenchman Antoine Vechte), the goldsmith was regarded purely as an artisan. For works of high art, manufacturers would commission designs from fashionable artists, many of whom paid little if any heed to the functional aspects of the objects or the

limitation of the material, creating sculptural designs to be made up by craftsmen whose skills they undervalued.

A different problem arose in relation to industrial or useful objects which were to be mechanically produced. All too often the designs were created with complete disregard for the capabilities of the machine, which were inevitably different from those of the craftsman. Machine production lent itself to simple, plain spun or turned shapes rather than to elaborate outlines and complex decoration, and in many cases the manufacturer had no choice but to compromise and modify the design to suit these limitations. It was not until Christopher Dresser began designing in the 1870s and 1880s that the implications of mechanized production were fully taken into account.

ROCOCO REVIVAL

The principal stylistic developments which followed a general abandonment of strictly classicizing models were predominantly revivalist and frequently eclectic. The first to emerge was a renewed interest in naturalism, closely allied to the already burgeoning revival of the Rococo. A particularly early example (1826) is the salt by John Bridge in the Victoria & Albert Museum, London, formed as a sea urchin supported on a coral stem and standing on a rock base. Pure examples of the style, however, are rarely to be found in silver. More often the style is represented by somewhat inappropriate naturalistic ornament applied to classicizing forms. This is especially noticeable in the table centre-pieces produced in the 1830s and 1840s. Frequently set on a triangular base, adorned with acanthus leaves, shells and stylized scrolling foliage, the stems are often formed as naturalistic vines, or trees decorated with ill-proportioned figures and putti. Closely allied to this use of naturalism was an interest in Renaissance ornament. The work of the Mannerist goldsmith Wenzel Jamnitzer, who cast animals and foliage from

PAIR OF CANDLESTICKS, WILLIAM PITTS, LONDON, 1809 (H33.3cm/13in)

The stems incorporate eagles and the bases include the heads of lions, dolphins and dragons. (TOP)

SILVER-GILT VASE, JOHN S. HUNT FOR HUNT & ROSKELL, LONDON, 1846 (H52cm/20½in), AND MIRROR PLATEAU, STORR & MORTIMER, LONDON, 1856 (D47.5cm/18½in)

This piece exhibits the progression from classic shapes towards a greater naturalism. (ABOVE)

COMPOTE STANDS, STEPHEN SMITH
AND WILLIAM NICHOLSON, LONDON,
1860 (H29.2cm/11½in)

*Based on 18th-century porcelain, these stands
epitomize notions of an ideal, bucolic past.* (RIGHT)

SILVER-GILT SAUCE BOATS WITH
LADLE AND SUGAR BASKET WITH
TONGS, WILLIAM SMITH, CHESTER,
1885 (H18.5/7¼in and 16.8cm/6½in) (BELOW)

life, could now be emulated not only by
casting, but also by electrotyping. Indeed, in
its most extreme form, the striving after
perfect copies of nature led to natural
objects, such as leaves, birds and insects,
being electroplated.

Also allied to the Rococo Revival was the
style frequently referred to as Old French, a
confused style that encompassed not only
elements of the Rococo, but also of the late
classical Baroque of the court of Louis XIV.

Journal of Design put it in 1850: 'All beauty of
form, all excellence of modelling, is lost in
the glitter of the metal where burnishing is
employed, and compositions that would
have been truly works of Art in bronze
become toylike when thus wrought.' Technology, some of it very new, helped to
overcome the problem. Acids and abrasives,
which create a dead, milky white surface,
were frequently used, combined with burnished areas to form a contrast. The tech-

INKSTAND, CHARLES THOMAS AND
GEORGE FOX, LONDON, 1852
(H9cm/3½in)

*Formed as a garden pond, the circular base is finely
chased with water lilies and mounted in the centre
with a cast and chased lily bud. Some of the finest
examples of Victorian naturalism were produced by
members of the Fox family who supplied a number of
the most important retail outlets of their day.*

Principal amongst its exponents was the
firm of Robert Garrard, which on the demise
of Rundell, Bridge and Rundell succeeded
first to the position of 'Royal Goldsmith' in
1830 and then to that of 'Crown Jeweller' in
1843. Whether by deliberate intent or a
whim of taste, Garrard's never generated the
same impetus in the field of design as their
predecessors. However, this did not prevent
the firm producing some magnificent pieces
of plate. Most imposing were their testimonials made in recognition of the services,
particularly the public services, of the recipient. The usual practice with such pieces
was to incorporate appropriate decoration,
allowing tremendous scope for the imagina-
tion of the designers and sculptors involved.

Equestrian and figure groups were the
most popular, although sculptural work of
this kind was open to criticism because of
the distorting effect of reflection. As the

nique of oxidizing the surface, which creates
a grey-blue-black colour with bronze-like
reflective qualities, was used to great effect
by Antoine Vechte (1799–1868) on his Titan
Vase of 1847, the pre-eminence of which was
acknowledged in the Exhibitions of 1851,
1855 and 1862.

These sculptural groups occasioned an
additional interest in Renaissance ornament
and, indeed, the employment of artists and
sculptors in the manufacture of plate was in
conception an idea which appealed to the
Victorian Renaissance man. Thus Henry
Cole, in the guise of his pseudonym Felix
Summerly of Summerly's Art Manufacturers, commissioned silver from the artist
Richard Redgrave. (Such works included a
christening mug, decorated with a frieze of
angels, a popular design which continued to
be produced for many years.) This was not a
new idea – Rundell's employed the sculptors

THE TITAN
VASE, ANTOINE
VECHTE,
LONDON, 1847
(H75cm/29½in)

*The figures are
embossed and have been
oxidized to overcome
the problems of
reflection.* (FAR LEFT)

SCULPTURAL
GROUP OF ST
GEORGE AND
THE DRAGON,
C.F. HANCOCK,
LONDON, 1875
(H70cm/27½in)

*The group has been
frosted to reduce
reflection. Much of the
modelling for Hancocks
was by McCarthy while
the designs were by
Lami, Marochetti and
Monti.* (LEFT)

John Flaxman (1755–1826), Thomas Stothard (1755–1834), E.H. Baily (1788–1867) and William Theed (1804–91); but the fact that a third party should feel the necessity to improve the work of goldsmiths indicates that the firms themselves had little artistic input at that date.

GOTHIC REVIVAL

The most significant stylistic development was the Gothic Revival, already in evidence some years earlier. The most important protagonist of the style was without doubt Augustus Welby Northmore Pugin. Discovered in 1827 in the Print Room of the British Museum by John Gawlor Bridge of Rundell's, Pugin (1812–55) was a gifted youth who also worked for Sir Jeffry Wyatville, then remodelling Windsor Castle for George IV. A notable example of his designs for Rundell's is a group of silver-gilt cups of 1826, 1830 and 1836 (see the cup by Bateman, right), their stems based on the designs of Albrecht Dürer, whose work he had been copying at the time of his first meeting with Bridge. In 1838 Pugin entered into an arrangement with the Birmingham 'Medieval Metal Worker' and manufacturer of church furnishings, John Hardman, who was to produce most of Pugin's designs. Puginesque silver continued to be made by the firm of John Hardman Powell.

Pugin, who converted to the Church of Rome in 1835, was a child of his time, a period of intense reappraisal of Christian liturgy within the Church of England and of Catholic Emancipation led by the Oxford Movement and followed by the Tractarians

SILVER-GILT CUP, WILLIAM
BATEMAN, LONDON, 1836 (H28cm/11in)

CLOCK, BAPST &
FALIZE, PARIS,
1881 (H45cm/17¾in)

*This French, Neo-
Gothic silver, gold and
hardstone clock, set
with enamels, was
designed in Louis XII
taste by Lucien Falize
II for Alfred Morrison
(Falize's greatest
English patron). The
modelling is by M.L.
Chedeville, the
goldsmith's work by
Bapst & Falize, and
the clock movement by
Le Roy et Fils.*
(ABOVE)

CLARET JUG, R.A. GREEN, DESIGN
BY WILLIAM BURGES, LONDON, 1865
(H27.9cm/11in) (ABOVE)

and the Cambridge Camden Society. The use of the Gothic style was considered not only ecclesiologically correct, being both pre-Lutheran and predating the aberrations of classicism which had turned churches into basilicas, but also essentially a British style. Despite the work of Viollet-le-Duc in France and the eccentricities of Ludwig II in Bavaria, England was the principal exponent of the Gothic, from the New Palace of Westminster to the smallest church.

The major problem faced by the Gothic revivalists in Britain was that although they had a great deal of architecture to work from, there was a singular lack of Gothic church plate as the vast majority had been destroyed during the Reformation. Pugin looked to the Continent for inspiration where the great German treasuries, such as that at Aachen, were largely intact, but followers of the Cambridge Camden Society were striving for a pure English Gothic and found their output restricted and inhibited by the tiny number of objects available as source material. As the style became popularized and played an increasingly important role in the design of domestic as well as display plate, much rather dubious 'Gothic' was produced. Such pieces were justifiably criticized as 'abominations' or 'Brummagem Gothic' by Pugin, as were many of the poor designs being imported from Italy.

Pugin himself explained the problems of such pieces in *The True Principles of Pointed or Christian Architecture*: 'Neither relative scale, form, purpose, nor unity of style, is ever considered by those who design these abominations; if they only introduce a quatrefoil or an acute arch, be the outline and style of the article ever so modern and debase, it is at once denominated and sold as Gothic' (p. 24). Since architecture was the principal source of design it is not surprising that much work relied heavily upon it for inspiration. Tea and coffee services were produced where the 'designer' had simply taken a Gothic tower and added the necessary spout or handle. The same procedure was adopted for inkstands, candlesticks and condiment sets. Dubious as such designs are, they do have a quirky charm. The same

cannot be said of the many examples where Gothic decoration has simply been added to an existing form to make it fashionable.

Pugin was invited by the commissioners of the 1851 Great Exhibition to design the Medieval Court. It is, however, not without significance that his post was taken by William Burges (1827–81) for the comparable Exhibition of 1862. In effect, the late Gothic style of Pugin, which had its roots in the fourteenth century, had been replaced by Burges's muscular interpretation of the late Romanesque/early Gothic of the thirteenth century. With even less source material to work from, such pieces became a more intellectual exercise, relying on scholarship.

In contrast to Pugin's Gothic style William Burges's plate was stronger and frequently more secular. While Pugin was content with translating architectural motifs to plate, and inventing metalwork unknown in the late Medieval period, Burges's designs are replete with iconographical and literary references to now obscure religious and mystical texts. To the modern eye Burges seems more imbued in the Medieval tradition, although his centrepiece, commissioned by the Marquess of Bute, is a crenellated disaster combining the extravagances of an eighteenth-century epergne (the use of which was in any case largely redundant by that date) with the skills of the castle architect. The piece, now in the Victoria & Albert Museum, was intended as a wedding present for Bute's friend George Breyd and made by Barkentin and Krall in 1880. As architect-designers, however, Pugin and Burges should not be considered in isolation. William Butterfield had a considerable influence in matters of design through the Cambridge Camden Society, as did George Edmund Street, who later took over from Butterfield as superintendent of the Society's plate scheme in 1856. Other designers were Sir George Gilbert Scott, who specialized in French Gothic, his pupil George Bodley, who later started the church furnishing business of Watts & Co., and John D. Sedding, whose use of naturalism was influenced by Ruskin. All designed plate for the churches they were building.

CENTREPIECE, PRESENTED BY THE
EAST INDIA CO., ROBERT GARRARD,
LONDON, 1846 (H72cm/28¼in)

craftsmen. L. Morel Ladeuil had trained in Paris before working for Elkington's, who employed the Parisian Emile Jeannest to lead their design studio and Albert Willms, who worked with J.V. Morel in London, to design Renaissance Revival models.

Great interest was shown in the major pieces produced in England during this period, in particular, the silver-gilt centrepiece designed by Prince Albert in 1842 for

ton (although by that date in the British Museum). Similarly classicizing pieces, frequently associated with eating and drinking and decorated to conform to the Bacchic festival with vines and putti, predominate in domestic plate during the second quarter of the century.

Inspiration was not confined to Europe. As travel increased and the British Empire expanded, India, the Middle East and China

SALTS, STEPHEN
SMITH AND
WILLIAM
NICHOLSON,
LONDON, 1862
(H29.2cm/11½in)

These salts are formed as cast figures of sikhs standing guard over the containers which are supported on palm trees. Each stands on a carpet-covered base and has a spoon with a palm-branch handle.

FURTHER
REVIVALS

Whilst England had been preoccupied with the Rococo and Gothic revivals, together with a developing interest in naturalism, France had in addition been pioneering Renaissance Revival pieces. In Paris, the firms of Froment-Meurice and Jean Valentin Morel were manufacturing plate influenced by the style of Fontainebleau, and the goldsmith Charles Duron produced gold-mounted hardstones in the Renaissance taste which were shown at the international exhibitions. J.V. Morel worked for a brief period in London, but by far the greatest Continental influence on English design of the period was provided by the influx of foreign

Queen Victoria, which featured four of her favourite dogs (Royal Collection).

From the 1840s onwards decoration considered appropriate to function became a feature of design. As a result cream jugs were decorated with recumbent cows and christening mugs with angels and children praying, fish carvers were pierced and engraved with fresh- and salt-water fish, and so on. Despite the prevailing taste for the Gothic, it must also be stressed that classicism prevailed for much domestic plate. Indeed, a revival of interest in Neoclassicism during the 1840s led to significant pieces of plate being produced in a taste which would have been considered unremarkable fifty years earlier. Thus at the Great Exhibition of 1851 the firm of C.F. Hancock showed a vase whose design was copied exactly from d'Hancarville's illustrations of the Etruscan vases in the collection of Sir William Hamil-

all provided sources for design. It could reasonably be said that any style of art which sprang from a culture considered at all 'civilized' was likely to be used at some point during this period. The mid-nineteenth century, however, usually mixed the various forms together, in some cases to such an extent that it is difficult to identify their precise sources. The most common approach was to embellish everything with the enduringly popular foliate and floral scrollwork of the Rococo.

It was perhaps the 1851 Great Exhibition in London which provided the supreme showcase for nineteenth-century eclecticism. The most successful of the many exhibitions of the century, with an attendance of over six million people, the goods on display represented a host of derivative styles and gave substance to the views of contemporary reformers and critics.

TRUE AND FALSE PRINCIPLES

For the British silver industry the years 1840 to 1880 marked a period of great expansion and, paradoxically, the beginning of a long, slow decline. As in so many trades in Great Britain, the expansion had been under way ever since the mid-eighteenth century, a fact confirmed by the opening in 1773 of assay offices at Birmingham and Sheffield. London aside, these two centres came to dominate the manufacture of silver wares during the nineteenth and early twentieth centuries. At the same time, the old assay offices at Dublin, Edinburgh, Glasgow and Chester continued to operate, as did those, for a time, at York, Exeter and Newcastle.

Apart from overall social and economic changes, much of the concentration of the silver trade's activities in London, Birmingham and Sheffield came about because of improved communication through the new railway system. In an age of increasing commercial enterprise, with manufacturers supplying home, colonial and foreign markets, efficient mobility was essential.

However, accelerated by a number of factors, including foreign competition and the growing popularity of porcelain and glass in place of silver, the industry's subsequent decay was inevitable, reaching its lowest ebb in the 1920s and 1930s. It was then that mass-production techniques, such as spinning (perfected in the Britannia metal trade a century before), were harnessed by some, mostly in Birmingham and Sheffield, to produce 'cobweb'–quality hollow wares. Tea sets, sugar casters and mustard pots made on this principle were certainly cheap, but manufacturers who sought to supply such goods were actually deepening the industry's problems. These men had been brought up in the days of Victorian factory building and were mesmerized by the illusion of an ever-growing market, an everlasting empire and a world of universal peace and prosperity.

A NEW AWARENESS OF ART AND DESIGN

On the threshold of this new age, as railway tracks began to connect all parts of the country and war with France was but a memory, there were those who determined to improve the public awareness of art and design. Great strides

FOUR-PIECE TEA AND COFFEE SET, CHARLES FOX, LONDON, 1836/37 (Coffee pot: 28cm/11in) (LEFT) AND A FOUR-PIECE TEA AND COFFEE SET, JAMES DIXON & SONS, SHEFFIELD, 1866/67 (coffee pot: H28cm/11in) (RIGHT)

had been made in the 1820s and 1830s in the area of factory reform and the management of the poor, so it seemed natural that the country's intellectual health should be addressed also. There followed several measures, including the appointment in 1835 of a Select Committee 'to inquire into the best means of extending a knowledge of the ARTS, and of the PRINCIPLES OF DESIGN among the People (especially the Manufacturing Population)'. The Committee's *Report*, published the following year, is a mine of information concerning the thoughts of contemporary artists, manufacturers and others on the subject. The Rococo Revival, at that time at the height of its popularity, was condemned on all sides. The architect and designer J.B. Papworth (1775–1847), for instance, blamed the overuse of asymmetrical scrolls with shells, flowers and foliage on the inability of manufacturers to copyright their designs. The absence of any protection, he maintained, induced them 'to seek a style of ornament capable of being executed with facility by workmen unpossessed of theoretical knowledge'. As if to emphasize his aversion to the Rococo Revival style, he added that it had been 'erroneously termed that of Louis XIV'.

Papworth's opinion is telling because he had once worked for Rundell's, the celebrated London goldsmiths on Ludgate Hill. That he should have disliked the Rococo so much is ironic, for at the beginning of the century it had been this firm, by the sale of second-hand silver and through its own plate-working activities, which had explored and fostered renewed interest in the style. Garrard's as much as Rundell's was to blame; both dealt in old plate, both were plate manufacturers and in 1809 both began simultaneously to produce the first reproductions of early and mid-eighteenth-century English silver. Yet it was Rundell's, with its enlightened policy of employing the best designers, modellers and craftsmen, to which several witnesses of the 1835 Select Committee referred as a worthy example. By then Rundell's was still a going concern, although barely so, all but one of the former partners having died or retired; it closed at Christmas 1843.

The Select Committee was successful in several ways, not least because it had given the subject of art and design a thorough reassessment. Indirectly, it was also responsible for the wave of interest which, activated by the considerable energies of civil servant Henry Cole (1808–82), gave birth to the Great Exhibition of 1851 and, ultimately, the South Kensington Museum (now the Victoria & Albert Museum). More immediate results, however, were the establishment of the Patent Office Design Registry, the initial Act of Parliament for which was passed in 1839, and the opening of the Government Schools of Design. It was at the first of these (located in London's Somerset House) that Christopher Dresser (1834–1904), that most original and influential of designers, began his education in 1848. Fifty years later, having published *The Art of Decorative Design* (1862), *The Principles*

of Decorative Design (1873) and *Japan: Its Architecture, Art and Art Manufacturers* (1882), he was praised by *The Studio* for his efforts in raising the national level of design, 'not by producing costly *bric-à-brac* for millionaires, but by dealing with products within the reach of the middle classes, if not the masses themselves'.

PAIR OF WINE COOLERS, SILVER-GILT, REILY & STORER, LONDON, 1845 (H38.5cm/15in)

London's workshops were already celebrated for their richly cast decorative silver by the time these coolers were made. Although their eclectic design is typical of the early Victorian period, the incorporation of mythological vignettes was traditional. In this instance, the plaques depict episodes from the tales of Bacchus and Ariadne.

A RELIANCE ON THE PAST

Not many designers working during the first fifty years of Victoria's reign were as clear-thinking as Dr Dresser. While the uncompromisingly plain wares he designed during the 1870s and 1880s for silversmiths and electroplaters, notably Elkington's, James Dixon & Sons and Hukin & Heath, enjoyed a vogue alongside the 'Japanese' goods of, for instance, the Worcester Porcelain Co., they were not to everyone's liking. In fact, the taste for the Rococo, far from withering away after the attack upon it at the Select Committee hearings of 1835, flourished with renewed vigour, especially when cunningly combined with old Baroque and eighteenth-

century Dutch styles for everything from tea sets to wine coolers. This taste for eclecticism, so carefully nurtured at Rundell's and Garrard's half a century before, now ran riot – as even the most cursory glance at *The Art Journal*'s generously illustrated catalogue of the Great Exhibition will prove.

Many of the goldsmiths' exhibits in 1851 and again at the International Exhibition in London in 1862 were breathtaking for their wonderful craftsmanship. But some visitors to these exhibitions, like the young William Morris .(1834–96), were horrified by the vulgarity of the displays. Others, like the artist Richard Redgrave (1804–88), were no less bemused, finding too many of the silver centrepieces and race cups 'treated merely as groups would be by the sculptor'; the surfaces, he observed, were overloaded with 'imitation of textures [and] laborious little-ness'. Chief among the perpetrators of this kind of work were London's leading manu-facturing and retail goldsmiths Garrard's (the Crown Jewellers since Rundell's demise), Hunt & Roskell (successors to Paul Storr's retail and manufacturing firm, Storr & Mortimer), and C.F. Hancock (a former employee of Hunt & Roskell). For their 1851 exhibit Garrard's mounted a huge show of testimonials and other large works in silver, mainly of the sculptural kind, which they had made during the previous thirty years or so. With a venerable history stretching back to the 1720s, when the business was founded by George Wickes, Garrard's intent was to flatter past clients at the same time as appealing for fresh commis-sions. One of their pieces, for instance, was a great tankard of 1846–7, which probably owed much to old German or Scandinavian vessels, many of which had passed through Garrard's own second-hand department. It was a form of outsize trophy to which they returned on a number of occasions, as with another massive tankard of 1862–3 and a third of 1888–9. As a statement of innova-tive design, therefore, Garrard's 1851 exhi-bit was all but worthless. Nevertheless, the firm was able to congratulate itself upon being awarded a Council Medal for its efforts, the jurors having declared its display, which also included jewellery, as manifesting 'manufacturing capabilities of the highest order, and an attentive study of all that can conduce to progress in this branch of national industry'.

Garrard's rivals were no less guilty of relying on the past. With the exception of Elkington's of Birmingham, patentees of the electroplating and electrotyping pro-cesses, and the Panton Street firm of Joseph Angell, all looked to their old productions to satisfy the demands of the Great Exhibi-tion. Even Smith & Nicholson, a business formerly connected to Rundell's as plate manufacturers, but now also retailers, was proud to show the Macready Testimonial which it had made in 1841 as a gift to the actor William Charles Macready. This object

typifies the early and mid-Victorian ideal of presentation plate. Although designed by Charles Grant, later to defect to Elkington's, its basic form was not unfamiliar to the Smith craftsmen; dozens if not hundreds of their centrepieces and candelabra had identi-cal triform bases embellished with similarly cast and applied anthemions and foliage. It seems likely that Grant's main contribution was the modelling of the figures, one of which, unusually, was a portrait of the recipient. Although such objects remained a staple part of the more important silvers-miths' output even after the First World War, the taste for them diminished rapidly after the 1860s. Nevertheless, some major testimonial plate was made.

SILVER INKSTAND IN THE FORM OF A DONKEY, JOSEPH ANGELL & SON, LONDON, 1842 (H19cm/7½in)

Sentimental sculptural silver for the desk and dining table first became popular during the 1820s. Silversmiths produced such objects throughout the Victorian and Edwardian periods. (ABOVE)

SILVER TANKARD, PARCEL-GILT, R. & S. GARRARD & CO., LONDON, 1846 (H50.5cm/20in)

Probably made as a racing trophy, this tankard appears to be that shown by Garrard's at the Great Exhibition of 1851. (LEFT)

THE GROWTH OF THE LUXURY TRADE

THE TAZZA OF MOORE, SILVER CUP ON SILVER-MOUNTED EBONIZED WOOD PLINTH, FROM DESIGNS AND MODELS BY RAFAEL MONTI, CHARLES FREDERICK HANCOCK, LONDON, 1864 (Overall H49.5cm/19½in) (LEFT)

KNIFE, SPOON AND PAIR OF GRAPE SCISSORS FROM A DESSERT SERVICE, SILVER-GILT, FRANCIS HIGGINS & SON, LONDON, 1863–70

The finest quality British silver spoons, forks and related table ware has always been made in London. During the Victorian period two firms in particular were noted for the excellence of their work: Chawner & Co. and Francis Higgins & Son. (BELOW)

Changes apparent in society as a whole, with rising standards of living and the greater spending power of the middle and lower middle classes, are apparent in a careful comparison between the precious metals and allied sections of the 1851 and 1862 exhibition catalogues. Large works by the leading firms, exemplified by Hancock's group of five silver cups nobly dedicated to the 'Poetry of Great Britain' and made from models, ironically, by the Italian sculptor Rafael Monti (1818–81), were still plentifully represented at the exhibition of 1862. On the other hand, the demand for small silver and silver-mounted wares and rich patterns in silver spoons and forks, the latter a specialist branch of the trade, was clearly on the increase.

By a curious chance of history, the manufacture of silver spoons and forks, with knives as a secondary branch, has for centuries been concentrated in London. With the encouragement of Rundell's and Garrard's customers at the beginning of the nineteenth century, these workshops, among them Eley, Fearn & Chawner, became the acknowledged masters of their craft. A series of retirements, bankruptcies and takeovers in immediate pre-Victorian times left only a few principal firms, chief of them being Chawner & Co. (absorbed by Holland, Aldwinckle & Slater in 1883), and Francis Higgins & Son. Although both Chawner's and Higgins's were renowned for the excellent quality of their work, some of the most interesting was carried out by the latter. In the 1840s and 1850s, for instance, Higgins's issued many unusual naturalistic novelties which were so lavish that the design completely subsumed the form. One of these charming objects, a parcel-gilt caddy spoon, was shown at the Great Exhibition. Its handle and bowl were

made to resemble water weeds caught on the edge of a shell. The *Art-Union* magazine (later *The Art Journal*) in 1848 praised the firm's productions as 'remarkable for their elegant simplicity, or elaborate and rich workmanship; manufactured too at a price which brings them within the reach of a class not absolutely wealthy'.

But over the next forty years or so manufacturers and designers of spoons and forks, not least Higgins's, began to lose their way. Traditional patterns, such as Fiddle and Old English, were joined by many others, from the attractive or merely pedestrian to the bizarre. Among the latter must be the salad servers with silver bowls and coloured porcelain lobster-claw handles that formed part of Rowland Ward's mounted lobster-shell table service made for the Fisheries Exhibition, South Kensington, in 1883. Operating from fashionable Piccadilly premises known as 'The Jungle', Ward was

a taxidermist who built a career on the spoils of birds and animals. Silver-mounted horse-hoof inkstands and deer-feet candlesticks were some of his best-selling lines – hardly surprising in a country where many more besides 'the upper ten thousand' were devotees of field sports.

The nineteenth-century luxury trade, of which Rowland Ward's was an example, flourished in London as nowhere else in the world at that time (except, perhaps, Paris). Ever since the middle of the previous century, Birmingham had been known for its silver and plated snuff-boxes, buttons and other small wares, but the best quality in such items had always been made in London. More specifically, the workshops of Soho and some in Clerkenwell threw their energies behind supplying the growing number of retail houses – many of which were fancy goods sellers as well as goldsmiths – clustered in Mayfair and Belgravia and along Piccadilly, Regent Street and Oxford Street. In spite of fluctuations caused by several financial depressions, the Victorian and Edwardian periods were exceptionally kind to this type of business. Jenner & Knewstub of St James's Street and Jermyn Street; Asprey & Co. and Walter Thornhill & Co. of Bond Street, and Payne & Son of Lowndes Street were just a few of the better-known retailers.

DESIGN FOR
SILVER-MOUNTED
NOVELTY,
PROBABLY FROM
THE WORKSHOP
OF T.W. DEE &
SONS AND
SUCCESSORS
H.W. & L. DEE,
LONDON, THIRD
QUARTER OF THE
19TH CENTURY

*These designs are from
a collection of several
hundred drawings.*

THE INDUSTRY
ABROAD

Competition for British silversmiths from abroad during the period 1840 to 1880 was certainly a reality, although not yet a serious threat. The political upheavals in both France and Germany at this time hampered expansion there until matters became more settled in the 1870s. In France, as had always been the case, the centre for the silver and jewellery trades was Paris. With few exceptions,

Probably the most accomplished small silver workers and gold and silver mounters working for these firms were H.W. & L. Dee of Soho. A collection of many hundreds of designs believed to have come from them were sold by Sotheby's in 1991. The drawings, a number of which were highly finished, showed great variety in their repertoire of mounted objects, from velvet purses, ladies' leather belts and chatelaines, to glass inkstands, claret jugs and *carte-de-visite* frames. Dee's must have had a reputation second to none within the Victorian goldsmiths' trade but the firm was certainly not alone, since the demand for high-class novelties of all kinds was able to support several dozen such businesses, both in London and Birmingham.

George Betjemann & Sons, dressing-case makers and small silver workers, supplied goods to retailers all over the country, but were eventually all but absorbed by Asprey. Barkentin & Krall, a firm with Scandinavian origins, almost failed as general silversmiths until becoming specialists in ecclesiastical work. Whether they tried this line because of various commissions received from the architect William Burges (1827–81) is not known; he designed an extraordinary group of vessels for them to make for his own use, including a silver-mounted abalone-shell dish paid for from fees received for his work on St Faith's, Stoke Newington, in 1872.

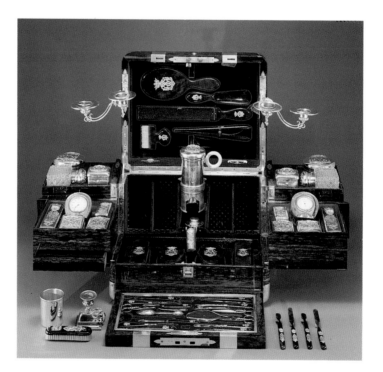

VELVET-LINED
CALAMANDAR
DRESSING-CASE
WITH SILVER
AND SILVER-
MOUNTED CUT-
GLASS AND
TORTOISESHELL
FITTINGS, THE
CASE WITH
RETAILER'S
LABEL *W.
THORNHILL 144
NEW BOND
STREET*, THE
FITTINGS
LONDON AND
PARIS, 1881 and
circa

The relationship between these and other such manufacturing firms and their retailers has only begun to be investigated within the last few years, largely in an effort to unravel the confusion caused by the so-called maker's mark which, in many instances, is no such thing. In former times this mark was also known as a name or owner's mark; under the provisions of the 1975 Hallmarking Act it is now more reasonably known as a sponsor's mark.

Parisian workshops specialized in pieces of the finest quality and also special commissions, as demonstrated by the output, for example, of F.-D. Froment-Meurice's firm or that of Rudolphi. Christofle et Cie, the equivalent of Birmingham's Elkington & Co., was founded in 1830 and grew to be France's largest manufacturing silversmiths and electroplaters. The industry in Germany, on the other hand, was very different, chiefly because it had no major centre until a

FOUR-PIECE TEA AND COFFEE SET, ELECTROPLATE, STAMPED *DESIGNED BY DR. C. DRESSER*, HUKIN & HEATH OF BIRMINGHAM, *c.*1880 (Coffee pot: H18cm/7in)

Christopher Dresser was praised by The Studio *for his efforts in raising the national level of design, 'not by producing costly bric-à-brac for millionaires, but by dealing with products within the reach of the middle classes, if not the masses themselves'. Unfortunately, the call for such refreshing new designs from the British silver industry was swamped by a growing demand at the end of the last century for 'Queen Anne' coffee pots and 'Adam's' salt cellars.*

very late period. As in Paris and London, the better firms congregated in the capital city; and Berlin supported a number of manufacturing-retail businesses such as Sy & Wagner, goldsmiths to the King of Prussia. German mass-production wares, however, were usually cheaper than those from Sheffield or Birmingham. Die-stamping and spinning were extensively used to produce light-weight goods. By the late 1870s manufacturers in the United States, many established in New York and Providence, Rhode Island, began for the first time to challenge their European counterparts. Encouraged by their government's new system of tariffs as well as a genuine interest in good design, some American companies amazed observers in London and Paris by the beauty and quality of their work. This was particularly true of the inlaid and coloured silver goods inspired by Japanese metalwork which Tiffany & Co. sent over for the Paris Exposition of 1878.

CONCLUSION

To any student of English silver, this complex period was one of increasing and unceasing activity. Silversmiths and their contemporaries in allied trades had never known a more commercially fruitful time. But there was an underly-

ing weakness, the foundations of which had been laid many years before, when goldsmiths, encouraged by a growing number of customers enthralled by styles of the past, began to manufacture reproduction wares. The industry's potential vitality, expressed briefly in wares made to Christopher Dresser's refreshing new designs, was eventually dissipated as batch- and mass-production was strangled by demands for 'Queen Anne' coffee pots and 'Adam's' salt-cellars.

PAIR OF CIGAR LIGHTERS, SILVER-GILT, THOMAS WILLIAM DEE & SONS, LONDON, 1866 (H16.5cm/6½in)

Given as a wedding present in 1866 to the Earl of Sefton by Albert Edward, Prince of Wales (the future Edward VII), these lighters are fine examples of the luxury goods in silver for which London was famous the world over. T.W. Dee & Sons were jewellery mounters, enamellers and specialist smallworkers in gold and silver who supplied the better firms in London's West End.

AMERICAN SILVER

A discussion of silver in the American colonies must acknowledge at the outset that precious metals were the very impetus for colonization. The earliest settlement in Virginia was peopled not by farmers and yeomen, but by gentlemen and aristocrats hoping North America would yield silver and gold as South America had done for Spain. Economically and stylistically, American silver developed in the image of its European, usually English, models. Numerous immigrant silversmiths provided stylistic tutelage in American workshops. Customs records leave no doubt that English silver was imported to the American colonies in substantial quantities, often retailed by American silversmiths. French silver and craftsmen were particularly influential in the classical period, when trade restrictions with Britain no longer applied to a newly independent country.

Throughout the eighteenth century, silver, largely an urban luxury, was produced mainly in three silversmithing centres: Boston, New York and Philadelphia. The fourth major city, Charleston, in South Carolina, was reliant on a planter economy; credit with London brokers made it simpler to purchase English silver. In the early 1800s Baltimore grew to majority as an urban centre hosting notable silversmiths, but was the last city to do so before manufacturers and retailers marketed nationally, and all but replaced workshop silversmiths. In the second half of the nineteenth century, international exhibitions informed American styles. The Arts and Crafts Movement briefly redirected the limelight back to the craftsman, but never to the exclusion of factory-made silver.

COFFEE POT, MARK OF TIFFANY AND COMPANY, NEW YORK, 1856–59 (H27.3cm/10¾in)

The use of a new technique, acid-etching, permitted innovative effects. Here the anthemia are depicted in positive and negative fields, that is, engraved on a smooth background, and defined in contrast to an etched background.

127

The goldsmiths and refiners who sailed on the first English ships for Virginia had little impact during the early years of colonization in seventeenth-century America, but within a few decades the services of their professional descendants were needed in colonies further north. This was not in order to refine and process ore, but to fashion objects for those colonials grown wealthy enough to store and enjoy their assets in the form of plate.

Silver was a practical and enjoyable repository for one's assets. Apart from their beauty and social status, silver vessels had an additional advantage as they could be redeemed for cash almost instantly at the nearest silversmith's shop. Furthermore, they were less vulnerable to burglary than a bag of coins, not only because of their more cumbersome size, but also due to the personalized engraving that adorned a large percentage of such pieces. Silversmiths were aware of the advertised descriptions of stolen silver, and were likely to apprehend the miscreant bringing them such items for cash. In comparison with land or business investments, where speculation could spell disaster, silver was a much safer and more accessible investment.

American silversmiths were not subject to the regulations of the Worshipful Company of Goldsmiths in London, but as a group they tended to abide by the guild's sterling standard throughout the eighteenth century. Because there were no assay offices in the colonies, only the maker's touch identifies most American silver prior to the nineteenth century, making dating less specific than was the case with British silver. In the nineteenth century an alloy known as 'coin' was also employed, consisting of 90 per cent silver and the remainder copper, the same alloy as coinage. The words coin, dollar, standard and premium, or the letters C or D, indicate this standard. Electroplated silver, offering the appearance of silver at considerably reduced cost, was available in the 1840s and thereafter. Nineteenth-century silver will frequently bear a retailer's mark in place of, or occasionally in addition to, a maker's mark.

MANNERISM

The earliest period of American silver, the seventeenth century, dates from the age of late Mannerism in Western fine and decorative arts. Anglo-American Mannerism was heavily reliant on northern European sources, Netherlandish in particular. Thus the style is readily identifiable in silver from both New

CAUDLE CUP, MARK OF JOHN CONEY, BOSTON, c.1690–1700 (H14cm/5½in)

John Coney was among the most talented and versatile silversmiths active in the colonies in the 17th century.

England and early New York (then known as New Amsterdam), where goldsmiths are documented by the mid-seventeenth century. The earliest works to survive are from a partnership in Boston, that of John Hull (1624–83) and Robert Sanderson (1608–93). A dram cup with their mark, dating from about 1651, presents attenuated twisted wire handles and chased panels of floral decoration that allude to more sophisticated grotesque ornament popular in Europe.

The term 'grotesque' originates from ornamental schemes discovered in the Roman emperor Nero's pleasure palace, the Golden House, dating from AD 64 and excavated in the late fifteenth century. Its vaulted rooms, deeply buried and therefore known as grottoes or caves, were highly decorated – the walls and ceilings were covered with fantastic creatures amid foliage and architectural ornament, tightly controlled in geometric compositions. The style came to be called grotesque in reference to its cave-like origins, and was embraced by artists for its decorative qualities. The grotesque gave licence to interpret nature rather than imitate it, encouraging the draughtsman to stylize foliage into ornamental compositions.

Both Hull and Sanderson had learned their craft in England, before emigrating to America in the 1630s. As Boston's founding silversmiths, they trained a number of the most significant artisans of the succeeding generation. A caudle cup marked by one of their apprentices, John Coney (1655/56–1722), and made in about 1690–1700, displays the attenuated caryatid handles and imaginative foliate composition found in Mannerist-influenced English silver of the Restoration period. Particularly droll is a cherubic creature emerging from the centre of a flower. Such two-handled cups were used for caudle, a thin porridge with sugar, spices and wine or ale, although they were undoubtedly employed for other foods and beverages as well.

Tankards, cups, spoons, beakers, porringers and jewellery were the most common incidences of silver among the 5 to 10 per cent of the population rich enough to own plate in seventeenth-century New England.

The tankard was a commodious drinking vessel for cider or ale, of large cylindrical form with a hinged lid and a substantial, curving handle. An example from about 1690–1700 has the characteristic drum shape, narrow baseband, corkscrew thumbpiece and flat cover of the early Boston genre. Marked by the German-born silversmith, William Rouse (1639–1709), it is distinguished by its engraving, an unidentified armorial in a scrolled acanthus sur-

land from the Mohawk Indians in 1685, and this beaker was in all likelihood an expression of his grateful thanks to Sanderson. The fantastic allegorical scenes engraved around it were copied from a collection of prints by Adriaen van de Venne (1589–1662), published in Amsterdam in 1655. The scenes in foliate wreaths represent Integrity (the ermine starving rather than discolouring his coat in the ring of surrounding mud), Industry (geese in a marsh) and Virtue (a

TANKARD, MARK OF WILLIAM ROUSE, BOSTON, c.1680–92 (H19.4cm/7⅝in)

Less than a dozen objects are known with Rouse's mark. This tankard is the outstanding member of the group and displays all the attributes of the finest Boston tankards of this period. (BELOW LEFT)

TWO-HANDLED BOWL, MARK OF CORNELIUS KIERSTEDE, NEW YORK, 1700–10 (H13.7cm/5⅜in, D25.4cm/10in) (BELOW)

round, and a carnation engraved on its lid. Rouse, a native of Wesel, came to Boston in the 1670s, possibly via England.

By contrast with Boston silver, plate from the Dutch colony of New Amsterdam (which became New York in 1664) was less conservative in its decoration. Early New York tankards frequently have bands of stamped and cut leafage around their base mouldings, and engraved lids, some with inset coins. The Dutch penchant for engraving in early New York silver is best appreciated in a tall beaker from 1685, perhaps the outstanding example of Mannerism in early American silver. Marked by Cornelius van der Burch (c.1653–99), the beaker is engraved with the date 1685 and the name of its recipient, Robbert Sanderson [sic], who served as interpreter for the Commissioner of Indian Affairs, Robert Livingston. The commissioner had procured a large tract of

vase of flowers). Above the scalloped baseband Magnanimity is symbolized by a serpent coiling around the legs of a stork, clutching in its beak a lizard who eats a spider (each animal stronger than its victim); Humility by a tortoise in the clutches of an eagle about to be dropped on the rocks below; and Faithfulness by a crocodile who defies Death on his back.

Another New York silver form reliant on Dutch examples is the two-handled bowl, or *brandewijnskom*, used for serving a brandy and raisin beverage on ceremonial occasions. The finest surviving example, marked by native-born Cornelius Kierstede (1674–1757), has the typical six-lobed shape adorned with chased floral panels. While its handles, in the form of caryatids, and stylized foliage remain Mannerist, the boldness of the chasing suggests the influence of the Baroque.

BEAKER, MARK OF CORNELIUS VAN DER BURCH, NEW YORK, 1685 (H20.3cm/8in)

MONTEITH,
MARK OF JOHN
CONEY, BOSTON,
c.1700–10

MONTEITH,
MARK OF JOHN
CONEY, BOSTON,
c.1700–10
(H21.9cm/8¾in,
D27.3cm/10¾in)

*Only two examples of
this form are known in
New England silver of
this period. The other,
also marked by Coney
and virtually unadorned,
contrasts with this
bowl, considered the
outstanding example of
American Baroque
silver.*

CHOCOLATE POT, MARK OF EDWARD
WINSLOW, BOSTON, 1700–10
(H23.2cm/9⅛in)

*This is the finest of three surviving chocolate pots in
the Baroque style, all of which are based on English
models. Engraved with the Hutchinson arms, it is
thought to have belonged to Thomas Hutchinson, a
wealthy merchant and civic leader.*

THE BAROQUE STYLE

The Baroque style transformed American silver at the end of the seventeenth century, introducing vigorous, sculptural ornament densely ordered in symmetrical compositions. The Mannerist penchant for chased and engraved grotesque ornament in panels or strapwork was supplanted by fluted surfaces and cast elements. The best of these pieces proclaimed the stature of their owners with an arresting monumentality. Such adornment added considerably to the cost of a vessel, but by 1700 Boston society boasted more than a few wealthy enough to imitate London fashions. For the successful merchant John Coleman, silversmith John Coney supplied a stunning punch bowl in the new and fashionable monteith form. Named after the Scottish earl whose scalloped cape hem resembled the rim, the monteith was described as 'a vessel or bason notched at the brims to let drinking vessels hang there by the foot, so that the body or drinking place might hang into the water to cool them' (quoted in Ward and Ward, eds., *Silver in American Life*, p.141). The masterpiece is taut with suspended motion, expressed in the tight gadrooning around its foot, and the reflective fluting of its bowl, which opens into a sumptuous brim of scrolling arches and urns crested with cherubic masks. The great drama of the piece derives from its magnificent cast lion's-head handles. So closely does Coney's achievement resemble the examples produced by English silversmiths during this period that one wonders if he employed a journeyman fresh from one of the London workshops.

The fluted and gadrooned surfaces and weighty cast and chased decoration characteristic of Baroque silver were introduced to English silver by French Huguenots, Protestants fleeing religious persecution under Louis XIV. Colonial American silversmiths adopted the style from English examples, favouring in general the less expensive and less challenging fluted decoration to more complex schemes. More typical of American Baroque silver than the Coney monteith is a chocolate pot dating from about 1700–10 and marked by Edward Winslow (1669–1753). By 1700 affluent American colonists had adopted the new custom of drinking exotic beverages. Tea from the Orient, coffee from the Middle East and chocolate from Central and South America had inspired new forms for their service. Chocolate pots are considerably rarer in American silver than those for tea or coffee, and are distinguishable from coffee pots only by their removable finials, which permitted the insertion of a stirring rod. The Winslow teapot has a chain to retain its removable finial. The teapot's curved surfaces are enhanced by fluting, animating the form and accentuating its volume. Applied sheet silver ornament, known as cut-card work, adorns its lid and spout, further references to the Baroque embellishment which was introduced into London silver by Huguenot craftsmen.

If most American Baroque silver relied on fluting to convey the style's sculptural vigour, a few pieces like the Coney monteith attest to the opulence attainable for wealthy

patrons. Another such piece is the sugar box marked by Edward Winslow and made for Lieutenant-Governor William Partridge of Massachusetts in 1702. Sugar was an expensive luxury, often eaten as a stimulant accompanying liquor before the fashion for tea and coffee. Perhaps because of sugar's consumption during courtship rituals, sugar boxes seem to have been symbolic of love, marriage and procreation; most surviving examples were presented as wedding gifts. This box was Partridge's gift to Daniel Oliver and his wife Mary Belcher on the occasion of their son's birth in 1702. Amid its rich Baroque fluting and acanthus decoration, typical of the genre, are iconographic symbols of chivalry and love – the mounted knight on the locking hasp and the circlet of myrtle on the lid. Winslow marked three other similar boxes, and a total of nine are known, all from Boston. These may perhaps have been inspired by the example brought by Elizabeth Glover from London to America in 1638, along with her collection of plate, and described as 'a great siluer trunke with 4 knop to st[a]nd on the table and with suger' (quoted in Fairbanks and Trent, eds, *New England Begins: The Seventeenth Century*, pp.370–71).

THE QUEEN ANNE STYLE

The Baroque was succeeded by a simpler, more restrained taste in silver, named after the monarch with whose reign it coincided in England – Queen Anne. It became popular in American silver in the 1720s, after the queen's death. Form and proportion took precedence over ornament, and the latter was usually limited to a restrained and elegant passage of engraving. Two teapots, one from New York and one from Boston, portray the apogee of the style for that form. The New York example, marked by Peter Van Dyck (1684–1751), was known as an 'Eight Square Tea-pot' when it was made in about 1720–35. Octagonal forms were popular in Queen Anne silver, as were smooth expanses, and curves balanced by reverse curves, all seen in the illustration above. Pear-shaped teapots, whether or not 'eight square', remained fashionable in New York after they had been discarded in Boston in favour of globular or apple-shaped pots, a form derived from English

SUGAR BOX, MARK OF EDWARD WINSLOW, BOSTON, 1702 (H14cm/5½in)

This sugar box is among the most ornate of the nine known from this period, all from New England. Its rounded casket shape, stepped lid and swirled fluting are typical of the genre. (ABOVE LEFT)

TEAPOT, MARK OF PETER VAN DYCK, NEW YORK, c.1720–35 (H18.1cm/7⅛in)

In March, 1727, a New York newspaper announced a lottery, for which one of the prizes was an 'eight square' teapot. This pot, admired for its elegant proportions, is the only example of the form to survive. (ABOVE)

SUGAR BOWL, MARK OF SIMEON SOUMAINE, NEW YORK, *c*.1738–45 (D11.9cm/4$\frac{11}{16}$in)

By this date, sugar was widely available and lockable boxes were no longer required.

TWO-HANDLED COVERED CUP, MARK OF JACOB HURD, BOSTON, 1744 (H38.3cm/15$\frac{1}{16}$in)

examples, which in turn were copies of Oriental prototypes. An example of the apple-shaped teapot is that marked by Jacob Hurd (1703–58) and made for Boston wine cooper James Townsend (1699–1738). The teapot displays masterful engraving of the Townsend arms in a Baroque mantle. An inscription below the armorial records the vessel as 'The Gift of James Townsend to Reb Mason 1738 [sic].' (Rebecca Mason was Townsend's half-sister.)

A similar marriage of form and ornament is encountered in a sugar bowl marked by New York silversmith Simeon Soumaine (1685–1750) for Elizabeth Cruger, whose initials form the engraved ciphers on the body and lid. The form itself was known in imported Chinese porcelain examples. Copying the circular perfection of the potter's facility at his wheel is more challenging with hammers, however, and Soumaine's effort is one of the masterpieces of American Queen Anne silver. The reel shape of the lid not only repeats the foot rim, but also serves as a foot for the cover of the sugar bowl which, when upended, cleverly doubles as a small tray.

Exquisite proportions also set apart a two-handled covered cup, marked by Jacob Hurd and presented to Edward Tyng, commander of the ship that vanquished a French privateer in the first naval battle of King George's War in 1744. The cup was commissioned that same year by a group of grateful Boston merchants. Tyng's award is a masterful composition of curves and reverse curves. The domed lid repeats the movement of the base; and the graceful scroll handles balance the height, as does the girdling midband. The engraved cartouche bears an inscription about the event amid a mantle of military regalia. Such cups were also known as 'bishops', for the spiced wine and citrus drink imbibed from them. Tyng's bishop was among the most monumental silver forms of its period, standing over 38 cm (15 in) in height, and yet remains the most graceful of its genre. It is an apt illustration of the American preference for silver as a medium for presentation objects, from the early days of settlement to the present.

TEAPOT, MARK OF JACOB HURD, BOSTON, 1738 (H14.6cm/5$\frac{3}{4}$in)

Apple-shaped teapots such as this one were derived from English examples, which in turn copied Oriental prototypes. A prolific maker, Jacob Hurd marked some of the finest silver of his time (see two-handled cup, above).

THE ROCOCO STYLE

By the late 1740s the Rococo taste began to influence American silver, at first in the asymmetrical cartouches engraved on Queen Anne forms, but by the 1750s in form and decoration as well. The Rococo was a renegade style defying conventional axioms of symmetry and order. Naturalistic ornament abounds, unfettered by restrictive compositional boundaries. Such asymmetrical compositions were intended to surprise and delight the eye grown jaded with regulation and composure in design. Mature Rococo silver relied on additional ornament – chasing, piercing, casting and engraving – as well as modifications to forms, and was therefore quite expensive. Not everyone could afford to indulge in its excesses, and simpler pieces continued to be made throughout the third quarter of the eighteenth century. Considering its additional cost, it is not surprising that the majority of the finest American Rococo silver forms are those devoted to the service of tea and coffee, prestigious social rituals. The third silversmithing centre, Philadelphia, asserted its superiority in this period over Boston, now in economic decline, and New York. Philadelphia was the largest and richest city in the colonies in the years prior to the Revolution, so it follows that much of the finest Rococo silver came from its shops.

A coffee pot-on-stand by Philadelphia silversmith Richard Humphreys (1750–1832) is a statuesque example of the double-bellied form preferred for tea and coffee accoutrements in the mature Rococo taste. This elegant, gravity-defiant profile was further dramatized when elevated on a stand, often ordered *en suite* for tea or coffee pots, but rarely surviving so. Handsome armorial engraving enhances both pot and stand, probably the work of a contracted engraver. Regrettably the arms, unidentified, have yet to shed light on the pot's original ownership.

The fullest expression of the Rococo style in silver called for repoussé decoration, known as chasing in period accounts, and requiring the services of a specially trained silversmith, the chaser. Such a specialist was undoubtedly employed by Joseph Richardson (1711–84) to decorate the magnificent teakettle-on-stand he supplied to the Plumsted family sometime around 1750. The quality and variety of the decoration suggest that the unknown craftsman was 'lately from London', from a workshop such as that of Paul de Lamerie, a hotbed of high Rococo silver design. The outstanding American expression of Rococo silver, the teakettle is alive with movement and feral drama. Faces, paws and plumage emerge from flowers and C-scrolls that bedeck the body and stand. The kettle's double C-scroll feet, a motif repeated in the handle, suggest a visual dance that is only restrained by

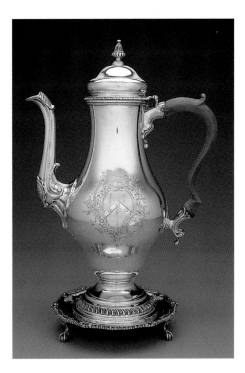

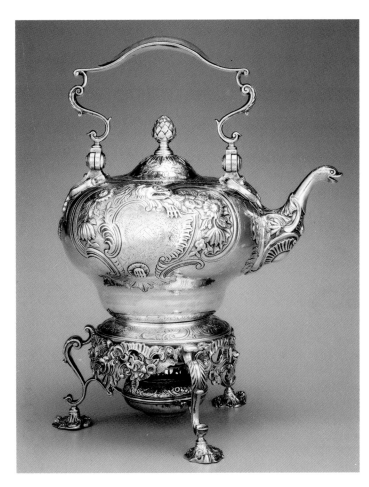

COFFEE POT ON STAND, MARK OF RICHARD HUMPHREYS, PHILADELPHIA, 1770–80 (H34.6cm/13⅝in, stand D17.2cm/6¾in)

At least in the thriving city of Philadelphia, records of imports of English silver leave no doubt that stands routinely accompanied teapots and coffee pots. The practice is not so easily documented in less prosperous Boston. (ABOVE)

TEAKETTLE ON STAND, MARK OF JOSEPH RICHARDSON, PHILADELPHIA, 1745–55 (H37.5cm/14¾in) (LEFT)

BASKET, MARK
OF DANIEL
CHRISTIAN
FUETER, NEW
YORK, 1754–69
(L37.8cm/14⅞in)

*Luxury forms such as
this basket are
exceedingly rare in
American silver. Only
two Rococo examples
survive, both made in
New York, along with
most of the pierced
silver of this period,
suggesting the existence
in New York of an
immigrant piercer from
one of the specialized
London workshops.*

flattened shell feet firmly anchoring the kettle in place. The decoration and composition of the piece argue for a hand more fluent in such work than that of Richardson, who apprenticed with his father in Philadelphia and was unlikely to have had sufficient experience with such ornament.

The contribution of foreign craftsmen is more easily identified in a basket bearing the mark of Daniel Christian Fueter (1720–85), who settled in New York in 1754. Born and trained in Bern, Switzerland, Fueter worked in London for two years before crossing the Atlantic. He was among the few foreigners who succeeded in opening his own shop, a move usually blocked by domestic silversmiths, who effectively controlled patronage; most foreigners worked as journeymen or even indentured servants for American smiths. Fueter may even have been the foreigner responsible for introducing the Rococo style to New York, since his arrival in 1754 predates any documented examples of New York Rococo silver. His basket could easily be mistaken for a London example; its elaborate piercing and castings are unrivalled in American silver of the period. The female masks on the handles are among the few incidences of human figural references in American Rococo silver.

EARLY NEOCLASSICISM

Economic hardships accompanying the American Revolution interrupted the full development of the Rococo style, and by its conclusion in 1783, the prevailing taste was Neoclassical. With its relentless symmetry and ornamental restraint, the style was in marked contrast to the vigorous Rococo, a new expression for a new country, and its roots in Graeco-Roman democracy only enhanced its appeal to citizens of the newborn republic. Classical shapes, fluting and reeding, and delicate engraved garlands – all in strictly symmetrical compositions – characterized the style. The American interpretation continued to rely on British example, in turn inspired by artists' and architects' renderings of the arresting discoveries at Herculaneum and Pompeii in the 1740s and 1750s. These excavations and others offered the first glimpses of Roman artefacts and domestic architecture. Their impact on designers, most notably the Englishman Robert Adam, resulted in an age of Neoclassicism.

Equally revolutionary, but uncelebrated

by comparison, was the introduction of new technologies in silver production. The Industrial Revolution was a snowball that began its descent in the late eighteenth century. By this period, rolling mills made sheet silver of uniform gauge available to silversmiths, relieving them of the first of several stages in their production process. For some forms this even alleviated the raising process, allowing the smith to fashion certain shapes by seaming sheet silver instead of laboriously hammering it up from the flat. The resulting reduction in cost facilitated greater consumption: silver services, almost unknown in the Rococo period, now became frequent residents of sideboards and tea tables.

A tea and coffee service marked by Christian Wiltberger (1766–1851) of Philadelphia includes a coffee pot, teapot, cream pot, sugar dish and slop bowl, all of fluted urn shape on pedestal feet. The initials of the service's owners, Bernard and Mary Raser, are framed in central laurel wreaths below borders of classical medallions, all in bright-cut engraving, a technique employing faceted, reflective incisions. The elevated urn shape of the Wiltberger tea and coffee pots is typical of Philadelphia silver of this period and contrasts with the compact, drum-shaped teapots favoured in New York and Boston. Although absent here, galleried rims frequently adorn the Philadelphia vessels, another regional characteristic.

A contemporary service from Boston marked by Paul Revere (1735–1818) typifies the style in New England silver. Made for John and Mahitabel Templeman in 1792, the service is one of the most complete to survive, and among the most extensive recorded in Paul Revere's daybooks, which listed a teapot and stand, tea caddy, sugar urn, cream pot, punch strainer, tea shell, six tablespoons and twelve teaspoons. The fluted oval forms of both caddy and teapot are associated with Boston Neoclassical silver, and were copied from imported English silver or Sheffield plated wares. New York examples are typically of similar shape but without fluting, and have higher lids rising from a concave shoulder band.

BASKET, MARK
OF SIMEON
BAYLEY, NEW
YORK, 1790–95
(L35.2cm/13⅞in)

*The angular shapes and
repetitive decoration of
this basket are in
contrast to those found
on its earlier Rococo
counterpart (see p.
134). (ABOVE)*

TEA SERVICE,
MARK OF PAUL
REVERE,
BOSTON, 1792
(Sugar box:
H24.4cm/9⅝in, teapot
L28.6cm/11¼in)

*Better known as the
patriot who, in 1775,
alerted the countryside
to the advance of
British troops prior to
the first skirmish of the
American Revolution,
Paul Revere was among
the most successful of
Boston silversmiths,
working in both the
Rococo and
Neoclassical styles.*
(ABOVE)

A particular style of engraved cartouche also distinguishes early Neoclassical New York silver, as seen on a basket marked by Simeon Bayley (*fl.*1784–99) and made for Edward and Mary Dunscombe. The swagged ermine drapery and streamers enclosing their initials comprise a design found repeatedly on silver by New York makers of this period and, like the fluted forms in Boston, was copied from English sources, in this case armorials. The basket itself, of angular shape and precise foliate piercing, contrasts with the earlier Rococo example by Daniel Christian Fueter.

TEA AND COFFEE SERVICE, MARK OF
CHRISTIAN WILTBERGER,
PHILADELPHIA, 1790–1800 (Coffee pot:
H35.5cm/14in, waste bowl D17.5cm/6⅞in)

*Philadelphia's penchant for ornament, undoubtedly a
reflection of the city's wealth, continued, even in the
more restrained Neoclassical taste.* (ABOVE)

TEA AND COFFEE
SERVICE, MARK
OF SIMON
CHAUDRON AND
ANTHONY
RASCH,
PHILADELPHIA,
1809–12 (Coffee
pot: H33cm/13in)

*The exquisite detail on
this service, and its
animal motifs, bespeak
its origins in the
workshop of French
emigrés.*

MATURE
NEOCLASSICISM

After the turn of the century, more extensive archaeological evidence contributed to more accurate renderings of classical forms and motifs. A predictable shift in taste also favoured increasingly vigorous, dramatic forms in the wake of restrained Adamesque elegance. Large firms, marketed by retailers in various cities, began to overshadow local workshops and the majority of fine silver from this period came from New York and Philadelphia. A tea and coffee service from around 1810 by the Philadelphia partnership of Simon Chaudron (1758–1846) and Anthony Rasch (1778–1857) exhibits the full shapes, ornamental bands and sculptural castings that identify mature Neoclassical silver. Animal motifs figure prominently in

this style, as seen on the spouts, ram's-head masks and hoof feet. The incurving triangular bases of the pieces are also signature elements, as are the stepped concave lids and bud finials. The sudden phenomenon of horizontal bands of ornament, seen here on the bases and shoulders, resulted from the invention of stamping mills that supplied such decoration by the roll. The service was ordered by Philadelphian George Mifflin Dallas, probably for his marriage to Sophia Nicklin in 1813, and may have been among the last commissions of the partnership, which separated in 1812. French-born Chaudron came to Philadelphia from Santo Domingo in 1793 or 1794, and advertised French silver plate among his wares. Bavarian-born Rasch was originally his indentured servant, and in due course became a partner in the firm from 1809 to 1812.

Chaudron was among the émigré craftsmen responsible for the direct French influence visible in this period, a predictable

result of close ties during the Revolution and open trade between the two countries thereafter. Such an influence is particularly evident in a pair of Philadelphia sauce boats marked by his colleague, Anthony Rasch, probably after the partnership, between 1812 and 1820. The extensive use of animal motifs, particularly the coiling serpents, relates the boats to French Empire silver. The vessels invoke drama and suspense as the snake leers threateningly toward the ram's-head spout. Diminutive winged-lion feet and a plinth with egg and dart decoration complete the classical vocabulary of the serving forms.

Presentation silver was especially prominent in this era, a taste fuelled by the war with England and an increasingly prosperous citizenry who rewarded naval heroes with silver. Among the firms specializing in such commissions was that of Philadelphians Thomas Fletcher (1787–1866) and Sidney Gardiner (d. 1827). The partnership

PRESENTATION VASE, MARK OF THOMAS FLETCHER AND SIDNEY GARDINER, PHILADELPHIA, 1824–5 (H60.3cm/23¾in)

SAUCEBOAT, MARK OF ANTHONY RASCH, PHILADELPHIA, c.1815 (L28.4/11³⁄₁₆in)

This sauceboat and its pair are among the most beguiling examples of American silver in the French Neoclassical taste. (BELOW)

was awarded the commission of a pair of monumental vases by a group of New York merchants for the state's governor, De Witt Clinton, in 1824. The vases celebrated not naval glory, but mercantile genius. Clinton had championed the Erie Canal, which channelled lucrative trade from the Midwestern states into New York City, making it the largest city in the United States by 1830. Fletcher and Gardiner modelled the presentation gift after one of the most famous classical icons of the time, the Warwick Vase, an antique marble excavated from Hadrian's Villa in 1770, and often copied in English silver. Fletcher, designer of the vases and probably the firm's principal designer, undoubtedly viewed some of the British versions during his eight-month sojourn in England in 1815, buying plate and visiting prominent silversmiths.

Weighing over 400 ounces (nearly 11.5kg) each and standing 60cm (2ft) in height, the vases differ from the antique original in

their smaller scale, the treatment of the base, the substitution of American scenes and the addition of covers with eagle finials. Views of the canal and allegorical representations of the arts and sciences fill the decorative panels. The addition of covers places them firmly in the two-handled covered cup tradition of American presentation silver, and suggests comparison with the Tyng cup, the most monumental form of its period eighty years earlier. The vases were presented to Governor Clinton in 1825.

That same year Clinton was the recipient of yet another masterpiece of Neoclassical silver when the citizens of the state, expressing their gratitude for the canal, presented him with a table plateau, marked by New York silversmith John W. Forbes (1781–c.1864). Just as Fletcher and Gardiner's interpretation of the Warwick Vase was entirely English in derivation, so the plateau was wholly French in inspiration. Although uncommon in American silver, the plateau

had become popular in French Empire table settings, and Forbes presumably copied a Parisian example when he made two of these grand centrepieces. Virtually identical, the other example was owned by the Hunter family of New York and now resides in the White House. Both are more than 150cm (5ft) in length and comprise three mirrored sections to reflect the service pieces and candlesticks placed thereon. Each plateau is rimmed by a pierced gallery of stamped ornament: winged lions and classical vases amid fruit and foliate borders. Resembling a reflective pool with a surrounding balustrade, each plateau is supported by six plinths resting on lion-paw feet, surmounted by American eagles and adorned with the figures of Pomona, goddess of the orchard, and Flora, goddess of flowers. Used to create a tablescape of watery reflections, flowers and fountain-like candelabra, these extravagant forms suggest the influence of formal garden design.

THE ROCOCO REVIVAL

Neoclassicism was succeeded by a move away from order and symmetry toward more romantic, picturesque modes. With advances in technology and the development of a consumer economy, the traditional dominance of a style cycle for two to three decades gave way to a panoply of choices competing for a patron's dollars. Fashion still dictated a preferred taste, and orchestrated a rough

Rococo ornament on silver in the second decade of the century, not long after the taste was revived in England. If not the innovator, Kirk certainly popularized his heavily decorated version – curvaceous, swollen forms virtually covered with repoussé ornament, that is, chasing applied from the interior and exterior of the vessel. Other silversmiths in Baltimore also worked in the genre; indeed the 'elaborate' type was known in the period as 'Baltimore silver' despite its manufacture in other cities.

The style gained a national following in the 1830s and retained it well into the 1850s. Outstanding examples of Kirk's interpreta-

ated, most of their expanses laboriously covered with repoussé flowers, C-scrolls, fantastic creatures and exotic Oriental landscapes. The intertwining C-scroll handles are cast as foliate vines supporting a bird at the lower handle juncture and a reclining hound at the upper terminal. They are also taller and more massive than their eighteenth-century counterparts. Even apart from the magnified drama of presentation silver witnessed in the Neoclassical period, American silver increased in scale and sets grew more numerous as a rising middle class amassed greater wealth, while technology and mass-production lowered costs.

PAIR OF EWERS,
MARK OF
SAMUEL KIRK,
BALTIMORE,
1830–46
(H42.2cm/16⅝in)

Primarily decorative in function, these ewers are archaic revivals of an earlier form that traditionally accompanied basins, and was employed to rinse greasy fingers between courses before the advent of forks in the 17th century.

chronology, but there was considerable overlap, and the remainder of the nineteenth century hosted a succession of revival styles. The Rococo, so antithetical to classical order, was revived as early as the 1820s in Baltimore, one of the last great eastern seaboard cities to develop. A thriving, expanding port in the early nineteenth century, Baltimore attracted numerous silversmiths, one of whom, probably Samuel Kirk (1793–1872), reintroduced chased

tion of the Rococo Revival are a pair of ewers predating 1846, the year his son joined the firm. Their exuberance far exceeds that of eighteenth-century American Rococo silver, an exaggeration typical of the nineteenth-century revival styles. Although of double-bellied Rococo form, they differ from the typical eighteenth-century version, with the upper belly mounted much higher and appearing as a swollen shoulder. No portion of their surfaces remains undecor-

KETTLE ON STAND, MARK OF BALL, TOMPKINS & BLACK, DESIGNED BY JOHN CHANDLER MOORE, NEW YORK, 1850 (H43.9cm/17⁵⁄₁₆in)

The industrial revolution, largely a 19th-century phenomenon, transformed the life and economy of Western cultures, which responded by taking stylistic refuge in historical revivals. This Rococo Revival kettle is an ironic tribute to one of the greatest technological advances of the age, the telegraph.

Rococo Revival silver was not unique to Baltimore; other manufacturers were quick to adopt the taste, but with less intensive decoration. A kettle-on-stand from 1850 is a fine example of the style outside Baltimore and suggests an intriguing comparison with its counterpart of *c*.1750 by Joseph Richardson (see p. 133, below). Designed by John Chandler Moore (*fl*.1827–51) for the New York firm of Ball, Tompkins and Black (*fl*.1839–51), the kettle stands more than 7.5cm (3in) taller than the earlier one. In addition its shape is more exaggerated, creating a repetitive, curvaceous profile, and the decoration is looser and more florid. Moore produced at least four such kettles; this one is distinguished by the figure of Zeus as the finial. The iconography of the god holding a lightning bolt was a reference to the innovation of the telegraph. The vessel was part of a service presented to the president of the New York and New England Telegraph Company, Marshall Lefferts, by the Associated Press, a newly founded consortium of six New York newspapers for, according to the inscription, 'advancing the cause and credit of the Telegraph System, the noblest enterprise of this eventful age' (Warren, Howe and Brown, *Marks of Achievement*, p. 93). In addition to the finial, the cover sports a gallery of telegraph lines and poles, and Zeus triumphs with an eagle over scenes of a train and a sailboat, slower forms of communication.

THE GOTHIC REVIVAL

Contemporary with the Rococo Revival was another romantic style, the Gothic Revival. Primarily an architectural style of the 1840s and 1850s, the Gothic had limited influence on the decorative arts in North America, far less than the Rococo Revival, for example. It was favoured for ecclesiastical silver, such as the silver and enamel chalice and paten made

for Trinity Church, New York, in about 1855, and marked by the New York partnership of Francis W. Cooper and Richard Fisher (*fl*.1855–62). The church had just commissioned a new chapel designed by the noted Gothic Revival architect Richard Upjohn, and the chalice and paten were ordered for its use. The design of these pieces is derived from Medieval prototypes but, like the Rococo Revival kettle-on-stand by Ball, Tompkins & Black, is more exaggerated in form and decoration.

Although never a widespread choice in domestic hollow ware, the Gothic Revival style was apparent in flatware patterns. By the mid-nineteenth century, machine technology permitted flatware to be stamped and drop-pressed, thus greatly speeding production, lowering costs and allowing any number of different patterns to be used. Designs and forms multiplied accordingly, and a guest at dinner was likely to find a bewildering array of spoons, knives, forks and serving cutlery, specialized for every course, a puzzle of etiquette, and all part of a massive flatware service.

THE RENAISSANCE REVIVAL

In the 1850s, as the Rococo once again outgrew favour, a taste for classicism re-emerged, only in this case based on Italian and French Renaissance sources. Designers raided the vocabulary of the first classical revival of the sixteenth and seventeenth centuries for compositions which, in their elaboration and combination of ornament, are unerringly nineteenth-century in appearance. Renaissance Revival silver was

CHALICE AND PATEN, MARK OF FRANCIS W. COOPER AND RICHARD FISHER, NEW YORK, *c*.1855, SILVER, SILVER-GILT AND ENAMEL (Chalice: H24.8cm/9¾in)

Scenes from the life of Christ are alternately engraved and enamelled in exquisite detail on both chalice and paten. The paten is actually of tazza form on a broad, circular foot with a stem and knop similar to those on the chalice.

FRUIT STAND,
MARK OF
GORHAM MANU-
FACTURING
COMPANY,
PROVIDENCE,
RHODE ISLAND,
1866
(H42.6cm/16¾in)

*'We arrived here at 9
o'clock this morning, all
is well, Thank God.
The cable has been laid
and is in perfect
working order.' So was
worded the first
transatlantic telegram
on 28 July 1866, sent
from England by the
cable's promoter, Cyrus
Field. This stand
commemorated the
realization of Field's
twelve-year dream.*

WATER JUG AND
STAND, MARK OF
SAMUEL KIRK
AND SON,
BALTIMORE, 1879
(Jug: H33.7cm/13¼in)

*Both the design and
ornament on these pieces
are traceable to 17th-
century sources, but the
elaboration of
decoration is a 19th-
century phenomenon.*

exhibited at the Crystal Palace Exhibition in London in 1851, with a considerable influence on American manufacturers. A return to classical urn shapes, adorned with masks, medallions, French Renaissance strapwork and classical borders, characterized silver of the 1860s and 1870s.

A fruit stand made in 1866 by the Gorham Company of Providence, Rhode Island, exemplifies the finest American interpretations of the style. The stand copies the form of a Renaissance tazza, an elevated serving vessel. A caryatid in classical drapery supports the bowl, which is flanked by cherubs. Portrait medallions adorn the base of the vessel, depicting Cyrus Field, recipient of the stand, and George Peabody, the donor, who presented it to Field in commemoration of his role in completing the transatlantic telegraph cable in 1866. Peabody's banking business in England benefited considerably from the cable. The Gorham Company, founded in 1831, was among the first silver companies in the nineteenth century to become mechanized, and it grew to be one of the largest silver firms in the world by 1900.

More illustrative of the French Renaissance strain of the Renaissance Revival style is a water jug and stand from 1879 by Samuel Kirk & Son, chased in the Kirk tradition of repoussé ornament. Differing from Kirk's earlier Rococo Revival expressions, the ornament here is symmetrical and ordered, if prolific. The stylized foliage and grotesque figures call to mind the Mannerist style which decorated the earliest American silver of the seventeenth century (and with good reason, since late Renaissance Mannerist ornament provided source material for Renaissance Revival designers as well). The most compelling aspect of the jug is its intriguing design, the spout and handle formed by an arching dolphin harnessed by the faun below. Martin Chapman has identified the source of the design, a print in *Livre de Vases* by the seventeenth-century French designer Jacques Stella (1596–1657).

Not all Renaissance Revival silver was so French in inspiration. A coffee pot (see p.126) made by Tiffany & Company in the late 1850s recycles antique vocabulary from

Greek precedents. The amphora-shaped body is decorated with a frieze of mounted horsemen and chariots similar to that on the Parthenon. Anthemion borders complete the vessel's decorative scheme, while the lid is surmounted by a helmet. The surface texture of the vessel was achieved with a new technique, acid-etching, which left a pitted, matt surface in contrast with burnished areas. Although Greek in inspiration, Tiffany titled the pattern Etruscan, evidence of the loose interpretation of terminology when marketing took precedence over historical accuracy. Tiffany was founded in 1837 by Charles Lewis Tiffany, and by the 1850s was a leading manufacturer of fine silver, hiring renowned designers and entering international expositions. By the end of the century their only rival in size and quality was the Gorham Company.

THE AESTHETIC MOVEMENT

As the pendulum of taste again swung clear of classicism in the late 1870s, it moved into a style altogether new in Western art, embracing the asymmetry and organic motifs of Japanese art. Conceived as a reform style in reaction to overly ornate preceding styles, it was called the Aesthetic Movement because of its emphasis on the aesthetic importance of domestic articles. The style was inspired by the opening of Japan to Western trade in 1854. Oriental art was not a new influence in Western decorative arts, but the primary sources in previous centuries had been Chinese and Middle Eastern artefacts. Occidental audiences were introduced to Japanese art at the 1862 International Exhibition in London, but American participation in the style was delayed by the Civil War. The Centennial Exposition in Philadelphia in 1876 effectively initiated the taste in the United States. The Japanese exhibit there was lauded as 'so subtle, free, and varied in decorative expression, so full of delicious

TILTING WATER SET, MARK OF SIMPSON, HALL, MILLER & CO., CONNECTICUT, *c*.1891, SILVER PLATE AND PORCELAIN (H60.3cm/23¾in)

PITCHER, MARK OF TIFFANY AND COMPANY, NEW YORK, *c*.1878, SILVER WITH COPPER AND GOLD (H22.5cm/8⅞in)

coquetries and surprises, that it never becomes stale or monotonous' (Ward and Ward, *Silver in American Life*, p. 177).

Some of the finest American silver in the Aesthetic taste differs from its British counterparts in the application of mixed metals, copied from Japanese example. While the regulatory guild in London did not permit the application of base metals to sterling standard plate, American silver manufacturers were not so constrained, and introduced copper and brass, as well as gold. A pitcher by Tiffany & Company of 1878 exemplifies the outstanding effects attainable with such a 'palette' of metals, as well as the naturalism characteristic of the *japonesque* style. Flora and fauna are depicted realistically, enlivening the piece with suspended motion. The dragonfly is airborne; the fish has just emerged from the waters; the reed appears to be growing up the neck of the pitcher. The effect is quite different from that of stylized ornament, which is governed by

the shape of a vessel and manipulated to adorn specific spaces. Equally novel is the surface treatment, rippling with hammer marks in imitation of sand-cast Japanese bronzes. The inspiration for such designs was provided by Oriental artefacts collected by the company and its chief designer, Edward C. Moore (1827–91). Tiffany exhibited a number of wares in the new style, including a pitcher of the same design, at the Paris Exposition of 1878, earning the firm considerable European acclaim. Gorham, Tiffany's major competitor, was equally active and accomplished in the Aesthetic style, although they did not exhibit at the 1878 exposition.

Not all Aesthetic Movement silver was as pure in its *japonisme* as the pitcher. Frequently Japanese motifs were combined with other elements, as seen on an electroplated tilting water set from about 1891, which mingles Egyptian sphinxes, camels and pyramids, as well as classical nudes and masks, with Japanese iconography. Such stylistic mixtures were more common in electroplated silver, designed for the broadest possible range of tastes. The process was far less labour-intensive than the fused plating or Sheffield process previously in use. Electroplated silver was first produced in the United States in the 1840s and was extremely popular with a burgeoning middle class anxious to acquire the accoutrements of the affluent. The mass marketing of this silver substitute included the use of trade catalogues; Simpson, Hall, Miller & Company illustrated this set in their 1891 catalogue for $56, roughly one-quarter of its price in solid silver (Ward & Ward, *Silver in American Life*, p. 82).

The set, originally fitted with two goblets, is an apt illustration of the plethora of highly specialized forms that characterized silver production in the second half of the nineteenth century. The tilting water set kept the contents cool in a double-walled porcelain vessel, and its self-contained pouring mechanism appealed to a society intrigued with mechanical devices.

While Japanese art was the chief influence in the Aesthetic Movement, other exotic Oriental cultures also held sway, as seen in the use of Egyptian motifs on the water set. Islamic art was a further variation on the theme, particularly influential for coffee services, and the elongated neck and spout of the Turkish coffee pot became a familiar form in the 1880s. Persian- or Turkish-style coffee sets were often highly ornate, embellished with enamelling and mounted stones. A Tiffany set from 1901 is intriguing for its combination of decorative techniques in both Islamic and Russian styles, an apt illustration of the eclecticism that emerged in the last quarter of the century.

THE COLONIAL REVIVAL

Contemporary with the Aesthetic Movement was a growing awareness of Colonial American artefacts. The 1876 Centennial Exposition in Philadelphia effectively launched the Colonial Revival, arousing enormous interest in the country's history. The earliest examples of Colonial Revival silver, patterned after eighteenth- and early nineteenth-century styles, date from the 1870s. It was a style that used a minimum of applied ornament and relied upon classic forms rather than decoration. The fashion gained popularity throughout the last quarter of the century, at first produced with standard mechanized techniques, and later, during the Arts and Crafts Movement, by hand, imitating process as well as style. A tea and coffee service from about 1885, by Black, Starr & Frost of New York, relates to earlier mature Neoclassical forms from about 1810 with classical shapes and reeded decoration, but betrays itself with telltale differences in scale and production. The tea- and coffee-pot shapes are more elongated than they would have been originally, particularly in their peaked lids. The thinner gauge of the silver and the stamping of the repoussé decoration betray mechanical production techniques. Colonial Revival silver has never gone out of production since the late nineteenth century, and remains popular today.

ECLECTICISM AND OTHER STYLES

Several factors contributed to the ever increasing array of choices confronting the late nineteenth-century silver patron. Reduced costs associated with mechanization, as well as the development of marketing and advertising, encouraged the consumer to update his silver more often

COFFEE SERVICE, MARK OF TIFFANY & CO., NEW YORK, *c.*1903, SILVER-GILT AND ENAMEL, AMETHYSTS (Coffee pot: H28cm/11in)

TEA AND COFFEE SERVICE, MARK OF
BLACK, STARR & FROST, NEW YORK,
c.1885 (Kettle: H27cm/10⅝in)

*A Colonial Revival service such as this one offered the
consumer a more sober alternative to sybaritic coffee
services in exotic styles, in an age when the moral role
of domestic art and artefacts was a subject of serious
consideration.*

and indulge in a variety of styles. Celtic
strapwork was part of a strain of Nordic
ornament employed at Tiffany – representing yet another romantic or exotic culture
with which to tantalize buyers. Their most
famous piece in this mode is the massive
Viking punchbowl, 51.4cm (20¼in) in diameter, made for the World Columbian
Exposition in Chicago in 1893, and now in
the collections of The Metropolitan
Museum of Art.

Sometimes current events inspired special
designs. A Gorham ice bowl with polar bear
handles is modelled as an iceberg, not merely
as a reflection of its function, but also in
reference to Antarctic expeditions and The
acquisition of Alaska in 1867. Gorham
introduced this design in 1870, and it
remained a top seller for 15 years (S.J.
Hough, 'The Class of 1870 Gorham Sterling
Ice Bowls, *Silver*, vol. 22, 1989, pp.30–33).
The bowl, which was accompanied by tongs
in a distinctive harpoon design, is another
example of a specialized vanity form. Ice was
a decidedly American luxury until the development of mechanical refrigeration in 1888.
A Bostonian had perfected techniques for
profitably shipping and storing ice, and it

ICE BOWL AND
TONGS, MARK OF
GORHAM MANU-
FACTURING CO.,
PROVIDENCE,
RHODE ISLAND,
1872 (H18.4cm/7¼in,
L28.5cm/11¼in)

*As increased travel
raised society's collective
consciousness of distant
places, Americans were
fascinated with
references to such lands,
whether to northern
climes or Oriental
meccas.*

became a fashionable accompaniment to
beverages that drew compliments from
European visitors.

The taste for exotic or romantic cultures
extended even to Native American motifs.
The American Indian became an increasingly romanticized icon once he ceased to
threaten the dominant white culture. Sou-
venir spoons were the most prolific occur-
rences of Indian-style silver, but Tiffany

produced some stunning designs in hollow
ware. Such silver was praised in Europe for
being 'essentially and wholly American'
(Carpenter, *Tiffany Silver*, pp.205–07). A
bowl by Tiffany is a beguiling imitation of an
Indian basket, 'woven' in copper and silver,
with turquoise-mounted handles. It was
exhibited at the Paris Exposition Universelle
in 1900 and at the Pan American Exposition
the following year in Buffalo, New York.

VASE, MARK OF TIFFANY & CO.,
NEW YORK, 1900, SILVER WITH
COPPER AND TURQUOISE (H19cm/7½in)

*American fascination with exotic cultures did not
overlook indigenous, native American-Indian motifs.
Pieces such as this were highly praised on the continent
as refreshingly American and non-derivative of
European styles.*

influencing the silver market and the plethora of styles available was the price of silver itself. The discovery of the Comstock Lode in Nevada in 1859 and other silver mines in the west added vast amounts of silver to the country's supply, effectively lowering the price. As a result of this democratizing phenomenon, silver for the upper classes became grander and grander, either in numbers or size. Enormous dinner services were made at Tiffany and Gorham, including hollow ware as well as flatware. Perhaps the most dramatic illustration of the increasing size of silver objects is in the realm of presentation silver. The price of silver decreased at the same time that enormous

NAVAJO
LEATHER BELT
WITH CONCHOS,
ARIZONA,
*c.*1910–20,
SILVER AND
TURQUOISE
(L120cm/47¼in)

*The Navajo silver
industry, founded to
cater to the tourist
trade, continues to
thrive for the same
reasons today.*

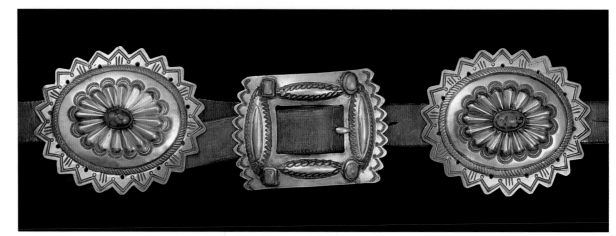

Although based on Indian designs, it bore no relation to Native American silver, which was far simpler.

Silver was introduced to American Indians by Europeans, but it was not embraced as a strong craft tradition until the late nineteenth century. The Navajo of the Southwest learned silversmithing from Mexican craftsmen in about 1860, and the craft soon spread to other tribes in the region. The Southwest tribes specialized in jewellery – belts, bracelets, necklaces and adornments – for which a thriving tourist trade soon developed. By 1900 silversmithing had become a full-time occupation for many Indians, who produced increasingly ornamental, turquoise-laden designs for

white patrons. Traders encouraged the cottage industry, providing tools and even commercial stamping dies after 1920. For their own use, the native Indians preferred less elaborate compositions, like concho belts. A favourite form adapted from Mexican silverwork, the belt consisted of several circular or oval conchos (from the Spanish *concha*, for 'shell') which were strung on a leather thong. Stamped or punchwork decoration, simple castings and mounted turquoise are characteristic of Navajo work. More elaborate use of turquoise dates from the 1920s and after, and distinguishes trade jewellery (Ward and Ward, *Silver in American Life*, pp.20, 116–19).

Another highly significant factor

fortunes were made in oil, railroads and other new industries, enabling a *nouveau-riche* elite to proclaim their new status with massive silver objects. Indeed, commemorative trophies could measure more than 60 cm (2ft) in diameter.

An apt example is a presentation plaque given in 1884 by a group of businessmen to James J. Hill for masterminding the bridge spanning the Mississippi River and linking Minneapolis and St Paul. Made by Tiffany & Company, the plaque weighs over 500 ounces (around 14kg) and measures some 86cm (34in) across. By virtue of its lobed shape and sculptural rim decoration, it appears at first glance to be Rococo Revival. A closer inspection reveals Renaissance

PRESENTATION
VASE (TO
EDWARD DEAN
ADAMS), MARK
OF TIFFANY &
CO., DESIGNED
BY PAULDING
FARNHAM, NEW
YORK, 1893–5,
GOLD, QUARTZ,
ROCK CRYSTAL,
PEARLS,
GARNETS,
TOURMALINES,
AMETHYSTS,
ENAMEL
(H49.5cm/19½in)

*Despite the European
styles manifested in this
vase, its commission was
emphatically patriotic.
An accompanying
booklet published by
Tiffany noted that
'every piece of material
used, and the artist and
his principal assistants,
are American, which
shows an independence
that many countries in
the old world might be
proud of'.*

from bankruptcy. Commissioned in 1893, the vase was not completed by Tiffany & Company until 1895, requiring the services of 3 draughtsmen, 15 modellers, 18 goldsmiths, 21 chasers, 12 finishers, 4 moulders, 3 turners, 2 enamellers, 3 stonecutters and 2 lapidaries (Warren, Howe and Brown, *Marks of Achievement*, p.146; Metropolitan Museum of Art, *Nineteenth-Century America*, p.281). The vase was designed by Tiffany's chief designer, Paulding Farnham, with references to more than one style: its classical urn shape and allegorical figures characterize the Renaissance Revival, while scrolling leafage suggests the Rococo and the mounted stones and enamelling recall Islamic-style services. In form the piece remains the two-handled covered cup that characterises presentation tradition.

THE ARTS AND CRAFTS MOVEMENT AND ART NOUVEAU

The movement for reform from ostentatious design began in the 1880s with the Aesthetic Movement. The cause was taken up with greater vigour in the Arts and Crafts Movement, which gained momentum in England in the last quarter of the century, eschewing machinery and mass-production in favour of the revival and preservation of handicraft traditions. These ideals, with some modifications, took root in the United States in the 1890s, and were in full bloom by the early 1900s. The tenets of simple, straightforward designs derived from nature, the use of honest, sincere materials, and quality craftsmanship did not dictate a particular style. Indeed, in France the movement was associated with Art Nouveau, a curving, sensual style never fully embraced in the United States.

Some of the earliest American silver in the

Revival elements as well, particularly the portrait medallion of Hill at the top. Indeed the rim is composed of intricately cast trophy heads of northwestern game, symmetrically arranged to punctuate vignettes from Hill's life. The use of animal iconography and the ordered placement also suggest the Renaissance Revival style. At the base of the design is a cipher of Hill's initials, woven in amongst the vines, which is more suggestive of the Rococo. The face of the plaque is exquisitely engraved and applied with sheet silver to depict a view of the bridge and Minneapolis. Tiffany's bill for this custom commission included $2,975, just in labour, at an average of 42 cents per hour (F.J. Puig, J. Banister, G.W.R. Ward and D. McFad-

den, *English and American Silver in the Collection of the Minneapolis Institute of Arts*, Minneapolis, 1989, pp.294–5).

In a competition of such conspicuous consumption, however, gold outranked silver, no matter how large the latter. Gold was rarely worked in the solid by American silversmiths, except for small personal items like jewellery, buttons, snuff-boxes and medals. Gold hollow ware is extremely rare and one of the largest examples known is also the outstanding example of its genre, presentation silver. The Adams Vase was the gift of the Board of the American Cotton Oil Company to their chairman, Edward Dean Adams, who worked without compensation to rescue the firm successfully

MONSTRANCE, MARK OF ARTHUR STONE, GARDNER,
MASSACHUSETTS, 1909, GOLD WITH AMETHYSTS, DIAMONDS,
PEARLS, GARNET, CRYSTAL (H39cm/15⅝in) (RIGHT)

MARTELÉ MIRROR, MARK OF GORHAM MANU- FACTURING COMPANY, PROVIDENCE, RHODE ISLAND, 1899 (H59.1cm/23¼in)

According to the company's archives, only two mirrors of this type seem to have been made. This example was a custom commission, ordered through the New York retailer, Theodore B. Starr. (RIGHT)

Arts and Crafts Movement was Colonial Revival in design, wrought by New England silversmiths copying their forebears. Evidence of the movement's widespread influence came in 1896 when the Gorham Company, one of the largest silver companies in the world and a fully mechanized one, decided to hire traditional silversmiths to produce a line of hand-wrought silver. The company selected Art Nouveau for the line as a fresh, new style that was not imitative but progressive, and named it Martelé (French for 'hammered'). Martelé was entirely handmade, raised and chased by various silversmiths, and therefore quite expensive. A dressing mirror from 1899, for example, required 327¼ hours of labour, 80 hours by the initial silversmith who crafted the basic form and a staggering 240 by the more specialized and highly paid chaser, who added the sinuous repoussé ornament; it

sold for $450 (discounted from $500) to a New York retailer, Theodore B. Starr. The line was successful despite Americans' basic mistrust of Art Nouveau lawlessness; indeed Martelé silver and Tiffany glass are almost the sole bastions of American Art Nouveau design. Of the nearly 4,800 Martelé objects recorded in company archives, only two such dressing mirrors are listed.

The Arts and Crafts Movement not only emphasized handcraftsmanship, but revered as well the workshop artisan, making and marking his or her own wares in small studios. Numerous such silversmiths flourished in this period; one of the most talented was Arthur J. Stone (1847–1938) of Gardner, Massachusetts. Stone was born in Sheffield, England, and trained in traditional silversmithing there and in Edinburgh, before emigrating to America in 1884. He employed several assistants and worked in

various guises of Arts and Crafts style, from Colonial Revival to Gothic to more progressive designs. While most Arts and Crafts silversmiths did not distinguish themselves as virtuoso craftsmen when judged by pre-industrial standards, Stone was the exception. His monstrance, made in 1909 for Boston's Church of the Advent, is an exquisite technical and aesthetic achievement. A sacred repository for the Eucharist, the vessel was designed by Frank E. Cleveland of the architectural firm Cram, Goodhue & Ferguson, noted for their Medieval designs, and hired by the church to complete its interiors. Stone and his assistants crafted the masterpiece in gold, mounted with 9 amethysts, 87 diamonds, 2 pearls, garnet and crystal (Warren, Howe and Brown, *Marks of Achievement*, p.139).

More typical of the movement's signature simplicity and rejection of elitist materials is

a covered standing cup, marked by the Petterson Studio of Chicago and dating from about 1912–14. John Pontus Petterson (1884–1949) was trained in his native Norway before settling in the United States in 1905. The elongated form, purposely visible hammer marks and a semiprecious stone mounted in the finial relate this cup to English works by Charles Robert Ashbee's Guild of Handicraft. Ashbee was well known in the United States, as were his designs; he had even visited Chicago on his American trip in 1900.

Among the most progressive designs in American Arts and Crafts silver is the Commonwealth coffee set, made in about 1930 by Porter Blanchard (1886–1973), working in Los Angeles. Blanchard began his silversmithing career in New England, near Boston, and was trained as a maker of flatware by his father. Both Blanchards were

members of the Boston Society of Arts and Crafts. Porter, intoxicated with tales of California, journeyed west in 1923 and established his own shop, joined by his father and brother shortly thereafter. Once in California he augmented his Colonial Revival repertoire with contemporary designs. Blanchard named all his designs and marketed them nationally, although as the movement abated his locus shrank back to southern California. At the height of his success he was forced to use machinery to assist in meeting orders, although finishes were applied by hand. Blanchard, like many other silversmiths, continued to make his living as a studio craftsman, long after the Arts and Crafts Movement had waned in the face of wars and the Depression. The heyday of the movement had ended by the 1930s, and national manufacturers resumed their virtual control of silver production.

COMMONWEALTH COFFEE SERVICE, MARK OF PORTER BLANCHARD, BURBANK, CALIFORNIA (COFFEE POT: H22.2cm/8¾in)

Porter Blanchard cited Ruskin and his followers for initiating the 'simpler, finer lines and plainer surfaces' that he favoured in his work. (ABOVE LEFT)

COVERED STANDING CUP, MARK OF THE PETTERSON STUDIO, CHICAGO, *c.*1912–14, SILVER WITH GARNET (H31.8cm/12½in)

Petterson was one of a number of Chicago silversmiths who collectively defined a progressive style of Arts and Crafts silver associated with that city, in contrast with the Colonial Revival mode favoured in New England. (ABOVE)

ARTS AND CRAFTS &
ART NOUVEAU

*I*nitially inspired by a revulsion to mechanical means of production, but subsequently also questioning the principles of nineteenth-century design, the movements we know as Arts and Crafts and Art Nouveau were born almost simultaneously in Britain, France, Germany, Austria, Denmark and America. Rooted ideologically in the ideas of Ruskin and Pugin, the Arts and Crafts Movement in Britain aimed to reassert the importance of craftsmanship, as epitomized by the Medieval guilds, an aim that was translated into practice by William Morris. The style established a tradition of vitality in the decorative arts which, in the 1890s, spread abroad as Art Nouveau – a deliberate attempt to create a new style in reaction to the academic historicism of the nineteenth century. These movements were transformed in time by the acceptance of modern industrial methods, but their legacy within the decorative arts is one that still continues.

JARDINIÈRE, TIFFANY & CO., NEW YORK, 1879
(H26cm/10¼in)

———

Edward C. Moore, artistic director of Tiffany's from 1868 until his death in 1891, was a keen student and collector of Japanese metalwork. The use of green and yellow gold and alloys of brass and copper on this piece show the extent of Moore's interest in the techniques of the Japanese craftsman.

'Arts and Crafts' and 'Art Nouveau' are expressions used to describe two of the styles emanating from a new philosophy of art which flourished in Europe and North America at the turn of the century. 'Arts and Crafts' is the name generally applied to the decorative arts of Great Britain and North America at that time, whereas 'Art Nouveau' usually refers to parallel developments in France and Belgium (although the term is often used loosely to describe the entire phenomenon worldwide). Slightly different styles emerged in other countries, among them 'Jugendstil' in Germany, 'Secessionstil' in Austria, 'stile Liberty' or 'stile floreale' in Italy, 'modernisme' in Catalonia and 'nieuwe kunst' in the Netherlands.

These various styles often appeared quite different, but they had a common tendency toward conventionalization and abstraction.

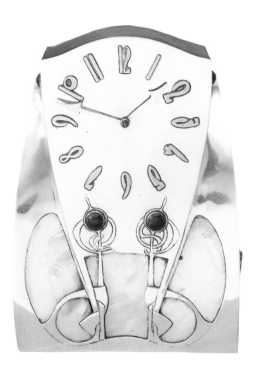

LIBERTY & CO.
CYMRIC
CLOCKCASE,
BIRMINGHAM,
1903 (H24.5cm/9½in)

*The almost abstract
treatment of the flowers
and leaves contrasts
with the more realistic
decoration of Slott-
Møller's mirror
(RIGHT). The two
objects indicate the wide
range of styles known as
Art Nouveau.
(ABOVE)*

MIRROR,
HARALD SLOTT-
MØLLER,
COPENHAGEN,
1898 (H27cm/10½in)

*Copenhagen silversmiths
A. Michelsen
manufactured this
ivory-handled mirror,
influenced by the
decorative arts of
Japan. (RIGHT)*

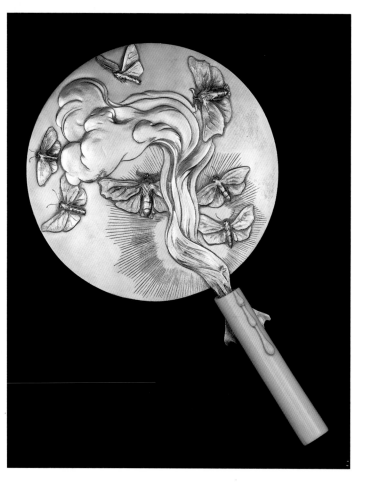

Most designers and decorative artists were inspired by natural forms but they never tried to imitate nature. Instead, they composed more or less formal arrangements of plants and animals treated in a more or less diagrammatic manner. They did not share their predecessors' reverence for historical styles. On the other hand, some of their designs were inspired by the art of other epochs or other cultures: Gothic, Celtic, Byzantine, Romanesque, Assyrian, Japanese, Chinese, Indonesian and American Indian. All these styles lean toward a formal, sometimes almost abstract, representation of the natural world. What modern designers at the turn of the century spurned was the style of the High Renaissance and its derivatives. The illusionistic representation of the material world, achieved by means of perspective and chiaroscuro, had dominated Western art since Raphael, but now it was deliberately abandoned by many artists and also designers.

If the change in the modern designer's attitude to the art of the past was fundamental, equally radical were new, widely held views about how decorative objects should be made. Industry was now condemned for lowering aesthetic standards by eliminating the artist from the processes of manufacture. In the production of silverware, methods such as spinning, pressing and die-stamping – which had become common practice – were regarded by many as inferior to raising, planishing (hammering) and chasing. The only way to introduce an element of art into modern silverware, many considered, was through the craftsman's hand.

Such integrity of art and craft was achieved by some silversmiths who forswore mechanical methods of manufacture. They adopted the modern aesthetic and made silverware by hand in the Art Nouveau style or one of its variants. Alternatively, the desired embodiment of artist and craftsman in one person was achieved when a designer working in the modern style learned the skills of the silversmith.

Besides these artist-craftsmen, there were also those Art Nouveau and Arts and Crafts designers who were content to 'carefully guide the hand that carries out the work', as English metalworker, designer and enameller Nelson Dawson stated in 1907. In addition, silver of the period was designed in one version or another of the modern style and mass-produced by industrial manufacturers. Although Dawson and many others deprecated what they saw as an unholy alliance between art and industry, believing that integrity of purpose and purity of expression were to be found exclusively in handwork, some designers were not willing to accept that good taste should be a privilege of those who could afford to pay for a unique piece of silverware. They accepted commissions from manufacturers or retailers to design modern silverware for a wider market, and as they learned to recognize the potential of the machine and to avoid its defects, their work assumed a dignity and integrity of its own.

ARTIST-CRAFTSMEN

GREAT BRITAIN

In 1885 Gilbert Leigh Marks (1861–1905) left the London silversmiths Johnson, Walker & Tolhurst, to which he had been apprenticed since 1878, and set up his own workshop. Here for the next twenty years he chose to make silver and other metalwork entirely by hand, an attitude that reflects the teachings of John Ruskin and William Morris. He would have been made aware of current aesthetic theory by two uncles, both eminent artists: Henry Stacy Marks (1829–98), a painter and designer involved in the decoration of pottery and furniture, and the painter,

modern style. Moreover, by combining the roles of designer and executant, Marks assured himself of a place in the Arts and Crafts Movement.

The architect Charles Robert Ashbee (1863–1942) started the Guild of Handicraft in 1888 as an extension of his teaching work at Toynbee Hall, a philanthropic foundation in the East End of London. Members of the Guild made leatherwork, furniture and metalwork, including silver. Neither Ashbee, who did most of the designing, nor the workmen had been trained as silversmiths. They learned techniques by trial and error and taught each other. Ashbee's designs were based on sixteenth-, seventeenth- and eighteenth-century silverware, although the shapes and decoration were freely adapted and restricted by the capabilities of the Guildsmen. The forms in which the metal was supplied by the silver merchants, that is

"CYMRIC" SILVER-WORK (Hall-marked). 27

CIGARETTE CASES.

No. 1. Silver Cigarette Case.
Size, 3½ by 2½ inches.
Price, £1. 2. 6.

No. 2. Silver Cigarette Case.
Size, 3½ by 2½ inches.
Price, £2. 10. 0.

No. 3. Silver and Enamel Cigarette Case.
Size, 3½ by 2½ inches.
Price, £1. 10. 0.

No. 4. Silver Cigarette Case.
Size, 3 by 2½ inches.
Price, £1. 17. 6.

Copyright.

Liberty & Co.   London & Paris.

LIBERTY & CO. CYMRIC CIGARETTE CASES, *c.*1900

Liberty catalogues issued at the turn of the century offered Cymric silverware at remarkably low prices, achieved by using production techniques such as pressing or spinning, rather than raising shapes.

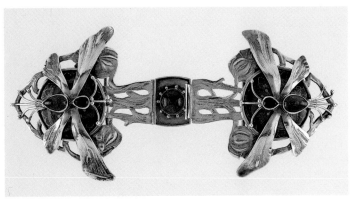

CLOAK CLASP, GUILD OF HANDICRAFT, UNMARKED, *c.*1902
(W13.75cm/5⅜in)

Most Guild of Handicraft silver jewellery designed by C.R. Ashbee incorporated enamels and semi-precious stones.

illustrator and poster designer Fred Walker (1840–75). Gilbert Marks made silver vessels usually decorated with chased and repoussé flowers in a manner recalling seventeenth-century styles, both the rich luxuriance of Jacobean ornament and the more stylized motifs found on William and Mary silver. Some of his work is so derivative, and sometimes the ornament is so naturalistic, that it is difficult to call it Arts and Crafts in style, but the pieces decorated with conventionalized plants, or with flowers treated in the Japanese manner, can be recognized as authentic expressions of the

untreated wire and balls, were exploited by Ashbee, who used them as decorative elements in many of his designs. During the 1890s professional craftsmen were taken on and the range of silver manufactured by the Guild expanded. Many pieces were decorated with enamelling and small cast figures, which supplemented the earlier reliance on repoussé ornament. Some of Ashbee's silver forms were instantly successful and soon became known across Europe and North America through exhibitions and illustrations in artistic magazines. The two most famous pieces were the loop-handled butter dish, or porringer, and the muffin dish with a dome-shaped cover, often given a wirework finial set with a semiprecious stone.

Henry Wilson (1864–1934) was an architect working in an essentially Arts and Crafts style when, during the 1890s, he turned his attention to metalwork and jewellery. From 1885 to 1891 he had been chief assistant to J.D. Sedding (1838–91), whose office in Oxford Street was next door to the shop of Morris & Co., and who had always encouraged a practical approach to the crafts among architects. Wilson, while completing the commissions in hand at Sedding's death, became more and more interested in the crafts of the silversmiths and metalworkers employed on the furnishings and decoration of Holy Trinity Church in Sloane Street, London. In 1895 he set up his own workshop where he designed and made silverware and jewellery, developing an original style which often featured elements of Byzantine or Romanesque art. He was an accomplished sculptor as well as architect and craftsman, and his work often incorporated cast figures. His technical expertise became formidable; in 1903 he published *Silverwork and Jewellery*, a workshop manual that was widely used for many decades. He investigated and acquired some of the skills of the Japanese metalworker, including the application of gold ornament to silver.

During the late 1890s a partnership was formed between Wilson and the enameller Alexander Fisher (1864–1936). Enamelling was a popular form of decoration among the artists and craftsmen working in modern styles at the turn of the century, not only in Britain but throughout Europe and North America. It was a craft that was quite easily mastered, and did not require sophisticated equipment. Furthermore, the Medieval quality of the colours, comparable to those seen in stained glass or illuminated manuscripts, appealed to the modern sensibility. Much Arts and Crafts and Art Nouveau silver was decorated with enamels, mother-of-pearl or cabochon-cut gemstones; too great a surface area of the shiny, reflective metal was found unattractive. Fisher was one of the most accomplished and influential enamellers of

the day, and many British and American pupils studied the craft at his school. Most of the sometimes quite elaborate silver frames in which his enamel plaques are often set, however, were probably the work of professional silversmiths, and partnership with Wilson would have provided Fisher with a more sympathetic executant. The enameller's skills would have been a useful addition to Wilson's decorative range. But their temperaments seem to have been incompatible, and the partnership quickly broke up.

Another young architect working in Sedding's office became a noteworthy silversmith and jeweller. John Paul Cooper (1869–1933) joined Sedding in 1889 and

COVERED DISH
AND SPOON,
GUILD OF
HANDICRAFT,
LONDON, 1902/03
(H9.75cm/3⅞in)

The looped wire handles are characteristic of the Guild's work. C.R. Ashbee had to design pieces which could be made by less skilled silversmiths.

became Henry Wilson's assistant when he took over after Sedding's death. Like Wilson, Cooper progressively turned his attention to the crafts, and he began designing plasterwork, metalwork and embroidery. When he was appointed to teach metalwork at the Birmingham School of Art in 1901, he went to Wilson's workshop for practical instruction. He taught at Birmingham until 1907, producing pieces of silver and jewellery for sale at the same time. In 1910 he built a house for himself at Westerham, Kent, with a workshop in the garden, and devoted the rest of his life to making fine silver and jewellery. His work was often embellished with exotic materials like shagreen, ivory, mother-of-pearl, coral and lapis lazuli.

Although he was inspired by Wilson's free translations of Medieval styles, the natural shapes of the materials that he incorporated often dictated the forms of his silver.

Cooper's silver and jewellery were sold by the Artificers' Guild through its gallery in Maddox Street, London. The Artificers' Guild had been formed in 1901 by Nelson Dawson (1859–1942) and the designer Edward Spencer (1872–1938), who employed a group of craftsmen to make up their designs at workshops in Chiswick. In 1903 Dawson left, and the enterprise was run thereafter by Montague Fordham, who already owned the gallery in Maddox Street. Neither Dawson nor Spencer was a silversmith, but they worked closely with their craftsmen. Most of Dawson's silver was loosely based on historical examples, and much of it was decorated with enamels. Spencer adopted a similar style to that of Henry Wilson and J.P. Cooper.

Montague Fordham had previously been a director of the Birmingham Guild of Handicraft, established in 1890 by Arthur S. Dixon (1856–1929). The Guild started as a course of evening classes in metalwork and design and was soon producing quantities of silverware. In 1895 larger premises were found and the Guild launched a journal, *The Quest*, which was hand-printed on its own press. Much silver made by the Guild was designed by Dixon in simple, functional shapes, often set with semi-precious stones.

Birmingham was second only to London as a centre for the manufacture of silverware in nineteenth- and twentieth-century Britain. The Vittoria Street School of Jewellers and Silversmiths offered the young men and women of the city practical training in the crafts of metalwork. Bernard Cuzner (1877–1956) was one of its pupils. Cuzner, who went on to study and later to teach at the Birmingham School of Art, designed jewellery in the Art Nouveau style before adopting a less flamboyant Arts and Crafts manner. By 1901 he was making spoons in a style derived from sixteenth-century English silver, with long, square-sectioned handles soldered to tear-shaped bowls. Over the years that followed, he showed increasing respect for the material itself and began to limit his decoration to simple borders around large areas of plain silver. Cuzner regarded machines as useful aids to the craftsman, and often designed silverware for industrial production.

Albert Edward Jones (1879–1954) was another native of Birmingham, and was born into a family of metalworkers. He learned the craft of the silversmith from Edward Webb at the firm of John Hardman before studying at the Birmingham School of Art. In 1901 he was working with the Birmingham Guild of Handicraft. When, in the following year, Jones set up his own workshop in Windmill Street, Birmingham, he insisted on making his silver entirely by hand and even refused to undertake any electroplating. The work he produced was very much in the Arts and Crafts idiom, but he failed to develop a personal style of his own. Many of his pieces were inspired by the designs of C.R. Ashbee.

After Birmingham, the city of Sheffield was the most important metalworking centre outside London. Omar Ramsden (1873–1939) was working there as a silversmith when he met Alwyn Carr (1872–1940) at evening classes organized by the local art school. In 1896 they both won scholarships to the South Kensington School of Art in London (now the Royal College of Art) and two years later set up their own workshop together, partly to execute a commission

PRESENTATION DISH AND COVER, HENRY WILSON, LONDON, *c*.1904 (H40.75cm/16½in)

Commissioned by the children of Susan and Charles Trask, to commemorate their parents' golden wedding, the iconography of this piece is as elaborate as its construction and decoration. It shows Wilson's considerable skills in the application of the small gold plaques to the silver.

that Ramsden had won for a mace for the city of Sheffield. Several other orders for ceremonial pieces followed, and they also started designing and making a wide range of domestic silver. Although much of their work was decorated in the Arts and Crafts style with repoussé ornament of Tudor roses, galleons and other motifs typical of the movement, they were quite prepared to accommodate clients who demanded more classical styles; nor were they averse to organizing their workshop and the many assistants they employed into a system of production that was virtually industrial. The partnership was dissolved in 1918. Ramsden continued to run the workshops, sometimes designing in an Arts and Crafts style.

FRANCE

The conditions determining the role of the silversmith in France during the 1890s were different to those prevailing anywhere else. The French craftsman had for centuries assimilated *le bon goût* which characterized the decorative arts of the nation, and an understanding of style as well as technical skill was expected of him. As a result, he was more highly regarded than his counterpart in Britain, where the distinction between designer and craftsman was more clearly defined. The expression of a single identity in a work of art, favoured by Morris, was also alien to the French notion of *haut luxe*, which expected an object to be worked on by different hands performing a variety of skills. Consequently, many silver objects made in France were embellished with enamels and semiprecious stones, and one of the principal tasks of the French silversmith was that of making elaborate mounts for glass or ceramic vases and other vessels.

SILVER-
MOUNTED
STONEWARE
VASE, LUCIEN
BONVALLET,
PARIS, c.1899
(H24.7cm/9¾in)

The vase, designed by Maurice Dufrêne (1876–1955) and made by Pierre Adrien Dalpayrat (1844–1910), was purchased in 1899 by the Musée des Arts Décoratifs, Paris, which then commissioned the silver mounting, designed by Bonvallet, from the firm of Cardeilhac.

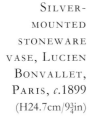

In the course of the 1890s, Art Nouveau was established as the dominant style of the French applied arts. It was characterized by asymmetrical arrangements of botanical ornament, often incorporating insects or birds. The inspiration was Japanese art, which was assiduously promoted in France by dealers, critics and artists. Prominent among the dealers was German-born Siegfried Bing; from 1888 to 1891 he published the magazine *Le Japon Artistique*, and a wide range of Japanese art was available at his Paris gallery. In 1895 he opened La Maison de l'Art Nouveau, where he offered modern objects and furnishings made in his own workshops and elsewhere.

From an early age Lucien Falize (1839–97) worked with his father, Alexis, who in 1838 had established a firm of jewellers in Paris. In 1862 they visited the international exhibition held in London and were highly impressed by a collection of Japanese art on

display. Lucien's fascination with the work of Japanese enamellers and metalworkers persisted, and in 1889 he wrote an article for *Le Japon Artistique* on Japanese jewellery. Although working mainly as a jeweller, Falize produced a considerable quantity of silver, most of which was decorated with flowers and other plants treated in a naturalistic manner inspired by Japanese art. At the Salon des Artistes Français of 1896 several pieces of carved cameo glass designed by Emile Gallé (another keen admirer of Japanese art), with Art Nouveau silver mounts by Falize, were among the most acclaimed exhibits. In common with most leading French craftsmen, as he became successful and employed more assistants, Falize progressively undertook more of the designer's role and less that of the actual maker, although he continued to supervise closely the execution of all pieces produced in his workshop.

Lucien Gaillard (b. 1861) worked for the family firm of jewellers, founded by his grandfather in 1840. He started his apprenticeship in 1878, and in 1881 he began a detailed study of the techniques used by Japanese craftsmen to colour and patinate silver and other metals, and their methods of

CUP, RENÉ LALIQUE, PARIS, c.1901
(H18.7cm/7½in)

The technique of blowing an opaline glass vessel into an openwork silver form was a radical alternative to the usual practice of French silversmiths, that of applying silver mounts to a glass vase or bowl.

using different metals together. He made bronze pieces 'dusted' with flecks of inlaid silver, often ornamented with insect or bird motifs. Another motif characteristic of Gaillard's style is a barbed form, which sometimes appears as silver applied to bronze and sometimes as repoussé ornament on silver vessels. He also made silver mounts for ceramics and glass, usually in botanical forms. In 1892 Lucien Gaillard took control of the family firm and in 1900 moved it to larger premises. Here Japanese craftsmen were employed. Production, however, was increasingly concentrated on jewellery.

COVERED CUP, PHILIPPE WOLFERS,
BRUSSELS, *c.*1899 (H20.4cm/8in)

Wolfers's skill is demonstrated by his use here of both
plique à jour *and* champlevé *enamels.* (RIGHT)

NAPKIN RING, HENRI HUSSON,
PARIS, *c.*1905 (D5.75cm/2¼in)

*Husson's silver reflects his interest in Japanese design
and metalwork techniques.* (BELOW)

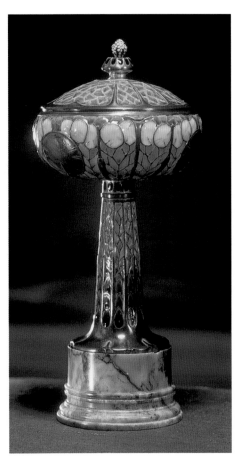

Henri Husson (1852–1914) was an innovative silversmith who specialized in producing copper vessels encrusted with silver or gold, probably inspired by Japanese metalwork. He decorated his work with insects and plants, chased or sculpted in high relief. Husson also manufactured items of domestic silver, and his work was cast in quantity and marketed by the firm of Hébrard, a foundry that ran a gallery in a fashionable quarter of Paris.

Principally a jeweller, René Lalique (1860–1945) made a variety of small objects in silver, such as scent bottles and handles for walking sticks. Toward the end of the 1890s he began to make a series of silver and glass cups. The glass, usually opaline, was blown into openwork silver carved in forms such as pine twigs and fir cones. The enameller Eugène Feuillâtre (1870–1916), who worked for Lalique until 1899, made silver and glass vessels using the same method, to which he added enamelling. For one piece the wings of three butterflies, which formed the openwork silver framework into which a glass vase had been blown, were given coloured markings in enamels. Most of Feuillâtre's silver, however, was completely covered with enamelled decoration. When Lalique began to make pressed glass objects in about 1910, some were embellished with silver mounts or clasps and hinges.

BELGIUM AND THE NETHERLANDS

In Belgium, the most prominent silversmith to work in the Art Nouveau style was Philippe Wolfers (1858–1929), who belonged to a family of jewellers and silversmiths. In 1892 he took over the family firm, but he maintained his own workshop where he produced Japanese-influenced pieces. During the 1890s he used floral forms for silver mounts on glass or copper vases, and decorated silver vessels with enamel plant or animal designs.

The floral, Japanese-inspired version of Art Nouveau that flourished in France and Belgium also spread to the Netherlands, but only at a commercial level. The Dutch silversmiths who can be considered artist-craftsmen generally worked in a geometric style developed by the architect and designer Hendrik P. Berlage (1856–1934). They treated natural motifs in a simple, diagrammatic manner, or otherwise used decoration consisting of abstract, linear forms such as circles, ovals and spirals.

The two most prominent silversmiths associated with the modern style in the Netherlands were Frans Zwollo (1872–1945) and Jan Eisenloeffel (1876–1957). Zwollo set up as an independent silversmith and metalworker in 1893 in Amsterdam. He joined the Theosophical Union of the Netherlands and in 1899 met the architects J.L.M. Lauweriks and K.P.C. de Bazel, who were also members. Zwollo made silver and copper mounts for the furniture they designed. His work – and decorative style – became closely linked to Lauweriks' career. Whereas in 1898 he had been producing silver in a rather tame, Oriental idiom, under the architect's influence he adopted a more modern manner based on Egyptian and Assyrian art. Both Lauweriks and Zwollo taught at the Haarlem School of Applied Arts, and when the former was appointed director of a handicrafts school at Hagen, Germany, he arranged for Zwollo to teach silversmithing there and to head the Hagen silver workshop, which was established by Karl Ernst Osthaus, a patron of several modern artists, designers and musicians. Lauweriks designed most of the silver that Zwollo made at Hagen, fluid, twisted forms with virtually no ornament. At the outbreak of the First World War in 1914, the two Dutchmen returned to the Netherlands. Zwollo set up a workshop at The Hague and reverted to the more geometrical style that he had first learned from Lauweriks.

Jan Eisenloeffel studied at the Amsterdam school for design instructors and in

COFFEE POT, JAN EISENLOEFFEL,
UTRECHT, *c.*1905 (H22.5cm/9in)

*Although a highly skilled craftsman, Eisenloeffel
liked to design silver for production by mechanical
processes. This simple but elegant coffee pot is
decorated solely with a geometrical pattern in enamel.*

1896 joined Hoeker & Son, a firm of
jewellers and silversmiths. He was employed
as a draughtsman, but gained workshop
experience and in 1898 visited St Petersburg
and Moscow to study Russian enamelling
techniques. On his return, Willem Hoeker
put him in charge of the metalwork section
of the Amstelhoek workshops which
Hoeker had founded in 1897. Here, ceramics, furniture and silver were made to
modern designs using mechanical as well as
manual processes. Eisenloeffel produced not
only handmade silver objects decorated with
sparse, geometric ornament in enamels, but
also lathe-spun vessels with machine-
engraved ornament. In 1902 he set up his
own workshop, where he continued to make
silver in the same style, which was retailed at
De Woning (The Dwelling), an Amsterdam
store selling modern decorative art.

GERMANY

The tradition of excellence established by
generations of goldsmiths and silversmiths
in Germany was maintained at the end of the
nineteenth century by a dwindling number
of craftsmen. Most of them loyally kept to
the historical styles which had consolidated
the reputation of their trade. Only a few
were inspired by contemporary aesthetic
theories to produce work in a modern style.
The fount of this style was Munich, where
elements of Japanese decorative art and
modern British design, together with an
environment of late Gothic and Rococo
forms, combined to produce a distinct and
original look in the graphic and applied arts.

Fritz von Miller (1840–1921) was born in
Munich, the son of a bronze founder in
whose workshop he received his initial
training in metalwork. He attended the
academies of art in Munich, Berlin and
Dresden before serving an apprenticeship
with the London goldsmiths Hunt & Roskell. He spent some time in Paris training as
a model-maker and enameller before returning to Munich, where in 1868 he was
appointed to teach silver- and goldsmithing
at the School of Applied Art, a position he
held until 1912. In 1876 he set up his own
workshop in Munich and soon gained a
reputation for elaborate silver centrepieces
in historical styles. In about 1895, however,
he began using conventionalized floral and
animal forms in his designs and developed a
philosophy of creativity which accorded
well with modern ideas. He gave up making
preparatory drawings or plaster models in
order to exploit spontaneous effects that
might occur in the process of manufacture.

COVERED GOBLET, ERNST RIEGEL,
MUNICH, 1903 (H24cm/9½in)

*Riegel combined traditional forms and techniques with
a modern decorative style. This piece was made while
he was still working in Munich, where Jugendstil had
flourished since the mid-1890s. The crowned birds in
the decoration may allude to* The Seven Ravens, *one
of the Grimm brothers' fairy tales.*

Among those whom von Miller influenced was Ernst Riegel (1871–1939), who
was his assistant from 1895 to 1900. Riegel
had been apprenticed to a silver chaser in
Kempten, Allgäu, and was selected by von
Miller for his great technical abilities. In
Munich he blossomed in the atmosphere of
artistic innovation into a talented Jugendstil
designer. In 1900 he established his own
workshop in the city and started making
silver that combined contemporary style
with traditional forms and techniques. For
instance, a goblet and cover made by Riegel
in 1903 incorporates opals set *à jour* and a
double-walled bowl with the outer wall
pierced and chased, techniques that had been
neglected for many years. The shape echoes
late Gothic apple-goblets, but the piece has
been fashioned in the form of a tree, treated
in a Jugendstil manner that recalls the work

SILVER-PLATED
BASKET, WIENER
WERKSTÄTTE,
VIENNA, *c.*1905
(H25.5cm/10in)

*Gitterwerk
(latticework) was a
speciality of the
Werkstätte.* (RIGHT)

TAZZA, JOSEF
HOFFMANN AND
EDUARD JOSEF
WIMMER,
VIENNA, *c.*1905
(H32.5cm/11in)

*This piece differs
greatly from
Hoffmann's more usual
geometric style.* (FAR
RIGHT)

of such artists as Otto Eckmann and Bernhard Pankok, whose decorative designs appeared regularly in the Munich magazine, *Jugend*, which lent the style its name. Riegel's frequent use of birds among thick foliage as an ornamental motif may well have been inspired by Persian decorative art, a notion that the occasional appearance of flamingoes and parrots tends to confirm.

In 1907 Riegel joined the artists' colony at Darmstadt, an enterprise supported by the Grand Duke Ernst Ludwig of Hesse. Here he made important items of silver and jewellery for the Grand Duke's family and entourage. He also won acclaim for his civic and ecclesiastical silver, which he continued to produce after his appointment as professor of goldsmithing at the Cologne School of Applied Arts and Handicrafts in 1912, a post he held for over 20 years.

Emil Lettré (1876–1954) studied at the Academy of Design in Hanau before working under von Miller in Munich. In 1905 he established a workshop in Berlin where he began to produce a series of remarkable silver vessels, the forms and decoration of which were many years ahead of their time. Spherical and cylindrical shapes, decorated with bands of wire soldered on to the body in wavy or arcaded patterns, and animals treated in a streamlined, geometric manner, all prefigure the decorative arts of the years between the two world wars. Everything produced in his workshop was handmade, although Lettré himself soon restricted his activity to designing.

In 1897 a group of Munich artists and designers, inspired by the example of Ashbee's Guild of Handicraft, founded the United Workshops for Art in Handwork (VWKH). Silversmiths were hired to make pieces designed by members of the group, and their work included silver mounts for enamelled copper bottles designed by Paul Haustein (1880–1944) and flatware designed by Richard Riemerschmid (1868–1957).

From 1900 the Belgian Art Nouveau designer Henry van de Velde (1863–1957) worked in Germany. A number of silver objects were executed to his designs by Theodor Müller, the court jeweller at Weimar, where van de Velde was appointed professor at a new school of applied art in 1904. Albert Feinauer, who taught silversmithing at the Weimar school, made some silver tea services designed by van de Velde.

AUSTRIA

Progressive decorative art in Austria at the turn of the century can be roughly divided into two phases. The earlier period, between 1897 and 1903, was dominated by a style of luxuriant curves and conventionalized flowers, related to Jugendstil, whereas after 1903, the year the Wiener Werkstätte were founded, a more austere, geometric manner prevailed. There seems to have been no outstanding Austrian silversmith who both designed and made silver in a modern style. During the earlier phase, designers had pieces made up by leading Viennese silversmiths. For example, Alfred Pollak made pieces designed by the architect Josef Hoffmann (1870–1956), and enamelled silver objects designed by the artist Koloman Moser (1868–1918) were executed in the workshop of Georg Adam Scheid.

When the Wiener Werkstätte were started in 1903, premises were quickly found to house workshops for the manufacture of silver and jewellery. Professional silversmiths were hired who worked in close collaboration with the designers. Like the VWKH in Munich, the Wiener Werkstätte were inspired by the Guild of Handicraft, and some of the workshops' output recalled Ashbee's silverware. More typical, however, was their rigidly geometric work. Hoffmann and Moser, co-founders of the Werkstätte and its principal designers, created a range of vessels made from silver pierced to form latticework. Hoffmann designed flatware with straight-sided, slightly tapering shafts, the spoons having circular or oval bowls and the tines of the forks arranged in a rectangle; the only ornament was a narrow band of spherical beading at the end of the handles. A more baroque manner characterized some of Hoffmann's later silver, for instance, bowls and tazzas with fluted sides; other pieces have overall chased ornament of dense foliage. The Wiener Werkstätte also made silver designed by Carl Otto Czeschka (1878–1960), which often featured chased spiral ornament, and Otto Prutscher (1880–1949), whose designs were characterized by

TEA AND COFFEE
SERVICE, OTTO
PRUTSCHER,
VIENNA, c.1913
(Teapot on stand:
H40cm/15¾in)

*Prutscher, an architect,
here successfully
combines geometrical
pattern with baroque
form.* (RIGHT)

VASE, JACOB
PRYTZ, OSLO,
c.1914 (H21cm/8¼in)

*Although the turquoise
stones with which this
piece is set link it
firmly to the art of the
early 20th century, the
exploitation of different
textures to achieve a
decorative effect looks
forward to the silver of
the 1950s.* (BELOW)

elaborate geometric ornament. Although the workshops endeavoured to keep down the price of many silver articles by using mechanized processes, much of the output was entirely handmade and several pieces were produced to order.

SCANDINAVIA

Two Danish silversmiths won international acclaim during the early years of the twentieth century. Mogens Ballin (1871–1914) was a painter who, in about 1900, opened a workshop where he made metalwork and jewellery entirely by hand. His silver was decorated with abstract, organic shapes, either chased or pierced, in a style reflecting the work of the architect and designer Thorvald Bindesbøll (1846–1908). In 1901 Georg Jensen (1866–1935) started working in Ballin's workshop. Although apprenticed to a goldsmith in the early 1880s, Jensen experimented with sculpture and pottery before reverting to metalwork. In 1904 he established his own workshop in Copen-

hagen and was soon making the silverware for which he became famous. His work was decorated with abstract, rounded motifs derived from Bindesbøll's ornament, to which he added bunches of fruit or flowers. From 1906 Jensen also made silver designed by the painter Johan Rohde (1856–1935), whose ornament was more restrained than Jensen's and helped to establish the international reputation of the firm. Such was the demand for his silver that Jensen felt obliged to introduce mechanical processes.

The Norwegian architect Torolf Prytz (1856–1938) designed silver bowls and tazzas decorated with naturalistic plant motifs in *plique-à-jour* enamels for J. Tostrup, a firm of silversmiths in Christiania (now Oslo). In 1900 some of these pieces were exhibited at the Exposition Universelle in Paris. Prytz was art director of Tostrup from 1890 to 1912, when his son Jacob (1886–1962) took over. Jacob's work for the firm included vessels which depended for their decorative effect on different textures given to the silver by chiselling or polishing.

UNITED STATES

Two features of the Arts and Crafts Movement in the United States are particularly pertinent to the silverware that was made under its aegis. First, many of the silversmiths were women. The taboos and inhibitions which restricted women's activities in most European countries were far less rigorously observed by American society, which prided itself on its respect for personal liberty. The other relevant aspect of the American Arts and Crafts Movement is the variety of styles it fostered. In the field of plate, the range included Colonial Revival, Art Nouveau, British Arts and Crafts, the Glasgow style of Charles Rennie Mackintosh, Gothic Revival and others.

In 1901 the Handicraft Shop was founded in Boston. Among the craftsmen who were provided with workshop facilities there was the silversmith Karl F. Leinonen (1866–1957). He had been born in Turku, Finland, and had settled in Boston in 1893. The shapes of his silver are simple and elegant, with scarcely any ornament. In contrast, the work of Elizabeth E. Copeland (1866–1957) is richly decorated with enamels and wire soldered on to the silver. She trained at the Cowles Art School in Boston under Laurin P. Martin, who had learned enamelling from Alexander Fisher. Copeland spent a short time at the Handicraft Shop, where she gained practical experience before setting up her own workshop in Boylston Street, Boston. She specialized in small boxes which she modelled on Medieval reliquaries, and she deliberately introduced a primitive look to show that they were handmade.

Mildred G. Watkins (1883–1968) also gained some practical experience of silversmithing at the Handicraft Shop. She had attended the Cleveland School of Art in her native Ohio, and returned there after her visit to Boston, where she also studied enamelling under Laurin P. Martin. She made jewellery and small items of silver, often decorated with *plique-à-jour* enamels and semiprecious stones; these were mounted in pierced openings given the forms of conventionalized flowers.

In 1900 Clara Pauline Barck (1868–1965) founded the Kalo Shop in Chicago. There she sold leather wares and simple jewellery made by herself and her friends. In 1905 she married George S. Welles, a businessman who made metalwork for a hobby. Together they established the Kalo Art-Craft Community, where instruction in metalwork skills was given. At first, only copper and brass items were made, but Clara Welles soon found trained silversmiths who made vessels and flatware to her designs and passed on their skills to other members of the community. The functional shapes of the silver, seldom decorated with more than chased or repoussé initials, and its sturdy construction fulfilled the Kalo Shop's motto: 'Beautiful, Useful and Enduring'. In 1911 Julius Olaf Randahl (1880–1972), a Swedish immigrant who had worked at the Kalo Shop, established the Randahl Shop where he made domestic silver, sometimes in the form of a simplified flower with small areas of chased and chiselled decoration.

Robert Riddle Jarvie (1865–1941) was a Chicago city clerk who, like George Welles, took up metalwork as a hobby and soon gained a considerable reputation for his tall, thin candlesticks in brass or copper. In 1905 he left his job and opened a workshop where, from about 1910, he concentrated on making plate, specializing in trophies and presentation pieces in an architectonic style. The decoration of his work owed much to the Arts and Crafts style promoted in the pages of *The Craftsman*, a magazine started in 1901 by the New York furniture designer Gustav Stickley. Jarvie also exploited the Glasgow style, which had been created by Charles Rennie Mackintosh and consisted of interlaced rectilinear forms, sometimes incorporating circular and heart-shaped motifs. The Prairie School architect George Grant Elmslie (1871–1952), who designed a few pieces made by Jarvie, was an ardent admirer of Mackintosh's work. Jarvie was commissioned by the Union Stockyard Company to design and execute the trophies awarded to the champion cattle breeders, and he complied with a series of punchbowls and other functional items.

TROPHY, ROBERT RIDDLE JARVIE, CHICAGO, 1912 (H25.4cm/10in)

The style of Jarvie's silver was largely influenced by the work of the Prairie School architects. This piece was commissioned by the Aero Club of Illinois.

COMMERCIAL
SILVER

The success of the Art Nouveau and Arts and Crafts styles encouraged manufacturers and retailers to provide their customers with items designed in the modern idiom. They were not troubled by the irony that the philosophy underlying the visual appearance of such objects precluded the techniques of mass-production and deplored any separation of the designer from the craftsman. While commercial exploitation pure and simple dictated the decisions of most manufacturers, some no doubt felt obliged to

TEA SERVICE,
BOUCHERON,
PARIS, *c.*1900
(Teapot:
W18.5cm/7¼in)

*The reputation of the
Parisian firm of
Boucheron had been
established by the lavish
diamond jewellery that
it made during the 19th
century. The quality of
this tea set shows that
many French
manufacturers managed
to retain high standards
of craftsmanship despite
using mechanical
processes.*

LIBERTY & CO. CYMRIC STAND,
LONDON, 1904 (H22.5cm/9in)

*Designed by Archibald Knox, this piece forms the
base of an oil lamp. The flat foot contributes to a very
effective design, as well as making the object cheaper
to produce.*

provide the public with reasonably priced
goods in a modern, decorative style. But
most firms of manufacturing silversmiths
continued to produce wares in a range of
historical styles which remained much more
popular than any artistic innovation.

In 1899 the London department store
Liberty's introduced 'Cymric' silver, most
of which was manufactured by the Birmingham firm of W.H. Haseler. Designers
included Archibald Knox (1864–1933),
Harry Silver (1881–1972), Oliver Baker
(1856–1936), a painter who was friendly
with the Haseler family, and the silversmith
Bernard Cuzner. Knox and Silver designed
in a style inspired by Celtic interlacing
patterns, whereas Baker's and Cuzner's
designs were influenced by antique English
utensils. Haseler used every mechanical
device – lathes, die-stamps, presses – in
producing 'Cymric' silver, which was sometimes given an ersatz handmade appearance
by hammering its surface.

In France, most manufacturers retained a
strong craft element in their production
processes. The Parisian firm of Cardeilhac
commissioned designs for silverware from
Lucien Bonvallet (1861–1919), who also
designed textiles and furniture. For Cardeilhac he created a series of vases in repoussé
copper and silver, as well as a large number
of mounts for ceramic and glass vessels, and
items of domestic silverware. For Boucheron, a leading Parisian firm of jewellers
and silversmiths, Lucien Hirtz (b. 1864)
designed elaborate items of silver decorated
with enamels (Hirtz had previously worked
for Falize). Paul Follot (1877–1941), although opposed to the mass-production of
objets d'art, designed a range of domestic
silver for La Maison Moderne, a store in
Paris run by the German art critic Julius
Meier-Graefe. For Siegfried Bing's gallery,
La Maison de l'Art Nouveau, silverware was
designed by Edward Colonna (1862–1948),
Georges de Feure (1868–1943) and Eugène
Gaillard (1862–1933), brother of the silversmith Lucien Gaillard.

The Dutch firm of J.M. van Kempen &
Son produced considerable quantities of
well-made Art Nouveau silver, some decorated with flowers treated in a naturalistic
manner and other pieces bearing more
restrained, geometric ornament. Van Kem-

pen's did not reveal the identity of their very
talented designers, who worked exclusively
in the firm's own studio.

In Denmark the architect Thorvald Bindesbøll designed silverware for the Copenhagen firm of A. Michelsen. His designs
usually featured undulating lines and
abstract motifs shaped like clouds or tad-
poles. The silversmith Mogens Ballin and
the painter Harald Slott-Møller (1864–1937)
also designed items for Michelsen. For the
Swedish manufacturers C.G. Hallberg, the
architect Ferdinand Boberg (1860–1946)
designed silver in an Art Nouveau style
influenced by Japanese decorative art.

Modern style was regarded in Germany as
a potential advantage in world markets, and
manufacturers were encouraged by the
government to employ designers with progressive ideas. Peter Bruckmann (1865–
1937), director of the manufacturing silversmiths Bruckmann & Söhne of Heilbronn,
played a leading role in the foundation of the
Deutscher Werkbund in 1907, an organization of manufacturers, businessmen,
designers and craftsmen, the purpose of
which was to promote the aims of German
industry and commerce. Bruckmann commissioned designs from Peter Behrens
(1868–1940), Hans Christiansen (1866–
1945), Joseph Maria Olbrich (1867–1908),

TABLE SILVER, HEINRICH VOGELER, BREMEN, c.1902

The 'Marguerite' pattern was one of several which Vogeler designed for the Bremen firm of M.H. Wilkens & Son. This sort of low-relief decoration on nearly flat surfaces is ideally suited to machine production. Vogeler held strong views in favour of the popularization of modern art and design.

CIGARETTE CASE, ANTOINETTE KRASNIK, VIENNA, 1902 (H8cm/3¼in, W7.8cm/3in)

Antoinette Krasnik, a pupil of Koloman Moser, designed a range of items in silver for A. Sturm, a Viennese firm of silversmiths. The diagrammatic treatment of the dragonfly (executed in enamel) demonstrates a move from the flowing Art Nouveau style popular in Vienna earlier to the geometrical style developed by the Wiener Werkstätte.

Paul Haustein and Emil Lettré, among others. Behrens, Christiansen and Patriz Huber (1878–1902) supplied designs in the modern idiom to Martin Mayer, a firm of manufacturing silversmiths in Mainz, and the prolific Behrens worked in addition for M.J. Rückert in the same city and M.H. Wilkens & Söhne of Bremen. Wilkens also made domestic silver designed by the architect Albin Müller (1871–1941) and the painter and graphic artist Heinrich Vogeler (1872–1942). Koch & Bergfeld, another firm of Bremen silversmiths, made flatware designed by Henry van de Velde.

In 1902 the Austrian manufacturing silversmiths Alexander Sturm made items designed by Antoinette Krasnik, a pupil of Koloman Moser. Geometric in style, they were sometimes decorated in enamel with conventionalized animals or flowers. Josef Hoffmann also designed for this firm.

In the United States, Tiffany and Company made a wide range of more or less ornate silver, most of it designed in-house. Under the artistic direction of Edward C. Moore (1827–91) the Japanese influence prevailed, in techniques as well as style, while during the 1890s the firm produced a range of bowls and vases decorated in niello with American Indian motifs. The 'Martelé' range of Art Nouveau silver was made by

the Gorham Manufacturing Company in Providence, under the artistic supervision of William C. Codman (1839–1923), and Unger Bros of Newark produced tableware designed by Philemon O. Dickinson in a floral Art Nouveau style.

TWIN CANDLESTICKS AND TEA CADDY, JOSEPH MARIA OLBRICH, HEILBRONN, c.1901 (H34.7cm/13½in)

Manufactured by P. Bruckmann & Son, these pieces illustrate industrial design in a modern style.

ART DECO

*D*uring the early years of the twentieth century new styles emerged both as a development of the Arts and Crafts and Art Nouveau movements, and in direct contrast to them. Led by Modernists such as Joseph Hoffmann and Koloman Moser in Austria, a crisp linear style evolved, while followers of Georg Jensen in Denmark and Dagobert Peche in Austria promoted more naturalistic forms. The beginnings of the machine age saw a renewed interest in industrial design, and although the notion of the artist-craftsman survived, especially in Britain, the benefits of mass-production were recognized worldwide. In consequence, firms such as Puiforcat in France and the Gorham Manufacturing Company in the United States dominated the market in factory-made goods. These styles are known collectively as 'Art Deco', after the Paris Exposition Internationale des Arts Decoratifs et Industriels Modernes of 1925. While Art Deco had in fact peaked in Europe by that date, the impact of the exhibition continued to be felt, especially in the United States, until war engulfed Europe in 1939.

CUP, GEORG JENSEN, COPENHAGEN, 1933 (H19cm/7½in)

An example of the elegant style with subtle decorative touches that marked much of the later work of the Danish silversmith Georg Jensen, whose working methods embraced both handmade and, to a lesser extent, mechanical processes.

163

The Art Deco, or Moderne, style in the decorative arts – roughly spanning the years from the mid-1910s (when it began to appear in Paris) to the 1930s (when it flourished most strongly in the United States) – was as evident in European and American silver design as it was in other applied arts. Typical characteristics of Art Deco objects include luxuriant materials, stylized floral motifs, geometric patterns, angular shapes and unmistakably contemporary adaptations – rather than mere duplications – of past styles, among them ancient Egyptian, classical Greek, Pre-Columbian, tribal African, French Baroque and Rococo.

AUSTRIA

At the same time that the Arts and Crafts Movement and the Art Nouveau style were in early eclipse, harbingers of Art Deco began to appear, most especially in the handmade silver output of about 1900–10 of the Wiener Werkstätte, founded by Moser and Hoffmann in 1903. By the 1920s, the handsome objects in hammered silver, gilt or white, of simple, often rigid geometric form, were joined by works in an ornate, baroque style. The chief exponent of this type of decoration was Dagobert Peche (1887–1923), the Wiener Werkstätte's co-director from 1917 until his death.

Among Peche's most elaborate designs were a silver-gilt jewel box surmounted by a fawn of 1920 and a silver box in the shape of an apple c.1918–20. Peche's energetic, dynamic creations, as well as the later fluted- and sometimes swirling-sided, often swollen-bodied and -stemmed, hammered silver vessels by Hoffmann, Eduard Josef Wimmer-Wisgrill and others, were a source of inspiration to silversmiths in several other countries, including France and the United States (where the Wiener Werkstätte had a short-lived New York branch).

Viennese designers in the Art Deco period also created jewellery and flatware,

JEWEL BOX, SILVER-GILT, DAGOBERT PECHE FOR THE WIENER WERKSTÄTTE, VIENNA, 1920 (H38.5cm/15⅛in)

Peche's unrestrained baroque- and rococo-style designs enlivened the Wiener Werkstätte's output.

BOWL, JOSEF HOFFMANN FOR THE WIENER WERKSTÄTTE, VIENNA, c.1920 (H19.1cm/7½in)

After the First World War, the Viennese architect-designer Josef Hoffmann eschewed his sleek, rectilinear metalwork designs of the early 1900s for more decorative and energetic, but still controlled and symmetrical, hammered silver vessels.

such as Hoffmann's fluted-column-handled flatware of c.1923–4, its pattern originally designed for the Primavesi family. The Wiener Werkstätte closed down in 1932, largely due to competition from factories.

SCANDINAVIA

The output during the Art Deco period of Danish silversmith Georg Jensen, who established a factory in Copenhagen in 1918, was highly prolific and extremely influential, as well as being profitable. It included examples of the decorated, floral type – many of these designed by Jensen himself – as well as purer, more geometric pieces created by Harald Nielsen (1892–1977), Johan Rohde (1856–1935) and Sigvard Bernadotte (b. 1907), among others.

Jensen's work was extensively displayed, admired and imitated throughout Europe and North America (it was exhibited at the 1925 Paris Exposition), and by the 1930s, retail outlets had been set up in Barcelona, Berlin, Geneva, London, New York and Paris. Indeed, the objects and flatware emanating from his factory, Georg Jensen Sølvsmedie, were arguably the most influential of all European silver pieces during the Art Deco period, providing inspiration both stylistically and technically, and in the fields of both handmade and mass-manufactured silver. The quality of Jensen workmanship, which was partly accomplished by machines, was impeccable and seamless.

Florally embellished Jensen silver of the 1910s to the 1930s comprised such objects as centrepieces, bowls, coupes, tureens, candelabra, cigar boxes, and coffee and tea services; their mainly glossy, rounded surfaces were enlivened with finials, knops, handles, stems, feet and other enhancements of Jensen's distinctive berry-and-tendril, bead-edged or other stylized organic type. Some objects were classically simple and elegant, such as a tureen of 1937; others were

smart and even slightly whimsical. Semi-precious stones such as amber were sometimes used, as they had been on the Art Nouveau pieces, and sterling and plated jewellery was produced in large numbers.

As early as 1920, Art Deco-style silver, distinguished for its pure form and surface texture, began to be designed by Georg Jensen Sølvsmedie, as well as pieces with subtle geometric or other embellishments. In fact, Johan Rohde's baluster-shaped pitcher design of 1920 was considered too avant-garde and did not go into production until 1925, after which versions in various sizes were produced. Dating from the mid-1930s were elegant centrepieces and smaller

shallow bowls by Harald Nielsen, with simple curled strapwork handles and hammered surfaces. The covered spout, fluted lid and reeded handle of Sigvard Bernadotte's 1937 design for Jensen, its cylindrical body engraved with a dense pattern of intersecting diagonals, might seem reminiscent of a teapot, but it is in fact a cocktail shaker with matching liqueur cups.

Art Deco flatware, with floral, beaded, geometric or other stylized decoration on the handles, was designed by Jensen as early as the 1910s. Johan Rohde's classic 'Acorn', or 'Konge', service of 1916 has a bold, organic pattern comprising foliate and scrolled forms, and the components of

'ACORN' FLATWARE, DESIGNED 1916, AND 'ACANTHUS' CARVING KNIFE AND FORK, DESIGNED 1917, BOTH JOHAN ROHDE FOR GEORG JENSEN, COPENHAGEN

ICE BUCKET, SIGVARD BERNADOTTE FOR GEORG JENSEN, COPENHAGEN, c.1930 (H20cm/8in)

Bernadotte designed for Jensen from 1930. Strict geometric forms and incised lines distinguished many of his creations for the Danish firm.

SOUP TUREEN, GEORG JENSEN, COPENHAGEN, 1928 (H36.3cm/14¼in)

The dense groupings of berries, beads and other organic forms attached to the hammered silver body and lid are classic Jensen motifs.

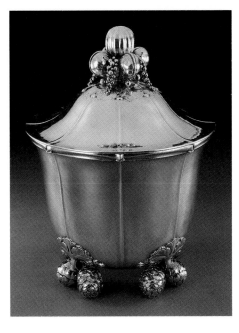

Georg Jensen's 'Beaded' pattern are simply but elegantly embellished by a necklace-like row of tiny silver beads; both are still made today. Harald Nielsen's 1926 'Pyramid' pattern and architect Oscar Gundlach Pedersen's 1931 'Parallel' (also known as 'Relief') pattern were in the geometric style, the handles of the former terminating in a three-stepped, ziggurat-like design, and those of the latter in simple parallel stripes.

In Sweden, Jacob Ångman (1876–1942) was the leading silver designer in the 1920s and 1930s. He began working for the Guldsmedsaktiebolaget (G.A.B.) firm in Stockholm in 1907, and thereafter almost single-handedly shaped the course of modern Swedish silver, influencing such important figures as Elis Bergh and Karl Wojtech. Ångman's mostly ovoid forms

TEA SERVICE,
JOHANNES
STELTMAN, THE
HAGUE, 1925
(Teapot:
H10.5cm/4in)

*Malcolm Campbell's
record-breaking racing
car at Pendine Sands
inspired this hammered
silver tea set with enamel
and semiprecious stones.*

were in the main smooth and undecorated but for their finials, which could take the shape of, for instance, a cornucopia of fruit standing on end.

BELGIUM AND THE NETHERLANDS

Wolfers Frères, established in Brussels in 1812, continued to produce gold, silver and jewellery throughout the Art Deco period, with significant designs created by Philippe Wolfers and his sons Marcel and Lucien. At the 1925 Paris Exposition, the elder Wolfers' range of 'Giaconda' silver was an early manifestation of the angular mode of Art Deco, and featured handles and finials of carved ivory (imported from the Belgian Congo). Another Belgian silver-making firm, Delheid Frères, also utilized ivory to enhance its tea and coffee sets, trays, and other vessels and objects, incurving, streamlined and rectilinear styles. Raymond Ruys's vase of 1930, executed by Raymond Delheid and shown at the 1930 Exposition Universelle in Antwerp, was a stunningly Modernist piece with horizontal and vertical striations and three long, fan-like feet.

Art Deco-period silver in the Netherlands was amazingly diverse for a small country, with several categories of design: handmade or anti-machine-made; Jensen-style classical; angular or rectilinear (with the occasional subtle added decoration); and ornamented Expressionistic. The latter related to the Amsterdam School and other Expressionist design and architecture of the 1910s and 1920s, and comprised a wide range of forms. These included the plastic, or figurative, e.g. the 60cm (2ft) high urn of 1918 with four caryatid-like attachments by Hendrik A. van den Eijnde (1868–1939); the fantastic or symbolic, one of the most extreme examples being the astounding tea service by Johannes Steltman (1891–1961); and the elegant bonbonnière of 1922 by J.A. Jacobs (1885–1968) of Heemstede, its squash-like form supported on an openwork, swagged-tendril foot.

GERMANY

German silver between the wars fell into a variety of schools, categories and movements, with elegant, Viennese-inspired pieces and floral, Parisian-style *objets* coexisting with the varied output – from coldly angular to strikingly classical and modern – of the influential Bauhaus, and a host of other types of handmade and machine-made wares.

The Deutscher Werkbund, founded in Munich in 1907, helped pave the way for the Bauhaus school of architecture and design set up by Walter Gropius in Weimar in 1919. In fact, the Werkbund's first exhibition, held in Cologne in 1914, included some silver by Gropius, elegant table pieces inspired by Viennese design. The Bauhaus based much of its educational philosophy on the Medieval guild, and its aim was to create pure, finely crafted, functional shapes devoid of decoration. The silver and other metal vessels made under 'Master of Form' Johannes Itten and Workshop Master Christian Dell (1893–1974) had a distinctly handmade look, whereas the objects produced after László Moholy-Nagy succeeded Itten were more Machine Age in style. Moreover, chromium, steel, nickel and 'German silver' (a nickel alloy) were the main metals used in production, rather than pure silver.

The highly functional, smoothly sleek, clean-lined vessels and appliances that emanated from the Bauhaus metal workshop in the 1920s and 1930s were created by the likes of Dell, Wolfgang Tümpel (1903–78), Wilhelm Wagenfeld (b. 1900), Josef Albers (1888–1976), Naum Slutzky, Gyula Pap and, perhaps the most notable of all, Marianne Brandt (1893–1983), who became the director of the metalwork studio when Moholy-Nagy left in 1928. Although Brandt's adjustable metal lamps are her lasting claim to fame, her coffee and tea service exhibited in Leipzig in 1927 are also remarkable for their simple geometric forms and practicality.

Elsewhere in Germany, the talented silversmith Theodor Wende (1883–1968) worked at the artists' colony in Darmstadt for a year from 1913 until the First World War, and from 1921 was professor at the Baden School of Arts and Crafts at Pforzheim. His streamlined and angular forms, such as a hammered silver mocha service with ivory handles and finials of 1930, showed a strong Cubist bent and a debt to the Parisian, Jean Emile Puiforcat.

Wende studied at Hanau's Royal Prussian Drawing Academy, as did Emil Lettré, whose designs (which he entrusted to artisans in his Berlin workshop) possessed an uncannily Modernist look. For example, an ovoid jar of 1906 was decorated with diagonals of ruffled tendrils of silver, its stepped lid topped with a handle in the form of a stylized stretched-out panther.

UNITED STATES

Innovative Art Deco silver in America was dominated by streamlined objects influenced by industrial design, but the general output of the many silver and plate factories was traditional and historicizing, with Colonial Revival objects to the fore. Following the 1925 Paris Exposition, some objects akin to those coming out of high-style France were produced, but these were

in New England, and both hired notable outside designers: the Gorham Manufacturing Company, founded in the early nineteenth century in Providence, Rhode Island, and the International Silver Company in Meriden, Connecticut, incorporated in 1898 by a number of independent silversmiths and silver and metal factories.

The Danish-born silversmith Erik Magnussen (1884–1961) added several important items to Gorham's inventory from 1925 to 1929, later working for the German firm

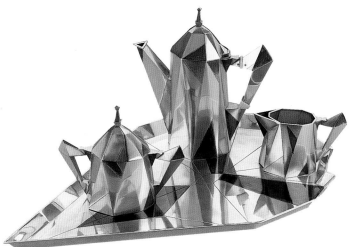

COFFEE SERVICE, ERIK MAGNUSSEN FOR GORHAM MANUFACTURING CO., RHODE ISLAND, 1927
(Coffee pot: H24.1cm/9½in)

Silver triangles alternate with gilt and oxidized ones on these unorthodox but nonetheless utilitarian pieces. Known as 'The Lights and Shadows of Manhattan', Magnussen's service, inspired by Cubism, caused a stir when it was first shown.

TEAPOT, THEODOR WENDE, PFORZHEIM, *c*.1925 (H24cm/9½in, W27cm/10½in)

This silver vessel has ivory details and a subtly hammered surface, as well as a strong functionalist nature, all of which are typical of the work of this German Bauhaus-influenced silversmith.

very few in number compared to sleek, machine-made wares. The influence of Georg Jensen, whose silver was first exhibited in the United States in 1915, was fairly considerable, especially in terms of handmade wares. Silversmiths were also inspired by the Craft Revival school of Great Britain, which was a continuation of the Arts and Crafts Movement.

The two most significant silver-making factories in the 1920s and 1930s were located

August Dingeldein & Söhne before striking out on his own. His elegant sterling and ivory covered cup of 1926 was a classic, formal vessel in the Danish taste, with a softly hammered surface and beads, volutes and fluted sections. A year later Gorham produced his stunning tea and coffee service, a controversial design boldly entitled 'The Lights and Shadows of Manhattan'. Although not in fact architectural in form, the dizzying array of faceted panels, made of gilt and oxidized burnished silver, contributed to producing a masterly tribute to the city of gleaming, stepped skyscrapers.

At divisions of International Silver, outstanding sterling and plated objects were mass-produced to designs by, among others, Donald Deskey, Lurelle Guild, Alfred G. Kintz, Gilbert Rohde, Eliel Saarinen and Gene Theobald. Rohde's tea service of about 1928 by the Wilcox Plate Company, of silver-plated Britannia metal and ebonized wood, comprised three wedge-like vessels and a round tray which, when not in use, formed a trim, cylindrical unit. Another such entity of around the same time was the paktong, or electroplated nickel silver, 'Diament' tea service by Theobald, its tall, rectilinear teapot flanked by a short creamer and sugar bowl. The romantically named 'Ebb Tide', 'Northern Lights' and 'Tropical Sunrise' bowls, platters, compotes and other vessels of 1928 onward, which made up Alfred Kintz's extensive 'Spirit of Today' line for the Simpson, Hall, Miller & Co. division in Wallingford, were more European and less Machine Age in their decoration.

One of International Silver's principal Art Deco achievements was a futuristic coffee urn of 1934 by Finnish-born architect Eliel Saarinen (1873–1950), whose commissions for the company included simple, elongated flatware and bowls as well. From the mid-1920s until 1933, he also designed more decorative pieces which were then made by hand by Arthur Nevill Kirk and Charles Price at the metal workshop of the Cranbrook Academy of Art in Bloomfield Hills, Michigan. The top of a Saarinen-designed, Kirk-made rectangular cigarette box of c.1930 included a tall finial surmounted by a roundel of a small figure blowing bubbles from a pipe.

A firm which made geometric plated silver was Bernard Rice's Sons, Inc., of New York, whose stepped 'Skyscraper' tea service, designed by Louis W. Rice in 1928, was produced in silver-plated metal in response to Erik Magnussen's Cubist tea and coffee service of 1927; that same year its so-called 'Apollo Studio' line of silver-plated accessories, such as mirrors and hairbrushes, was introduced. Reed & Barton of Taunton, Massachusetts, produced some silver vessels and other objects with bold ribbed and beaded decoration, but the rich, albeit belated Modernist output of Tiffany & Company. was especially notable, and considerably more innovative and daring than the bulk of its jewellery output of the time (although Art Deco-style accessories were made for the fashionable woman, as they were by many other firms). A smart ten-piece cocktail set, the shaker's top, tray's handles and goblets' feet studded with cabochon emeralds, was a surprising success at the firm's House of Jewels stand at the New York World Fair of 1939–40.

After moving to New York in 1926, German-born Peter Müller-Munk (1904–67) was employed briefly by Tiffany, but in 1927 he opened his own workshop, where he produced a fine body of one-off, custom-made Modernist vessels which made reference to various periods and styles. The scalloped rim of a bowl of about 1929 was elongated to create an architectural pattern of semicircular arches along the piece's outer wall, and the ivory crescent handles and stylized incised 'characters' on the rectangular faces of the vessels comprising a tea and coffee service of c.1931 were at once Oriental and primitive in appearance.

Multi-talented designer Kem (for Karl Emanuel Martin) Weber (1889–1963) opened a Hollywood design studio in 1927. Yet another designer for industry, Weber, a German émigré, created silver objects for several American firms, including stylish ebony-handled cocktail shakers and deep, round fruit bowls on fluted feet (with a black-nickel finish on the interior) for the Friedman Silver Company of New York.

Notable among the many American silversmiths and silver studios of the 1920s and 1930s were the Kalo Shop in Chicago, Margaret Craver in Boston, the Dane Peer Smed (who worked for a time for Tiffany), Briton Arthur J. Stone, who worked in Gardner, Massachusetts, and, in Chicago, Julius Randahl, Knut L. Gustafson and John P. Petterson. Standing well apart from the silver factories was William Spratling (d. 1967), a New Orleans architect-turned-designer who in 1925 set up a workshop in Taxco, Mexico, where he revived the silversmith's art of the area (and taught it to young Mexicans as well). Some of the vessels, utensils and jewellery he made were decorated with Aztec motifs, others with simple geometric designs.

GREAT BRITAIN

British silver mass-produced in the Art Deco period was largely in traditional or revivalist patterns, both hollow and flatware. Handmade, often hammered and enamelled, silver pieces, which had begun to be made in quantity at the start of the Arts and Crafts Movement, continued to be fashioned in large numbers throughout the 1920s and 1930s, indeed by many of the same individuals and guilds that had thrived several decades earlier. Modern-style silver in decorative Continental modes did appear, but the truly Modernist British silver of the time came out of the factories, not the studios or guilds. From 1925, the Goldsmith's Company took on an especially active role in the silversmith's trade. By means of studentships and sponsored exhibitions in Britain and France, it encouraged improvements in design and increased an awareness of, and stimulated the domestic market for, contemporary silver.

Specialist periodicals such as *The Burlington Magazine*, *The Connoisseur* and *Apollo*, all of which had started since the beginning of the century, and the long-running *Studio* and *Art Journal*, were especially instrumental both in publicizing developing trends in silver design and in recording new areas for the collector.

Somewhat ironically, it was a Briton, Christopher Dresser (1834–1904), who created the strongest and earliest harbingers of the Modernist style: from the late 1870s his functional teapots, toast racks, tureens and the like, their largely undecorated surfaces allying smooth curves with straight

TEA SERVICE,
HAROLD
STABLER, MADE
BY ADIE
BROTHERS LTD,
LONDON, 1935
(Teapots:
L19.8cm/7¾in)

*The designer and
teacher Harold Stabler
created this rectilinear
service for mass-
production in silver
and in electroplate.*

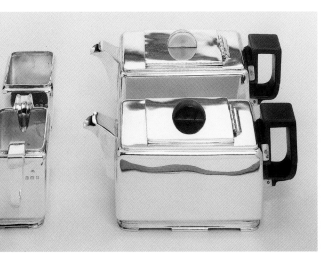

lines or even comprising pure geometric forms, were mass-produced in silver and electroplate by, among others, J.W. Hukin and J.T. Heath in Birmingham and London, James Dixon & Sons of Sheffield and Elkington & Company of Birmingham (designs were also sold to Boin-Taburet in Paris). Not surprisingly, his radical yet highly practical designs influenced metal-workers for generations, and some of these designs, such as one for a diamond-shaped electroplated teapot of 1880 by Dixon, could easily be mistaken for objects made a half century later. (Today, some of Dresser's silver creations are being reproduced by the Italian firm Alessi.)

The same English silver factories which produced these early Dresser pieces, as well as others which thrived in the nineteenth century, were still at work in the 1920s and 1930s. They were joined by more recently founded firms, and in the main their diverse outputs consisted of distinctly Modernist pieces, in addition to a substantial amount of reproduction wares. In 1922, Napper & Davenport of Birmingham produced the so-called 'Cube' teapot in silver with a wooden handle and finial; its compressed form appeared often in the 1920s and 1930s in the guise of ceramic teapots, but silver versions were far less popular. A silver, ivory and wood rectilinear tea service, designed by Harold Stabler (1872–1945) and made by Adie Brothers Ltd. of Birmingham in the

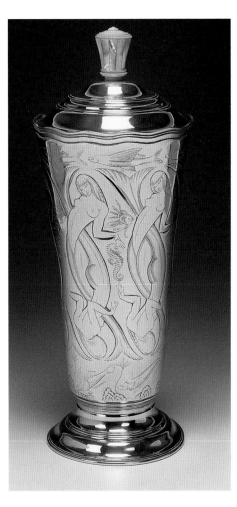

'MERMAID' CUP, R.M.Y. GLEADOWE, MADE BY WAKELY & WHEELER, LONDON, 1938 (H37cm/14½in)

mid-1930s, was also produced for a larger market in cheaper electroplate.

Wakely & Wheeler of London produced high-quality silver and electroplate, to designs by Stabler, R.M.Y. Gleadowe (1888–1944), Cyril J. Shiner (b. 1908) and other freelance and in-house designers. Two of the firm's sophisticated creations were Kenneth Mosley's footed conical vase of 1932, its lower section featuring an architectonic bas-relief, and Gleadowe's covered beaker of 1932, with swirling sides and a raised lid with scalloped circles. Altogether more decorative was the latter's 'Mermaid' cup of 1938, a tapered cylinder the body of which was engraved by George T. Friend with an underwater scene of sensuous mermaids, fish, sea horses and other marine life. Appropriately, the ribbed lip was topped with a finial sheathed in mother-of-pearl. Gleadowe also designed pieces for Edward Barnard & Sons, London's oldest silver factory (set up in 1689), as did Jane Barnard (b. 1902) for the family firm.

Mappin & Webb, established in 1863 in Sheffield, produced some of the most handsome Modernist silver in Britain in the 1930s. Keith Murray (1892–1981), a New Zealand-born architect who designed glass and ceramics as well as silver, created a classic – and not surprisingly architectonic – electroplated cocktail set for the company in around 1935. Less streamlined and more extravagant was Murray's covered cup of 1934–5 by the same firm, its straight-sided silver bowl with curved handles and its ivory finial comprising three graduated spheres. Architect Arthur E. Harvey (b. 1893), who headed the School of Industrial Design at the Birmingham School of Art, provided designs for Mappin & Webb as well as other factories, including Hukin & Heath and the Goldsmiths & Silversmiths Co. His jam pot of 1929 for Mappin & Webb, its glass body engraved with a stylized wave design, was topped with a stepped, conical lid (with glass knop) and accompanied by a simple silver spoon. A pepper mill for Hukin & Heath, designed in 1934, was in effect a fluted ivory column with a silver pedestal and top.

The leading British silversmiths of the Art Deco in the 1920s and 1930s, some of whom designed for industry as well as creating one-off pieces, included Charles Boyton, Leslie Durbin and H.G. Murphy. Bernard Cuzner and Edward Spencer were two silversmiths of the Arts and Crafts era whose later output included decidedly Modernist pieces. Bernard Cuzner (1877–1956), who designed for Elkington and other firms in the Art Deco period, was head of the Metalwork Department at the Birmingham School of Art from 1910 to 1942 and in 1935 wrote an important book, *A Silversmith's Manual*. Among his handsome Modernist objects was a tiny bowl (5.7 cm/2¼ in) in 1933, decorated on the outside with a niello design of crescents and semicircles. Londoner Edward Spencer (1872–1938), who designed ornate vessels with applied elements of other materials for the Artificers' Guild from 1903, latterly turned his hand to designing simple, geometric vessels, such as a biscuit jar of about 1935 with a stylized wave design on both its rim and the spherical knop of its lid.

The vessels and flatware designed and made by Charles Boyton (1885–1958) were unmistakably Modernist in taste and form, with some pieces obviously inspired by Jensen, others by Puiforcat. A sweetmeat dish of 1934, its bowl nearly flat, featured an ivory stem of three graduated rings, while another similarly shaped bowl included dense, stylized floral forms on its handles and stem. A tea set was made up of four cubic vessels and a rectangular tray, with not a single curve in sight, and the only diagonals formed by the triangular spouts.

Londoner Leslie Durbin (b. 1913) did not begin producing silver until the 1930s, but his largely ceremonial pieces, despite being official commissioned pieces, were strong modern statements. A tall covered cup made to celebrate the accession to the throne of George VI in 1936, for instance, included in its decoration stylized rampant lions on its triangular openwork handles.

Probably Britain's most innovative silversmith was Henry George Murphy (1884–1939), who had studied with Henry Wilson

CIGARETTE BOX, H.G. MURPHY, LONDON, 1933 (H11cm/4¼in)

Although strongly Machine Age in spirit, this box was handmade.

at the Central School of Arts and Crafts in London, where he later taught. Murphy had also worked in the Berlin atelier of Emil Lettré, whose proto-Modernist pieces without doubt influenced him. In 1913 he set up his own London workshop, The Sign of the Falcon, where he produced his own designs as well as those of others, including R.M.Y. Gleadowe and sculptor Eric Gill. Murphy's impeccably crafted vessels were largely plain forms enhanced with embossed geometric designs and elegant added elements, such as the ribbed ivory sphere on a cylindrical cigar box of 1934. A circular alms dish designed by Eric Gill, with eight panels of inscriptions (from the Gospel of St John) and religious scenes, was made in 1930 by Murphy's student E.B. Wilson. Other Murphy designs featured spiral fluted sides and beadwork, recalling earlier Viennese and Danish silver. Another Central School of Arts and Crafts teacher, A.R. Emerson (b. 1906), executed the designs of A.E. Poulter, such as a square-section biscuit box engraved with blossoms and a cylindrical tobacco jar with four bands of foliate forms alternating with rows of parallel lines.

FRANCE

It is no surprise that Paris, the birthplace of the Art Deco style, should have been the producer of the finest Art Deco silver. Since the eighteenth century Parisian silversmiths had been making outstanding works in gold and silver, and the emphasis on fine craftsmanship and innovative design continued throughout the first thirty years of the twentieth century.

Without doubt the most accomplished – and influential – French Art Deco silversmith was the Parisian Jean Emile Puiforcat (1897–1945), who came from a family of gold- and silversmiths and studied with both his father and the sculptor Louis Lejeune. He first showed his work in 1921, at the Société des Artistes Décorateurs. A year later he set up his own workshop and in the Paris Exposition of 1925 exhibited both hollow ware and flatware, which were universally admired. His first publicly displayed works in 1921 were two tea services, one with fruit knops and chased berries and leaves in the manner of Georg Jensen, the other undecorated and a sign of things to come. For Puiforcat eventually came to prefer the effects obtained by the simple play of light on the angles and surfaces of a work of art to any added 'contortions in imitation of natural vegetation'. Moreover, he abandoned the rather traditionalist Société des Artistes Décorateurs for more radical, avant-garde designers, showing with Les Cinq from 1926 to 1928, and in 1930 helping to found the Union des Artistes Modernes – its motto was '*le Beau dans l'utile*' – whose members included the committed anti-decoration Modernists Le Corbusier, Pierre Chareau, Robert Mallet-Stevens, René Herbst and Eileen Gray.

Despite his identification with the Modernists, Puiforcat firmly believed in the

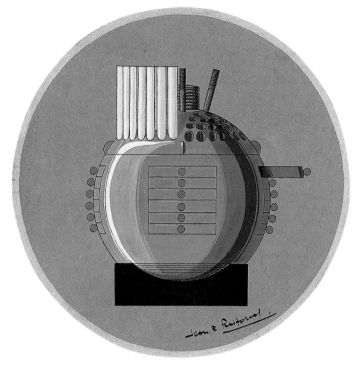

ancient mystical precept of the 'golden number', and duly attempted to uncover the mystery of harmonics in his pieces, which he saw as a blend of mathematics and creativity, a modern manifestation of the Platonic ideal of form through mathematical harmony. Nearly all his geometric forms were preceded by precise drawings detailing the ideal mathematical proportions of the objects. Early pieces often included added elements of precious and semiprecious stones, ivory and precious wood, while later vessels eschewed expensive materials for glass and such, or otherwise tended to be pure, unadulterated (except perhaps with gilt-silver) geometric exercises. Their glossy, seamless surfaces sometimes seemed quite futuristic-looking – as well as uncannily akin to those which could only be 'created' by a machine (such comparisons indeed were made by critics, and much to the master's irritation, who believed the machine to be without a soul).

Puiforcat's oeuvre included the full range of vessels and flatware, from candlesticks to clocks, bonbonnières to tea services, door hardware to table lamps. His love of perfect

COVERED BOWL, JEAN PUIFORCAT, PARIS, 1930–40 (H25.1cm/9⅞in)

A silver-gilt band and finial heighten the drama of this bowl by the leading Art Deco silversmith, Puiforcat. He sought perfection in design through geometric harmony, and this simple, spherical essay in silver is indeed a supreme achievement. (ABOVE LEFT)

DRAWING FOR A SMOKING CASE, JEAN PUIFORCAT, PARIS, 1935

The Parisian silversmith's careful planning included preliminary drawings. This spherical cigarette container on a stand is fitted with secret drawers and slots. (ABOVE)

VASE, JEAN PUIFORCAT, PARIS, c.1927–8 (H37.5cm/14¾in)

This stylish silver and glass vase was made by France's leading silversmith and sold by Saks Fifth Avenue, the fashionable New York department store. Although marked by asymmetry, the three hemispherical openings adhere to Puiforcat's refined sense of geometry. (LEFT)

TEA SERVICE BY
TÉTARD FRÈRES,
ON TRAY BY
SAVARY, PARIS,
both *c*.1930 (Tray:
L63.5cm/25in)

*Substantial knobs and
handles of exotic
palisander wood are a
part of this elegant,
subtly rectilinear tea
service by one of Paris's
finest silver firms; silver
and the same type of
wood comprise the tray,
which sports stepped
Art Deco handles.*

and geometric forms was self-evident: in a round soup tureen with an upright jade ring for a finial; in an octagonal vegetable dish with handles and finial like miniature piano keys of ivory; in a clock comprising twelve connecting circles of silvered metal enclosing Modernist numerals on marble rounds; and in an ivory, ebony and silver chess set, the chessmen taking on abstract geometric forms. His tea sets especially presented striking essays in geometry, such as a set of 1937, the leitmotif of which was the circle: the four cylindrical vessels comprised half-cylindrical spouts and half-moon shaped handles to which semicircles of rosewood were attached; similar handles flanked the oblong rosewood tray.

After Puiforcat, the creations of the venerable Paris firms Cardeilhac and Christofle are noteworthy. Maison Cardeilhac, founded in 1802, was run by Jacques and Pierre Cardeilhac from 1927. Pure geometric forms in the Puiforcat mode were produced, as were decorated, luxury wares. Orfèvrerie Christofle, set up in 1827, commissioned work from several notable designers of the Art Deco era, among them Maurice Daurat, Maurice Dufrêne, Paul Follot, André Groult, Jean Serrière, Louis Süe and his partner André Mare, the Dane Carl Christian Fjerdingstad (1891–1968) and the Italian Gio Ponti (1892–1979). Its varied output included revivalist, florid, geometric

ELECTROPLATED 'DAUPHIN'
CANDLESTICK, GIO PONTI FOR
CHRISTOFLE, PARIS, *c*.1927 (H20cm/7⅘in)

*The Italian architect and designer Gio Ponti created
several* objets-d'art *besides this candleholder, adorned
with a dolphin, for Maison Christofle, the long-
established French firm whose speciality was
electroplate. In 1926 Ponti also designed a house for
Tony Bouilhet, head of Christofle.*

and streamlined objects, as well as whimsical figurative pieces, like Louis Süe's Cubist squirrel sweetmeat dish and automobile ashtray, and Fjerdingstad's swan-form gravy boat. An octagonal coffee pot by André Groult had a stepped lid, while the pots in Henri Bouillet's tea and coffee service were elongated cylinders with thin hoop-like handles. Christofle produced much of the silver and 'Christofle silver' (as their electroplate was sometimes called) for the *Normandie*, the floating Art Deco palace of the French Line.

Tétard Frères was a late arrival among Paris silver firms, having been set up in 1880, but its Art Deco designs, especially those by Jean Tétard, were stunning geometric-based pieces rivalling those of Cardeilhac and Christofle. Some of the most starkly angular and dramatically Modernist silver and silver-plated metal pieces were produced in Paris by Maison Desny, which operated for a mere six years (1927–33). A futuristic cocktail set, for example, included a rocket-ship-like shaker and six glasses with conical bowls atop up-ended conical feet.

Other prominent names in French Art Deco silver were Gérard Sandoz (b. 1902), a jeweller who produced some fine tea sets, cigarette cases and other objects both plain or decorated with coloured enamel; Jean Goulden (1878–1947), primarily known for his boxes, clocks, lamps and vessels decor-

Surtout-de-table, Silvered-metal, Desny, Paris, *c.*1925
(Tray: L76.2cm/30in)

Maison Desny, a short-lived Paris firm (1927–33), produced a variety of startlingly original pieces. This table-centre is a simple reworking of an elaborate dining-table accessory which originated in late 17th-century France.

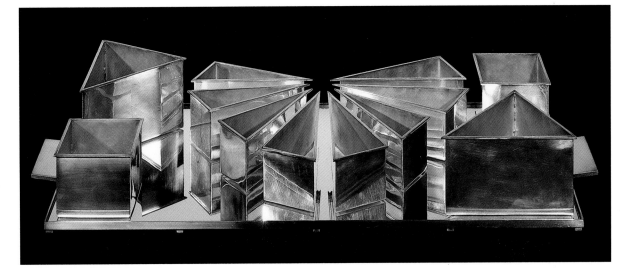

ated with Cubist-inspired coloured enamel patterns; Jean Dunand (1877–1942), whose superb lacquered objects included some silver jewellery with red and black geometric motifs; Jean Després (1889–1980), whose hand-wrought jewellery, objects and flatware had a distinctive machine-inspired look; Albert Cheuret, renowned for his Modernist silver and silvered-metal clocks, including one with the look of a stylized Egyptian headdress; Georges Fouquet (1862–1957) and his son Jean Fouquet (b. 1899), goldsmiths whose oeuvre included geometric-patterned cigarette boxes and jewellery; and Raymond Templier (1891–1968), who created silver objects in the geometric mode, such as cigarette cases enhanced with shagreen and eggshell lac-

quer, two popular, luxury Art Deco materials. Manufacturer-retailers like Boucheron, Cartier, Chaumet, Van Cleef & Arpels and Louis Vuitton also included Art Deco silver objects among their extensive inventories.

The late 1930s, and the onset of the Second World War, marked the end of the Art Deco style; the ornate Parisian version had already lost much of its appeal by the late 1920s, but its offshoot, 'Streamline Moderne', thrived considerably longer, especially in the United States. In terms of silver, the war led to a severe downturn in the production of both studios and factories, many of which – if they survived at all – turned their attention to making base-metal goods for the war effort or simple stainless steel utilitarian ware for domestic use.

Mantel clock, silvered-metal and onyx, Albert Cheuret, Paris, 1925 (L42cm/16½in)

Little is known of Cheuret, who designed several Art Deco timepieces. The pyramid shape of the clock recalls ancient Egypt, a prime source of inspiration for Cheuret, and the gathered sides are a clever conceit imitating cloth. (ABOVE LEFT)

Cigarette case, Raymond Templier, Paris, 1930 (H12.8cm/5in)

A pattern in coloured lacquer and a network of incised lines decorate this silver case, which has to be opened flat to be appreciated fully. Despite their extravagant materials, Templier's Art Deco jewellery and other works are not incompatible with a Machine Age aesthetic. (ABOVE RIGHT)

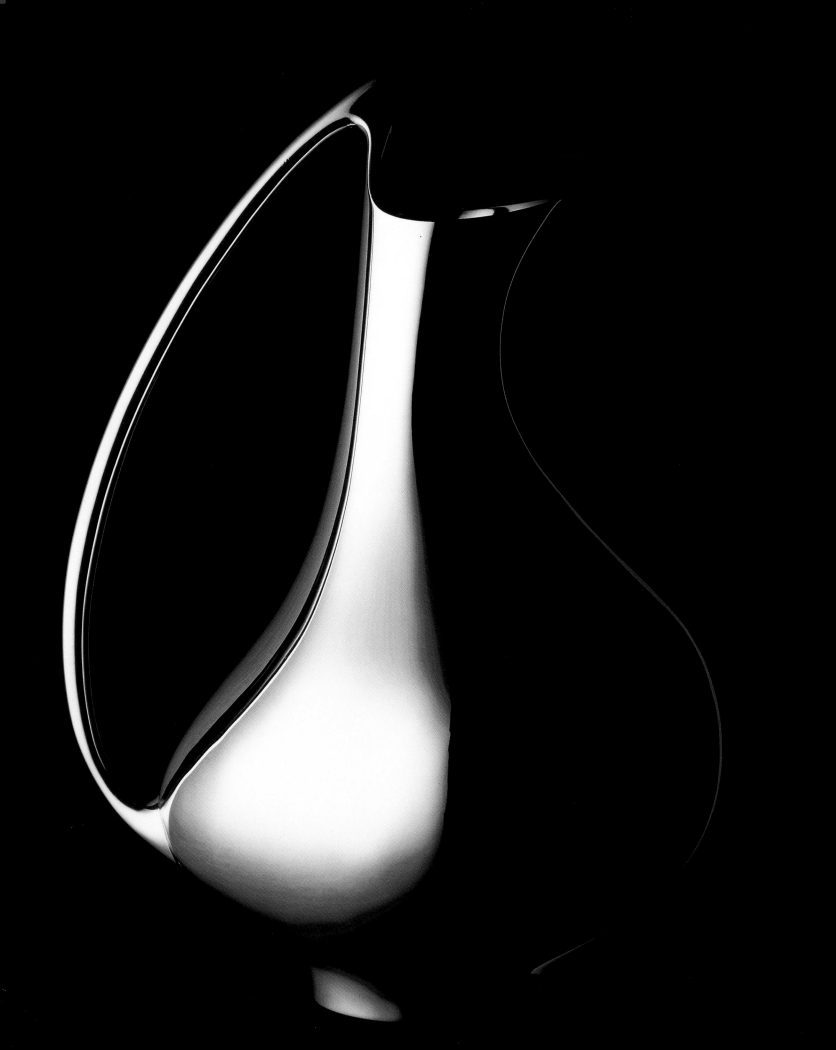

POST-WAR SILVER

The destruction in Europe, both economic and industrial, wrought by the Second World War, not only limited the means by which silver was produced but also severely restricted the market. As a result, many goldsmiths turned their talents to designing wares in stainless steel, a new medium developed by the Sheffield firm of Firth Brown for the armaments industry. Much of the impetus for new design was lost in those countries most affected by the war and the lead was taken by Scandinavia, notably Sweden where a strong tradition of contemporary design already existed. With the post-war boom in education and the growth of civic pride in the rest of Europe came the rise of the corporate client: new universities and polytechnics, rebuilt cities and successful businesses. Goldsmiths worldwide were again required to produce plate, regalia and presentation pieces in a style to match the new confidence reflected in the British slogan coined in 1951, 'Britain can make it', which united that new breed, the industrial designer, with the traditional artist-craftsman.

JUG, *ANDEN*, HENNING KOPPEL FOR GEORG JENSEN,
COPENHAGEN, 1951 (H29cm/11½in)

This jug heralded a series of lyrical, sculptural silver designs by Koppel which were produced by the firm of Georg Jensen during the following fifteen years. Koppel's free-flowing curves, which combined a dynamic rhythm with supreme utility, came to exemplify the very best of Scandinavian silver design.

The industrial reconstruction throughout Europe in the immediate post-war period promised the opportunity of an accelerating and even closer integration between the crafts and industrial practice. In the first two decades after the Second World War, this ambition seemed to be realized with the increasingly diversified role of the silversmith. In Scandinavia in particular, but also in Britain, Italy and elsewhere, silversmiths were not only encouraged to practise their craft but also to engage in design for industry. Two examples which serve to illustrate this point are the careers of the silversmiths Sigurd Persson and Robert Welch.

One of the most important Swedish silversmiths of the post-war generation, Persson (b. 1914) has equally enjoyed an illustrious career as an industrial designer, creating, for example, a range of stainless steel products. (This medium was developed initially for the armaments industry.) The success of Scandinavian stainless steel wares, almost invariably designed by trained silversmiths, appeared to epitomize the value of a close and continuing cooperation between art and industry, both of which prospered as a result of this relationship. Subsidized by his earnings from industry, the silversmith was given the freedom to pursue his craft, while industry, by engaging the skills of the trained artisan, was able to pursue and enhance its profits.

By the early 1980s, Perrson was designing a set of cutlery in his suburban Stockholm studio that would eventually be sold in the NK (Nordiska Company) department store in the city centre. But instead of being manufactured in Eskilstuna a few kilometres away, the cutlery was in fact produced by a factory in South Korea. Indeed, the fragmentation of production has become increasingly a feature of late twentieth-century industry. The lower manufacturing costs offered by the Far East, combined with an improved ease of communication and more advanced distribution networks, have undermined the traditional European manufacturing centres and exploded the myth, prevalent since the early nineteenth century,

COFFEE POT, SIGURD PERSSON, STOCKHOLM, 1991 (H23cm/9in)

Sigurd Persson's illustrious career as a silversmith, industrial designer, jeweller and glass designer has spanned the last fifty years. His work ranks amongst the most distinguished of the post-war period.

that the quality of design alone would be the salvation of national industries.

In Britain this has been even more acutely realized. The Sheffield manufacturing industry, for example, is a mere shadow of its former self. Robert Welch (b. 1929), who worked as a consultant designer for over 25 years for the Midlands stainless steel company, Old Hall Tableware, found himself writing an obituary for the firm in 1983. Viners of Sheffield was one of the biggest manufacturing stainless steel companies in Britain, employing up to a thousand workers and the services of the distinguished silversmith, Gerald Benney (b. 1930), as consultant designer, at the height of its success in the 1960s. The company no longer exists.

In the early 1990s, individual silversmiths find themselves operating in a niche market. Many of the large manufacturing firms that would have previously directly employed their talents no longer exist or have become largely retail outlets. A new generation of British silversmiths have embarked on successful careers running small workshops producing innovative silver hollow ware to

commission. Rod Kelly (b. 1956) is establishing himself as a formidable chaser, and his work now features in major collections. Alex Brogden (b. 1954) also works independently, making a range of objects that feature elemental forms, often produced in part by electroforming. Brogden's work has led to several important commissions from the Italian retailer, Bulgari, which are sold in their stores around the world, and this reflects another interesting facet of silversmithing in the late twentieth century: the increasing globalization of certain aspects of silver design.

Alessi, the large Milanese manufacturer of stainless steel tableware, has taken this aspect a stage further. In 1979 it established a small independent division within the company, Officina Alessi, to act as a research department for the company. Their first experiment was the Tea and Coffee Piazza series, launched in 1983, a group of 11 limited edition silver tea and coffee sets designed by an international group of Post-Modern architects, including Michael Graves and Richard Meier from the United States, Kazumasa Yamashita from Japan,

Paolo Portoghesi and Aldo Rossi from Italy, and the Austrian Hans Hollein. The international impact of this group of objects proved enormous. Their importance crystallized the issues at the core of the Post-Modern debate and finally exploded an argument of functionalism which had dominated the great majority of progressive silver design for much of the century. Despite the severely impractical aspect of some of these objects, they have become

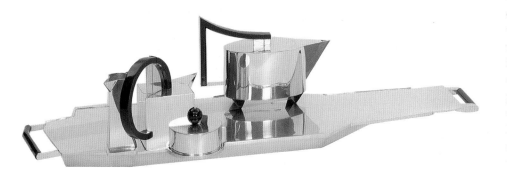

traditions have contributed to important developments and distinctions which have led others to emulate their achievements. At the end of the twentieth century, silversmithing has polarized. Progressive design is either in the hands of the small craftsman-silversmith supported by a craft guild with a continuous history since the Medieval period, or it lies within the realm of a few distinguished, large-scale manufacturers still surviving within Continental Europe.

icons of late twentieth-century design which serve as tableaux much like the display plate that characterized the sixteenth and seventeenth centuries.

Another important contributor to modern Italian silver design is Vicenza-based Cleto Munari, who has also manufactured a silver collection by an international group of architects and designers. Architects designing for silver is not in itself a new idea, but the idea of architectural silver presented within an international context is a late twentieth-century innovation. The Italians, above all, have relied on the architectural profession to supply them with designs for their innovative silverware. The international operations of both Munari and Alessi also beg the question of how important national distinctions are to a discussion of late twentieth-century silver. Increasingly, these distinctions are being eroded. Now the biggest exporters of silver and goldsmiths' work, the Italians have demonstrated that they can successfully commission designs from one national culture and manufacture it in another for sale throughout the world. And yet national cultures and

TEA AND COFFEE SERVICE, HANS HOLLEIN FOR ALESSI, ITALY, 1983 (H18cm/7⅛in) (TOP)

CARAFE AND GOBLET, ANGELO MANGIAROTTI FOR CLETO MUNARI, VICENZA, 1981 (Carafe: H24cm/9½in; goblet: H13cm/5in) (ABOVE)

GREAT BRITAIN

A decisive element in the success of British contemporary silver is the post-war renaissance of London's Royal College of Art, established in 1837 to provide trained designers for industry. However, for much of the nineteenth century, the college failed to make any significant impact. Between 1837 and 1948 there were constant controversies over the curriculum and how to construct and cultivate a fruitful relationship with industry. In turn, industry found that it could safely ignore the college, and in fact the major developments in metalwork in the latter part of the nineteenth and early twentieth centuries, such as C.R. Ashbee's Guild of Handicraft, were entirely independent of the influence of the Royal College of Art. Between the two world wars matters scarcely improved. Despite its earlier resistance to the fine arts, the college achieved distinction as a post-graduate institution for painting and sculpture, but this only provoked even further criticism from those whose ambition was to raise the design standards of British crafts and industry. The meeting of these requirements was not even attempted by the college. The Design and Industries Association published a trenchant memorandum in 1934 criticizing art education's 'bias toward the fine arts' and its 'divorce from industry, which is equally a divorce from the needs of our time'.

The Second World War intervened before any effective reforms could be introduced. By 1946 the college found itself facing the prospect of closure but it was reprieved by the Ministry of Education. Deciding to act on a report it had commissioned, this time from the fledgling Council of Industrial Design, it appointed Robin Darwin (1910–74), Professor of Fine Arts at Durham University, as Principal of the Royal College of Art. He was charged with the task of reforming the curriculum to provide specifically for the needs of industry. Darwin reorganized the college departmental structure so that it conformed more closely to industrial disciplines. Departments which required craftsmen demonstrators were provided with them, and it was by this means that the influential silversmith Leslie Durbin (b. 1913) came to be a part-time tutor at the college.

But of even greater importance was Darwin's selection of departmental heads, to whom he gave the freedom to develop their own curriculums. For the head of Silversmithing and Jewellery, he appointed

Robert Goodden (b. 1909), who trained as an architect and was in private practice until his appointment to the Royal College in 1948 (he began his training as a silversmith while a student at the Architectural Association). Goodden's achievement was to create a course that equally served the needs of both the mass-production metalwork industries and the craft of silversmithing.

For the Royal Pavilion at the Festival of Britain in 1951, Goodden designed the tea and coffee service used by King George VI and Queen Elizabeth at the opening ceremony. Rich in nautical and maritime imagery, the vessels' basic forms were essentially Neoclassical, the decoration completed with rhyming couplets engraved on the neck of each vessel. The service was made by Leslie Durbin, who trained with Omar Ramsden and at the Central School, London. Durbin also produced his own

silver designs, combining simplicity with a degree of sumptuousness and decorative detail not entirely conforming to the current taste for plain, simple forms.

Three eminent silversmiths who graduated in the 1950s from the Royal College of Art were Gerald Benney, Robert Welch and David Mellor. Benney also trained under Dunstan Pruden in the workshop complex at Ditchling, Surrey, founded by Eric Gill, and at the Brighton College of Art. He

started his own workshop in 1955 and by 1957 was appointed consultant designer to Viners of Sheffield, a major producer of base metal hollow ware and flatware. Benney relies on strong geometric forms in his work, which in the 1950s incorporated an increasing use of attenuated shapes and showed some Scandinavian influence. From the early 1960s, he returned to a more formal, symmetrical style, enriched by a textured surface and, occasionally, deep, lustrous enamel. A Martini jug and six tankards designed by Benney and produced in pewter by Viners in 1958 also has a soft, textured surface as its main decorative element, thus illustrating that the practice of the craft of silversmithing had a direct and interdependent relationship with Benney's activities as an industrial designer. The value of this relationship has also been stressed by his contemporary, Robert Welch, who has worked equally successfully in both disciplines and who wrote in his book *Hand and Machine* (London, 1985) that 'each area can enrich the other to a very important degree'.

Welch studied under Cyril Shiner and R.G. Baxendale at the Birmingham College of Art before continuing with his postgraduate work at the Royal College. He had become interested in stainless steel production while a student at Birmingham: in 1954 he won a scholarship to visit Sweden, which further stimulated his interest, and he made a special study of the material during his last year at the Royal College. In 1955 he was appointed as a consultant designer to Old

FESTIVAL OF BRITAIN TEA SERVICE, DESIGNED BY ROBERT GOODDEN AND MADE BY LESLIE DURBIN, LONDON, 1951 (H25.7cm/10¼in)

This service was made for the use of King George VI and Queen Elizabeth at the opening of the Festival of Britain in May, 1951. (ABOVE)

COFFEE SERVICE WITH ONE-GALLON COFFEE POT, ROBERT WELCH, BIRMINGHAM, 1960

Hall Tableware in the Midlands, a post he held for the next 25 years, during which time he won three Design Council Awards. His career has spanned the requirements of industrial design and the craft of silversmithing, disciplines in which he has been equally successful.

David Mellor (b. 1930) studied silversmithing at the Sheffield School of Art and

STATE PATRONAGE

State patronage was nonetheless an important element in the support of British post-war silversmithing which operated in several ways. The enormous expansion in university education in Britain and throughout the Commonwealth created a demand for new regalia. Several silversmiths, includ-

ing Gerald Benney, Desmond Clen-Murphy (b. 1924), Stuart Devlin (b. 1931) and Alex Styles (b. 1922) designed and made the new maces as well as other ceremonial silver that was required on formal occasions in the university calendar.

The post-war 'Assistance to Craftsmen Scheme' introduced by the Chancellor of the Exchequer, Sir Stafford Cripps, provided a

the Royal College before finishing his studies at the British School in Rome. In 1954 he set up his own workshop and design consultancy. The direction of his career was established when, as consultant designer to Walker and Hall, he was awarded a Design Council Award in 1957 for his 'Pride' cutlery service, followed by another Award for an accompanying tea service launched in 1959. His ceremonial silver has enjoyed equal distinction. Important commissions have included a large candelabrum for the City of Sheffield and a range of silverware and cutlery for the Ministry of Works to supply British embassies abroad, the latter an example of enlightened government patronage. Unfortuately, only one embassy, Warsaw, received a full complement of Mellor's 'Embassy' range before the Ministry of Works abandoned the scheme in a cost-cutting exercise.

COFFEE POT, *EMBASSY*, DAVID MELLOR, LONDON, 1963 (H17.1cm/6¾in)

This coffee pot forms part of a service which was the result of a limited competition held by the Ministry of Public Buildings and Works in 1961 for a set of tableware to be used in British embassies abroad. (ABOVE LEFT)

TEAPOT, GERALD BENNEY, LONDON, 1987 (H13.3cm/5¼in)

This teapot of silver-gilt, blue enamel and ivory is a typical example of Gerald Benney's mature style. The textured surface is a treatment which he first used on a chalice in 1957 and has since become very much a feature of his work. (ABOVE)

MACE, ALEX STYLES, LONDON, 1958

This mace was commissioned from Garrard's, who engaged their chief staff designer, Alex Styles, to execute the piece. The city arms are fully modelled and contained within the branches of the head. (LEFT)

more indirect form of patronage. The silver trade in particular was crippled by the very high rate of purchase tax levied on the maker's cost price to the retailer; at one time it was as high as 133 per cent. In these circumstances it was quite impossible for silversmiths to employ apprentices, if they managed to survive at all. The Chancellor's scheme granted purchase tax exemption to individual commissioned pieces of silver (although up to five repeats were permitted), provided each piece was approved by two panels of expert judges as a fine example of contemporary design and hand craftsmanship. The purchaser of each exemption was obliged to sign a deed of covenant with the Crafts Centre (which administered this scheme), agreeing it would not be sold to a third party. Furthermore, there was an obligation for all these pieces to bear the names of the designer and craftsman if these did not correspond to the maker's or sponsor's mark, so they were unusually well documented. The scheme continued until 1962 when, with the reduction in purchase tax, it was no longer considered necessary.

THE GOLDSMITHS' COMPANY

The London Goldsmiths' Company deserves particular praise in its continuing efforts to support the craft. In 1925 it began its own collection of contemporary silversmiths' work, which has now grown to be the biggest and most comprehensive representation of British twentieth-century silversmiths' work in the world. Through a vigorous programme of exhibitions, involvement in trade affairs and awarding of scholarships, it has sustained an unequalled level of institutional patronage.

Regarding university regalia, the Goldsmiths' Company was instrumental in introducing clients to the appropriate designer-craftsman for each particular project. More recently, the Dean and Chapter of Lichfield Cathedral relied heavily on advice from the Company for the commissioning of their modern church plate. The collection, which represents a broad cross-section of the most distinguished designer-craftsmen practising in Britain today, includes not only work by well-established names such as Gerald Ben-

ney, Brian Asquith, Keith Redfern and Stuart Devlin, but also represents work by younger silversmiths, such as Grant Macdonald, Rod Kelly, Alex Brogden and Lexi Dick. Similarly, the Goldsmith's Company is represented on the committee responsible for commissioning modern silver for the British prime minister's residence, 10 Downing Street.

Individuals such as Louis Osman (b. 1914) have benefited from the support of the Company throughout their careers. Osman, who graduated from the Bartlett School of Architecture in 1935 and trained as a medallist before turning to silver, works within an Arts and Crafts tradition. He is one of the few major silversmiths of his generation who neither studied at the Royal College of Art nor had any experience of industrial design. While Benney, Welch and Mellor illustrate that the distinction between craft and industrial design can at times be a very fine one, Osman removes his work into the sphere of fine art. His past collaborations, such as that with Graham Sutherland on the altar cross for Ely Cathedral in 1964 (orga-

DISH, ALEX BROGDEN, LONDON, 1990 (D42.5cm/16¾in)

Alex Brogden's current metalwork designs reflect a stylized abstraction that stems from a childhood interest in classical archaeology. (ABOVE)

ALMS DISH FOR LICHFIELD CATHEDRAL, ROD KELLY, LONDON, 1991 (D51cm/20in)

This alms dish forms part of the collection of modern church plate, commissioned by Lichfield Cathedral in 1991. The inscription, cut by Stanley Reece, reads 'All things come of thee O Lord and of thine own do we give thee'. (RIGHT)

nized by the Goldsmiths' Company), has given his work a powerful, expressive richness, quite unlike the cool, intellectual statements of his contemporaries.

Many successful silversmiths received their first commissions from the Goldsmiths' Company for its own collection of modern plate. An attenuated design by Stuart Devlin for a coffee service, effortlessly blending silver with a modern material, nylon, was purchased by the Company in 1959. This set was executed while Devlin was still under the influence of Scandinavian design. Later his style increasingly relied on richly textured surfaces and a combination of costly materials that entailed some sacrifice of formal discipline. The Amity Cup was a commission awarded to the young jeweller and silversmith, Kevin Coates (b. 1950), in 1981 by a past Prime Warden of the Company, Robert Goodden, to commemorate the ancient friendship that existed between the Goldsmith's and Fishmongers' companies. This represented a departure in English silversmiths' work from the previous generation's abstract formalism, for the form of the double stem of the cup (as an illustration of the ring of friendship) and the modelled figures of the two companies' creatures, the leopard and the luce, represent a symbolic interpretation of a theme.

One-man shows, such as the retrospective of the work of Alex Styles (b. 1922) in 1987 commemorating his association with the London firm of Garrard's, honour illustrious careers and demonstrate the innova-

THE PRINCE OF WALES'S CROWN, LOUIS OSMAN, LONDON, 1969 (H26.5cm/10½in, L28.8cm/11⅜in)

This crown, commissioned by Goldsmiths' Hall for the investiture of the Prince of Wales at Caernarvon Castle on 1 July 1969, was designed and made by Louis Osman. Made of pure gold, the body is electroformed with embellishments of four crosses and four fleur-de-lis, set with 75 square-cut diamonds and 12 emeralds. The engraving is by Malcolm Appleby, the enamelling by Dilys Osman.

COFFEE SERVICE, STUART DEVLIN, LONDON, 1959 (H33cm/13in)

This service was made by the London silversmiths Wakely & Wheeler, to a design by Stuart Devlin. By combining silver with a new material, nylon, which is heat resistant, Devlin was able to dispense with the traditional handle altogether and create this attenuated design which betrays contemporary, Scandinavian influence.

AMITY CUP, KEVIN COATES, LONDON, 1981 (H14.7cm/5¾in)

This cup was commissioned by the Prime Warden of the Goldsmiths' Company from 1976 to 1977, Professor Goodden, and was to be used in celebration of the ancient friendship between the Goldsmiths' Company and the Fishmongers' Company, represented by a leopard and fish respectively.

TEA SERVICE, HOWARD FENN,
LONDON, 1991 (Teapot: H14.5cm/5¾in)

*Howard Fenn graduated from the Sir John Cass
School of Art in 1979. His work has a distinctive
character which combines bold clear lines and
sculptural massing.*

tive side of the work of the major retailers
and manufacturers in the trade. By such
activities, the Goldsmiths' Company serves
well the interests of the silversmithing
profession and gives British silversmiths'
work an unequalled integrity, vitality and
pre-eminence.

SCANDINAVIA

Scandinavian design in the twentieth
century has been lauded for a variety
of apparently conflicting qualities:
for both its sophisticated grace and unman-
nered charm; as a reflection of socially
humanistic values as well as for its pure
aesthetic beauty; at once for its innovative
boldness and its conservative traditions. In
the later nineteenth century, an increasing
Nordic nationalism led to a renewed interest

in traditional crafts and respect for quality of
production. The Stockholm exhibition of
1930 brought Scandinavia to worldwide
attention as a supplier of elegant, inexpensive mass-produced goods. Although not
immediately applicable to the silver trade, it
established in the public mind the Scandinavian interpretation of functionalism; that
utility was the proper basis for design, which
in turn led to the progressive refinement of
form throughout the decorative arts for the
next three if not four decades.

The dominant force in silver was the
Copenhagen firm of Georg Jensen, started
in 1904. Jensen's simplified version of Art
Nouveau, based on thoroughly developed
basic forms, was taken a stage further by the
silversmith Kay Bojesen (1886–1958), who
had served his apprenticeship with Jensen
and was influenced by him in his early work.
But he built on this achievement by assimi-
lating the new fashion for simplicity combined with utility, first demonstrated at the
1930 Stockholm exhibition. In his mature
work of the 1950s, the qualities of common
sense and practicality combined with artistic
and technical perfection are evident.

Bojesen attracted many talented designers
to his workshop including architect Magnus
Stephensen (b. 1903), who had a genius for

making the simplest household article
attractive. He combined this with an attention to detail reminiscent of Japanese industrial art at its best. In the 1950s he worked for
Jensen, where he began to depart from the
severe functionalist aesthetic he had practised earlier. His work took on a more
sculptural quality, in part a response to
working alongside one of the most brilliant
designers employed by Jensen after the war,
Henning Koppel (1918–81). His series of
silver *anden* jugs (literally 'duck' in Swedish
and resembling a duck's breast in outline),
designed for Jensen in the early 1950s,
provided the benchmark for a succession of
silver designs that were to transform international perceptions of Scandinavian craft
and design. The uniform characteristic of his
work can be summarized as the functional
giving way to the sculptural if there is an
aesthetic advantage to be gained. Koppel
never found his lack of training in the craft
of silversmithing a hindrance but it must be
recognized that the success of his free-form
designs was achieved with the support of
expert craftsmen in the Jensen workshops,
especially Harald Nielsen, who provided
much valuable criticism and advice.

Sweden, too, contributed to the success
of Scandinavian silver design in the post-
war period. Perhaps the two most important
silversmiths of this generation are Sigurd
Persson and Birger Haglund. Persson, the
son of a silversmith, grew up in Helsingborg
where he learnt his craft. He studied art in
Munich before the war and afterwards in
Stockholm, where in 1942 he set up his own
workshop. His thematic, thorough treatment of a series of objects and jewellery
shows a clarity and control which, despite
certain features, like the swan-like curved
spouts of his coffee pots or wide-open
orifices with their hint of the organic world,
provide a series of cool, definitive, intellectual, abstract statements. His achievements
have been justifiably ranked as equal to those
of the Jensen silversmithy and yet his scale
of operation is modest by comparison. Since
the 1940s he has also worked as an industrial
designer (one of his most successful designs
was a set of cutlery for Scandinavian Airlines

in 1959) and from the latter part of the 1960s he has also worked as glass designer at the Kosta glassworks. His success in these commercial aspects of his career has enabled him to subsidize and continue his silver-smithing workshop.

Birger Haglund (b. 1918) was trained as a silversmith by master craftsmen in Köping and Kristianstad as well as working for Erik Fleming at the Atelier Borgila. In the 1940s he set up a workshop in Stockholm, but abruptly left for Johannesburg, where he stayed for four years and made his fortune. This he squandered as he witnessed with horror the encroaching policy of apartheid. His career in South Africa had to be abandoned when the police moved in on his workshop on the grounds that he was paying his workers excessively high wages. Forced to return home in 1952, he spent the next four years working exclusively as a jeweller until he began to receive commis-sions for church plate. His silverwork of the 1960s was characterized by a series of free forms and at the Crafts Exhibition in Stockholm in 1964 he displayed such unusual innovations as coffee pots and ladles with acrylic handles in bright colours and bold combinations. At the end of the 1960s he travelled to Afghanistan for the United Nations, which proved to be a turning point for him. Witnessing craftsmen in the Kabul bazaar who could rapidly produce objects out of brass and copper with considerable ingenuity, concentrating on the essentials and disregarding superficial scratches and abrasions on the metal, he lost the desire for perfection that had been so deeply ingrained by his early training. On his return to Stockholm in 1976, he started to produce hollow ware in thin, shimmering silver which retained the scratches and marks left by his tools.

Finland also made an important contribu-tion to the success of post-war Scandinavian silver. In the 1950s Tapio Wirkkala (1915–85) reorganized the production at Kultakes-kus, Finland's largest precious metals com-pany, while simultaneously gaining an inter-national reputation as a glass designer with Iittala. He became the leading figure in Finnish design and played an important role in influencing the rising generation as artis-tic director of the Institute of Industrial Arts. Prestigious commissions for the Fin-nish Presidency and for the cutlery used by the state airline, Finnair, helped consolidate his reputation as a silver designer. The style of his work at first had naturalistic overtones but progressively became more formal as his designs became simpler. Wirkkala had no formal training as a silversmith. An excep-tional draughtsman, he never executed his designs but left that to the professional silversmiths in the Kultakeskus (although by becoming familiar with production tech-niques he frequently offered suggestions as to the appropriate finish).

By the late 1960s, Scandinavian design was beginning to lose its homogeneity and influence. The close interdependence between craft and industrial design was starting to fall apart. Many designers in the traditional art industries were beginning to face retrenchment because of economic decline. More ominously, a new critical attitude was emerging which began to question social and economic traditions that had served Scandinavian industry so well since the war and the craft movement, highlighting the negative aspects of indus-try, began to gather broad support among artists. Gradually, industrial design and the traditional crafts began to draw apart. Inevi-tably the craft discipline became a separate one, in part encouraged by the younger generation of artist-craftsmen in the early 1960s who found that, in the improving economic conditions, they could ignore the role of the industrial designer altogether. In the 1970s, the decline of manufacturing industry throughout Western Europe in the face of competition from the Far East simply hastened the specialization of each role and the confident assumptions of the 1950s of the integrity of craftwork and industrial design were now irretrievable.

The visual character of Scandinavian design of the 1950s and the 1960s is best summed up as a delicate balance between the organic and hard-edged abstraction. By the late 1960s, the organic had triumphed, giving silversmiths such as the Swedes Bengt Liljedhal (b. 1932) and Olle Ohlsson (b. 1928) an opportunity to exercise an informality and directness that challenged the sleek, sophisticated forms of the pre-vious decade. The next two decades repre-sented a reaction against the glossy perfec-tionism which had given Scandinavian silver its distinctive quality in the 1950s. Suddenly, the artistic nature of the object had become more important than its func-tion. However, the craft revival was not confined to Scandinavia. In Britain, it was stronger still and since the 1970s, Britain has retained its ascendancy in silver craftsman-ship which it had lost with the demise of the Arts and Crafts movement.

BOWL, BIRGER HAGLUND, STOCKHOLM, 1985 (L20.2cm/8in)

After 1976, Birger Haglund's direction changed from perfectionist idealism to the production of simple pieces which retained the scratches and marks left by his tools.

OTHER COUNTRIES

Germany faced bigger problems than most countries over the reconstitution of its industry and industrial culture after the war. Carl Pott (b. 1906), who in 1937 took over his father's firm in Solingen, represents one of the most consistent success stories of German post-war silversmithing. Trained initially in his father's factory, he studied at the technical school in Solingen and subsequently at the Research Institute for Precious Metals in Schwäbisch-Gmünd. The style of his work is characterized by a simple austerity which reflected a return to progressive German design, in particular that of the Bauhaus

COFFEE POT AND
TRAY,
FRIEDRICH
BECKER,
GERMANY, 1985
(H20cm/7⅞in)

Friedrich Becker's early engineering training contributed to his characteristic style: clear-cut geometric forms and a technical precision. (RIGHT)

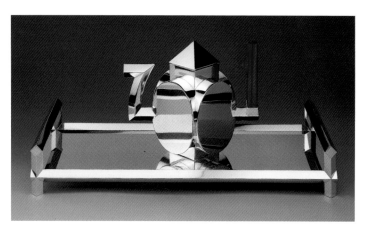

TEA AND COFFEE SERVICE, *COMO*,
LINO SABATTINI, MILAN/PARIS, 1957,
(H20.8cm/8¼in)

Lino Sabattini (b.1925) is one of the most distinguished designers of contemporary Italian silverware. Self-educated during the Second World War, he operated an independent studio in Milan between 1956 and 1963 while at the same time acting as a consultant designer to the French firm of Christofle, which produced this electroplated tea service between 1960 and 1970. (ABOVE)

during the interwar years, rather than an experimentation with new departures.

The work of Friederich Becker (b. 1922) and Sigrid Delius (b. 1927) represents the most academic approach to late twentieth-century German silver design. Like Pott, their education was firmly grounded in the traditional apprenticeship system and completed by extensive academic study. Their work is characterized predominantly by abstract formality, executed with perfect precision. The technical education of German goldsmiths remains consistently thorough and the regular organization and sponsorship of the European Silver Triennale by the Deutsches Goldschmiedehaus in

the traditional goldsmithing centre of Hanau since 1965 has given German goldsmiths' work an international dimension.

Neither France nor North America has made decisive contributions to international silver design in the late twentieth century. The Parisian firm of Christofle commissioned a few avant-garde designs in the 1950s, but their most successful works were not by French designers but the Italians Lino Sabattini and Gio Ponti. In the United States, Tiffany tended to rely on the strength of its former reputation while craft silver, like that of John Marshall (b. 1936), which has gained international attention, inclines toward an exaggerated expressiveness.

One of the most remarkable examples of thriving silversmithing activity in the last two decades has been Australia. Since colonization in the late eighteenth century, and in particular after the discovery of gold at Bathurst, New South Wales, in 1851, there has been a small but steady flow of European silversmiths migrating to Australia and establishing businesses in the larger cities.

The fortunes of such men as J.M. Wendt, Edward Fischer and Henry Steiner were directly linked to the rising pastoral and mining fortunes in the late nineteenth century. Some impressive commissions – including centrepieces, presentation objects and church plate – were undertaken by them, often incorporating naturalistic representations of exotic local flora and fauna. But at the time this work only aroused local interest; with a small population in a predominantly Anglocentric culture, the prestigious commissions tended to be placed with London goldsmiths.

The economic recession of the 1890s did little to encourage an indigenous silversmithing tradition, and the worldwide depression of the 1930s virtually extinguished it. In the post-war period training opportunities had to be re-established from scratch. In Melbourne Victor Vodica, an immigrant from Czechoslovakia, founded a gold and silversmithing course at the Royal Melbourne Institute of Technology, for a number of years the only formal training offered in Australia. When Dutch silversmith Wal van Heekeren arrived in Sydney in 1968, he set up his workshop for private tuition and, in 1972 the Norwegian Ragnar Hansen (b. 1945) joined the Sturt Metal Workshop at Mittagong, New South Wales, essentially an amateur organization offering craft instruction to those who wished to pursue such activities as hobbies rather than as a profession. In 1973 Hansen was appointed to set up gold and silversmithing courses at the School of Art at the Tasmanian College of Advanced Education and later, in 1981, he was invited by the Canberra School of Art to establish Australia's first and only post-graduate school for silversmithing and jewellery. In 1984 he was joined by Johannes Kuhnen (b. 1952), a young German gold- and silversmith who had been apprenticed to Friederich Becker and subsequently studied under Sigrid Delius in Dusseldorf.

The new initiatives in Australian silversmithing and jewellery were entirely European-inspired. Ragnar Hansen's early Australian work in particular echoed the smooth, flowing lines of 1950s Scandinavian silver, which became progressively more exaggerated and sculptural throughout the 1970s and early 1980s. The deliberate deformation of the surface and ultimately the form itself, combined with details such as handles and knops of local Australian

COFFEE POT AND TEAPOT, JOHANNES KUHNEN, CANBERRA, 1991 (H27cm/10⅝in)

The quality of Johannes Kuhnen's work is distinguished by a cool sculptural precision and an experimentation with new materials, illustrated by these two vessels which combine sterling silver with stainless steel, anodized aluminium and nylon.

woods, is a development which occurred entirely since Hansen's arrival in Australia. In this respect, he echoes and extends the tradition established by the husband-and-wife team of Helge Larsen (b. 1929) and Darani Lewers (b. 1936). On his arrival in Australia in 1961, Larsen, a Dane, introduced rational forms, warm surfaces and a rich combination of materials. Unhampered by the traditional guild restrictions of their European colleagues, Larsen and Lewers have extended the range of their work by experimenting with new materials and combining them with traditional techniques. Their 1989–91 sterling silver coffee service with coloured acrylic details demonstrates this fusion. Johannes Kuhnen reflects the cool precision of modern German practice, using a combination of simple geometric forms executed with superb precision. Responsible for introducing anodizing to Australian metalworkers, his technical virtuosity has had an enormous impact on contemporary Australian designs.

The establishment of several major craft centres, most notably the Jam Factory in Adelaide and the Meat Market in Melbourne (their rather prosaic names deriving from the former function of these buildings), has provided experimental centres as an alternative to the art-school structure and a

subsidized outlet for craftwork. The distinguished German goldsmith, Frank Bauer (b. 1942), was engaged by the Jam Factory between 1975 and 1979 and has since made Adelaide his base. Bauer, who comes directly from the Bauhaus tradition, continues to experiment with basic geometry.

The interchange between Europe and Australia is now no longer in one direction. Two graduates from the Canberra School of Art, Susan Cohn (b. 1952) and Robert Foster (b. 1962), have caught the attention of European sponsors. Cohn's design for a series of hollow ware of perforated matt coloured metal combined with sterling silver was issued by Alessi in 1992. Using a combination of simple, abstract forms and coloured metals, Robert Foster was one of three participants (along with Michael Rowe of Great Britain and Werner Bünck of Germany) in an exhibition of modern silver at the Museum für Angewandte Kunst in Cologne in 1992. Along with the regular participation of Hansen and Kuhnen in the European Silver Triennale and the increasing representation of Australian metalwork in public collections, both at home and abroad, the wheel has now come full circle and in the field of contemporary metalwork Australia can rightly consider itself part of the international mainstream.

FORGERIES, FAKES AND CONCOCTIONS

'Fakes reflect the history of taste more accurately than any other available body of material' (Mark Jones, 'Facing up to Fakes', *Burlington Magazine*, June 1989). The validity of the role of fakes is now so well recognized that the British Museum organized in 1990 an exhibition entitled 'Fake, the Art of Deception'. The history of silver fakes or forgeries stands apart from those in other media, however, because for hundreds of years most consumers have been protected by law against fraudulent goods.

To answer the question, 'What is a fake?', it has to be understood that much depends on the motive of the creator of the forgery or altered piece: was it fashioned with the intention of deceiving, or was it created honestly but subsequently considered illegitimate through change of circumstance? Did Reinhold Vasters (1827–1909) know from the start that pieces crafted by him or from his designs were passed off as masterpieces of Medieval or Renaissance art? The works of the nineteenth-century silversmiths Antoine Vechte and Antonio Cortelazzo may also have been sold as 'old' by the dealers who commissioned them. Indeed, many forgeries, including those of Vasters, can now be considered works of art in their own right. Some are of good quality and some are beautiful, while others are poor pastiches of earlier objects.

The attitude to fakes and forgeries also reflects the state of knowledge at a given time, and reassessment is constantly necessary. For example, until research was done on British Colonial silver, which identified the marks used by silversmiths in places such as India, Jamaica and Canada, as well as those appearing on China trade silver, many pieces now accepted as fine examples of Colonial work were thought to bear false English marks. No doubt other such mistakes will come to light in the course of time and further confusions will arise. For instance, future connoisseurs may consider today's commercial copies of the works of Vienna Secessionist Josef Hoffmann and Art Deco master Jean Puiforcat to be forgeries, although they are not created to deceive.

Sometimes even specialists have difficulty recognizing fakes and forgeries; indeed, learning to identify these deceptions is a never-ending process. However, with today's greater understanding and knowledge of the subject, it is difficult to believe the verdicts on some objects in the past. One of the finest pieces made for the English collector William Beckford was an agate cup and cover with jewelled silver-gilt mounts by James Aldridge, 1815. Acquired by the Victoria & Albert Museum at the Hamilton Palace sale of 1882 as a Renaissance work of art, the piece was subsequently regarded as an embarassing late nineteenth-century forgery until the hallmarks were read and the piece reassessed in the late 1960s as an important revivalist work. Hundreds of pieces made by, for example, the Swiss firm Bossard in the late nineteenth and early twentieth centuries have misled collectors in the past. Doubtless many of these were honestly made as reproduction or revival pieces, but others were very possibly dishonestly marketed from the start. Other popular lines from Holland included such items as brandy bowls, windmill cups or toys and a huge variety of spoons, created in a variety of earlier styles and sometimes

DESIGN FOR A CUP WITH SILVER-GILT MOUNTS, REINHOLD VASTERS, LATE 19TH CENTURY (H33.5cm/13in)

One of the large quantity of surviving designs by Reinhold Vasters, most of which are for Renaissance-style mounted pieces. This is in the style of 16th-century German cups which often incorporated a coconut, ostrich egg or similar rarity.

passed off at the time of manufacture as antique pieces.

The present-day difficulty is to understand which of these pieces were originally sold as 'old' and which have become 'old' through the confusion of subsequent generations. Hugh Tait of the British Museum has written that an object 'cannot be classed as a "fake" if the intention was not to deceive'.

Throughout the nineteenth century objects were produced to furnish countless mansions built in Gothic, Renaissance or 'Jacobethan' style. Some were outright forgeries and fakes, some were objects altered to meet current taste and some were concocted from bits of old silver with new additions.

Some splendid forgeries were produced in the nineteenth century, and it is now

THREE 19TH-CENTURY PIECES IN 16TH/17TH CENTURY TASTE (Cup and cover: H32cm/12⅝in) (BELOW LEFT)

TWO MOUNTED TIGERWARE JUGS, ONE RIGHT AND ONE WRONG (Smaller jug: H21.5cm/8½in)

The jug on the left is not old: the silver mounts are probably 19th-century. (BELOW)

However, it is difficult to ascertain the manner in which a newly made piece might have been sold.

Until the late eighteenth and early nineteenth centuries, when the fashion for revivalist pieces developed, silversmiths tried to defraud the public only by using below-standard silver or in some other way attempting to circumvent the hallmarking laws, such as by 'duty dodging' (see p.190). When collectors began to show an interest in antiquarian objects, it was not just the objects for which they were looking that were in short supply; so, too, was knowledge. Hallmarking was not properly understood and even William Beckford could fall prey to dealers offering 'the work of Cellini'.

recognized that the practice was widespread at the beginning of the century, not just in the later decades. An early example is a tigerware jug in the Victoria & Albert Museum, whose stoneware body was proved, on analysis, to have been made twenty years either side of 1800, although its genuine mounts, which have been altered to fit the ceramic body, are dated 1576. In 1896 the Louvre purchased the gold Tiara of Siataphernes, supposedly a magnificent Greek relic from the third century BC; in fact, it had been made only a short time before by Israel Rouchomovski in Odessa. The 1911 auction catalogue of the collection of J. Bossard in Lucerne is filled with dubious pieces, as was the collection of the

dealer and collector Frederic Spitzer. The British Museum and the Victoria & Albert Museum were two institutions duped by the work of the nineteenth-century forger Louis Marcy, while members of the Rothschild family were among the many collectors who bought the work of Reinhold Vasters. A large group of Vasters's designs survives in the Victoria & Albert Museum and research on these has helped transform thinking on 'historicist' pieces.

Silver which deceives can be divided into three main categories: forgeries, fakes and concoctions. Many are straightforward attempts to deceive and defraud, but others are not so simply defined.

FORGERIES

QUALITY OF METAL

The systems of marking that developed throughout Europe from the thirteenth century were introduced to safeguard the public, in law, against poor-quality silver (that is, to guarantee the purity of the alloy). At certain times the rules were upheld more rigorously than others, but for the most part the standards were observed because the penalties were severe. An entry in the minutes of the Worshipful Company of Goldsmiths in London for 1596 tells of John More and Robert Thomas, who marked silver plate that was far below standard with counterfeit marks and who were each 'sentenced to be set in the pillory at Westminster . . . where they were each to have an ear cut off and then to be led through Foster Lane where they had made the fraudulent plate and finally to the Fleet prison until they each paid a fine of 100 marks' (J.S. Forbes, 'Forgery of Hall Marks', *Worshipful Company of Goldsmiths Review 1971–2*).

PHOTOGRAPH FRAME (H21.5cm/8½in)

A recent example of faking by electroforming: the marks for Birmingham, 1901, and the damage on each side of the original frame have been reproduced. Frames made in the late 19th or early 20th century were usually of thin sheet silver with stamped decoration.

Spectrographic analysis can detect the age of silver from impurities in the metal, and work is also being done on analyzing silver from the different countries where it was mined, linking this information with the dates a mine was worked. Recent forgers are thought to have gone to the trouble of melting down old pieces to create their own works, thus attempting to avoid detection by spectrographic analysis, but their methods are by no means foolproof.

METHOD OF MANUFACTURE

One of the signs of forged silver that is easiest to detect is anachronistic manufacturing methods, for example, pieces may have been spun instead of having been hand-raised or cast. One example was a tankard bearing the forged marks of the American silversmith Jacob Hurd. This piece also has poor patina, a feature that is difficult to reproduce convincingly.

Today, modern casting methods, involving the use of latex moulds and, for small parts, centrifugal casting, make it more difficult to detect forgeries because it is possible to reproduce a piece exactly, including clear marks. The only significant difference between the forgery and the original is a slight shrinkage. A giveaway on these pieces can be the placing of the marks. If several spoons or candlesticks, for example, come from the same mould, the marks and, of course, any damage, will be identically positioned, whereas there would be some individuality about pieces which were 'right'. Weight, too, can be an indication of an object's dubious nature; for example, a piece that is wrong will be too heavy, too light or incorrectly balanced compared to one that is 'right'.

MARKS

FORGERY. The most consistently attempted offence over the centuries has been that of forging marks. In countries with a system of hallmarking, the assay master is responsible for seeking out offenders. In the United Kingdom he upholds the Hallmarking Act

of 1973. The aforementioned punishment meted out in sixteenth-century England was extremely severe, but in 1757 forging hallmarks was a crime punishable by death (this was later amended to transportation). However, English authorities in the eighteenth century were at times remarkably lax and much silver has survived unmarked or without the full complement of marks. A consistent offender was the London silversmith Edward Feline, who apparently had his own set of punches in the 1740s. By comparison, very little unmarked French plate from the eighteenth century has survived.

In the United Kingdom, the Forgery Act of 1913 allowed a maximum of 14 years' imprisonment. In 1971 a Sheffield silversmith found guilty of forging marks was given a two-year sentence, and in the 1980s a forger specializing in spoons was caught. Hitherto the faker has tended to copy the marks of well-known silversmiths, such as Paul Revere and Joseph Richardson in the United States, and Paul Storr and Hester Bateman in England.

Perhaps the most blatant case in England in the past hundred years was that of Charles Twinam, who was found guilty of forging silver, and Reuben Lyon, who was fined £3,090 for selling Twinam's pieces in 1898 and 1899. Because of the large quantity of forgeries that were sold before the pair's deception was eventually discovered, Twinam's work still appears from time to time on the market.

TRANSPOSING AND PLACING MARKS. Marks can be removed from one object and inserted into another, a common method of faking. Sometimes the marks become stretched in the process; other clues are seams or patches around the marks, or marks put in the wrong place. In striking marks on silver, the assay masters followed long-held traditions over where they should be placed (see pages 194–5). In the United States, too, where there was no authorized system of marking, silversmiths were fairly consistent in this practice. When a piece bears forged or transposed marks, the mis-

FOUR PROBLEM PIECES OF ENGLISH AND IRISH DESIGN (Cup: H33cm/13in)

The caster was made in the 20th century in early 18th-century style; the fake marks are wrongly positioned on the base. The candlestick is of a type made in large numbers in the 1750s. Although it may have been cast from an original, the finish is unconvincing and it bears fake marks. The cup and cover, a duty dodger made c.1725, bears inserted marks. Dish rings were popular in Ireland in the 18th century but the Rococo decoration here is typical of the late 19th century; it has inserted marks (see below for details of marks). (RIGHT)

BASE OF CANDLESTICK

The marks are from forged punches and are relatively easy for the trained eye to detect. The finish of the underside is also different from its 18th-century prototype. (BELOW)

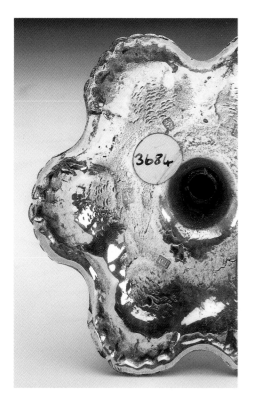

UNDERSIDE OF CUP

Removal of the foot reveals the circular disc bearing marks for 1705, inserted to avoid paying duty.

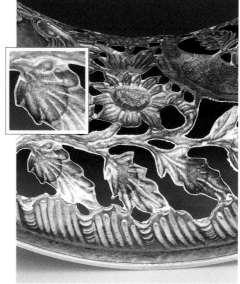

UNDERSIDE OF DISH RING

Three seams, or 'patches', indicate where marks have been inserted (see enlargement).

BASE OF A
TANKARD
BEARING
AUTHENTIC
MARKS,
EXETER, 1741

Above the hallmarks, in a triad, are the contemporary engraved initials of the owners of the piece. Such initials can be helpful in identifying armorials. Below the marks is the scratchweight, which should always be checked against the current weight to ensure that nothing has been added, for example strengthening features such as an added rim or plating on the inside.

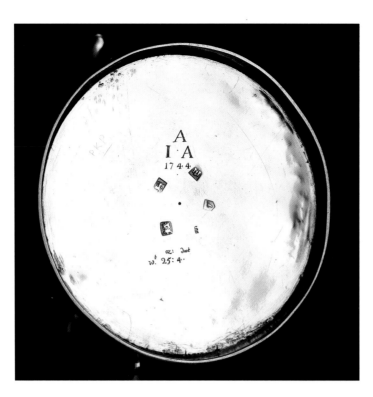

REMOVING MARKS. It is easy to blame forgeries and problem pieces on the people who made them. They are not always responsible, however: unscrupulous dealers may be the culprits. Certain combinations of marks will identify an object as being from the nineteenth century, whereas only one or two of the set might be more difficult to detect as not coming from the sixteenth, seventeenth or eighteenth century. The practice of removing marks selectively is less common on English silver but does appear on pieces made on the Continent, where the marking systems are more complicated and thus not as well understood.

DUTY DODGERS. Between 1719 and 1758 a tax of 6d per ounce was levied on silver made in England. In order to avoid this, silversmiths sometimes inserted marks from another piece, either of earlier date or of very much lighter weight, into their work. This

take is often made of putting them in the wrong place. Custom also varies from place to place about marking the separate pieces that make up a whole object.

CASTING MARKS. This has been mentioned earlier with regard to modern methods of casting. The other technique used to reproduce marks on an object is electroforming.

PSEUDO-HALLMARKS. In the late nineteenth and early twentieth centuries, several manufacturing silversmiths on the Continent marked their wares with pseudo-hallmarks, attempting to copy those of earlier times. As hallmarking regulations were less strictly enforced at that time, there was no attempt to stop the practice. The chief protagonists in Germany were the firm of B. Neresheimer & Söhne of Hanau and Berthold Müller. The Augsburg pineapple, a small Gothic 'n' (for Nuremberg) and a lion rampant are the marks most frequently struck on their wares; all are easily distinguishable from earlier marks. More difficult to judge is a range of mid-eighteenth-century Augsburg marks, using the pine-

apple and date letter in one punch, which are found on late nineteenth-century pieces. The Netherlands, the other major late nineteenth-century manufacturing centre, had no laws forbidding the striking of old marks in addition to current ones. Problems arise when the new set has subsequently been removed in order to confuse.

THREE BEAKERS (Tallest: H17.8cm/7in)

The 18th-century German beaker (left) has added chasing; the early 17th-century Swedish beaker (centre) has added engraving; the beaker (right), one of a pair with fake English marks for 1616 and 1634, was probably made no earlier than the 1950s by cutting down a chalice or cup.

practice was most commonly used on hollow ware, often on pieces of high quality or considerable weight. Another way of lessening the tax was to have the body of a cup legally marked but to avoid duty on the cover. This could be done either by leaving it unmarked or by having the maker's mark stamped four times, in imitation of the full set of marks.

FAKES

CHANGE OF FUNCTION

As fashions change, so do the objects that people use in their homes. If something is outmoded, it is perfectly understandable that it should be altered to suit a new purpose or the prevailing taste. A possible early example is a cylindrical salt presented

permitted to alter the function of a piece or to add parts to it; unless additions are assayed and hallmarked, the piece cannot be sold legally.

Other alterations are undertaken to change an object of little value into a more desirable collector's piece. Examples of these are spoons that have been made into forks, dessert spoons that have been turned into apostle spoons and plain snuff-boxes that have become castle-top vinaigrettes.

ADDED ENGRAVING AND CHASING

Throughout the nineteenth century, in order to meet the demands of fashion cheaply, silversmiths frequently decorated an old piece of silver in the current taste. From the 1820s onward, chased and engraved Rococo and Mannerist decoration was added to a range of items. This is not

tion of tastes in collecting. An example of the latter is the flat-chasing of chinoiserie scenes in the taste of the 1670s and 1680s, a practice that achieved considerable popularity among collectors in the early twentieth century. Suitably interesting pieces of 'seventeenth-century chinoiserie' were devised to lure the unwary buyer (several examples of these can be seen at Polesden Lacey in Surrey).

The practice of changing a coat of arms or initials to suit a new owner is perfectly legitimate, and has been carried out by succeeding generations. It detracts from an object's desirability in the eyes of collectors, however, if the engraving is not contemporary with the piece. Highly dubious, though, are the methods used by some dealers to 'improve' their stock by smartening up worn engraving. Sometimes this is extremely difficult to detect, unless the crispness of the engraved armorials is at variance

THREE ENGLISH PIECES ALTERED IN THE 19TH CENTURY (Larger tankard: H20.6cm/8in)

The tankard (left), 1680, has an added spout and ivory filets. The mug (centre), 1734, has later gilding inside. The tankard (right), 1770, has an altered body shape, added spout and ivory filets. All have 19th-century chasing.

to the Goldsmiths' Company in 1632 by Richard Rogers, which may have started life thirty years earlier as a clock salt. Some of the most commonly found altered pieces are tankards and mugs made into jugs, dinner plates or salvers reshaped and bearing new borders, and snuffers trays made into inkstands. In England, however, it is not

illegal in England, providing the function of a piece is not changed, but it does affect its value today. Only occasionally, when the chasing is of high quality, can the chaser be said to have improved an older piece.

There is a distinction between this early to mid nineteenth-century practice of later chasing to follow fashion, and the exploita-

with a rather worn cast or chased border. Even worse is the engraving of armorials, in the correct style, in a previously empty cartouche or on to a plain piece. A recent example was a set of three salvers by Edward Feline of 1723 which appeared on the market in 1968 with blank cartouches and again in 1986, this time with arms added.

GILDING AND PLATING

In the Middle Ages a widespread practice was to gild latten (brass) and pretend it was silver-gilt. This was most commonly practised on spoons, and records are littered with the punishments meted out to offenders. The Ordinances of Goldsmiths in London of 1305, stated 'that no one shall make a hanap [cup] of copper or latten gilt; that no one shall gild any work of copper or latten nor set real stones therein, except for church ornaments' (Charles Oman, 'The False Plate of Medieval England', *Apollo*, LX, pp. 74–5, 1952). There is also a range of objects, notably cups and some mounted pieces, many from Germany, which might have fooled people but which were probably sold honestly to those who could not afford the precious metals. Nowadays this would not deceive many, but gilding is used (often combined with chasing) to cover up repairs. Harder to detect is the plating of silver (usually on the inside) to strengthen a piece weakened by repair, the removal of engraving or dechasing. This is not faking, merely a deceitful practice if not explained by the seller. It is illegal in England, however, if the silver added exceeds 5 grams in weight.

CONCOCTIONS

'The practice of revitalizing broken or otherwise damaged works of art, particularly those made of precious metals, and of creating for them new, congenial settings has a long tradition and is not in itself illegitimate. Difficulties arise, however, if deceptively optimistic descriptions and pedigrees are attached to the results' (see Dr. Yvonne Hackenbrock, 'Reinhold Vasters, Goldsmith', *Metropolitan Museum Journal, 19/20*, 1986). Mounted pieces and delicate Renaissance works have been prime targets for the 'improver', and it is a small step from repair to fabricating a large proportion of a piece. Cups whose finials, figure stems and bases can easily be replaced are the usual vehicles for this

UNMARKED SILVER-GILT DISH WITH LATE-17TH-CENTURY BORDER (H44cm/17¼in)

This dish was altered in the 1830s when the centre was soldered to the border. The band of strapwork and foliage is contemporary with the chased armorials which are those of the 4th Earl of Ashburnham, a renowned collector.

'JONAH AND THE WHALE' SALT CELLAR, 16TH CENTURY (H31.4cm/12½in)

This German piece is unmarked; it has been extensively altered, notably by adding the female figure – work known to have been done before 1857.

practice; they were probably the type of object most easily sold to collectors. Doubtless some were passed off as fine examples of old plate, sometimes with old marks transposed and often with their surfaces nicely gilded to cover up problem areas.

Some concocted pieces, however, were properly marked, such as the range of toilet boxes in late seventeenth-century taste made by William Elliott in the 1820s, with early plaques set into the lids; a dish of 1822 by Edward Farrell in Baroque taste centred by a seventeenth-century panel; and many cups, goblets and tankards incorporating seventeenth- and eighteenth-century ivories. A third option would be to remove all trace of the marks.

Over the centuries forgers and improvers have created a great many problem pieces. Collectors and specialists puzzle over them, deprecate them and are amused by them; undoubtedly life would be duller without them. But at some time a purchaser has been duped and the law has been broken. Forgery is slowly being eliminated and, on the whole, the practice is now rare due to stringent controls and the relatively small financial gain made by the faker. The game is not worth the candle.

SELECT BIBLIOGRAPHY

EARLY SILVER

Baratte, F. and Painter, K. (eds), *Trésors d'orfèvrerie gallo-romaines*, Paris, 1989

Bothmer, D. von, *Greek and Roman Treasury*, New York, 1984

Clark, G., *Symbols of Excellence: Precious Materials as Expressions of Status*, Cambridge, 1986

Dalley, S., *Mari and Karana: Two Old Babylonian Cities*, London, 1984

Dodwell, C.R., *Anglo-Saxon Art: A New Perspective*, Manchester, 1982

Galanina, L. and Grach, N., *Scythian Art: The Legacy of the Scythian World, Mid-7th to 3rd Century BC*, St Petersburg, 1986

Mundell Mango, M., *Silver from Early Byzantium: The Kaper Karaon and Related Treasures*, Baltimore, 1986

Oliver, A., Jr., *Silver for the Gods: 800 Years of Greek and Roman Silver*, Toledo, Ohio, 1977

Vickers, M. (ed.), *Pots and Pans: a Colloquium on Precious Metals and Ceramics in the Muslim, Chinese and Graeco-Roman Worlds, Oxford, 1985*, Oxford, 1986

THE MEDIEVAL PERIOD

Campbell, M., 'Gold, silver and precious stones' in Blair, J. and Ramsay, N. (eds), *English Medieval Industries*, London, 1991

Campbell, M., *Medieval Enamels*, London, 1983

Dodwell, C.R. (ed.), *Theophilus De Diversis Artibus*, London, 1961

English Romanesque Art 1066–1200, exh. cat., London, 1984

Fritz, J.M., *Goldschmiedekunst der Gotik in Mitteleuropa*, Munich, 1982

Les Fastes du Gothique: le siècle de Charles V, exh. cat., Paris, 1981

Lightbown, R.W., *Secular Goldsmiths' Work in Medieval France*, London, 1978

Rhein und Maas: Kunst und Kultur 800–1400, exh. cat., Cologne and Brussels, 1972

Swarzenski, H., *Monuments of Romanesque Art*, London, 1953

Taburet-Delahaye, E., *L'Orfèvrerie Gothique au Musée de Cluny*, Paris, 1987

The Golden Age of Anglo-Saxon Art, exh. cat., London, 1984

RENAISSANCE AND MANNERISM

Bimbenet-Privat, M., *Les Orfèvres Parisiens de la Renaissance 1506–1620*, Paris, 1992

English Silver Treasures from the Kremlin, exh. cat., Sotheby's, London, 1991

Frederiks, J.W., *Dutch Silver*, The Hague, 1952–61

Glanville, P., *Silver in Tudor and Early Stuart England*, London, 1991

Hayward, J.F., *Virtuoso Goldsmiths and the Triumph of Mannerism 1540–1620*, London, 1976

Kohlhausen, Heinrich, *Nürnberger Goldschmiedekunst des Mittelalters und der Dürerzeit, 1240 bis 1540*, Berlin, 1968

Oman, C.C., *The Golden Age of Hispanic Silver 1400–1665* Victoria & Albert Museum, London, 1968

Pechstein, K., *Goldschmiedewerke der Renaissance*, Kunstgewerbemuseum, Berlin, 1971

Tait, H., *Catalogue of the Waddesdon Bequest in the British Museum*, vol. II *The Silver Plate*, vol. III *The Curiosities*, London, 1988 and 1991

Wenzel Jamnitzer und die Nürnberger Goldschmiedekunst 1500–1700, exh. cat., Nuremberg and Munich, 1985

BAROQUE, ROCOCO AND NEOCLASSICISM

Babelon, J. *et al*, *Les Grands Orfèvres de Louis XIII à Charles X*, Paris, 1965

Blair, C. (ed.), *The History of Silver*, London, 1987

Bradbury, F., *History of Old Sheffield Plate*, London, 1912

Catello, Elio and Corrado, *Argenti Napoletani dal XVI al XIX secolo*, Naples, 1973

Di Natale, M.C., *Ori e Argenti di Sicilia dal Quattrocento al Settecento*, Milan, 1989

Erikson, S., *Early Neoclassicism in France*, London, 1974

Fornari, S., *Gli Argenti Romani*, Rome, 1968

Goodison, N., *Ormolu: The Work of Matthew Boulton*, London, 1974

Grimwade, A.G., *London Goldsmiths 1697–1837. Their Marks & Lives*, 3rd ed., London, 1990

Paul de Lamerie, exh. cat., London, 1990

Hernmarck, C., *The Art of the European Silversmith 1430–1830*, London and New York, 1977

Lankheit, K., *Florentinische Barockplastik. Die Kunst am Hofe der Letzten Medici 1670–1743*, Munich, 1962

Lightbown, R.W., *Catalogue of Scandinavian and Baltic Silver in the Victoria & Albert Museum*, London, 1975

Nocq, H., *Le Poinçon de Paris. Repertoire des maitres-orfèvres de la juridiction de Paris depuis le Moyen-Age jusqu'a la fin du XVIII siècle*, Paris, 1926–31

Rowe, R., *Adam Silver 1765–1795*, London, 1965

Schliemann, E. (ed.), *Die Goldschmiede Hamburgs*, Hamburg, 1985

Schroder, T., *The National Trust Book of English Domestic Silver 1500–1900*, London, 1988

Seling, H., *Die Kunst der Augsburger Goldschmiede 1529–1868*, Munich, 1980

Rococo. Art and Design in Hogarth's England, exh. cat., London, 1984

Snowman, A.K., *Eighteenth-century European Gold Boxes*, London, 1990

Triomphe du Baroque, exh. cat., Brussels, 1991

THE NINETEENTH CENTURY

Bouilhet, H., *L'Orfèvrerie française aux XVIIIe et XIXe Siècles*, Paris, 1908–12

Bury, S., 'The Lengthening Shadow of Rundells', *The Connoisseur*, February, March, April, 1966

Carlton House. Past Glories of George IV's Palace, exh. cat., London, 1991–2

Clark, K., *The Gothic Revival*, 2nd ed., 1950

Culme, J., *Nineteenth-Century Silver*, London, 1977

Culme, J., *The Directory of Gold and Silversmiths, Jewellers and Allied Traders 1838–1914*, Woodbridge, Suffolk, 1987

Dennis, F., *Three Centuries of French Domestic Silver*, Metropolitan Museum of Art, New York, 1960

Victorian and Edwardian Decorative Art, exh. cat., London, 1972

Oman, C.C., 'A Problem of Artistic Responsibility', *Apollo*, March, 1966

Pickford, I. (ed.), *Jackson's Silver and Gold Marks of England, Scotland and Ireland*, Woodbridge, Suffolk, 1989.

Snodin, M., 'J.K. Boileau, a forgotten designer of silver', *The Connoisseur*, June, 1978

Victorian Church Art, exh. cat., London, 1971

Wardle, P., *Victorian Silver*, London, 1963

White, J., *The Cambridge Movement*, 1962

Young, H., 'A further note on J.J. Boileau, "a forgotten designer of silver"', *Apollo*, October, 1986

AMERICAN SILVER

Buhler, K., *American Silver 1655–1825 in the Museum of Fine Arts, Boston*, Boston, 1972

Buhler, K. and Hood, G., *American Silver: Garvan and Other Collections in the Yale University Art Gallery*, New Haven, Connecticut, 1970

Carpenter, C.H., Jr., *Gorham Silver 1831–1981*, New York, 1982

Carpenter, C.H., Jr. and Carpenter, M.B., *Tiffany Silver*, New York, 1978

Fales, M.G., *Early American Silver*, New York, 1970

Hood G., *American Silver: A History of Style 1650–1900*, New York, 1971

Metropolitan Museum of Art, *Nineteenth-Century America: Furniture and Other Decorative Arts*, New York, 1970

Safford, F.G., 'Colonial Silver in The American Wing', *The Metropolitan Museum of Art Bulletin*, 41 (Summer 1983)

Ward, Barbara M. and Ward, Gerald W.R. (eds), *Silver in American Life*, New York, 1979.

Warren, D.B., Howe, K.S. and Brown, M.K., *Marks of Achievement: Four Centuries of American Presentation Silver*, Houston, 1987

ARTS AND CRAFTS & ART NOUVEAU

Hiort, E., *Modern Danish Silver*, Copenhagen, 1954

Krekel-Aalberse, A., *Art Nouveau and Art Deco Silver*, London, 1989

Leidelmeijer, F. and Cingel, D., *Art Nouveau en Art Deco in Nederland*, Amsterdam, 1983

Naylor, G., *The Arts and Crafts Movement*, London, 1990

Schweiger, W.J., *Wiener Werkstatte, Design in Vienna 1903–1932*, London, 1984

ART DECO

Bonneville, F. de, *Jean Puiforcat*, Paris, 1986

Bouilhet, T., *L'Orfèvrerie française au 20ème siècle*, Paris, 1941

Moller, J.E.R., *Georg Jensen, The Danish Silversmith*, Copenhagen, 1985

Rotterdam, *Silver of a New Era, International Highlights of Precious Metalware from 1880 to 1940*, exh. cat., 1992

POST-WAR SILVER

Chadour, B. (ed.), *Eighth European Silver Triennale '86*, Hanau, 1986

Hiort, E., *Modern Danish Silver*, New York, 1954

Hughes, G., *Modern Silver Throughout the World*, London, 1967

Lutteman, H.D. and Lindkvist, L. (eds.), *Contemporary Swedish Design*, Stockholm, 1983

Mazzariol, G. and Giannetti, A., *Silver and Architects in the Cleto Munari Collection*, Padua, 1986

McFadden, D., *Scandinavian Modern Design*, New York, 1980

Moller, V.S., *Modern Danish Silver*, New York, 1954

Persson, S., *Sigurd Persson Silver*, Stockholm, 1979

Poutasuo, T. (ed.), *Finnish Silver*, Helsinki, 1989

Welch, R., *Hand and Machine*, London, 1986

FORGERIES, FAKES AND CONCOCTIONS

Bly, J. (ed.), *Is it Genuine?*, London, 1986

Forbes, J.S., 'Forgery of Hall Marks', *Worshipful Company of Goldsmiths Review 1971–2*, London, 1992

Glanville, P., 'Tudor or Tudorbethan', *ISJFS Catalogue*, London, April 1989

Hackenbrock, Y., 'Reinhold Vasters, Goldsmith', *Metropolitan Museum Journal 19/20*, New York, 1986

London, *Fake, The Art of Deception*, exh. cat., 1990

HALLMARKS AND STANDARDS

Since, for most of its history, silver has been used either as specie or as plate convertible into coin, it has been necessary to regulate the proportion of silver in the silver alloys used to make both plate and coin.

The earliest system of marking silver plate appears to have been developed in France in the thirteenth century although earlier, as yet unintelligible, marks were struck in Byzantium. A comparable system was adopted in England, although the remainder of Europe had more or less local rules which varied from town to town. This survey is intended for guidance only and researching any hallmark should be undertaken using the standard work on the country or town where a piece was made.

FRANCE

Until the Revolution of 1789, the standard of silver alloy used in France was 95.8 per cent pure silver. Marks denoting the town guild appear as early as 1272, with maker's marks appearing after 1378, and being made obligatory some fifty years later. Until 1789, and probably as late as 1796, the maker's mark on French plate comprised the maker's initials and a device to distinguish the mark from that of a maker with the same initials. Certain towns incorporated additional specific symbols into the maker's mark, such as Paris which used a crowned fleur-de-lys and two small dots (*grains de remède*) in all maker's marks from 1493.

From 1677 additional marks indicated the obligation to pay tax on a piece of silver (the *charge* mark) and the payment of tax (the *dècharge* mark). The three marks – the maker's mark, mark of the guild (the date letter) and the *charge* mark – were struck on the incomplete piece of silver whereas the *dècharge* was struck after completion.

After 1797 new regulations were established. Maker's marks were struck in the form of a lozenge and two standards of silver (95 per cent and 80 per cent) were introduced. In addition excise marks were struck to indicate duty paid at assay. Different marks were also used in Paris and the provinces. The system was changed in 1809, and again in 1819, following the theft of punches from the mint. In 1838 the standard and excise marks were combined.

ENGLAND

The first documentary evidence of hallmarking in England occurred in 1300 with the introduction of the leopard's head to indicate sterling standard (92.5 per cent). In 1363 each goldsmith was required to have his own mark, at first a device and later his initials. In 1478 the system of date letters using a 20-letter alphabet (j and v–z being excluded) was introduced in London; in 1544 the lion passant was added to denote sterling silver and the leopard's head became the London mark. Between 1697 and 1720 a new standard (Britannia or New Sterling at 95.8 per cent) was made obligatory. Maker's marks were changed to the first two letters of a goldsmith's surname, while the figure of Britannia and a lion's head erased replaced the leopard's head and lion passant. This standard remained optional after 1720.

In 1784 an additional mark indicating the payment of duty was added. This was the monarch's head in profile which continued to be struck until 1890. Outside London, various provincial centres used their own system of marks used to guarantee the Sterling or Britannia standards.

GERMANY

To speak of Germany as a nation before the late nineteenth century is inaccurate. The area we now call Germany comprised city states, principalities, electorates and bishoprics, each of which had its own system of hallmarking. However, the two principal cities where goldsmithing had a great tradition were Nuremberg and Augsburg.

NUREMBERG. It is clear that some form of hallmarking existed in Nuremberg in the late fourteenth century. It is unclear, however, whether the town mark, the letter N in Roman script, was used before the 1460s. By 1511 the standard of silver had been set at 14 lots (87.5 per cent). By 1541 the town mark and a system of recording maker's marks, either a device or initials, had been incorporated. Yet no system of date letters was used until 1766, and even then the letter was only changed every three or four years. The system appears to have been abandoned in the post-Napoleonic period.

AUGSBURG. Goldsmiths are recorded in Augsburg since at least the early thirteenth century, but it was not until 1529 that the town mark, a 'pineapple', was introduced. The form varied and in 1735 a date letter was introduced into the base of the pineapple. As with Nuremberg, maker's marks were at first devices, or a merchant's mark, and later initials. The system of hallmarking appears to have died out in Augsburg in the second quarter of the nineteenth century. In 1884 a federal mark, a crown and crescent moon, was introduced throughout Germany to denote 80 per cent pure silver.

RUSSIA

The guild system in Russia was particularly well regulated in Moscow and St Petersburg. The Moscow goldsmiths either belonged to the Silver Row, or the Kremlin Armoury, where court goldsmiths worked. In 1700 the Silver Row was incorporated with the Armoury and the imperial eagle was introduced as the assay mark. In 1741 this was, in turn, replaced by the arms of the city, St George and the dragon. Two guilds existed in St Petersburg, one for native Russians and the other, established in 1714, for foreigners. The mark for the town was the arms of the city (crossed anchors and a sceptre). The marks found on Russian silver until 1899 were the maker's mark in the form of maker's initials, the assay mark in the form of the arms of the city and, usually, the date and a standard mark. This last mark, for silver, was normally '84' being the equivalent of 87.35 per cent pure silver (the Russian pound contains 96 zolotniks).

Under a *ukase* of 1882, introduced in 1896 but not actually in practice until 1899, the marks were rationalized. The maker's marks were unchanged but the standard marks and town marks were combined in an oval depicting a head of a girl wearing the *kokoshnik*, the traditional Russian headdress. This head was reversed to face right in 1908, and abandoned in 1917. In 1927 a similar head, but in a worker's scarf, with a hammer was introduced. A star enclosing a hammer and sickle replaced the head in 1958.

OTHER EUROPEAN COUNTRIES

Most other European countries use, or used, some form of hallmarking to regulate silver standards. Those such as Italy, Holland and part of Switzerland adopted the French system when under Napoleonic rule, and a version of that system was often adopted after 1814. Scandinavian countries used a system comparable to that of the German towns although Stockholm introduced a system of date letters as early as 1689.

UNITED STATES OF AMERICA

No unified system of hallmarking exists for the United States. Individual makers used marks, mostly initials, or sometimes a complete name, and it is possible therefore to identify the towns in which pieces were made if the location of the maker is known. Modern American silver is frequently marked 'Sterling', but this mark is applied by the maker and should not necessarily be considered a guarantee of standard.

FRANCE

 Maker's mark of François-Thomas Germain

 Charge *mark for Paris, 1756–62*

 Standard or guild mark for Paris, 1753–4

 Paris *décharge 1756–62*

  Maker's mark of Martin-Guillaume Biennais

 Tax mark for Paris, 1798–1809

 Standard mark for Paris, 1798–1809

ENGLAND

 Maker's mark of Paul Storr

 Town mark of London

 Standard mark for sterling silver

 London date letter for 1796–7

 Maker's mark of Paul de Lamerie

 Town mark of London

 Standard mark for Britannia standard

 London date letter for 1716–17

GERMANY

 Maker's mark of Hans Ulrich

Town mark of Nuremberg

Maker's mark of Philipp Stenglin

Town mark of Augsburg

RUSSIA

 Maker's mark of Pavel Sasikov

Town mark of Moscow

Mark of the assay-master André Titov, 1787

Standard mark for silver (87.35%) 1899–1908

GLOSSARY

acanthus Decoration based on a stylized form of the thick, scallop-edged *Acanthus spinosa* leaf. Of classical origin, it was used during the Renaissance and Baroque periods and extensively on Neoclassical silver, generally as a border pattern.

acid-etching Method by which a pattern or matt surface is made on silver by allowing acid to corrode and remove the surface. An acid-resistant substance is used to cover areas where the acid is not wanted.

alloy A mixture of two or more metals. Silver, too soft to be used in its pure state, is alloyed with a **base metal**, usually copper, to make it hard enough to be used. The presence of copper in silver also facilitates electro-gilding.

annealing Process by which metal is made malleable by repeated heating. Annealing prevents metal becoming brittle and cracking while it is being shaped by the **raising** process.

antependium A hanging for the front of an altar.

anthemion Decorative motif of Greek origin, based on the radiating pattern of a stylized honeysuckle flower and leaves. Associated chiefly with the Neoclassical style.

applied decoration Ornamental detail, such as **cut-card work** or intricate pieces fashioned by **casting**, made separately and attached to the completed object.

aquamanile Ewer, sometimes in the shape of an animal, used to hold water for washing the hands in either a secular or religious context.

arabesque, or **moresque** Pattern of abstract, interlaced foliage made on silver by **acid-etching** or **engraving**. Originating in Saracenic metalwork, it is characteristic of Mannerist silverware, particularly that made in Germany.

assay The testing of the quality of a silver object to ascertain that the proportion of silver and copper in the **alloy** meets the legal standard.

auricular Decorative style consisting of curious shell- and ear-like forms and incorporating sinuous monsters. It was developed in Holland in the first quarter of the 17th century by Paulus van Vianen and often used by his brother Adam and nephew Christian van Vianen.

baluster Vase shape derived from Renaissance architecture and used for the stems of goblets, the shafts of candlesticks and other vertical members.

bas relief See **relief**.

base metal 1. Any metal besides the precious metals (gold, silver, titanium and platinum etc.). Distinguished from them by being corruptible, or susceptible to tarnish and corrosion. 2. The metal onto which gold or silver is **plated**.

beading Border decoration consisting of a row of small, closely set hemispheres.

bombé Literally 'blown out'. A pronounced convex shape, seen for example in tureens and other vessels, particularly in the Rococo style.

bonbonnière A small lidded box for sweets, usually decorated and without hinges. Term not used until *c.*1770. Up to that date the term *boite à bonbons* was used to describe boxes for comfits or dragees for sweetening the breath.

brandwijskom A Dutch two-handled bowl used for the ceremonial serving of a raisin and brandy beverage.

bright-cut engraving See **engraving**.

Britannia metal An alloy of tin, antimony and copper resembling pewter. Sometimes used as the **base metal** in **electroplating**. Not to be confused with **Britannia standard**.

Britannia standard Properly called 'New Sterling'. The **standard** of silver, higher than **sterling standard**, denoting a proportion of 95.8 per cent pure silver as used in France (see **alloy**). An Act making this standard compulsory from 27 March 1697 to 1 June 1720 was introduced to prevent coinage being melted down and used for **plate**. Britannia standard silver, marked with the figure of Britannia, continued as an optional standard after 1720.

buffet An array of silver, for display rather than use, in the eating room. The term derives from 'buffet', a tiered sideboard on which the silver was set out.

burnishing Smoothing and polishing silver, and concealing joins, by cleaning it with soft soap, then sand and water; rubbing it with a series of different burnishers (steel, agate and bloodstone); then polishing it with jeweller's rouge, a mildly abrasive cleaning agent.

cartouche An ornamental scroll-edged panel, itself sometimes incorporating decoration.

cassolette or *athénienne* See **perfume burner**.

caster A cylindrical, pear- or vase-shaped vessel with a pierced cover, used for sprinkling sugar or spices. If in a set of three, one may have a 'blind' or blanked off cover, usually for powdered mustard.

casting bottle A bottle or flask for rose water, sprinkled through a pierced cover. These small items were considered the height of luxury in the 16th century.

casting Shaping metal by pouring molten metal into a mould. See also *cire perdue*.

caudle cup Two-handled bowl for individual servings of caudle (a gruel made with spice, wine and sugar), but more usually used for display on a **buffet**.

centrepiece or **épergne** Often elaborate piece of silverware for the dining table. Generally a combination of candleholders, sweetmeat baskets, **casters** and cruets, normally used for the dessert.

chasing Method of impressing linear decoration into silver with a blunt-ended punch, or chaser, struck with a hammer from the front. Used alone, it is known as flat-chasing, but was also used in conjunction with **embossing**.

châtelaine Device for carrying keys, a watch and other small objects, and intended to hang from a woman's belt.

chevron Zigzag pattern, a heraldic device.

chinoiserie Decoration consisting of a European adaptation of Oriental motifs such as pagodas, fretwork, birds, mandarins and coolies. Highly fashionable during the 1680s in England and the Rococo period.

ciborium 1. Free-standing shrine used in pagan religion. 2. Covered goblet used to contain the host during Mass.

cire perdue Method of **casting** metal, usually small objects for use as applied ornamental detail. A model of the desired shape is carved in solid wax or wax covering a rough clay mould, which is then encased in an investment, or covering, of plaster. When the whole is heated, the wax runs out leaving a cavity into which molten metal is poured. On solidifying, the metal takes the shape of the original wax model.

claws-and-ball foot Foot in the shape of claws or talons grasping a ball.

crater Bowl for serving wine, used in and before classical times.

credenza Sideboard or **buffet** for the display of fine metalware, especially in Renaissance Italy.

cut-card work Form of **applied decoration** on silver. It is cut from flat sheets of silver and usually takes simple foliate shapes. It was much favoured by Huguenot silversmiths in the late 17th to early 18th century and is associated with Queen Anne style.

Cymric Style of silver having a handmade appearance and incorporating Celtic and Art Nouveau elements. Designed by various craftsmen, including Archibald Knox (1864–1933), and sold through Liberty & Co. from 1899.

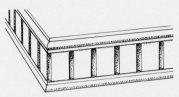

dentil ornament Decoration consisting of a series of equally spaced square or rectangular tooth-like blocks, a feature originating in classical architecture.

diaper pattern Trelliswork of squares or lozenges, sometimes enclosing other decoration.

die stamping Method of stamping metal into a steel die, originally developed by medallists but used during late 19th century for producing decorative details.

double cup Two goblets, the bowl of one inverted over that of the other and joining at the rim. It was a piece which might be presented as a wedding gift, or used in a ceremony of welcome, particularly in 16th-century Germany.

dram cup Small cup of variable shape and size, for small draughts of spirit.

drop pressing See **die stamping**.

écuelle Shallow bowl for individual servings of soup, or semi-liquid food, having, on silver examples, two flat, horizontal handles and a cover.

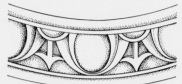

egg and dart Decoration, of classical origin, consisting of **ovolo**, or egg, shapes alternating with arrowheads.

electroforming or **electrotyping** Process by which a replica of an object is made by using an electrical current to deposit a thin layer of metal into a mould of that object. A negative mould of the object to be replicated is made in a water-resistant substance such as latex, or 'gutta percha'.

electroplating Process by which an electrical current is used to deposit a thin layer of silver on an article made in **base metal**, usually copper or **nickel silver**. Developed in the 1830s and patented by Elkington & Co., it was a revolutionary advance that brought silver within reach of the middle classes.

electrotyping See **electroforming**.

electrum A natural **alloy** of gold and silver used chiefly in classical times.

embossing or **repoussé** Method of producing raised ornament on metal by hammering or punching the inner side. Embossed decoration was often outlined with **chasing** to give it definition.

enamel An opaque or translucent glass substance, coloured with metallic pigments, that can be fused onto metal, usually at about 800 degrees C. It has been used as decoration in a variety of ways: *basse taille* (translucent enamel covering **engraving**); *champlevé* (enamel dropped into shallow depressions cut into the metal); *cloisonnè* (enamel divided by narrow ribbons of metal); *en ronde bosse* (covering decorative details in the round); and *plique à jour* (like *cloisonnè* but without the metal backing, so that light shines through). Enamel can also be painted with enamels of contrasting colour.

engraving Method of decorating metal by cutting thin furrows with a graver or burin, thereby removing a small amount of metal. In bright-cut engraving, the graver cuts into the silver a faceted groove that sparkles as it catches the light.

épergne See **centrepiece**.

fake An item made with the intention of deceiving the owner that it is of another date or origin.

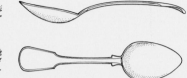

Fiddle pattern Violin-shaped termination to the handle of spoons and forks. Introduced in the 18th century and one of many patterns for **flatware** popular in Europe and America.

filigree Tracery of fine silver, gold or copper wire, featuring geometric or figurative motifs.

finial Decorative detail surmounting a lid or terminating the handle of a spoon. In the latter case it is also known as a **knop**.

flat-chasing See **chasing**.

flatting machine or **mill** Device, developed in the 1740s, for turning ingots into sheet metal by mechanical means as opposed to manual hammering.

flatware Term, of American origin, denoting knives, forks and spoons for use at table and as distinct from **hollow ware**.

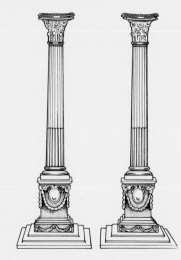

fluting Decoration consisting of concave vertical channels. In spiral fluting, the channels coil round the shape they decorate.

fly punching Method of decorating **Sheffield Plate** by piercing it in such a way as to prevent the underlying copper from being visible in the holes. This was accomplished by using the **punch** to drag some surface silver over the copper exposed by the piercing.

forgery Something made in fraudulent imitation of another object, style or type of object, with the intent to deceive a prospective buyer and offered for sale, usually at a high price.

gadrooning Decoration consisting of convex lobes, either straight or curved, and used chiefly for edging.

gauge The thickness of sheet metal.

gemellions Shallow bowls, usually used in pairs, for washing the hands at table, particularly favoured during the Middle Ages.

gilt Entirely covered in gold. See also **parcel gilt**.

guilloche Decoration consisting of undulating lines counter-entwined to produce a continuous figure-of-eight pattern. Taken from classical architecture, it was a popular form of decoration from Renaissance times onward.

guilloché Engraved, engine-turned decorative pattern; when covered with transparent enamel that reveals the pattern beneath, the technique is known as *tour à guillocher*.

hallmark The mark identifying the hall, or assay office, where silver was taken for **assay**, but now applied to any standard or tax mark on precious metals other than the maker's mark. Aside from the hallmark (or town mark), English silver usually bears a **standard** mark (indicating that the silver content of the metal meets legal requirements); a date mark (indicating the year in which it was taken for assay); and a sponsor's mark (identifying the person who sent it for assay). See also **Britannia standard**, **sterling standard**, and Hallmarks and Standards, p. 194.

hanap A large **standing cup**.

hollow ware An American term for receptacles such as cups, goblets, punch bowls, teapots and cream boats, as distinct from **flatware**.

Huguenot silversmiths French and Dutch Protestants who took refuge in England after the revocation of the Edict of Nantes (1685). Their work is characterized by bold and elegant shapes and they brought with them decorative techniques familiar on the Continent.

japonisme European adaptation of Japanese style and motifs such as chrysanthemums, blossom, bamboo, birds and fans, especially associated with the Arts and Crafts and Aesthetic movements.

joaillier French term for a member of the guild of *marchands-orfèvres-joailliers*, literally craftsmen entitled to make and sell goldsmiths' work and jewellery. The *joailliers* tended to produce the latter, a term which also encompassed gold boxes and objects of vertu.

key pattern Repeating motif of straight lines, usually at right angles, derived from classical Greek architecture.

knop Decorative swelling in the stem of a goblet or termination to the shaft of a spoon handle.

lathe-finishing, **lathe-turning** and **lathe-spinning** See **spinning**.

Martelé Literally 'hammered'. The trade name of a variety of Art Nouveau silver entirely handmade at the Gorham Company in Rhode Island, United States, at the end of the 19th century.

mask The term used in architecture and the decorative arts for a face without a body.

mauresque See **arabesque**.

mazer Shallow wooden drinking bowl with a broad silver rim or other **mount**, so-called from the High German word *Masa*. Widely used, mainly in northern Europe, from the Middle Ages to the early 16th century.

mercury gilding Process by which an amalgam of gold and mercury is applied to the prepared surface of metals to be gilded under heat. The mercury is evaporated by the heat as free mercury vapour, leaving a film of gold deposited on the object. Also known as fire gilding, the technique was in use from AD300 (although known in China 600 years earlier) and was used universally for good quality gilding until supplanted by electroplating in about 1840.

monstrance Vessel, usually made of gold or silver, in which the host, or communion wafer, is displayed for veneration.

monteith Large circular or oval bowl for water, with a scalloped rim for holding glasses by the foot so that they could be cooled or rinsed in the water. The name is said to derive from a Scotsman, Mr Monteith, who wore a cloak with a scalloped edge.

moresque See **arabesque**.

Mosan School The first great tradition of Western European enamelling and metalworking, which flourished in the Meuse valley in the 12th century. Most surviving Mosan enamels date from between 1140 and 1180. See also **Rhenish School**.

mount A casing or fitting, usually in gold or silver, added to protect or enhance an object made of another material, for example, ivory, rock crystal, coconut, wood or porcelain, or to make it into a serviceable article.

nef Vessel in the form of a rigged sailing ship, used in royal and noble households mostly during the Middle Ages and originally intended to hold the personal eating utensils, and even a napkin, of the owner. Of lavish workmanship, it served as a status symbol and had a ceremonial as well as a utilitarian function.

nickel silver An **alloy** of copper, zinc and nickel developed by Elkington & Co. in the 1840s and used as the **base metal** in **electroplating**. Proportions vary, but usually 2:1:1 to 3:1:1.

niello An amalgam of copper, silver and sulphur making a black waxy substance. It is usually inlaid into engraved designs in gold or silver and, as such, was popular in the Middle Ages, in 19th-century Russia and during the Art Deco period.

ogee A double, or S-shaped, curve.

Old English pattern Particular design of the handle of spoons and forks, in which the stem is plain and the terminal curves slightly backwards.

Old Sheffield Plate See **Sheffield Plate**.

openwork Pierced decoration effectively forming a network of silver and producing a delicate effect. It was used, for example, in bread baskets, fruit bowls and fish slices.

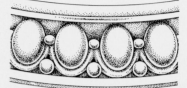

ovolo Pattern of repeated convex oval or egg shapes, of classical origin and often used in the 15th and 16th centuries, mostly as border decoration.

palmette Fan-shaped motif derived from the frond of a palm tree. Extensively used in the Neoclassical period.

parcel gilt Decoration of silver where part is covered in gold, creating a contrast between the gilding and the colour of the underlying material.

patina The surface sheen produced on silver: 1. naturally, as a result of handling, tarnish and minute scratches over many years. 2. Artificially, for decorative purposes.

patinate To create a **patina** by artificial means, usually for decoration.

pax Devotional plaque offered by the priest for the congregation to kiss.

perfume burner A small brazier for burning aromatic pastilles or evaporating liquid perfumes.

piercing Method of decorating metal by punching, or sawing, a design through it.

planishing Process of eliminating imperfections in silver after **raising**. A convex-faced hammer is used to smooth out previous hammer marks and even out the **gauge** before **burnishing**.

plate The traditional term for wrought silver and gold, both religious (church plate) and secular. It is now erroneously used to denote **plated silver**.

plateau A long low platform for the centre of a dining table. It usually stood on small feet and was often made of mirror glass in several sections so that it could be shortened or lengthened at will.

plated silver Silver plated on to a **base metal**. See **electroplating**, **electroforming** and **Sheffield Plate**.

pointillé or **pouncework** A type of decoration where the metal is struck with a pointed punch, either to form an overall ground pattern or to form lines of dots.

porringer A bowl, perhaps originally for individual servings of soup, stew or porridge, but frequently used for display on a **buffet**.

pot-à-oille or **pot-oglio** French term for a tureen on stand in which a certain ragout, or *oglio*, fashionable in 18th-century France, was made or served.

punch Implement with which a **hallmark** or various kinds of decoration, such as **chasing** or **embossing**, are impressed into silver and other metals.

putto From the Latin *putus* meaning 'little man', a child-like figure much used as a decorative motif in the Renaissance and Neoclassical periods.

pyx A small, circular lidded box in which the host is kept.

raising Making **hollow ware** from sheet metal by hammering and rotating it against a wooden or metal stake.

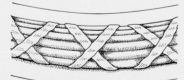

reeding Parallel, convex moulding suggesting bundled reeds.

relief Decoration raised from the surface of metal. Bas-relief is only slightly raised.

repoussé See **embossing**.

Rhenish School The second great Western European school of metalworking and enamelling (after the Mosan School), situated around Cologne and the Lower Rhineland. Rhenish enamels show Mosan influence, though with a preference for greens and blues.

rocaille Literally 'rockwork'. Exuberant, often exotic motif used either as ornament or as an integral part of an object. An essential part of the Rococo style.

rolling mill Mechanical device for turning an ingot of silver into a sheet by passing it through a series of rollers. Developed in the late 17th century, rolling was a swifter method than hammering and produced sheet silver of a finer, more even **gauge**.

serpentine Of undulating plan (or horizontal outline) usually consisting of a convex sweep flanked by concave curves. Not as pronounced as a **bombé**.

Sheffield Plate Sheet metal made by fusing silver to one or both sides of an ingot of copper and rolled to sheet form. The technique was developed by Thomas Boulsover, a Sheffield cutler, from 1742 and used commercially during the second half of the 18th century and first half of the 19th, notably by Matthew Boulton. Old Sheffield Plate is generally taken to mean plate made during that period, Sheffield Plate referring to that made subsequently.

silvered Plated with silver.

silver gilt Silver plated with gold.

silver plate See **plate**.

spinning Method of shaping **hollow ware** by pressing sheet silver into a wooden or metal former or 'chuck', rotating on a lathe. Known since ancient times but superseded by other methods, spinning was revived in England *c*.1820. It is especially practical for thin gauge silver of relatively simple form.

spun silver See **spinning**.

standard The quality of silver, measured by the proportion of pure silver to copper in the **alloy**. See also **Britannia standard** and **sterling standard**.

standard mark Mark punched onto silver at **assay**, certifying that its **standard** meets legal requirements.

standing cup A tall goblet on a knopped or baluster stem, with or without a cover. A prestigious piece with ceremonial associations.

steeple cup A goblet on stem, with a cover surmounted by a tall, narrow **finial** resembling a steeple.

sterling standard The **standard** of silver predominantly used in Britain, being 92.5 per cent pure silver.

strapwork Type of ornamental pattern in architecture and the decorative arts consisting of interlacing bands or straps, virtually invented by Rosso Fiorentino at Fontainebleau.

surtout de table Term used in France (and in England) to describe an elaborate centrepiece for a dining table.

swag or **festoon** A suspended garland of fruit, foliage or flowers, ribbons or drapery, characteristic of the Renaissance and Neoclassical periods.

taperstick A holder for a taper, similar to a small candlestick.

tazza A shallow-bowled cup or dish on a stem with a central knop (so shaped to afford a secure grip), originating in Renaissance Italy.

thurible A container on chains in which incense was burned.

triton Mythological figure with man's head and torso and dolphin's tail, sometimes shown holding a trident or conch shell.

troy weight Named after the French town of Troyes. System used to express weight of precious metals. Twelve troy ounces (as opposed to 16oz in Avoirdupois) make up 1lb, and the troy ounce is divided into 20 pennyweights, or 31.104 grammes (as opposed to 28.352 grammes in the Avoirdupois ounce).

turning See **spinning**.

trelliswork Decoration consisting of a band of intersecting straight lines, similar to the **diaper pattern** and popular in Ireland, but used mainly in the period 1735–7. It is found on jugs, the covers of kettles and the rims of salvers.

Vitruvian scroll Wave-like motif repeated to form a border decoration. Of classical origin, it was widely used on 18th-century silver.

white silver Neither **gilt** nor **parcel gilt**.

windmill cup Goblet in the shape of a miniature windmill, the body of the mill acting as the bowl when the windmill was inverted. It was used in wagers, the object being to drink a cupful before the sails had stopped revolving.

wine cooler 1. Oval cistern for steeping bottles or flagons of wine in ice or iced water and usually set on the floor beneath a **buffet**. 2. Vase, bucket or barrel-shaped vessel in which to chill a single bottle of wine, frequently with a liner to keep the water from wetting the bottle. This form, which stood either on the table or on the sideboard, is first encounterd in the late 17th century and gradually replaced the cistern.

wirework Silver, or **silver-plated** wires of cylindrical, square, rectangular or triangular section, made up into items such as fruit baskets, toast racks and centrepieces.

BIOGRAPHIES

Adam, Robert (1728–92): Scottish architect and designer, working principally in London, who was chiefly responsible for introducing the Neoclassical style to Britain after his return from Italy in 1758.

Algardi, Alessandro (1598–1654): Italian sculptor, working in Rome in the Baroque style. Also made models and designs for fine domestic and church plate.

Altenstetter, David (c.1547–1617): German enameller who worked with Augsburg goldsmiths and clockmakers, producing plaques decorated in translucent enamels featuring animals, flowers and foliage.

Angell, Joseph (fl.c.1800–c.1851/3): Son of a weaver, Angell was a London silversmith, apprenticed to Henry Nutting in 1796. He registered his first mark in 1811 from an address at 55 Compton Street, Clerkenwell, London, and set up in partnership with his nephew in 1831. Joined by other members of the family, the firm continued under various styles all of which incorporated the name Angell.

Ångman, Jacob (1876–1942): Swedish silversmith, very influential in his own country and internationally acknowledged for his functionalist designs. Worked for Guldsmedsaktiebolaget, Sweden's largest silver manufacturer, from 1907 until his death.

Artificers' Guild: Enterprise established in 1901 by Nelson Dawson (1859–1942), a painter, silversmith, jeweller and metalworker, and taken over by Montague Fordham and Edward Spencer in 1903. Silver and other metalwork was made by members of the Guild, mostly to Dawson's designs. The Guild closed in 1942.

Ashbee, Charles Robert (1863–1942): English silver designer, leader of the Arts and Crafts Movement in the 1880s and influential in the promotion of the Art Nouveau style. Ashbee founded the Guild and School of Handicraft in 1888 and registered the mark of the Guild of Handicraft in 1898.

Asprey & Co.: Major London retail and manufacturing jewellers and silversmiths. Founded in 1781 by William Asprey, a descendant of a French Huguenot family. Now run by the sixth generation of the family.

Auguste, Robert-Joseph (c.1723–1805) and **Henry** (1759–1816): French silversmiths, father and son, working in Paris in the Rococo and Neoclassical styles. Robert-Joseph worked for Madame de Pompadour, Louis XVI, Catherine the Great and other royal patrons. Henry received several major commissions for pieces for Napoleon's coronation in 1804.

Baier, Melchior (master 1525 – d. 1577): With **Ludwig Krug** (c.1490–1532), Baier was one of the two most important Nuremberg silversmiths of the second quarter of the 16th century. Both were instrumental in the formation of the south German Renaissance style.

Ball, Tompkins & Black: Firm of New York silversmiths, most prominent in the mid-19th century, dealing in presentation pieces and other silver, some of it made by **John Chandler Moore**. Now trading as Black, Starr & Frost.

Ballin, Claude I (c.1615–78): French goldsmith who worked for Louis XIV, specializing in grand pieces in the Baroque style. Much of his secular work was destroyed when quantities of royal plate were melted down in 1689.

Ballin, Claude II (1661–1754): Nephew of Claude Ballin I. *Orfèvre du roi* to Louis XV, he worked in the Rococo style but regarded rocailles as excessively ornate. Much of his work was destroyed in 1789, when quantities of royal plate were again sent for melting.

Ballin, Mogens (1871–1913): Danish painter and metalworker who established a studio in Copenhagen in 1899 and made pewter and silver vases, lamps, jewellery and other objects in Art Nouveau style.

Barnard, Edward & Sons Ltd: Firm of London silversmiths descended from a business established by Anthony Nelme c.1680. Edward Barnard I (apprenticed 1781 – d. 1853/5) joined the firm in 1773, his descendants continuing today.

Bateman, Hester (1708–94): London silversmith producing mostly flatware and tableware. Her son Jonathan, who joined the family business in 1769, took it over on her retirement in 1790, working in partnership with his brother Peter.

Bateman, William I (1774–1850): Grandson of **Hester Bateman**. Took over the Bateman workshop in 1805 and produced lavish, highly decorated pieces during the Victorian period.

Baur, Tobias (c.1660–1735): Augsburg silversmith known for his travelling services (luxury toilet items and tea wares packed in chests), often with agate and enamel decoration.

Benney, Gerald (b. 1930): British silversmith who studied at Brighton College, Eric Gill's Catholic Guild of St Joseph and St Dominic, and the Royal College of Art, where he later became Professor of Silversmithing and Jewellery. In 1959 he was commissioned to provide the altar plate for Coventry Cathedral; some years later he developed the silver surface which was to become his 'trade-mark' – a textured surface which does not show finger marks. Holds warrants from several members of the Royal family.

Bernini, Gian Lorenzo (1598–1680): Italian sculptor, painter, architect and designer who worked mostly in Rome and was the pre-eminent figure in the development of the Mannerist style. His patrons included the Borghese and Barberini families, and he was principal artist to the papal court. Of his designs for silver – which include a reliquary for Queen Henrietta Maria of England (1636) and a pair of candlesticks for St Peter's, Rome (1673) – none has survived.

Besnier, Nicolas (fl.1714–54): French silversmith working in the Régence and, later, the Rococo style. *Orfèvre du roi* during the Régence period.

Biennais, Martin-Guillaume (1764–1843): Owner of a prominent and prosperous Parisian workshop which employed some 600 craftsmen and produced silver, gilt bronze, jewellery and furniture, much of it made to the designs of **Percier** and **Fontaine**. Was the largest supplier to Napoleon, notably of tableware and travelling sets in which the workshop specialized. Also received commissions from other royalty and nobility in Europe. On his retirement in 1819, the silver and bronze-making side of the business passed to his assistant **Jean-Charles Cahier**.

Biller family: Leading Augsburg silversmiths who produced mostly secular silver in the Baroque style. The most notable are Johann Ludwig I (1656–1746) and II (1692–1746), Albrecht (1663–1720), Johannes (1696–1745) and Johann Jacob (d. 1723).

Birmingham Guild of Handicraft: An association of metalworkers formed by Arthur Dixon (1856–1929) in 1890. Produced silver and other metalwork designed mostly by Dixon and Claude Napier-Clavering.

Black, Starr & Frost. See **Ball, Tompkins & Black**.

Bodendick, Jacob: German silversmith who settled in London in the 1660s and ran a large and prolific workshop in which he employed mostly foreign craftsmen. Noted as a superb embosser of silver.

Bridge, John (1755–1834): See **Rundell, Bridge & Rundell**.

Cahier, Jean-Charles (1772–after 1849): French silversmith who, after a period working with **Martin-Guillaume Biennais**, set up independently, specializing in church silver. His later work, in neo-Gothic style, often incorporates enamel and filigree.

Cardeilhac: Parisian firm of retail and manufacturing jewellers and silversmiths, founded in 1802. Produced pieces in Art Nouveau style and, in the early 20th century, was one of several firms which promoted the Modernist style. Amalgamated with **Orfèvrerie Christofle** in 1951.

Cellini, Benvenuto (1500–72): Major Italian sculptor and goldsmith, the leading exponent of the Mannerist style. Born in Florence, he worked in Rome as a medallist and goldsmith (1519–39) and at Fontainebleau in France for François I, returning to Florence in 1545. Also wrote his famous *Autobiography* and *Treatise on Goldsmithing*. Despite his fame, only one example of his goldsmith's work is known to survive.

Christofle. See **Orfèvrerie Christofle**.

Cortelazzo, Antonio (1819–1903): Italian metalworker from Vicenza, renowned for his display pieces in silver, gold and, steel, with elaborate damascening and enamel.

Crespin, Paul (1694–1770): A London silversmith of French Huguenot parentage. Received commissions from the Portuguese royal family as well as from the English nobility. In 1720, with other Huguenot silversmiths, he made a service for Catherine the Great of Russia.

Cuzner, Bernard (1877–1956): Birmingham designer and silversmith, an influential figure in the Arts and Crafts Movement. Designed and made Cymric silver for **Liberty & Co.** around 1900.

Dawson, Nelson (1859–1942): English painter, silversmith, jeweller and metalworker. Founded the **Artificers' Guild** in 1901, becoming its director in 1903.

Delaunay, Nicolas (*c*.1655–1727): French silversmith and medallist, one of the great protagonists of the classical Baroque under Louis XIV, and certainly the most important goldsmith of the 17th century.

Deutscher Werkbund: An alliance of artists, designers and manufacturers founded in Munich in 1907 to improve and promote industrial design while involving the creative artist.

Devlin, Stuart (b.1931): Australian silversmith who settled in London in 1965. His work, for royalty and industrial bodies as well as for private clients, embraces a wide range of objects and styles. Received a Royal Warrant as Goldsmith and Jeweller to Her Majesty the Queen in 1982.

Dinglinger, Johann Melchior (1664–1731): A major German goldsmith, working in the Baroque style with a Mannerist flavour. Worked mostly for Augustus the Strong. His major works are preserved in the Green Vaults, Dresden.

Dixon, Arthur: See **Birmingham Guild of Handicraft**.

Dixon, James & Sons: Firm of Sheffield silversmiths founded in 1806. In 1829, began making Sheffield plate and Britannia metal wares; by the mid-19th century a major exporter to America. Produced solid silver and plated wares and pewter.

Dresser, Dr Christopher (1834–1904): Birmingham ceramics and silver designer and writer on the decorative arts. His concern with function, simplicity and good design with minimal decoration was combined with a desire to explore techniques of mass-production. His designs for plated silver were bought by **Hukin & Heath**, **James Dixon & Sons** and **Elkington & Co**.

Dürer, Albrecht (1471–1528): Nuremberg painter, engraver and goldsmith. His designs and studies for metalwork include richly decorated covered cups. One of his designs was also the model for a silver-gilt standing cup by **Rundell, Bridge & Rundell**, made 1826–7.

Duvivier, Claude (1688–1747): Parisian silversmith. Maker of a Rococo candelabrum modelled exactly on one of **Juste-Aurèle Meissonnier**'s designs.

Elkington & Co.: Leading firm of Birmingham silversmiths founded in 1830s. Patented or acquired patents for electroplating and other processes and developed various mechanical production processes. Some of its plated ware was designed by **Christopher Dresser**. Now part of British Silverware Ltd.

Falize, Lucien (1839–97): Born in Paris of Belgian parents, Falize was a goldsmith who worked in Medieval, Renaissance, Rococo and other historical styles. Became interested in Japanese design and also worked in the Art Nouveau style.

Fauconnier, Jacques Henri (1776–1839): Parisian silversmith notable for initiating the Renaissance Revival style in French metalwork.

Flaxman, John (1755–1826): Leading English sculptor who provided Neoclassical designs for Wedgwood and models for silver to be made by **Rundell, Bridge & Rundell**.

Fletcher & Gardiner (*fl*.1809–38): American firm of silversmiths in which the partners were Thomas Fletcher (1787–1866) and Sidney Gardiner (*fl*.1809–27). Based first in Boston; then, from 1811, in Philadelphia, making silver in the Empire style and specializing in presentation pieces.

Fogelberg, Andrew (*c*.1732–93). Silversmith, probably of Swedish parentage, who settled in London in the early 1770s. Noted for his restrained classical style and use of cameo-like medallions to decorate silver.

Fontaine, Pierre-François-Léonard. See **Percier, Charles and Fontaine, Pierre-François-Léonard**.

Forbes, John Wolfe (1781–*c*.1838): The most prominent member of the second generation of an American silversmithing family of Dutch or Scottish descent. Noted for making the Empire-style Forbes Plateau in New York in 1820–5, now in the White House.

Froment-Meurice, François Désiré (1802–55): The leading French silversmith and jeweller of his time, highly fashionable with the Parisian aristocracy. Specialized in Revivalist styles such as Gothic, Mannerist and Rococo.

Gaillard, Lucien (b. 1861): Parisian silversmith and jeweller. Often used horn, ivory and precious stones in his silver designs and was an exponent of the Japanese technique of mixed metals.

Garrard & Co.: Major London retail and manufacturing silversmiths descended from George Wickes, established in 1741 (see **George Wickes**). Appointed Royal Goldsmiths in 1830 and became Crown Jewellers in 1843. Was amalgamated with the Goldsmiths & Silversmiths Co. in 1952, now part of the Asprey Group. Known for tableware, trophies and commemorative pieces.

Gentile da Faenza, Antonio (1519–1609): Italian silversmith and assayer to the papal mint. Also made much ecclesiastical silver, very little of which survives with the exception of St Peter's altar plate.

Germain, François-Thomas (1726–91): French Rococo silversmith, the son of **Thomas Germain** whose workshop he inherited. *Orfèvre du roi* from 1748 until his bankruptcy in 1764.

Germain, Pierre II (?1716–83): French silversmith apprenticed to **Thomas Germain**, **Jacques Roettiers** and **Nicolas Besnier**. Known mainly for his *Elements d'Orfèvrerie* (1748), an influential pattern book of Rococo silver.

Germain, Thomas (1673–1748): Prominent French silversmith, and one of the creators of the Rococo style in silver. Made *orfèvre du roi* in 1723. Immortalized by Voltaire in *Les Vous et les Tu*.

Giardini, Giovanni (1646–1721): The leading Roman goldsmith of the Baroque period whose *Disegni Diversi*, a book of designs, was first published in 1711. Most of his surviving pieces are ecclesiastical.

Goldsmiths, The Worshipful Company of: London livery company set up in 1238 in Foster Lane in the City of London (where it still remains) to enforce standards of gold and silver, and operate the London assay office. The institution now also has an educational, promotional and charitable function.

Gorham Manufacturing Co.: Leading firm of American retail and manufacturing silversmiths founded in 1831 in Providence, Rhode Island. Took up drop-pressing and electroplating in the mid-19th century, making much High Victorian-style silver, and introduced Martelé ware in the 1890s. Merged with Textron Corporation in 1967.

Guccio di Mannaia (n.d.): Italian goldsmith and enameller, known from a signature on a Gothic enamelled chalice that he made between 1288 and 1292 for Pope Nicholas IV.

Guild of Handicraft: Guild of artist-craftsmen founded in 1888 by **C.R. Ashbee**. Produced silver in simple designs and jewellery, often in Art Nouveau style. Liquidated in 1907.

Harache, Pierre I (*fl*.1682–*c*.1698) and **II** (1653–1717): French silversmiths, father and son, among the first Huguenots to settle in London. Their work is of a high standard, often decorated with figurative and applied ornament.

Haseler, W.H. & Co.: Manufacturers of silver, jewellery and other metalwork established in Birmingham in 1870. Made Cymric silver for Liberty & Co.

Heming, Thomas (1722/3–1801): London silversmith working in the Rococo and Neoclassical styles. Appointed Royal Goldsmith to George III in 1760, but sacked for overcharging. His workshop also supplied dinner and dessert services and candelabra to Catherine the Great of Russia.

Hoffmann, Josef (1870–1950): Austrian architect and designer. His designs for silver and jewellery, based on simplicity and functionalism, were executed by the **Wiener Werkstätte**, of which he was a member.

Holbein, Hans (1497/8–1543): Important German painter and notable designer, especially of gold and silver in elaborate Renaissance style. Worked for Henry VIII from 1533 onwards.

Hugo d'Oignies (*fl*.1187–1238): Metalworker of the Mosan School, who worked in a monastery at Oignies, near Namur, Belgium. Noted for his applied filigree work that bridges the Romanesque and Gothic styles.

Hukin & Heath: Firm of Birmingham silversmiths established in 1875. Noted for silver-mounted glassware and Japanese-style silver, some of it designed by **Christopher Dresser**.

Hull, John (1624–83): Leading silversmith of English birth who settled in Boston, Massachusetts, in 1635. Founded Hull & Sanderson *c*.1652, which among other items produced spoons, beakers and church plate.

Hunt & Roskell: Major London silversmiths and successors to the firm founded by **Paul Storr** in 1822 as Storr & Co., later Storr & Mortimer, becoming Mortimer & Hunt in 1839 and Hunt &

Roskell in 1844, when it reached the peak of its success. Acquired by J.W. Benson in 1889, closed in 1928 and reopened in 1922 as part of the Asprey Group.

Hurd, Jacob (1703–38): American silversmith making mainly domestic silverware, but also some church plate, in Boston, Massachusetts.

International Silver Co.: Connecticut firm of manufacturing silversmiths trading under this name since 1898 and now one of the largest in the world. Its antecedent was the Meriden Britannia Co., founded by H.C. Wilcox in 1852, which took over other silversmithing and electroplating concerns, thus assuming its present name.

Jamnitzer, Wenzel (1508–85): The greatest of the Nuremberg goldsmiths in the Mannerist style. A master of engraving, enamelling, modelling and embossing, and noted for his naturalistically cast decoration in gold and silver, in the form of insects, reptiles, shells and other natural and fantastic subjects.

Jensen, Georg (1866–1935): Danish silversmith renowned for his simple designs and the clean flowing outlines of his tableware and cutlery. Also florally embellished pieces. Founded in 1916, the firm which bears his name has retail outlets throughout the world.

Kierstede, Cornelius (1675–1757): New York silversmith of Dutch descent, whose work, mostly tableware, shows considerable Dutch influence.

Kirk, Samuel (1783–1872): Founded Kirk & Son Inc. of Baltimore in 1815, the oldest surviving firm of American silversmiths. Specialized in vessels richly decorated in repoussé work.

Knox, Archibald (1864–1933): English textiles and metalwork designer. Responsible for much of the Celtic Revival pewter and silver sold by **Liberty & Co.** from 1898.

Krug, Ludwig (c.1480–1532): With **Melchior Baier**, was one of the two most important Nuremberg silversmiths of the early 16th century.

Lalique, René (1860–1945): Leading French jeweller and glass-maker in the Art Nouveau and Art Deco styles. Also made silver scent bottles and other small objects, and glass vessels with silver mounts fashioned in natural forms.

Lamerie, Paul de (1688–1751): French Huguenot silversmith, the most highly acclaimed of his time, who came to London as a child in 1689. Was apprenticed to **Pierre Platel** in 1703 and set up independently in 1713, becoming goldsmith to George I in 1716. His early work is in the relatively plain Queen Anne and Huguenot styles, but by the 1730s he had begun working in the Rococo style, of which he became the leading exponent in England.

Liberty & Co.: Retailing firm established in London by Arthur Lazenby Liberty in 1875. Employed various avant-garde designers, including **Christopher Dresser** and **Archibald Knox**, and led the way in promoting Japanese style, Art Nouveau and Cymric and Celtic Revival silver.

Mappin & Webb Ltd: Leading firm of London retail and manufacturing silversmiths and jewellers, founded in 1774 by Jonathan Mappin of Sheffield, which later took over Stephen Smith & Co. Produced some outstanding Art Deco silver during the 1930s. Now part of the Asprey Group.

Marks, Gilbert (1861–1905): London designer and silversmith working mostly in Art Nouveau style, his silver often featuring relief decoration of fruit and flowers.

Marot, Daniel (1633–1752): Influential Huguenot architect and designer who developed his own variant of the Baroque style. Became Court architect and 'designer-in-chief' to William III, working for him at the palace of Het Loo in Holland and following him to England in 1694, where he also worked at Hampton Court. The style he created was disseminated through his books of designs, notably in Holland and England.

Meissonnier, Juste-Aurèle (1695–1750): The great protagonist of the Rococo, Meissonnier was born in Turin, but moved to Paris in 1714 where he worked at the Mint. In 1724 he was appointed *orfèvre du roi* and two years later '*dessinateur*' of the King's Chamber and Cabinet. A polymath, Meissonnier was both architect, designer, painter, chaser and medallist. Amongst his patrons was the Duke of Kingston, for whom he designed a pair of tureens and a candelabrum which bear his signature. The only piece struck with his maker's mark, however, is a gold and lapis lazuli snuff-box of 1728.

Mellor, David (b. 1930): Industrial designer in silver and stainless steel. His flatware and hollow ware are remarkable for their elegant plainness. Was chairman of the British government's Craft Council until 1984. Runs a factory near Sheffield and has one retail outlet in Manchester and two in London.

Moore, John Chandler (fl.1827–51): New York silversmith, specializing in presentation pieces in Rococo Revival style which he made chiefly for **Ball, Tompkins & Black**.

Morel-Ladeuil, Léonard (1820–88): French silversmith who studied under **Antoine Vechte** and from 1859 until his death worked for **Elkington & Co.** as a designer of electroplate in Renaissance Revival style.

Moser, George Michael (1706–83): Leading London gold-chaser and enameller of Swiss origin, and the decorator of many snuff-boxes and watches. Was influential in the development of the Rococo style in England. Was drawing master to the young George III, manager and treasurer of St Martin's Lane Academy, and founder-member of the Society of Arts. Became the first Keeper of the Royal Academy in 1768.

Moser, Koloman (1868–1918): Austrian painter and designer in the Art Nouveau style. A founder of the **Wiener Werkstätte** (1903).

Nicholas of Verdun (fl.1181–1205): Goldsmith and enameller of the Mosan School and one of the greatest Medieval craftsmen in the early Gothic style. His work heralded a new classicism.

Odiot, Jean-Baptiste-Claude (1763–1850): French silversmith who also periodically served in the Republican army. His work, in the Empire style, is characterized by much use of applied ornament in the form of classically inspired human figures and animals. His workshops, which sometimes used the designs of **Percier** and **Fontaine**, occasionally supplied Napoleon, but his major commissions came from royal patrons in Rome, Russia, Sweden and Bavaria.

Orfèvrerie Christofle: Parisian manufacturers of metalwork founded in 1827 by Pierre Christofle. Acquired the monopoly of the French electroplating industry in the 1840s. Also notable producers of Art Deco silver.

Peche, Dagobert (1887–1923): Austrian designer, most notably of silver in a loose Art Deco style with an element of fantasy and a handcrafted look. Joined the **Wiener Werkstätte** as artistic director with **Hoffmann** in 1915.

Percier, Charles (1764–1838) and **Fontaine, Pierre-François-Léonard** (1762–1853): French architects, interior decorators and designers who, working in partnership, created the French Empire style, disseminating it through their *Recueil des décorations intérieures* (1801, reissued 1812).

Persson, Sigurd (b. 1914): Swedish silversmith and industrial designer, a major contributor to the development of Scandinavian silver in the 1940s and later.

Petzolt, Hans (1551–1633): The greatest Nuremberg goldsmith after **Wenzel Jamnitzer**, whose Mannerist style he followed before returning to the simpler styles of the early 16th century.

Platel, Pierre (c.1664–1719): French Huguenot silversmith who settled in London in the late 17th century. Master of **Paul de Lamerie**. One of the leading exponents of the Huguenot style, maker of several important pieces, including the Chatsworth gold ewer and basin.

Pugin, Augustus Welby Northmore (1769–1832): Major English architect and designer, highly influential in developing the Gothic Revival style. Designed silver for **Rundell, Bridge & Rundell** and Hardman's, and church plate derived from 15th-century prototypes.

Puiforcat, Jean (1897–1945): French silversmith in the Art Deco style, noted for his stylishly simple, slightly geometric silver aimed at a wealthy clientèle. Virtually created the Modern style in French silver in the 1920s.

Ramsden, Omar (1873–1939): Leading English silver designer. Was influenced by the Arts and Crafts Movement and Art Nouveau but also made silver in Elizabethan, Queen Anne, Georgian and other revivalist styles.

Revere, Paul (1735–1818): The best-known American silversmith, famous for his patriotism during the American Revolution. A prolific maker, he produced much tableware in Georgian and English Neoclassical styles, as well as the 'Sons of Liberty' bowl, made on the eve of the Revolution.

Richardson, Joseph (1711–84): The second generation of a family of American silversmiths working in Philadelphia, and the most prolific. Made a range of domestic silver, and personal items to be presented as gifts to American Indians.

Ritter, Christoph (d. pre-1573): The first of several generations of a distinguished family of Nuremberg goldsmiths. Noted as the maker of an elaborate salt surmounted by a scene of the crucifixion, made for the Nuremberg City Treasury in 1551.

Roettiers, Jacques (1707–84): Flemish silversmith, working first in the Rococo style, then, from the 1780s, adopting the Neoclassical style. Succeeded **Nicolas Besnier** as *orfèvre du roi* in 1737, a title to which his son Jacques-Nicolas (b. 1736) in turn succeeded in 1772.

Rollos, Philip (*fl.*1697–1710): Huguenot silversmith who settled in London in the late 17th century (his first mark is recorded in 1697). Known for several handsome and elaborate pieces in typical Huguenot style, including wine coolers, ice pails and two-handled cups.

Rosso Fiorentino (1494–1540): Florentine painter and designer and virtual inventor of strapwork. Worked in Fontainebleau and was commissioned to design much elaborate silver for the palace of François I of France. These pieces have not survived but are known through the engravings of René Boyvin (*fl.*1542–69).

Rundell, Bridge & Rundell: Firm of London silversmiths which, under other names, can trace its origins to the mid-18th century. Under Philip Rundell (1746–1827) and John Bridge (1755–1827), who were joined by Edmund Waller Rundell, Philip Rundell's nephew, in 1805, the firm prospered. It reached its peak in the first half of the 19th century, when it held the Royal Warrant as Crown Jewellers and produced many prestigious pieces. As well as making its own silver, the firm was supplied by subsidiary factories managed, among others, by Benjamin Smith, Digby Scott and Storr & Co., in which **Paul Storr**, Philip Rundell and John Bridge were the original partners. After John Bridge's death in 1834, the firm became Rundell, Bridge & Co. It closed in 1843.

Salviati, Francesco (1510–63): Florentine painter, goldsmith and designer in the Mannerist style. His designs for gold, silver and bronze were widely imitated.

Sanderson, Robert (1609–93): London-born silversmith who emigrated to America *c.*1635–8. Worked in partnership with John Hull in Boston and produced mostly ecclesiastical plate.

Sbarri, Manno di Sebastiano (1536–76): Florentine goldsmith who worked in the Mannerist style. Probably studied under **Benvenuto Cellini**. Maker of fine pieces decorated with rock-crystal plaques and lapis lazuli.

Sedding, John Dando (1838–91): Architect and designer in the neo-Gothic style, a follower of **A.W.N. Pugin**. Designed church plate.

Spencer, Edward. See **Artificers' Guild**.

Sprimont, Nicholas (1716–71): Belgian Huguenot who arrived in England before 1742. Worked as a silversmith only *c.*1742–7. Received commissions from Frederick, Prince of Wales, but *c.*1749 relinquished silversmithing to become manager of the Chelsea porcelain factory in partnership with Charles Gouyn, a jeweller.

Storr, Paul (1771–1844): Eminent and prolific English silversmith whose workshop produced pieces in the Neoclassical and Rococo Revival styles. In 1807 he was one of the founding partners in Storr & Co., which, as a subsidiary of **Rundell, Bridge & Rundell**, supplied the latter with silver. In 1818 Storr became a partner in Rundell, Bridge & Rundell but left to open his own workshop in 1819. In 1823 he founded Storr & Mortimer, which became Mortimer & Hunt after his retirement in 1839.

Tatham, Charles Heathcote (1772–1842): English architect and designer who studied in Rome (1794–7) and played an important part in formulating the Regency style. Published his *Designs for Ornamental Plate* in 1806.

Tétard Frères: One of several leading Parisian retail and manufacturing firms who dealt in Art Nouveau silver and, in the first decades of the 20th century, produced and sold silver in the clean-lined Modernist style associated with **Jean Puiforcat**.

Thelot, Johann Andreas (1655–1734): Augsburg goldsmith and chaser noted for elaborate, highly sculptural reliefs on silver.

Tiffany & Co.: America's leading firm of silversmiths and jewellers, founded in New York in 1837 by Charles Lewis Tiffany (1812–1902). Under his son Louis Comfort Tiffany (1844–1933), the firm became renowned for designing and producing Art Nouveau silver. Now has branches in Paris and London as well as throughout the United States.

Valadier, Luigi (1726–85): Distinguished Italian silversmith, whose family owned a workshop in Rome. Studied in Paris in 1754, and in Rome made ecclesiastical pieces, and tableware in Rococo and Neoclassical styles. His son Giuseppe (1762–1839), a precocious draughtsman who became an architect and silversmith, took over the workshop on his father's death, producing silver in Neoclassical style.

Van Vianen family: Adam (1565–1627), his brother Paulus (1570–1613) and son Christian (1598–*c.*1666). Notable family of Dutch silversmiths who devised the Auricular style. Incipient in the work of Paulus, it was taken up and developed by Christian and Adam.

Vasters, Reinhold (1827–1909): German goldsmith and restorer. Also the author of a large number of designs for jewellery, silver and *objets de luxe* in Renaissance and Gothic styles. From these he is known to have designed and made forgeries that were acquired as genuine by many major museums and collectors.

Vechte, Antoine (1799–1868): French silversmith who worked for **Froment-Meurice** and **Carl Wagner** in Paris, and from 1849 to 1862 for **Hunt & Roskell** in London, for whom he made chased and embossed silver in a highly sculptural style that anticipated the Renaissance Revival. Some of his work was acquired by national museums as genuine Renaissance silver.

Vries, Hans Vriedeman de (1527–1604): Flemish painter and designer, and Antwerp town-planner, de Vries was influential through his Mannerist designs which he published in 1565.

Wagner, Carl (1799–1841): German silversmith and jeweller who settled in Paris in 1830. Important in the development of the neo-Renaissance style in silver. Also revived Renaissance-style niello work and patented his own method of niello decoration.

Welch, Robert (b. 1929): English silversmith and designer in stainless steel and other metals. Worked in Sweden and Norway in the mid-1950s, then established a workshop in England. Has made many important pieces for **The Worshipful Company of Goldsmiths** and other institutions including the Victoria & Albert Museum, for which he made a candelabrum in 1980.

Wickes, George (1698–1761): Leading London silversmith the quality of whose work has been likened to that of **Paul de Lamerie**. With Edward Wakelin he founded Wickes & Wakelin in 1747, the firm supplying Frederick, Prince of Wales, the dukes of Chandos, Devonshire and Norfolk and other aristocracy. Following Wickes's withdrawal from the firm in 1759, it underwent various changes in partnership and eventually became **Garrard & Co**.

Wiener Werkstätte: Craft studio founded by **Josef Hoffmann** and **Koloman Moser** in Vienna in 1903. Specialized in handmade silver and jewellery and other items in Art Nouveau and Art Deco styles, some to designs by **Dagobert Peche**. Closed in 1931.

Willaume, David I (1658–1741): French Huguenot silversmith who settled in London in 1686. His clientèle included the wealthiest patrons of the period but his fortunes were also boosted by money-lending. The work of his son David Willaume II (1693–1761), who was also involved in the family banking business, shows markedly less Huguenot influence.

Wilson, Henry (1864–1934): English designer of furniture and metalwork in the Arts and Crafts tradition, his designs for metalwork combining Byzantine and Medieval elements.

Winslow, Edward (1669–1753): American silversmith of Boston, Massachusetts, who made mainly domestic silver but also some church plate.

Wolfers, Philippe (1858–1929): Belgian sculptor, goldsmith and jeweller working in revivalist and Art Nouveau styles, his jewellery and silver often incorporating ivory. Worked for the family firm Wolfers Frères, jewellers and silversmiths of Brussels.

Wyatt, James (1746–1813): Celebrated English architect in the Neoclassical and Gothic styles whose designs were used by Matthew Boulton in silver, Sheffield plate and ormolu.

INDEX

ACKNOWLEDGMENTS

The publisher thanks the following photographers and organizations for their permission to reproduce the photographs in this book:

4–5 Scala, Florence; **4** left Bauhaus-Archiv, Berlin; **6 & 9** E.T. Archive, London; **14** Scala, Florence; **16** Bridgeman Art Library, London/British Museum; **17** above left Louvre, Paris/© Photo: R.M.N.; **17** below Metropolitan Museum of Art, New York; **17** right Purchase, Joseph Pulitzer Bequest, 1966; **17** centre Louvre, Paris/© Photo: R.M.N.; **18** below Metropolitan Museum of Art. Purchase, J.Pulitzer Bequest, 1946 & Bequest of Walter C. Baker, 1971; **18** centre Louvre, Paris/© Photo: R.M.N.; **18** above & **19** right Lee Boltin Picture Library, New York; **19** left National Museum of Athens; **20** left Lee Boltin Picture Library, New York; **20** right E.T. Archive, London; **21** left Ekdotike Athenon SA, Athens; **21** below right Courtesy of George Ortiz/Photo: D. Widmer, Basel; **21** centre Courtesy of Michael Vickers; **22** above & below Lee Boltin Picture Library, New York; **23** Toledo Museum of Art, Ohio. Purchased with funds from the Library Endowment. Gift of E.D. Libbey; **24** E.T. Archive, London; **25** left Louvre, Paris/© Photo: R.M.N.; **25** right Bridgeman Art Library,

London/Giraudon/Louvre; **26** Left Louvre, Paris/© Photo: R.M.N.; **26** right Antiken Museum/Bildarchiv Preussischer Kulturbesitz, Berlin; **27** right Art Museum, Princeton University. Purchase, Carl Otto van Kienbusch, Jr. Memorial Collection; **27** centre Cliché Musées de Vienne, G. Renaux; **27** above Musée des Beaux Arts de Lyon/Photo: Laurent Sully-Jaulmes; **28** below E.T. Archive, London; **28** above Römermuseum, Augst/Photo: D. Widmer; **29** below Mas, Barcelona; **29** above Bibliothèque Nationale, Paris; **30** right Scala/Museo Archeologico, Florence; **30** left & **31** Römermuseum, Augst/Photo: D. Widmer; **32** below E.T. Archive, London; **32** above Courtesy of the Byzantine Collection © 1992; Dumbarton Oaks, Trustees of Harvard University, Washington DC; **33** below National Museum of Ireland, Dublin; **33** above Bridgeman Art Library, London/British Museum; **34** Chorherrenstift Klosterneuburg, Stiftsmuseum/Photo: Gabriel Hildebrand, Rikfoto **38** above Hildesheim Cathedral; **38** below Wallace Collection, London; **39** Statens Historische Museum, Stockholm; **40** right & left The Trustees of the British Museum; **41** below Les Musées Royaux de Beaux-Arts de Belgique, Brussels/Photo C. Valkenberg; **41** above The Trustees of the British Museum; **43** above Syndication International/Louvre; **43** below right By courtesy of the Board of Trustees of the Victoria &

Albert Museum, London; **43** below left Metropolitan Museum of Art, New York. Gift of J. Pierpont Morgan, 1917; **44** above left Kunsthistorisches Museum, Vienna; **44** below Canterbury Cathedral Treasury/Photo: Ben May **44** above right & **45** By courtesy of the Board of Trustees of the Victoria & Albert Musuem, London; **46** left National Museet (National Museum of Denmark), Copenhagen; **46** centre & right By courtesy of the Board of Trustees of the Victoria and Albert Museum, London; **47** By courtesy of the Board of Trustees of the Victoria & Albert Museum, London; **48** left Edimedia, Paris; **48** right Metropolitan Museum of Art, New York. The Cloisters Collection, 1952; **49** By courtesy of the Board of Trustees of the Victoria and Albert Museum, London; **50** left Abbatiale Saint-Taurin/Photo: Georges Kischinewski, Evreux; **50** right Louvre, Paris/© Photo: R.M.N.; **51** left Scala, Florence/Orvieto Cathedral; **51** right Scala, Florence/S. Francesco (Tesoro) Assisi; **52** below Metropolitan Museum of Art, New York. The Cloisters Collection, 1953; **52** Above Musée Historique Lorrain, Nancy/Photo: Gilbert Mangin; **53** left Cleveland Museum of Art, Ohio. Gift from J.H. Wade, 24.859; **53** right By courtesy of the Board of Trustees of the Victoria & Albert Museum, London; **54** The Trustees of the British Museum; **55** below Museo degli; Argenti, Florence/Photo: Marcello Bertoni; **55** above By courtesy of the Board of Trustees of the Victoria & Albert Museum, London; **58** Musées d'Art et d'Histoire, Geneva; **58** Biblioteca Nazionale Marciana, Venice/Foto Toso; **60** left Museo degli Argenti, Florence/Photo: Marcello Bertoni; **60** right Scala, Florence/Museo dell'Opera del Duomo, Florence; **61** right Courtesy of Timothy Schroder; **61** left The Royal Collection, St James's Palace/© H.M. The Queen; **62** left By courtesy of the Board of Trustees of the Victoria & Albert Museum, London; **62** right Ashmolean Museum, Oxford; **63** right The Trustees of the British Museum; **63** centre Kunsthistorisches Museum, Vienna; **63** left Graphische Sammlung Albertina, Vienna; **64** Private Collection; **65** below Offentliche Kunstsammlung, Kunstmuseum, Basel; **65** above right Private Collection; **65** above left Los Angeles County Museum of Art. The Arthur & Rosalinde Gilbert Silver Collection; **66** left Courtesy of Timothy Schroder; **66** right Kremlin Museum, Moscow; **67** left Courtesy of Timothy Schroder; **68** left The Governing Body, Christ Church, Oxford; **68** right Museo Nazionale di Napoli/Photo: Fabrizi Parisio; **69** Kunsthistorisches Museum, Vienna; **70** above left Germanisches Nationalmuseum, Nuremberg; **70** above right Schweizerisches Landesmuseum, Zurich; **70** below Schatzkammer der Residenz, Munich; **71** right & left The Trustees of the British Museum; **72** left The Worshipful Company of Goldsmiths, London; **72** centre & right Kremlin Museum, Moscow; **73** Norfolk Museums Service (Norfolk Castle Museum); **74** below left Partridge Fine Arts PLC, London; **74** above Los Angeles County Museum of Art. The Arthur & Rosalinde Gilbert Silver Collection; **74** below right Museo degli Argenti, Florence/Photo: Bazzechi; **75** left Los Angeles County Museum of Art. Gift of William Randolph Hearst; **75** right Christie's Images, London; **76** centre Thyssen-Bornemisza Collection, Lugano, Switzerland; **76** below Kunsthistorisches Museum, Vienna; **76** left Staatlichen Museen zu Berlin/Bildarchiv Preussischer Kulturbesitz; **77** National Gallery, London; **77** left Rijksmuseum, Amsterdam; **78** Calouste Gulbenkian Museum, Lisbon; **80** Instituto Nazionale per la Grafica, Rome; **81** left Museu de São Roque, Lisbon/Photo: Wis Filipe Candido de Oliviera; **81** right Christie's, Geneva; **82** right Scala, Florence/Capella dei Principi, Florence; **82** left Westminster Cathedral/Photo: A.A. Barnes/© Conran Octopus; **83** Devonshire Collection, Chatsworth. Reproduced by permission of the Chatsworth Settlement Trustees; **84** left The Royal Collections, Stockholm/Photo: Hakem Lind; **84** right Inventaire General SPADEM 1992/Photo: Alain Maulny/Cathédrale de Poitiers; **85** right By courtesy of the Board of Trustees of the Victoria & Albert Museum, London; **85** left The Royal Collection, St James's Palace/© H.M. The Queen; **86** above The Trustees of the National Museums of Scotland, 1992; **86** below Christie's, London; **87** By courtesy of the Board of Trustees of the Victoria & Albert Museum, London; **88** left Stadt Museum, Ingolstadt; **88** right Staatliche Museen zu Berlin/Bildarchiv Preussischer Kulturbesitz; **89** left & right The Trustees of the National Museums of Scotland, 1992; **91** below Louvre, Paris/© Photo: R.M.N.; **91** above Founders Society, Detroit Institute of Arts; **92** below Arquivo Nacional de Fotografia, Museu Nacional d'Arte Antiga, Instituto Portugues de Museus, Lisbon; **93** right Cleveland Museum of Art, Ohio. Leonard C. Hanna Jr. Fund, 77.182; **93** above Musées des Arts Decoratifs, Paris; **94** centre Cooper Hewitt Museum, National Museum of Design, Smithsonian Institution, anon. gift/Photo: Steve Tague, courtesy of Art Resource; **94** left Arquivo Nacional de Fotografia, Museo Nacional d'Arte Antiga, Instituto Portugues de Museus, Lisbon; **94** right Courtesy of Peter Fuhring; **95** above Alekis Kugel Collection/Photo: Jean-Loup Charmet; **96** right & left The Royal Collection/St James's Palace/© H.M. The Queen; **97** above Museu de São Roque, Lisbon; **97** below right Bayerisches Nationalmuseum, Munich; **97** below left By courtesy of the Board of Trustees of the Victoria & Albert Museum, London; **98** above Drottn-

ingholm, Sweden/Photo: National Swedish Art Museum; **98** below Los Angeles County Museum of Art. Lent by Mr & Mrs Arthur Gilbert; **100** centre © National Trust 1991; **100** above left Courtesy of James Lomax; **101** below right Temple Newsam House (Leeds City Art Galleries); **101** left & above right By courtesy of the Trustees of Sir John Soane's Museum, London; **102** above Temple Newsam House (Leeds City Art Galleries); **102** below Temple Newsam House (Leeds City Art Galleries); **103** left The Toledo Museum of Art, Ohio; **103** right & **104** left Courtesy of the Museum of Fine Arts, Boston. Theodora Wilbour Fund in memory of Charlotte Beebe Wilbour; **105** left Courtesy of the Museum of Fine Arts, Boston. Gift of Mrs Horatio A. Lamb; **105** right Private Collection. Photo courtesy of the Artemis Group; **108** right Christie, Manson & Woods Ltd, London; **108** left Staatsgalerie Stuttgart; **108** centre Staatliche Museen zu Berlin/Bildarchiv Preussischer Kulturbesitz; **109** & **110** Christie, Manson & Woods Ltd, London; **111** The Royal Collection, St James's Palace. Courtesy H.M. The Queen; **112** below Christie, Manson & Woods Ltd, London; **113** above The Board of Trustees of the National Museums & Galleries of Merseyside, Liverpool Museum; **116** below Phillips Fine Art Auctioneers, London: **116** above right Christie's, New York; **117** above left The Worshipful Company of Goldsmiths, London; **118** below By courtesy of the Board of Trustees of the Victoria & Albert Museum, London; **126** Courtesy of the Museum of Fine Arts, Boston. Marion E. Davis Fund; **128** Courtesy of the Museum of Fine Arts, Boston, The E. J. Holmes Collection, Bequest of Mrs E. J. Holmes; **129** left The Los Angeles County Museum of Art. Gift of Florence Alden Stoddard & Katherine Alden Stewart; **129** above right The Metropolitan Museum of Art, New York. Samuel D. Lee Fund, 1938; **129** below right Yale University Art Gallery. Mabel Brady Garvan Collection; **130** below The Metropolitan Museum of Art, New York. Bequest of A.T. Clearwater, 1933; **130** above & **131** right Yale University Art Gallery. Mabel Brady Garvan Collection; **131** left Courtesy of the Winterthur Museum, Delaware; **132** below, above left & above right, Yale University Art Gallery. Mabel Brady Garvan Collection; **133** above Courtesy of the Museum of Fine Arts, Boston. Gift in memory of Dr George Clymer & his wife Mrs Clymer; **134** Courtesy of the Museum of Fine Arts, Boston. Decorative Arts Special Fund; **135** below Courtesy of the Museum of Fine Arts, Boston. Gift of John Favorid in memory of Bertha Sease Favorid and Bishop John Heyl Vincent; **135** above left Museum of the City of New York, 32.237.6. Gift of George Elsworth Dunscombe/Photo: John Parnell; **135** above right Minneapolis Institute of Art; **136** Courtesy of Winterthur Museum, Delaware; **137** right Metropolitan Museum of Art, New York, Fletcher Fund, 1959/Photo: Schechter Lee; **137** left Metropolitan Museum of Art, New York. Purchase, L.V. Bell & Rogers Funds, Anon. & R.G. Goelet Gifts; and Gifts of Fenton, L.B. Brown and of the grandchildren of Mrs Ranson Spaford Hooker, in her memory, by exchange, 1982 (1982.4). Photograph by Paul Warchol, 1984; **138** left High Museum of Art, Atlanta. Virginia Carroll Crawford Collection, 1984.168.1 & 2; **138** right Metropolitan Museum of Art, New York. Gift of Mrs F.R. Lefferts, 1969; **139** Courtesy of the Parish of Trinity Church, in the City of New York; **140** above Museum of the City of New York, 34.346.2. Gift of Newcomb Carlton/Photo: John Parnell; **140** below Maryland Historical Society, Baltimore; **141** left Yale University Art Gallery, Millicent Todd Bingham Fund; **141** right Courtesy of Museum of Fine Arts, Boston. Private Collection; **142** Collection High Museum of Art, Atlanta. Virginia Carroll Crawford Collection, 1984.168.1–5; **143** Los Angeles County Museum of Art. Gift of Anna Bing Arnold; **143** Los Angeles County Museum of Art. Gift of Theodore G. & Eleanor S. Congdon; **144** below Yale University, Peabody Museum of Natural History; **144** above Collection High Museum of Art, Atlanta. Virginia Carroll Crawford

Collection, 1984.170; **145** Metropolitan Museum of Art, New York. Gift of Edward D. Adams, 1904; **146** left Los Angeles County Museum of Art. Decorative Arts Acquisition Fund; **146** right Private Collection; **147** left Los Angeles County Museum of Art. Purchased with funds provided by the Decorative Arts Council; **147** right Los Angeles County Museum of Art. Gift of Max Palevsky & Jodie Evans; **150** below Danske Kunstindustrimuseet, Copenhagen/Photo: Ole Woldbye; **151** left Stapleton Collection, London; **154** right Hessisches Landesmuseum, Darmstadt; **154** left Musée des Arts Decoratifs, Paris; **156** left Hessisches Landesmuseum, Darmstadt; **156** right Stadtmuseum, Munich/Photo: Wolfgang Pufer; **158** below Vestlandske Kunstindustrimuseum, Bergen (The West Norway Museum of Applied Art); **159** Courtesy of the Decorative & Industrial Arts Collection, Chicago Historical Society; **161** above Deutsches Klingenmuseum, Solingen/Photo: Foto Manufaktur; **161** below right Private Collection/Photo: Institut Mathildenhöhe, Darmstadt; **161** above centre Badisches Landesmuseum, Karlsruhe; **164** above Metropolitan Museum of Art, New York. Gift of Jennifer Johnson Gregg, 1976/Photo: Schechter Lee; **164** below Metropolitan Museum of Art, New York. Purchase, anon. Gift, 1978; **166** Haags Gemeentemuseum/Photo: Museum Boymans-van Beuningen; **167** left J. Alistair Duncan/Barry Friedman Ltd, New York; **167** right Gorham Inc, United States; **169** above By courtesy of the Board of Trustees of the Victoria & Albert Museum, London; **170** The Worshipful Company of Goldsmiths, London; **171** above left Metropolitan Museum of Art, New York. Purchase Edgar Kaufman, Jr. Gift, 1972; **171** below Virginia Museum of Fine Arts, Richmond. Gift of Sydney & Frances Lewis; **171** above right Société Puiforcat; **172** below Musée Bouilhet-Christofle, Paris/Photo: Jean Michel Kollar; **173** below right Musée des Arts Decoratifs, Paris; **173** above J. Alistair Duncan/Primavera Gallery, New York; **174** Georg Jensen Museum, Copenhagen; **176** Professor Cleto Munari Design Associati, Vicenza; **177** below Cleto Munari Design Associati, Vicenza; **177** above & **178** above By courtesy of the Board of Trustees of the Victoria & Albert Museum, London; **178** below Master, Fellows & Scholars of Churchill College, Cambridge/Photo: A.A. Barnes/© Conran Octopus; **179** above right, above left, below left & **180** left The Worshipful Company of Goldsmiths, London; **180** right Lichfield Cathedral/Photo: David Cripps; **181** below left The Worshipful Company of Goldsmiths, London; **181** above National Museum of Wales, Cardiff/© H.M. The Queen; **181** below right The Worshipful Company of Goldsmiths, London; **182** © Howard Fenn; **183** Statens Konstmuseer, Stockholm (National Swedish Arts Museums); **184** below Prof. Friedrich Becker; **185** City of Hamilton Art Gallery, Victoria, Australia; **186, 187** left & **190** below By courtesy of the Board of Trustees of the Victoria & Albert Museum, London; **192** below The Trustees of the British Museum; **192** above Christie's, New York.

Sotheby's, Geneva
92 above

Sotheby's, London
1, 2, 10, 12, 42, 67 right, **95** below, **104** right, **106, 112** above, **113** below left & right, **115** above, **115** below, **116** above left, **117** below, **119** left, **120, 121, 122** above, **122** below, **123** below, **123** above, **124** above, **125** below, **150** above, **151** right, **152, 153, 155** left, **155** right, **157** right, **157** left, **158** above, **160** left, **160** right, **162, 165** left, **165** above right, **169** below, **172** above, **173** below left, **184** above, **187** right, **188, 189** below right, **189** above right, **189** below centre, **189** below left, **190** above, **191**.

Sotheby's, New York
78, 99, 117 above right, **118** above, **119** right, **124** below, **125** above, **148, 165** below right.